THE ONE AND ONLY:
THE BALLET RUSSE
DE MONTE CARLO

Constan

JACK ANDERSON

The One and Only:

The Ballet Russe de Monte Carlo

DANCE HORIZONS,
NEW YORK, 1981

ISBN 0-87127-127-3

Library of Congress
Catalog Card Number 81-67267

Printed in the United States
of America

Dance Horizons,
1801 East 26th Street,
Brooklyn, N.Y. 11229

Frontispiece:
Alexandra Danilova and
Frederic Franklin in
Massine's *Le Beau Danube*.
Photo: Constantine Photos

*To
my mother,
who first took me to the Ballet Russe,
and
to all the artists of the Ballet Russe*

ERRATA   *The One and Only: The Ballet Russe de Monte Carlo*

Page 96   Line 1: for "Leon Danielian" read "Frederic Franklin";
line 2: for "Frederic Franklin" read "Leon Danielian";
also p. 290 line 31: for "Leon Danielian" read
"Frederic Franklin." (Franklin danced the premiere of
Danses Concertantes on the opening night of the
company's season, then injured himself on the
second night.)

Page 121   Line 22: for *"Concert Barocco"* read *"Concerto
Barocco."*

Page 149   Line 12: for "October 1950" read "October 1951."

Page 156   Line 14: for "George Rouault" read "Georges
Rouault."

Page 291   Line 1: for "Frederic Franklin" read "Nicholas
Magallanes"; line 3: for "Nicholas Magallanes" read
"Herbert Bliss."

Page 309   Last bibliographical entry: for *"Oxford History"* read
"Oxford Dictionary."

CONTENTS

PART II.

Life in the Company

LIST OF ILLUSTRATIONS

ix

Roland Guerard as the Mormon Apostle, and his five wives in Marc
    Platoff's *Ghost Town.*
Alicia Markova and George Zoritch in Fokine's *Les Sylphides.*
Group from Massine's *Rouge et Noir.*
Alexandra Danilova and Marc Platoff in Ashton's *Devil's Holiday.*
Nini Theilade in Massine's *Bacchanale.*
Group from *Bacchanale.*
Alexandra Danilova in Fokine's *Igrouchki.*
Scene from Massine's *Saratoga* with Nicholas Beriozoff, Vladimir
    Kostenko, Roland Guerard, Frederic Franklin, Alex-
    andra Danilova, Tatiana Chamié, and Sviatoslav
    Toumine.
Lubov Roudenko and Ian Gibson in Massine's *The New Yorker.*
Michel Katcharoff as Dr. Coppelius.
Nijinska's *Chopin Concerto* with Maria Tallchief, Nathalie Kras-
    sovska, Ruthanna Boris, and Gertrude Tyven.
Alexandra Danilova and group in Nijinska's *Snow Maiden.*
Group from Nijinska's *Etude.*
The Russian Sailors' Dance in Schwezoff's *The Red Poppy* with
    George Verdak, Herbert Bliss, Alan Banks, Alexander
    Goudovitch, Nikita Talin, and Alfredo Corvino.

FOLLOWING PAGE 200:
Alexandra Danilova in *Song of Norway* surrounded by Alfredo
    Corvino, Alexander Goudovitch, Alan Banks, Serge Is-
    mailoff, and Michel Katcharoff.
Maria Tallchief, Nicholas Magallanes, and Mary Ellen Moylan in
    Balanchine's *Danses Concertantes.*
Merriam Lanova, Bernice Rehner, Myrna Galle, Sonja Taanila, Pa-
    tricia Wilde, Constance Garfield, Joy Williams, and
    Pauline Goddard in Balanchine's *Serenade.*
The Pas de Sept from Balanchine's *Le Bourgeois Gentilhomme.*
The funeral scene from Page and Stone's *Frankie and Johnny* with
    Frederic Franklin, Ruthanna Boris, and Pauline God-
    dard.
Alexandra Danilova, in *Mozartiana* costume, with George Balan-
    chine and Frederic Franklin.
The masquerade costumes from Balanchine's *Night Shadow.*
Alexandra Danilova and Nicholas Magallanes in Balanchine's *Night
    Shadow.*
Rachel Chapman and George Balanchine play the score for

Raymonda while Barth Cummings, Peter Deign, Harding Dorn, and Claire Pasch listen.

Alexandra Danilova in Balanchine's *Raymonda.*

Alexandra Danilova, Frederic Franklin, and Nikita Talin in Ruth Page's *The Bells.*

Leon Danielian and Ruthanna Boris in Boris's *Cirque de Deux.*

Mary Ellen Moylan.

Yvonne Chouteau and Vida Brown in Bettis's *Virginia Sampler.*

Alexandra Danilova and Oleg Tupine in *Paquita.*

Oleg Tupine and Yvette Chauviré in Lifar's *Roméo et Juliette.*

Yvonne Chouteau as Juliet.

Alan Howard and Nina Novak.

Gertrude Tyven.

Group from Massine's *Harold in Italy* with Teri de Mari and Leon Danielian.

Alexandra Danilova as the Sugar Plum Fairy in *Nutcracker.*

Nathalie Krassovska and Jean Yazvinsky in *Scheherazade.*

Moscelyne Larkin as Odette in *Swan Lake.*

Rachel Chapman, staff pianist.

Sophie Pourmel, wardrobe director.

PREFACE
TO THE
BALLET RUSSE SERIES

SINGULAR in connotation, multiple in its manifestations and sometimes the one or the other in name, Ballet Russe (or The Ballets Russes) is a species which has, it seems, become extinct. Serge Diaghilev was its principal creator. He built on two existing foundations, Russia's excellence in academic theatrical dancing at the turn of the century and the high esteem in which the art was held there.

Before the coming of Diaghilev, the Russian ballet's foreign reputation was based largely on the reports of European dancers, musicians and theater people of all sorts who worked in Russia as well as on the limited though direct evidence of Russian soloists and small groups that had been dancing in the West with increasing frequency since the middle of the nineteenth century. Good as this reputation was, only cognoscenti and professionals were aware of it.

Diaghilev was not the first to conceive of showing Russian ballet abroad on a grand scale. Plans for a Paris season by the Ballet of the Imperial Maryinsky Theatre of St. Petersburg had been made at least three times. On the first occasion, in 1890, Marius Petipa's *The Sleeping Beauty* — touchstone of Russian dance classicism — was to be presented at the Eden Theatre. The engagement was canceled suddenly when, on reconsideration, the Eden was judged to be "not among the first theatres" of Paris. On the second and third occasions, the Maryinsky troupe was to dance two ballets in Paris. A contract with Sarah Bernhardt's theatre was initially drawn up for the period of 15 May 1904 to 1 June, then was redrafted for 1905, and finally was canceled altogether when the Russia-Japan War became serious.

One can only speculate what the reception or repercussions might have been if the Maryinsky's ballet had preceded Diaghilev's to Paris. In the one instance before the advent of Diaghilev's and Pavlova's troupes, when *Sleeping Beauty* was seen outside Russia in an apparently authentic version, the reviews had been highly favorable. Nevertheless, the production, at La Scala in 1896, typically lasted only that season and the consequences for Italian ballet were nil.

When tours from the Maryinsky finally did take place, in 1908 and 1909 — the latter overlapping Diaghilev's first Paris season, it was to Northern and Central Europe. Only about twenty dancers were in these troupes, organized with Maryinsky permission though they were not strictly "official." Anna Pavlova was the prima ballerina both times. Adolph Bolm was premier danseur for the first tour and Nicolas Legat for the second. Elsa Will, [Lubov] Egorova, Mikhail Oboukhoff and Eugenia Eduardova danced prominent roles. Typical programs consisted of a long ballet (*La Fille Mal Gardée, Giselle,* a *Swan Lake* in just three acts, or *Paquita*) followed by assorted divertissements. Alexander Schiriaieff was principal ballet master. Petipa's only credit was as the author of *Swan Lake,* not specifically as the choreographer, and Lev Ivanov's name did not appear in the program listings at all.

These "Maryinsky" performances seem to have been popular everywhere. Critically, they were more successful in Berlin than in Vienna because (according to the Viennese) the Berliners were fed up with their epidemic of barefoot dancers and the Berlin ballet wasn't as good as it had once been. (The Vienna ballet was still considered "perfection.") Some of the Viennese critics ascribed the lack of impact of the big Russian works to the small size of the company. Pavlova and Eduardova were singled out for praise even though Pavlova and several other Russian women were found wanting as beauties. They were seen as being too thin. The company as a whole was deemed merely average, and the manner of presentation so old-fashioned that it was thought unlikely Russia would play a significant role in the sorely-needed reformation of the art of ballet. Judging by this response, the Maryinsky might not have taken Paris by storm even in full force.

Diaghilev came to the idea of displaying the Russian

ballet in Europe through his other Russian promotions: art exhibits, concerts, opera. At first, the Ballet Russe was something of an afterthought for him, even an economy. Yet, once the idea had been launched, he undoubtedly realized the impact it might have. What was lacking in European ballet was esteem more than technique. To have the Russian ballet judged as art, not just entertainment, Diaghilev had to transform it. Otherwise, the verdict might have been the same as for *Sleeping Beauty* in Milan or Mathilde Kchessinska's guest appearances at European opera houses: "good" or even "better," but not "unique."

What changed Russian ballet into Ballet Russe were compact works, balanced programs, and music, scenery and costumes of modern taste and independent vitality. The organizational characteristic that came to typify the Ballet Russe was itinerancy.

How original were these ingredients? Balanced "menus" of one-act ballets had been developed in European opera houses at the end of the nineteenth century. The integrated independence of action, music and visual design was receiving attention everywhere — in drama, opera, modern dance and, conservatively, in the work of a few other ballet companies. Even the traditional balletic traits of which Russia was so proud, musically-developed choreography and plastic dance strength, were not totally unavailable elsewhere. There is no doubt, however, that Diaghilev's recipes for combining these staples were the most varied and successful. No one before him in dance had created so intense an atmosphere of bold glamor.

Diaghilev's success infuriated the advocates of modern dance. They argued that his reforms were not really dance innovations but matters of packaging and presentation. The balletomane Viennese, who had found the touring Maryinsky able but old-fashioned, commented favorably on the folk dance vitality and male strength of Diaghilev's company. They dismissed the classical technique as correct but simple.

Were such commentators right in fact but wrong in feeling? It can be argued that they were insensitive to the potential of the classical dancing and choreography shown by the Diaghilev company which made this strain of ballet capable of further evolution. On the other hand, it may be that the dance development of the later twentieth century, with its emphasis on movement itself, was not derived from the typical content of Diaghilev's dance theatre but, instead, from an application of his recipes to classical Russian and European remnants and to modern dance ideas.

After the Ballet Russe became established, other traveling troupes began to copy Diaghilev. Italian stagioni, that had dominated tour circuits previously, imitated Diaghilev without acknowledging the example. Eventually they were driven out of the field by Ballet Russe troupes. These began to multiply even during Diaghilev's lifetime, and following his death it seemed for a while that "every other day another Ballet Russe is born." The success, too, of the largest of the modern dance troupes to tour, Kurt Jooss's, was partly due to its combination of Ballet Russe theatricality with the concert format: Jooss scheduled serious musical interludes instead of intermissions between his visual dramas.

What made the perpetual novelty of the Ballet Russe's presentations possible was itinerancy. Diaghilev became independent of any one public, theatre management, patron and (to some extent) dance tradition. Of course, this also made this enterprise risky. Nevertheless, the life span of Ballets Russes — from 1909, past Diaghilev's death in 1929, to circa 1965 — is remarkable. The Ballet Russe survived world wars, revolutions, depressions. What finally killed the species, it could be contested, was the resurgence of resident ballet companies and a new aesthetic chauvinism.

Among the dead, the Diaghilev company's life has been memorialized in numerous volumes. So has that of the touring Pavlova, especially in John and Roberta Lazzarini's book. Boris Romanoff's Russian Romantic Ballet and its rooted offshoot, the London Festival Ballet, were major subjects in *Braunsweg's Ballet Scandals.* It was time that the stories of other Ballet Russe troupes be told.

The impossible dream of documenting all the others was Mary Ann Liebert's. While working as performing arts editor at Marcel Dekker, she asked me to pick a Ballet Russe and write it up. Busy, I declined. She then asked me at least to help her by locating other writers and mapping their territories. Having grown up on latter-day Ballet Russe companies and being "born again" one night on seeing Alexandra Danilova dance her royal purple Black Swan, it was difficult to refuse the request. So, I found two poet/critics to pan and sift for the largest and longest lasting of the post-Diaghilev troupes: Kathrine Sorley Walker for Col. de Basil's Original Ballet Russe and Jack Anderson for Sergei Denham's Ballet Russe de Monte Carlo.

Neither of these companies aspired to reform Diaghilev's reformation or pretended to embody in movement the soul of a nation. Initially, they drew their personnel from people who had been with Diaghilev or been trained by Russian emigrées. The Paris studios of former Maryinsky ballerinas were the most productive but Russian teachers in Berlin, London, Vienna and other world capitals were also asked to audition their pupils.

In practice, the de Basil remained cosmopolitan to the last, traveling from country to country and continent to continent. When forced by circumstances to linger a while in one part of the world, as in South America during World War II, de Basil added local dancers to counteract the inevitable attrition and eventually produced a work advertised as the first Brazilian ballet, Vania Psota's *Yara*. By all accounts, the new dancers soon began to look à la Russe and the new choreography, despite its "native" traits, used these merely to spice familiar Russe formulas.

Denham's company, gradually and to the management's chagrin, became known as the "American" Ballet Russe. It remained itinerant, nevertheless, but mostly in the confines of North America with the United States serving as home range. During the course of World War II, Americans became the majority among the dancers. Most of them, though, had trained in the Russian "school" and they remained the majority even after the war. Some of the new works which Denham commissioned or revived, Agnes de Mille's *Rodeo* and Ruth Page's *Frankie and Johnny*, for instance, were landmark Americana. However, the directorate viewed and used them interchangeably with the caractère/demi-caractère ballets of Léonide Massine. Hindsight, perhaps, makes American dance traits apparent in George Balanchine's *Ballet Imperial* (now known as *Piano Concerto No. 2*) and *Night Shadow* (now known as *La Sonnambula*), but these works appealed to audiences of the day because they were about the glamour, sophistication and intrigues of foreign courts.

In reading Sorley Walker's and Anderson's books, it becomes apparent that the de Basil and Denham companies not only served to link the Diaghilev nights with the re-awakening of resident ballets but were ends in themselves for many artists and for large, diverse publics. As such, there is no doubt that these Ballets Russes were of importance to dance history and the cultural life of the twentieth century. To some extent, they still are. The dancers formed by the extinct Ballets Russes companies have become today's teachers and mentors.

George Jackson
Editor for the Ballet Russe Series,
Washington, D.C., May 1981

INTRODUCTION
AND
ACKNOWLEDGMENTS

THERE was once a ballet company that liked to call itself "The One and Only" in its advertisements. And for its devoted fans, that company, the Ballet Russe de Monte Carlo, was truly "The One and Only." Founded in 1938 as a result of legal and artistic squabbles, it flourished until 1962, when it quietly disbanded. During most of that time, it was essentially an American company, although it bore a foreign name and perpetuated a cosmopolitan style of dancing. Also during most of that time, it was beloved by balletgoers from coast to coast. Occasionally referred to as the Monte Carlo for short or, more frequently, just as the Ballet Russe, it was one of the most respected dance companies in the United States.

Yet, since 1962, many of its accomplishments have been overlooked or forgotten and to young dancegoers it is only a name and a legend. And even the legend has grown hazy. During my research for this book, I discovered that several of my New York acquaintances who had never seen the Ballet Russe entertained misconceptions about it. Some assumed that its offerings resembled the programs of divertissements given by Soviet concert dance troupes. Although the Ballet Russe, like most Western ballet companies, was influenced by the bravura of the first Soviet dancers who arrived here in the 1950s, it nevertheless grew out of a tradition of Russian dancing somewhat different from that of the

Soviets. Other friends revealed that they thought the Ballet Russe presented nothing but a few classical warhorses over and over again. Certainly, the repertoire did contain tried-and-true favorites that audiences never stopped clamoring to see. Yet in these days when the word "classics" increasingly refers to full-evening productions, it should be pointed out that all the Ballet Russe's classics were short enough to share a bill with at least one other work.

Perhaps it is not surprising that some people should now find the Ballet Russe mysterious. The Ballet Russe was a touring organization that in its heyday went to lots of places—including lots of surprising places—in the United States and Canada. But it did not go everywhere. It did not visit Europe after 1939 and it made few Latin American appearances. Moreover, after 1950 (except for one long season at the Metropolitan Opera House in 1957) its New York performances were restricted to a few nights annually at the Brooklyn Academy of Music. As a result, many dancers of the Ballet Russe never achieved international reputations. Yet the company contained artists who could be favorably compared with well-known members of globetrotting companies. Similarly, after 1939, the Ballet Russe repertoire was unknown in Europe and sometimes it was only scarcely known to New York audiences, even though that repertoire included some unusual ballets. However, if the Ballet Russe was a stranger to London and Paris during most of its existence, its dancers and repertoire were familiar in Chicago, Boston, and Kansas City, in St. Louis, Milwaukee, San Francisco, and Cleveland, in Toronto, Ottawa, and Montreal, and in Seattle, Portland, Los Angeles, and Houston. The Ballet Russe was not only familiar in such cities, it was welcome and beloved.

Ballet Russe programs emphasized variety. During the company's best seasons the repertoire contained classical and contemporary, serious and comic, dramatic and lyric ballets. The Ballet Russe always knew how to please the crowds (which is why the crowds kept coming back to see it), but it was also able to intrigue the intelligentsia. The Ballet Russe was actively involved in many important choreographic developments. Thus it promoted the symphonic ballet, championed neo-classical abstraction, and made excursions into Americana and modern dance. There was even a time when John Martin of the *New York Times*—a critic who was by no means always a fan of classical ballet—was able to call the Ballet Russe America's most experimental company.

Through changes of fortune and taste, the Ballet Russe

managed to survive because of an extraordinary mixture of talent, style, pluck, luck, and esprit de corps. And always, wherever it went, the Ballet Russe made people excited about ballet.

Oh yes, it most certainly did that. I am one of the hundreds, perhaps thousands, of balletgoers who can say, "The Ballet Russe de Monte Carlo was the first ballet company I ever saw." In 1950 I was a high school student in Milwaukee who, though fascinated by books and art and music, had seen little live theatre and, outside of recitals by local dancing schools, no dance at all. One day I read in the newspaper that two ballet companies were coming to town, Ballet Theatre and the Ballet Russe de Monte Carlo. I decided I wanted to find out what ballet was like, but my parents, who controlled my allowance, told me that I would be permitted to attend only one performance by only one of those troupes.

Never having heard of either of them before, I chose to attend the Ballet Russe de Monte Carlo. Why? Partly (and I almost blush to admit it) because of its glamorous-sounding name. My choice therefore bolsters the arguments of all those managers and impresarios who claim that whereas Ballet Theatre is an austere name with little box office appeal, Ballet Russe de Monte Carlo may be the greatest name ever invented for a ballet company.

The Ballet Russe program I attended consisted of *Coppélia*, the Bluebird pas de deux, and *Birthday*, and I chose it because the music of *Coppélia* was already familiar to me from recordings. At that performance I was able to see Alexandra Danilova and Frederic Franklin in *Coppélia*, Ruthanna Boris and Leon Danielian in the Bluebird, and Mary Ellen Moylan and Oleg Tupine in *Birthday*. Perhaps, for dramatic effect, I should say that I was bowled over, swept off my feet, carried away. But in truth I wasn't. Rather, and possibly more importantly, that performance simply whetted my curiosity about ballet. It made me decide that ballet was something I wanted to see again.

I did. I kept going back to see ballet—not only the Ballet Russe, but other companies as well. I saw the Ballet Russe through good seasons and bad. There were times when other companies aroused more passionate enthusiasm in me. Yet I never stopped attending the Ballet Russe. I could not imagine a dance season without it. The Ballet Russe de Monte Carlo was an important part of my dancegoing life.

Writing this book has therefore been a labor of love. I

have tried to chronicle the company's always lively, and often tumultuous, history. But since the Ballet Russe introduced ballet to many areas of the country, this is more than an account of dancers and choreographers. I have also concerned myself with manners and morals, with politics and publicity campaigns, with critical taste and popular sentiment. Even the superficially frivolous anecdotes that one may find here have been included in the hope that, in addition to being entertaining, they may also be instructive and reveal something of what it was like to be a ballet dancer—and, for that matter, a balletgoer—in America between 1938 and 1962.

Many people have helped me write this book, and I extend gratitude to them all. Irina Pabst (Mrs. Robert E. Pabst) was kind enough to allow me to pester her, month after month, with questions about her father, Sergei J. Denham, director of the Ballet Russe, and she introduced me to her daughter, Stephanie Fenwick, who told me what it was like to have a Russian ballet director as a grandfather. Michael Subotin, Denham's old friend and business associate, allowed me to rummage through the files of the Ballet Foundation: many thanks to him and to Anna Kisselgoff, who translated for me Subotin's biography of Denham from the Russian. Thanks, too, to Tatiana Massine, daughter of Léonide Massine, who secured permission for me to view her father's films, now housed in the Dance Collection of the New York Public Library.

The former members of the Ballet Russe to whom I spoke proved enormously helpful. The company's legendary stars, Alexandra Danilova and Frederic Franklin, provided me with much information. Leon Danielian seemed always ready to answer questions, and I recall with great pleasure my long conversations with such ballerinas as Ruthanna Boris, Nathalie Krassovska, and Mia Slavenska. Yvonne Chouteau and Rochelle Zide allowed me to read the diaries they kept as young dancers with the Ballet Russe; Robert Lindgren let me read the letters home that his mother had carefully preserved all these years; Igor Youskevitch provided me with a copy of an unpublished essay he had written on Russian ballet; and Michel Katcharoff let me read his memoirs. Nina Novak took time to write me from her present home in Caracas, Venezuela. Among the dancers who let me consult their scrapbooks and collections of memorabilia are Charles Dickson, Roman Jasinski, Moscelyne Larkin, Milada Mladova, Eugene Slavin, James Starbuck, and Sonja Taanila (who also showed me the scrapbooks of her sister, the late Gertrude Tyven). Most of the people mentioned were also delightful conversationalists, and so were such other former Ballet Russe dancers, choreographers, and staff members as Meredith Baylis, Valerie Bettis, Joy Williams Brown, Eugénie Delarova, Agnes de Mille, M. Hornyak, Marcel Fenchel Luipart, Alexandra Nadal, Duncan Noble, Ruth Page, Sophie Pourmel, Gilbert Reed, Nikita Talin, Maria Tallchief, Miguel Terekhov, and Raven Wilkinson.

There were many weeks when I haunted the Dance Collection of the New York Public Library. Genevieve Oswald, the Dance Collection's curator, and her staff did much to make my labors there pleasant and productive. I would also like to thank the staff of the newspaper room of the San Francisco Public Library and of the Hoblitzelle Theatre Arts Library of the University of Texas at Austin (with special thanks to Jane Combs, the ever helpful administrative assistant of the library's Humanities Research Center). Special thanks also go to George Verdak, who allowed me to do research in his truly remarkable private dance history archives in Indianapolis.

Among the people who have helped track down pieces of information for me are Giora Manor in Tel Aviv, Graham Jackson in Toronto, Grace Doty in Oakland, California, and Viola Hegyi Swisher in Los Angeles. Reminiscences, advice, and information have also come from Ann Barzel, Laura Clandon, Selma Jeanne Cohen, Edwin Denby, Gage and Richard Englund, Judith Brin Ingber, Robert Joffrey, Lincoln Kirstein, Robert Lawrence, P.W. Manchester, Maurice Seymour, Paul Taylor, Walter Terry, David Vaughan, Kathrine Sorley Walker, and Sallie Wilson. George Jackson was my enthusiastic and helpful editor, and finally, I wish to thank George Dorris, not only for his many suggestions, but for his infinite patience over the past three years, during which time I have discussed the writing of this book with him, virtually page by page, paragraph by paragraph.

Except as noted below, all photographs in this volume are from the collection of the Ballet Foundation and are reproduced here with the kind permission of the trustees of the foundation. Other photographs are from the following sources: the Three Companions in *St. Francis*, collection of Marcel Fenchel Luipart; Alicia Markova and George Zoritch in *Les Sylphides*, collection of George Zoritch; group from *Serenade*, collection of Joy Williams Brown; Rachel Chapman and George Balanchine at the piano, collection of Robert and Sonja Lindgren.

In general, I refer to ballets in this book under the titles by which they are best known to English-speaking audiences. If a ballet is known under different titles in England and America, I have usually chosen to emphasize the American title, since the Ballet Russe de Monte Carlo spent most of its time in America.

Jack Anderson
New York City, 1981

PART ONE

The Life of the Company

1 BIRTH OF THE COMPANY

Ballet RUSSE DE MONTE CARLO. Was there ever a more magical name for a ballet company? As a name, it sounds like a press agent's inspired invention. Yet the company which called itself that from 1938 to 1962 came by its name honestly. Initially its dancers were primarily of Russian descent, and even after it had become largely American in personnel and had pronounced itself an American institution, it emphasized a Russian tradition extending from the innovations of the Diaghilev Ballet back to the classicism of the Maryinsky. There was even a time when it possessed official connections with Monte Carlo.

The company had its origin in both the mysteries of the law courts and the glare of publicity. If certain other matters had gone otherwise, it might not have existed at all. For before there was a Ballet Russe de Monte Carlo, there already was a Ballets Russes, a Ballets Russes which for a few seasons also had been entitled to call itself "de Monte Carlo." This was the Ballets Russes organized in 1932 by René Blum and Colonel W. de Basil. Though that company, for various legal technicalities, modified its name several times, it was usually known for short as the de Basil company. And it was one of the balletic success stories of its time. Filling the gap left by the death of Diaghilev and the dispersal of his company, it brought together some of Diaghilev's former dancers along with a host of newcomers, including the much publicized

3

child prodigy "baby ballerinas." Its repertoire included Diaghilev revivals and ambitious new works, the most significant being the controversial symphonic ballets of Léonide Massine—who was, in effect if not in title, the company's artistic leader. The company triumphed in London and then, under Sol Hurok's shrewd management, took America by storm.

Yet by the mid-1930s there were signs of trouble within the company. There were dissensions so fierce that lawsuits seemed inevitable and dancers' loyalties were being claimed by rival factions. Aware that she might be called up as a witness in any court case involving the de Basil company, ballerina Alexandra Danilova once assured a friend, in her own special English, "I will tell the truth, the whole truth, and nothing is the truth!"[1]

Sorting out the truths in these disputes between some unusually contentious people and in a company notorious for intrigue is no easy matter. But it does appear that for several seasons professional relations between Massine and de Basil had been deteriorating. Massine had long wanted the title of artistic director, but de Basil had refused, desiring no rival in his company's directorate.[2] The most he was willing to concede was to grant Massine the position of *collaborateur artistique* in his 1934 contract.[3] To make matters worse, de Basil, a wily man who sometimes appeared to love intrigue as much as he did ballet, actually encouraged a certain amount of dissension because he could then, after a period of internecine squabbling, step in and as general director squelch the opposition, thereby—or so he may have hoped—strengthening the impression he liked to give as a man of power.[4]

One way by which de Basil tried to prevent Massine from gaining too much power of his own was to commission ballets from Bronislava Nijinska and to groom young David Lichine as choreographer. But Massine found ways to retaliate. In 1937 he contacted George Balanchine (then director of the American Ballet) about the possibility of pooling resources to establish an international company with dual headquarters in America and Europe.[5] Though nothing came of this, it was clear that Massine was growing restless and that he was willing to let influential people know it. Massine met with concert manager David Libidins and some potential patrons in the spring of 1937, and everyone who attended the meeting was sworn to secrecy—or so the *New York Times* reported to all its readers.[6] The patrons then founded a sponsoring organization known at first as World Art and later as Universal Art, the name in either case being an homage to *Mir Isskustva (The World of*

Art), the progressive Russian art magazine founded by Diaghilev in 1899.[7] While Massine was to be artistic director of the proposed new company, its general director would be a Russian-born banker who had adopted the American name of Sergei (occasionally written as Serge) J. Denham.

Comparatively few people knew much about Denham. It was perhaps this obscurity that made balletomane Robert Pitney skeptically remark when he heard rumors about a new company, "Hmm, Serge Denham? denim, serge? . . . Then it *must* be made up out of whole cloth."[8] Possessing a love of ballet that went back to his childhood, Denham was intrigued by the glamour which made it so different from the mundane world of business.

Eugénie Delarova remembers that when the de Basil dancers were returning to Europe after their "first or second" American tour, she was walking her dog on deck one morning and talking to it in Russian when a man approached and, also speaking Russian, said, "You must be one of the dancers! It is an honor to meet you." The man was Denham, who in his enthusiasm hosted a cocktail party for Delarova, Massine (at that time her husband), and other company members. Denham seemed delighted just to be able to entertain them.[9] Now he was about to hold an executive position with a new ballet company.

Eventually, one of his personal assistants in his business dealings in organizing the ballet would be his niece, Tatiana Orlova, who later married Massine.[10] Within the de Basil company itself he had a devoted ally in the person of Tatiana Chamié, who helped recruit dancers for the new troupe. Michel Katcharoff (then dancing with de Basil) recalls that when the company was in New York Denham would often come to Chamié's performances, stop backstage, and take her out to a late supper. When Denham complained that he found his banking job tedious, it was Chamié who urged him to take an active interest in ballet and to persuade his friends in finance and high society to support the art.[11]

Multilingual and well read, Chamié was never a star (though reportedly a good character dancer). Yet to this day she remains something of a legend. A member of a Syrian family living in Odessa, she left Russia with her parents at the time of the revolution and grew up in Paris. She appeared with the Diaghilev and de Basil companies (and then with the Ballet Russe de Monte Carlo), her career as a dancer lasting until 1943, when she opened a school in New York at which she taught until her untimely death from spinal meningitis in 1953 at the age of forty-eight. During her teaching years she was famous for giving open houses that were held every Wednesday night at her studio, which became a popular gathering spot. Ballet people met there to exchange gossip and hatch schemes.[12]

She regaled her students with stories, stories they still love to repeat. It was said that she had total choreographic recall and was a stickler for accuracy. As a company member, Chamié usually appeared only in corps roles but she would watch other dancers. If someone—even a principal—modified the choreography she was likely to hiss in the middle of a performance, "That's wrong!" Her outburst usually caused the culprit to revert shamefacedly to the original steps. That is, Chamié might do this if she were awake, for it is said that there were times when, having to hold a pose as a sylphide or swan maiden for a long time, she would actually doze off on stage.[13] Yet Denham trusted her judgment so much that, after her death, *Dance News* commented, "Both at the time of her active connection with the Ballet Russe de Monte Carlo and after her resignation, her role in that organization was far greater than it seemed to the casual observer."[14]

Among the backers of the proposed new company was millionaire Julius Fleischmann of Cincinnati, heir to a fortune in yeast, liquor, and coffee. A 1920 graduate of Yale, Fleischmann was known not only as an arts patron but also as a sportsman. In 1928, at a cost of $625,000 he built the 225-foot diesel yacht *Camargo*, at that time America's largest and most costly pleasure craft.[15] Julius Fleischmann, known familiarly as "Junkie," was probably the company's most loyal backer, unflaggingly supporting the Ballet Russe de Monte Carlo from its inception to its demise.

While plans for Massine's company were being made, Massine was still a member of the de Basil ballet. So when Denham approached Sol Hurok, at that time managing de Basil, to urge him to become involved with the hypothetical new group, Hurok replied that he would be interested only if he could be absolutely certain that Massine would be artistic director.[16] At the time, however, *Variety* suggested that Hurok's interest in a new company was not exclusively due to his admiration for Massine's artistry. The theatrical newspaper speculated that Hurok came to support the new troupe so that his name could adorn publicity posters in big letters, de Basil in the past having always stipulated that his own name figure more importantly in announcements than Hurok's. Hurok suffered from "hurt ego," claimed *Variety*.[17] For whatever reason, Hurok now found himself simultaneously involved in the internal affairs of two rival organizations. This was not to be the only time in the history of the Ballet Russe de Monte Carlo when Hurok would be involved in competing projects.

A company promised to him, Massine proceeded to plan a repertoire. As might be expected, he thought of a repertoire featuring his own ballets. Now that his contract with de Basil was scheduled to expire 15 September 1937, Massine desired exclusive rights to all his ballets, including those he had choreographed for de Basil. De Basil would have none of this.[18] The result of their disagreement was a case tried in London's Chancery Court. It opened on 9 July 1937 with a discussion of an issue that still vexes us today—whether the choreographer, as the "author" of a ballet in some sense should therefore also be considered its owner.[19] Massine adopted a lofty, even slightly sentimental, attitude toward creativity, one harking back to Romantic notions about artistic genius: "I am the servant of nobody. I devise my ballets as and when I can, and when the spirit moves me."[20]

According to the London *Times*, however, Mr. Justice Luxmoore took a rather different attitude toward the matter. He noted that Massine's ballets fell into three groups: first, those created before 1 June 1932 (that is, before Massine's association with de Basil); second, those created under a contract with de Basil which ran from 17 November 1932 to 10 August 1934; third, those created after 10 August 1934, under a contract which stated that Massine shall compose "such dances and ballets as may be suitable to and may be required by the director for the purposes of the Ballets Russes," and which further stated that Massine will give his "full and exclusive services to the director," and not produce ballets, plays, or films elsewhere.

Bearing these distinctions in mind, Justice Luxmoore ruled that copyright for all ballets in the first category belonged with Massine, and if de Basil wished to produce them he had to secure them from Massine. The ballets in the other categories, however, went to de Basil—who, said Justice Luxmoore, had engaged Massine to supply choreography, whereas he had supplied all the ballet's other components. Ballet being a composite art, it could not exist without choreography, nor could choreography exist without its allied arts. Consequently, ruled Justice Luxmoore, "It would be strange if Colonel de Basil, having paid for the supply of that necessary ingredient [choreography] for his ballet, was himself prevented from using it at the termination of the agreement."[21]

De Basil took another form of action against Massine in 1937 by acquiring the choreographic services of Michel Fokine. As when he had hired Nijinska and encouraged Lichine, this tactic was one by which de Basil tried to insure that Massine would not gain undue authority during the time in which he was still under contract. By setting Massine and Fokine in rivalry, de Basil could strengthen his own position as leader and arbitrator.[22] Moreover, in Fokine, de Basil had gained the acknowledged master of modern ballet, and his presence would suggest that the company had not suffered a catastrophic artistic loss with Massine's departure.

Although Massine's contract was to expire in September 1937, Hurok persuaded him to remain for an October season at the Metropolitan Opera House and for part of the American tour which followed.[23] Massine stayed on for several months, giving his last performance with the de Basil ballet in San Francisco on 30 January 1938, on a program which included Nijinska's *The Hundred Kisses* and his own *Symphonie Fantastique* and *Le Beau Danube*.[24]

Many of Massine's fellow company members soon had to make their own decisions as to whether to remain with de Basil or to follow Massine. Some had few second thoughts. Thus Danilova says, "De Basil was not a man of culture. He had silly ideas—you know, he always kept saying we should do a ballet about Mickey Mouse. Massine, though, was a great choreographer. Between the two, the choice was obvious." Other dancers had good reasons for continuing with de Basil. One of them, Roman Jasinski, explains that, despite his admiration for Massine, he did not wish to risk the uncertainties of a new company. In the financially precarious 1930s there had been several grandiose balletic projects that had never materialized: how could he be sure that Massine's would not be another? The de Basil company, despite its peculiarities, was a stable organization of proven artistic merit. Jasinski—and others—stayed.

The prospect of two Ballets Russes set balletomanes agog. *The Dancing Times's* American correspondent breathlessly wondered, "Which group will open first? Will there be battles in the aisles?"[25] Arnold L. Haskell thundered his disapproval: "Massine's departure will not only damage the company as a whole, but Massine himself perhaps even more. It has taken all of five years' hard work and sacrifice to build up this magnificent ensemble. . . . It would take more than five years . . . to create another such."[26]

But Haskell was considered a champion of de Basil. Massine's group remained undaunted, Denham confidently announcing,

> Our aim is perfection. We have set ourselves an ideal—the Diaghileff standard of ballet—and hope to achieve it.
> Ever since Diaghileff died ballet has become a commercial

enterprise. We hope to be rich enough to divorce the commercial aspect from the artistic one, so that art will not have to be influenced by commercial consideration.

But at the same time we believe that a ballet company must be self-sustaining and pay its own expenses.[27]

Hurok, too, waxed optimistic: "American audiences are now ripe for the very best products which modern ballet has to offer . . . and they are ready to accept startling innovations in their stride."[28]

Many new ballets were announced, some of which never got beyond the preliminary announcements. It was said that Balanchine would work with the company, reviving his version of Poulenc's *Aubade* and creating a new ballet about the life of Paganini to music by Vincenzo Tommasini.[29] During the 1930s there were several ballets—among them Ashton's *Apparitions,* Nijinska's *La Bien-Aimée,* Massine's *Symphonie Fantastique,* and Balanchine's *Transcendence* —about tormented, even demonically possessed, artistic genuises, and for years there had been talk of a ballet about Paganini. Eventually, there would be such a ballet—but it would not be by Balanchine. Eventually, too, there would be a new ballet score by Tommasini—but it would not accompany choreography about Paganini.

The most far-ranging project of the time was the formation, with World Art's cooperation, of a subsidiary body known as Ballet Guild, Inc. It was hoped that the guild would hold annual contests for the best new scenario, musical score, and scenery and costume designs for a ballet, and that the winning entries in each category would be put into production by Massine. The guild would also sponsor an annual work chosen by its members without respect to the terms of the contests. Mrs. Arne Horlin Ekstrom (dance writer Parmenia Migel) headed the executive committee, while additional committees were formed to judge décor and music.[30] Although, as it turned out, the Ballet Guild's contests never really enriched the repertoire, the very existence of such a group suggested the seriousness of the Massine company's intentions.

By early 1938 it seemed inevitable that there would be two Ballets Russes. In de Basil's company were such dancers as David Lichine, Irina Baronova, Tatiana Riabouchinska, Tamara Grigorieva, Olga Morosova, Nina Verchinina, Lubov Tchernicheva, Sono Osato, Yurek Shabelevsky, Paul Petroff, Yurek Lazowski, and Roman Jasinski. By winning some dancers over from de Basil and hiring others from elsewhere, Massine would eventually acquire Alexandra Danilova, Tamara Toumanova, Alicia Markova, Mia

Slavenska, Eugénie Delarova, Lubov Rostova, Nathalie Krassovska, Jeannette Lauret, Milada Mladova, Nini Theilade, Igor Youskevitch, Serge Lifar, Frederic Franklin, George Zoritch, Michel Panaieff, Roland Guerard, Marc Platoff, Simon Semenoff, and Jean Yazvinsky.[31] Not only was World Art, Inc. bringing a new company into being, it also purchased an existing company. On 19 November 1937 it bought René Blum's Les Ballets de Monte Carlo for $30,000, plus an additional $10,800 to remiburse Blum for the expense of creating three new works. As part of the agreement with Blum, the new company would present five weeks of ballet in Monte Carlo each spring from 1938 to 1941.[32]

Les Ballets de Monte Carlo had come into being as the result of an earlier feud with de Basil—this one with his former associate, René Blum, who severed his connection with de Basil in 1935.[33] The autocratic de Basil and the mild-mannered Blum found each other incompatible, and Blum was alarmed at de Basil's increasing preoccupation with American touring at the expense of concern for the company's Monte Carlo seasons.[34] If quarrels with Massine would lose de Basil a choreographer, his quarrels with Blum had lost his company a home.

Diaghilev had been granted the right to use the name, Ballets Russes de Monte Carlo, from the Prince of Monaco, who offered the company a place to work at the Monte Carlo Opera. The contract called for an annual spring season in Monte Carlo, but left the company free for other commitments during the rest of the year.[35] After Diaghilev's death, Blum took over the unexpired contract, at first booking itinerant dancers, then in 1932 forming a permanent company with de Basil.[36] Blum, brother of French Socialist premier Léon Blum, is almost universally remembered as a gentle man of exquisite taste and liberal views who never failed to help a dancer afflicted with financial or personal problems.

By severing his connection with de Basil, Blum prevented de Basil's company from having a secure and comfortable spring headquarters. Dancers looked forward to Monte Carlo. After the rigors of touring, it was a place where they could relax. The climate was genial and the pace leisurely, there being only four ballet performances a week—three evenings plus a Sunday matinee. The Café de Paris, opposite the Casino, became the dancers' favorite haunt. The Casino itself, however, was closed to them since, like all employees of the Principality of Monaco, they were forbidden to gamble there. Yet a few managed to sneak in and, if they were discreet about their gambling, no one seemed to mind. Everybody adored Monte Carlo—even the ordinarily quarrelsome "ballet mothers" who accompanied their dancing daughters on tour. On a terrace outside the Opera was a bench which became notorious as the roosting place for dancers' mothers who, denied admission to rehearsals, could nevertheless watch proceedings through the open windows of the rehearsal hall.[37]

As an independent entity, Blum's group existed only two years, 1936 and 1937. It opened its season in Monte Carlo 3 April 1936 with Nicolas Zverev as ballet master and a company headed by Vera Nemchinova, Marie Ruanova, Nathalie Krassovska (then billed as Natalie Leslie), Helene Kirsova, Anatole Vilzak, Anatol Oboukhoff, and André Eglevsky. At the end of that year, George Gué became ballet master. Gué, who also spelled his surname Gé, was a St. Petersburg-born Finnish dancer who had been ballet master at the Helsinki Opera before joining Blum's company. He served as ballet master for the Royal Swedish Ballet during World War II and later returned to Helsinki to direct the Finnish National Ballet.

In 1937, after some dancers had left the company, Blum's principals included Nana Gollner (who thereby became the first American ballerina of a Ballet Russe), Nina Tarakanova, Krassovska, Jeannette Lauret, Eglevsky, Grant Mouradoff, and Michel Panaieff. Productions included the second act of *Swan Lake,* a *Coppélia* staged by Nicholas Zverev (a former Diaghilev dancer who had also served as ballet master in Kaunas, Lithuania), Gué's *Un Soir* (Florent Schmitt), Balanchine's *Aubade,* and Boris Romanoff's versions of *Nutcracker* and *El Amor Brujo.* What gave the company its special distinction were its ballets by Fokine, all staged under the choreographer's personal supervision. From the Diaghilev era came *Les Sylphides, Carnaval, Spectre de la Rose, Scheherazade, Prince Igor,* and *Petrouchka,* while ballets that Fokine revived which had been originally produced under other auspices included *Les Elfes, Igrouchki,* and *Jota Aragonesa.* Most significantly, Fokine created three new works for the company: *Don Juan* (Gluck) and *L'Épreuve d'Amour* (attributed to Mozart), both 1936, and *Les Éléments* (Bach), in 1937.[38]

Proudly announcing its association with Fokine, Blum's Ballets de Monte Carlo opened a London season at the Alhambra, 15 May 1936. With the company came the rumor that the young English choreographer Frederick Ashton would create a new ballet for it, *Epsom,* with music by Marcel Delaunay and décor by Raoul Dufy.[39] But that rumor proved only a rumor. Discussing the season, *The Dancing Times* remarked, "With the outstanding exception of Vera Nemchinova the company at present appears to possess no dancer with a personality and a technique that will grip an audience but, as a compensation for this, it has a *corps de ballet* which, under the guiding hand of Fokine, has risen to heights of perfection which are a joy to watch."[40]

After a British tour, the company departed 11 September for South Africa, remaining there until 17 December. In February and March of 1937 it toured Britain again, returning to Monte Carlo for a season beginning 1 April. On 31 May it opened at the London Coliseum.[41]

There were those observers who thought that it had declined a bit since its last visit, *The Dancing Times* finding that the company "did not quite live up to the reputation they had established last year. The *corps de ballet* . . . were a trifle 'hard' and at times inclined to be ragged and among the principals 'personalities' were missing."[42] Blum's company closed 1937 with another British tour.[43] And then, in a sense, it was no more, for it had been purchased by World Art for Massine. De Basil, meanwhile, had hired Fokine, thereby bringing about a paradoxical situation: the Monte Carlo troupe had a large Fokine repertoire, but Fokine himself was now associated with de Basil; and while de Basil's repertoire contained Massine's most acclaimed ballets of the 1930s, Massine was now associated with the Monte Carlo company.

Among Blum's dancers who stayed with the company under Massine's direction, one of the most important was Nathalie Krassovska, who became a ballerina of the Ballet Russe de Monte Carlo. Of part-Russian, part-Scottish descent (hence her occasional use of Leslie as surname), she came from a dancing family, her grandmother having been a member of the Bolshoi, while her mother was Lydia Krassovska of the Diaghilev Ballet. Nathalie Krassovska danced with Balanchine's Les Ballets 1933 and as Lifar's partner on a South American tour. When both Blum and de Basil expressed interest in her, her mother decided she had better join Blum's company because David Lichine was in de Basil's and he had the reputation of being a "wolf." In the Blum company she came under the influence of Fokine, who once declared that he considered Krassovska "the most nearly perfect dancer" for *Les Sylphides*.[44]

However, if this remark is quoted to Krassovska, she will exclaim, "Oh, but he never said that to my face! In rehearsal it was all different: he screamed, I cried. He was the most demanding man I have ever worked with." He spent hours polishing choreography. Rehearsing *Les Sylphides,* Fokine told his dancers that "you must feel to the ends of your fingers," and he made them aware of the importance of tiny details: "he even told you how far into the distance it was proper for you to look." It was while working for Blum's company that Fokine started making little changes in *Les Sylphides,* much to the horror of dancers familiar with the ballet from performances by the Diaghilev company. Gradually, alternate versions of passages developed, each with its champions. Disputes between dancers who had been associated at different times with Fokine continued season after season in the Ballet Russe de Monte Carlo, and Ruthanna Boris remembers how it used to amuse Americans in the company to hear argumentative Russians shout about "Fokine-this" and "Fokine-that," since, given its Russian pronunciation, the name Fokine sounds disconcertingly like an English-language obscenity.

Of Fokine's creations for Blum, two attracted considerable attention and remained for a short time in the repertoire of the new Ballet Russe de Monte Carlo: *Don Juan* and *L'Épreuve d'Amour.* The more imposing was the former, first produced in London on 25 June 1936, with designs by Mariano Andreù. It was Fokine's version of the Don Juan ballet which Gaspero Angiolini had choreographed to a Gluck score in 1761 and which comes down to us in reputation as a major example of eighteenth-century *ballet d'action.* Commentators often make much of how, unable to find a complete Gluck score anywhere, Fokine and his assistant scenarist Eric Allatini scoured Europe until Allatini finally obtained an old manuscript in Germany. However, dance and music critic Robert Lawrence finds it peculiar that no one Fokine and Allatini encountered in their searches ever pointed out to them that the complete score had actually been published by Universal Edition of Vienna in 1923, edited by Robert Haas.[45]

The swiftly paced scenario tells of how Don Juan's serenade of Elvira is interrupted by the arrival of her father, the Commander, who is killed by Don Juan in a duel. During the course of a banquet given by Don Juan, the Commander's ghost appears several times to invite the Don to visit him in the cemetery. Fearing nothing, Don Juan accepts the invitation. When, despite the Commander's warnings, the Don refuses to repent, he is carried off to hell by furies. Fokine's Don Juan was Anatole Vilzak, while his comic valet, Sganarelle, was Louis Lebercher; Jeannette Lauret was Elvira and Jean Yazvinsky, the Commander.

All reports of the ballet emphasize its mimetic quality. Thus C.W. Beaumont praised the opening for being "pure choreo-

drama, a mime scene not 'walked,' but one in which every movement flows in harmony with the mood and rhythm of the music."
Fernau Hall, on the other hand, considered it "a ponderous and
prosaic type of mime." Several critics thought that some of the
divertissement dances at the banquet—including a gypsy dance, a
dance in which boys cavort like monkeys, and a dance in which
girls play with enormous tambourines—were, while clever in
themselves, not quite in keeping with the work's historical period.[46]

A film of *Don Juan* exists in the New York Public Library
Dance Collection, a silent rehearsal film utilizing only a minimum
of scenery and with the cast in practice dress. This rendition
seems, in several senses, a silent film. Not only is it literally silent,
lacking music, but the gestures Fokine devised resemble those of
actors in good silent movies. Though often large-scaled, they are
seldom melodramatic. Nor do they resemble the conventional
mime of nineteenth-century ballet. They remain legible in outline
and clear in dramatic motivation. In contrast to their gravity, the
banquet divertissements, though possibly anachronistic, stand
out like bright baubles of movement. These dances suggest the
superficial glitter of Don Juan's life as a libertine, while the terrible
battle of good and evil in which he participates is conveyed by the
austerities of the mime.

L'Épreuve d'Amour, which was premiered 4 April 1936
in Monte Carlo with Vera Nemchinova as the Chinese maiden,
André Eglevsky as her lover, Jean Yazvinsky as her tyrannical
father, and Helene Kirsova as a butterfly, also attracted critical
interest. A bit of *chinoiserie,* its score, once attributed to Mozart, is
now considered to be that of *Der Rekrut,* a divertissement with
music by various composers given in Vienna in 1838.[47] The ballet
concerns an avaricious Mandarin who wishes to have his daughter
marry a rich ambassador rather than the youth she really loves.
The youth and his friends first rob the ambassador, then restore
his wealth, causing the Mandarin to veer from lack of interest back
to desire for the proposed match. Realizing that it is only his wealth
that is coveted, the ambassador departs, leaving the lovers free to
marry.

The ballet won admirers. Beaumont found that, with its
designs by André Derain, it possessed the charm of porcelain
vases. Fernau Hall thought it expertly crafted, Fokine successfully
concealing the weaknesses of Blum's young, inexperienced company through the establishment of a picturesque atmosphere. As
part of the Ballet Russe de Monte Carlo's repertoire, it created less
stir in America, although Grace Robert regarded it affectionately.

She attributed its comparative lack of success here to the change in casting by which Lubov Roudenko replaced Kirsova as the butterfly which flutters through the Mandarin's garden (this, she claimed, was "like asking Mae West to play Ariel") and to "the effects of an ill-natured and ill-informed review by a music critic turned dance critic for the evening."

The critic she alluded to was surely Jerome D. Bohm of the *New York Herald-Tribune*, who called it one of Fokine's "weakest efforts," adding, "Aside from the fact that the action hardly ever links up with the course of the music, the choreographic invention is so feeble in its utilization of clichés that a further account of its ineptitudes seems futile." In 1939 the ballet became a casualty of World War II, for the company, trying to flee Europe before catastrophe overtook it, left the scenery and costumes behind in a Paris warehouse. After four decades, Michel Katcharoff, who eventually became régisseur of the Ballet Russe de Monte Carlo, still maintains, "This was one of Fokine's finest works that never really reached the large audience it deserved."[48]

When World Art, Inc., acquired Les Ballets de Monte Carlo, René Blum theoretically remained a co-director of the new company. In fact, however, he had less and less to do with it. When war seemed imminent he refused to leave his beloved Paris, despite the warnings of friends, and with the German occupation of France he was persecuted by the Nazis and deported to the Auschwitz concentration camp, where he died in 1942.[49]

The political troubles of Europe did not appear to dampen the spirits of the dancers who assembled in Monte Carlo in 1938 to prepare for the debut season of Massine's new company. When young British dancer Frederic Franklin walked into the rehearsal hall for the first time, he found more than a hundred dancers milling confusedly about, few of whom were actually under contract. These dancers included those who thought they had been promised, or said they had been promised, or wished they would be promised positions with the troupe. Eventually, Massine arrived and sorted things out, and the company got down to business rehearsing for a Monte Carlo season which ran from 5 April to 15 May 1938. During that year's spring and summer engagements, the company consisted of approximately 70 dancers.

Massine bore the title of *maître de ballet* (which in Europe tends to indicate much more authority than "ballet master" does in America). His lieutenants included Boris Kochno, *collaborateur artistique;* Jean Yazvinsky, *régisseur;* and David Libidins, *directeur administratif.* Denham was listed as *président du conseil d'administration.* The conductors were Marc-César Scotto, Efrem Kurtz, and Anatole Fistoulari. Programs featured Fokine ballets from the Blum repertoire, *Le Beau Danube* (a Massine work not controlled by de Basil), and the premieres of two new Massine ballets so dissimilar that, whether one liked them or not, they forced one to acknowledge his choreographic versatility: *Gaîté Parisienne* and *The Seventh Symphony.*[50]

Gaîté Parisienne, which had been advertised under tentative working titles of *Gay Mabille* and *Tortoni* (the latter being a popular Second Empire café), was the brainchild of Comte Etienne de Beaumont, who provided its slight scenario, as well as its scenery and costumes. He told Massine that he wanted to do a ballet to Offenbach in the style of the paintings of Franz Xaver Winterhalter, a society painter of the Second Empire.

With the cooperation of Offenbach's nephew, they examined operetta scores and, in search of ideas for designs, poked about antique shops on the Boulevard Raspail until they found a faded roll of wallpaper with an ostrich-feather pattern which was copied for the top border on the backdrop. Roger Desormière was first asked to compile the score, but when he was unable to complete the project he entrusted it to Manuel Rosenthal. Rosenthal's arrangement, however, was turned down by Massine, who accused him of insufficient respect for Offenbach. Rosenthal then suggested that their mutual friend Igor Stravinsky pass judgment on the score. Stravinsky, far from being censorious, advised Massine, "Léonide, if you reject this score you are an idiot; you will be rejecting what must be the greatest success of your career."[51]

Stravinsky was right. Other Massine ballets have been more exalted, others more academically perfect. Indeed, the faults of *Gaîté* are obvious: it has little subtlety and there are several false climaxes. Nevertheless, few Massine ballets have been more popular or durable. After its Monte Carlo premiere, 5 April 1938, Hurok, who was in the United States, anxiously inquired about the merit of the new work he was planning to import to America. Eugénie Delarova wrote back, "It is not only bread, it is bread and butter."

Gaîté's sole rival in popularity is probably *Le Beau Danube,* and, because both are frothy ballets in an operetta style, they are often compared. Curiously, *Gaîté's* reputation is higher in America than it is in Europe. When the Ballet Russe de Monte Carlo played London in the summer of 1938, Massine's great champion Ernest Newman called *Gaîté* a "mad and lovable entertainment."

Other critics were less enthusiastic. Haskell thought it had "little wit or true feeling of period," while *The Dancing Times* condescendingly referred to it as "a merry inconsequential romp, marred a little by the rather vulgar Can-Can." Beaumont recognized it as "the Parisian sequel to the Viennese *Beau Danube*," but thought it possessed "neither the homogeneity nor the charm of the earlier work."

Though the British sniffed with slight disdain, America capitulated to *Gaîté Parisienne* from the moment it shared the bill with *Giselle* at the Ballet Russe de Monte Carlo's New York debut 12 October 1938. Like Beaumont, John Martin compared *Gaîté* with *Beau Danube*, but came to different conclusions: "In 'Gaîté Parisienne' Massine has effected a companion to his popular 'Beau Danube' of other seasons, but the new work is so vastly superior to the old that there is no comparison. . . . It is . . . fresh as a daisy, extraordinarily skillful and inventive. . . ." Russell Rhodes, the American correspondent of *The Dancing Times*, agreed: "The ballet is in every way superior to *Le Beau Danube*."[52] Whatever quirks of national taste may be involved here, this has remained a widespread American opinion. Though *Beau Danube* has been cherished, *Gaîté Parisienne* has been the ballet which carries with it an almost sure-fire guarantee that it will send an audience home stirred to a pitch of happy excitement.

There is scarcely a story to *Gaîté*. The action merely brings together some people who might have gathered one night in a popular Parisian café. They include a vivacious Flower Girl, an even more vivacious Glove Seller and her admirer, a Baron, various officers, *cocodettes*, men and ladies about town, and an excitable and gullible little tourist from South America on his first trip to Paris. This character, the Peruvian (derived from a similar character, the Brazilian, in Offenbach's operetta *La Vie Parisienne*), was originally played by Massine in a droll, eye-rolling manner which reminded some spectators of Eddie Cantor.[53] Whoever portrays him, the choreography requires the character to burst into the café, all agog, suitcases still in hand. Somewhat prosaically, Massine says the Peruvian carried his luggage because he is a jewelry salesman and his bags contain his wares.[54] Other commentators have seen this detail as evidence that the Peruvian is so eager to sample the pleasures of the City of Light that he has come straight to the café upon his arrival in town, without bothering to check his luggage.

The role of the Glove Seller has been indelibly associated with Alexandra Danilova. Yet she did not create it. That honor went to Nina Tarakanova, Danilova stepping into the part at later performances. By universal assent, all those who saw the two interpretations feel that, whereas Tarakanova played the Glove Seller as naive, Danilova's Glove Seller was a sophisticated woman who, in Frederic Franklin's words, knew full well that that basket of hers contained "all kinds of stuff—contraceptives, everything." At first, Danilova remembers, Massine seemed slightly jealous of her success in the role, yet apparently was placated when she went to him and said, "My success is really your success, because I couldn't have been any success at all if it hadn't been for your choreography." Danilova in *Gaîté* became one of the attractions of the Ballet Russe, and the ballet often concluded a season's opening night performance. On the opening night of the company's 1941 season in New York, when Danilova made her first entrance she was given a spontaneous ovation which stopped the show.[55] Such show-stopping ovations thenceforth became a tradition of every opening night *Gaîté* with Danilova.

Gaîté's most elaborate ensemble number was a can-can which company publicists liked to hint was not only rousing, but slightly risqué. Apparently some audiences found it so. A Hartford critic wrote that the ballet's highlight was "the much talked of can-can, which, with some unexpectedness, actually was very shocking indeed. We should not have believed that a garter and a hint of flesh could have been so almost obscene. But it was danced with such grace, such remarkable skill, and such abandon that it became part of so swiftly moving a picture it could not be truly offensive."[56]

The Seventh Symphony was sterner stuff. It was what Massine termed a symphonic ballet, a ballet in which a famous piece of concert music was given choreographic realization, usually of an allegorical or symbolic nature. Here, to the Beethoven symphony that Wagner once dubbed the "apotheosis of the dance," Massine depicted nothing less than the creation and destruction of the world. The first movement showed the spirit of creation joyfully summoning the creatures of earth to life, while the second, with its procession of lamenting women carrying the inert body of a young man, suggested that this idyll had been shattered by the coming of death. In the third (which was to introduce Igor Youskevitch to America) gods disported themselves in the sky. On earth, however, in the fourth movement, mankind gave itself up to debauchery until divine judgment sent fire to consume the world.

Seventh Symphony was the fourth of Massine's essays in the symphonic idiom, and by this time balletgoers had grown familiar—perhaps too familiar—with his customary treatment of concert music. "Once again Léonide Massine put forward his theory that symphonies should be Massine as well as heard," the London *Daily Herald* quipped after the work's British premiere. And while the same paper called the experiment "magnificently justified," the work did not receive the adulation which had gone to the symphonic ballets created for de Basil: *Les Présages*, *Choreartium*, and *Symphonie Fantastique*. True, it had defenders. The articulate Ernest Newman noted, as did some of Massine's detractors, that Beethoven did not intend anything like Massine's scenario when he wrote the music. Yet, for Newman, "the astonishing thing is the extent to which Beethoven's music lends itself, both in general and in detail, to the choreographic conception of Massine."

Other critics were more guarded. *The Dancing Times*, though it found "the whole thing . . . a stupendous work," at the same time felt that it lacked the dignity and mystery of Ninette de Valois's ballet on a similar theme, *Création du Monde*, and thought that the choreography given Frederic Franklin as the creation spirit "rather suggestive of a conjurer waving his wand and producing rabbits from a hat." Virtually no one liked the way in which fire was personified by a female ensemble dressed in red rags. Giving a hint of what would soon be a widespread change of attitude in the estimation of Massine, Francis Toye snapped, "At the risk of hurting the feelings of a sincere and sensitive artist, Massine must be told that we have had enough of these symphony ballets. Not because of their lack of reverence to Beethoven and all that—I would be the first to applaud them if I thought the result satisfactory as ballet—but because they are a bore." In only a decade taste would change so much that when the Ballet Russe tried reviving *Seventh Symphony* in 1948 John Martin felt free to dismiss it as "foolish almost to the point of embarrassment."[57]

Like the can-can in *Gaîté Parisienne*, one scene in *Seventh Symphony* was held to be in questionable taste. This was the doleful second movement in which, though no reference was made to Christ's Crucifixion in the program note, the lifeless young man on stage was carried about in poses recalling religious paintings of the Descent from the Cross. In this day of rock musicals based upon the Bible, it is hard to imagine such a scene causing any hullabaloo. But British and American critics clucked over it. Charles Dickson, who created the part of the youth, says that most audiences saw a toned down version of the original, for in Monte Carlo his body had been painted a moldy green, making him appear as though he had been exhumed. The unpleasant look of this coupled with the religious issue occasioned so many protests that the body paint was soon abandoned.

Even before Massine's dancers had opened their Monte Carlo season, one last attempt was being made in New York to reunite the Ballets Russes. The prospect of two rival companies was being looked upon with consternation, especially by the socialites who had been loyal patrons of the old Ballets Russes. Now, they could not decide to which Ballet Russe they ought to contribute in the future, de Basil's or Massine's. Exasperated, Denham wrote his French representative, Jacques Rubinstein, on 15 March 1938:

> All my time has been taken up by bargaining, waiting, fighting, and conferences. . . .
> I found everything in a uproar—society split wide open into two groups—pro-World Art, and pro-Basil—fighting each other, and bringing the situation to a complete mess. You can well understand that all this was wonderful fuel for the newspapers which started to print all sorts of nonsense about the two organizations, their leaders, etc.
> It would not have been so bad after all, all this noise ("Noise is the price of fame . . .") if it had not so handicapped our financial campaign by giving a very fine excuse to people who otherwise would have wanted to subscribe not to do anything, claiming their inability to decide on which is which.
> Add to all this, the fact that Mr. Hurok got scared and lost his wits! He was running daily to our offices here, claiming that he could not book our company, that our adversaries had got ahead of him and that the local managers were raising a good deal of trouble, etc. Whether all this was truth or lies . . . is anyone's guess, but summing up all these factors, it was evident that something had to be done, and the only solution which presented itself was some kind of arrangement for a merger.[58]

Lawyers representing both factions began to meet. Once, with Hurok in attendance, they worked through the night at the offices of Washburn, Malone, and Perkins (the attorneys for Universal Art). After hours of discussion, hamburgers were sent for, then the conferees went back to business until the building closed for the night. The meeting adjourned to the St. Regis Hotel, of which ballet patron Prince Serge Obolensky was an executive. Finally, a verbal agreement was reached which convinced Hurok that he had "the finest ballet company under my wing that had ever existed, finer even then Diaghilev."[59] On 24 April 1938 the *New York Times* announced the merger of the de Basil and Massine troupes, the new company to be run by a board of governors (one of whom would be de Basil), an executive committee, and an artistic council headed by Massine.[60]

Difficulties still remained, however, For one thing, bringing Massine's dancers together with those of de Basil would result in an enormous company, and discharging any of those dancers would not be easy, since they all could claim that they were under contract. Early in negotiations, Denham had foreseen this and suggested the eventual formation of a second company, "A sort of preparatory company . . . which would have their own engagements outside of America and Covent Garden."[61] Despite problems, a merged Ballet Russe seemed possible, a company that would officially bow 20 June 1938 at Covent Garden. *The Dancing Times* rejoiced at the prospect, adding, "It almost seems too good to be true."[62]

It was. The companies never merged. Both de Basil and Massine had second thoughts. Yet on the appointed day, 20 June, a "Season of Russian Ballet" did open at Covent Garden. This was, in effect, a season by the de Basil company, although de Basil's name was no longer mentioned in the announcements, the company having been reorganized under the improbable title of Educational Ballets Ltd. by a board of directors including Victor Dandré, Serge Grigorieff, and Gerald Sevastianoff.[63] The Massine faction tried to take legal action against de Basil to restrain him from producing Massine's *Symphonie Fantastique, Boutique Fantasque,* and *Three-Cornered Hat,* and Fokine's *Coq d'Or,* rights to all of which, it was claimed, had been assigned during previous negotiations to Universal Art. De Basil's lawyers argued that the whole affair was a mixup owing to the Colonel's lack of linguistic proficiency. Not being fluent in English, he simply did not understand what he was agreeing to when he made his negotiations (as may indeed have been the case, since it is hard to understand what the Colonel thought he might have gained for himself by signing away the rights of these ballets to Universal Art). Furthermore, the Colonel's attorneys pointed out, de Basil "is no longer connected with the performance of any of these ballets at Covent Garden."[64] Presumably, reorganizing de Basil's directorate so that the company could exist without de Basil was an attempt to keep within the strict letter of the law and thereby to preserve the repertoire. In any event, the de Basil ballet—minus de Basil—did move into Covent Garden, and on its opening bill was one of the disputed ballets,

Coq d'Or. Legal wrangling between de Basil and Universal Art would continue until 1947.

Left with a contract with Universal Art, Hurok proceeded to organize his own ballet season. Covent Garden being unavailable, he rented the historic Drury Lane Theatre nearby, where his press agent found himself using the chair in which Richard Brinsley Sheridan had written *The School for Scandal.*[65] On 12 July 1938—a night when Educational Ballets Ltd. was dancing at Covent Garden—the Ballet Russe de Monte Carlo began dancing at Drury Lane. The ballet war was underway.

NOTES FOR CHAPTER 1

1. A.E. Twysden, *Alexandra Danilova,* p. 107. (For complete citations of book titles, see the Selected Bibliography.)
2. S. Hurok, *S. Hurok Presents,* p. 117.
3. "Law Report, July 30," London *Times,* 31 July 1937.
4. Fernau Hall, *An Anatomy of Ballet,* p. 408.
5. "Hold Your Hats," *Dance,* March 1937, p. 22.
6. Léonide Massine, *My Life in Ballet,* p. 204; and John Martin, "The Dance: New Ballet Alignments," *New York Times,* 23 May 1937.
7. Ballet Russe de Monte Carlo souvenir program book, 1958-59.
8. Lincoln Kirstein, *Blast at Ballet,* p. 61.
9. Conversation with Eugénie Delarova. Henceforth, all statements for which no printed source is given were made in conversation with the author.
10. S. Hurok, *S. Hurok Presents,* p. 126.
11. Michel Katcharoff, unpublished autobiography, p. 37.
12. "Tatiana Chamié Dies in New York," *Dance News,* December 1953, p. 10.
13. Conversation with Gage Bush Englund.
14. "Tatiana Chamié dies in New York," *Dance News,* December 1953, p. 10.
15. "Julius Fleischmann Dies at 68; Stage Producer and Art Patron," *New York Times,* 24 October 1968.
16. S. Hurok, *S. Hurok Presents,* p. 128.
17. "Ballet Battle Blooming," *Variety,* 25 August 1937.
18. "Choreography to Court," *Time,* 30 August 1937.
19. "Russian Ballet Lawsuit," London *Daily Telegraph,* 10 July 1937.
20. "M. Massine and His Ballets," London *Daily Telegraph,* 24 July 1937.
21. "Law Report, July 30," London *Times,* 31 July 1937.
22. Fernau Hall, *An Anatomy of Ballet,* p. 409.
23. "Date set for Massine-de Basil Split," *Dance,* September 1937, p. 21.
24. "Ballet Appears Twice Today," *San Francisco Chronicle,* 30 January 1938; and Alfred Frankenstein, "Massine Dances His Farewell to De Basil Troupe," *San Francisco Chronicle,* 31 January 1938. (Some reference sources incorrectly give the place of Massine's farewell as Oakland, California.)
25. Russell Rhodes, "The Future of the de Basil and Massine Companies," *The Dancing Times,* March 1938, p. 788.
26. Arnold L. Haskell, "Balletomane's Log Book," *The Dancing Times,* July 1937, p. 413.

27. "Hurok Signs New Attractions," *Dance*, October 1937, p. 23.
28. Russell Rhodes, "The New 'Ballet Russe,' " *The Dancing Times*, January 1938, pp. 524-525.
29. Russell Rhodes, "The Future of the de Basil and Massine Companies," *The Dancing Times*, March 1938, p. 788.
30. John Martin, "The Dance: Miscellany," *New York Times*, 6 March 1938.
31. S. Hurok, *S. Hurok Presents*, pp. 129-130.
32. "Blum Ballet Sold to Company Here," *New York Times*, 20 November 1937.
33. Michel Fokine, *Memoirs of a Ballet Master*, p. 271.
34. S. Hurok, *S. Hurok Presents*, p. 116.
35. George Amberg, *Ballet: The Emergence of an American Art*, p. 39.
36. S. Hurok, *S. Hurok Presents*, pp. 106-107.
37. Life in Monte Carlo: A.E. Twysden, "Under War Clouds," *The American Dancer*, January 1940, p. 15; André Eglevsky, "The Ballet," *Harper's Bazaar*, October 1938, p. 127.
38. Blum personnel and repertoire: Ballets de Monte Carlo souvenir program book 1937; Michel Fokine, *Memoirs of a Ballet Master*, p. 272; Arnold L. Haskell, *Dancing Around the World*, p. 342; S. Hurok, *S. Hurok Presents*, pp. 128-129; "The Sitter Out," *The Dancing Times*, April 1936, pp. 5-6; "The Sitter Out," *The Dancing Times*, December 1936, p. 262; advertisement, *The Dancing Times*, June 1937, p. 330.
39. "The Sitter Out," *The Dancing Times*, May 1936, p. 123.
40. "The Sitter Out," *The Dancing Times*, June 1936, pp. 247-248.
41. Blum itinerary: "The Sitter Out," *The Dancing Times*, August 1936, p. 477; "The Sitter Out," *The Dancing Times*, December 1936, p. 262; "Le Prochaine Saison des Ballets de Monte Carlo," *Eclaireur de Nice*, 2 February 1937; "The Sitter Out," *The Dancing Times*, June 1937, p. 277.
42. "The Sitter Out," *The Dancing Times*, July 1937, pp. 409-410.
43. Francis B. Savage, "The Blum Ballet," *The Dancing Times*, November 1937, p. 148.
44. Anatole Chujoy, "Dance in Review," *Dance News*, March 1945, p. 10.
45. Robert Lawrence, *The Victor Book of Ballets and Ballet Music*, p. 163.
46. Don Juan: Cyril W. Beaumont, *Complete Book of Ballets*, pp. 608-613, Fernau Hall, *An Anatomy of Ballet*, p. 95.
47. Horst Koegler, *The Concise Oxford Dictionary of Ballet*, p. 182.
48. Reviews of *L'Épreuve d'Amour:* Cyril W. Beaumont, *Complete Book of Ballets*, pp. 605-608; Fernau Hall, *An Anatomy of Ballet*, p. 95; Grace Robert, *The Borzoi Book of Ballets*, p. 119; Jerome D. Bohm, "2 Works Added to Repertoire of Ballet Russe," *New York Herald-Tribune*, 16 October 1938; Michel Katcharoff, unpublished autobiography, p. 42.
49. Horst Koegler, *The Concise Oxford Dictionary of Ballet*, p. 78.
50. Monte Carlo season and staff: "The Sitter Out," *The Dancing Times*," April 1938, p. 4, and June 1938, p. 285; program, Théâtre de Monte Carlo, Avril-Mai 1938.
51. Genesis of *Gaîté Parisienne:* Russell Rhodes, "The Future of the de Basil and Massine Companies," *The Dancing Times*, March 1936, p. 788; Léonide Massine, *My Life in Ballet*, p. 205; Manuel Rosenthal, program notes for Angel record S-37209.
52. Comparisons of *Gaîté Parisienne* and *Le Beau Danube:* E.N., "The Week's Music," London *Sunday Times*, 17 July 1938; Arnold L. Haskell, "Ballet at Drury Lane," *The Bystander*, 27 July 1938; "The Sitter Out," *The Dancing Times*,

August 1938, p. 516; Cyril W. Beaumont, *Supplement to Complete Book of Ballets*, pp. 47-48; John Martin, "New Work Marks Opening of Ballet," *New York Times*, 13 October 1938; Russell Rhodes, "New York Letter," *The Dancing Times*, December 1938, p. 319.

53. Arnold L. Haskell, "Ballet at Drury Lane," *The Bystander*, 27 July 1938.

54. Léonide Massine, *My Life in Ballet*, p. 205.

55. Anatole Chujoy, "Dance in Review," *Dance*, December 1941, p. 22.

56. Marian Murray, "Ballet Russe, with Many New Dancers in 'Coppelia' and 'Gaité, 'Enchants Bushnell Audience," *Hartford Times*, 30 November 1938.

57. Reviews of *Seventh Symphony*: S.F., "Most Daring Ballet," London *Daily Herald*, 13 July 1938; E.N., "The Week's Music," London *Sunday Times*, 17 July 1938; "The Sitter Out," *The Dancing Times*, August 1938, p. 516; Francis Toye, "Ovation for Massine," London *Daily Telegraph and Morning Post*, 13 July 1938; John Martin, "Ballet Russe Opens Its Season, Returning to the Metropolitan," *New York Times*, 20 September 1948.

58. Letter from S.J. Denham to Jacques Rubinstein, 18 March 1938.

59. S. Hurok, *Impresario*, pp. 202-204.

60. John Martin, "The Dance: Ballet Union," *New York Times*, 24 April 1938.

61. Letter from S.J. Denham to Jacques Rubinstein, 18 March 1938.

62. "The Sitter Out," *The Dancing Times*, June 1938, p. 267.

63. "The Sitter Out," *The Dancing Times*, July 1938, p. 387.

64. "De Basil Enjoined by English Court," *New York Times*, 22 June 1938.

65. S. Hurok, *Impresario*, pp. 207-208.

2 THE MASSINE YEARS (1938-1942)

THE 1938 London ballet war between Educational Ballets, Ltd. and the Ballet Russe de Monte Carlo may have been a war for managers, critics, and balletomanes. For the dancers, it was, in Roman Jasinski's words, "a ball."[1] By and large, the members of the rival companies remained friends during the managerial altercations, and they were delighted to be in the same city together. Moreover, since jobs were scarce in the 1930s, the existence of two large companies meant additional employment opportunities.

Dance fans took things more seriously. Dashing back and forth between Covent Garden and Drury Lane, often spending part of an evening in one theatre and the remainder in the other, they argued the merits of the two organizations. Gallerygoers partial to de Basil took to scribbling derogatory comments on posters advertising Massine's company, which opened 12 July at Drury Lane.[2]

If the ballet war was largely a polemical struggle, there nonetheless were some genuine skirmishes within the Ballet Russe de Monte Carlo. Principally, these involved Serge Lifar, who had been invited to stage *Giselle* and to dance Albrecht, with Alicia Markova, Tamara Toumanova, and Mia Slavenska alternating in the title role. All three ballerinas wished to dance the first London *Giselle*, the honor going to Markova. Yet Markova's costumes proved mysteriously unready, not only at dress rehearsal but on the morning of the performance. As a precaution, she took to the theatre the *Giselle* costumes she had worn with the Markova-Dolin Ballet. When the wardrobe staff finally brought the *Giselle* costumes to her dressing room, they did not fit, and the wardrobe ladies explained that they had been told another ballerina would do the opening *Giselle*, with Markova dancing later performances. Markova went on in the Markova-Dolin costumes, though Lifar protested that the costumes did not harmonize with the rest of the production.

Lifar's Albrecht failed to please audiences in London and, later, in New York. It was partly a matter of style. To Anglo-American taste, Lifar was what Frederic Franklin has called "a drooly sort of dancer," fond of flamboyant gestures, and in the second act "when he stood on one side of the stage, it looked as though his cape still hadn't finished coming out of the wings on the other." Lifar could also be guilty of bad manners. In *Giselle* he insisted upon taking every bow with his ballerina, never allowing her a solo call. Once, audiences kept demanding Markova alone until the stage manager grabbed Lifar by the elbows and restrained him while Markova went out to acknowledge her admirers.[3]

Besides appearing in *Giselle*, Lifar staged a new production (with décor by Eugène Berman) of *Icare*, his controversial ballet based upon the myth of Daedalus and Icarus. It was intended to prove dance an autonomous art which need not depend upon music. Therefore the choreography had been set to rhythms conceived by Lifar and arranged for percussion by J.E. Szyfer. Ballet-goers were divided on *Icare's* merits. For Fernau Hall the choreography "consisted for the most part of a series of repetitions of a single classroom step, followed by a series of repetitions of another step: the percussion section of the orchestra simply hammered out the obvious rhythms of each step in turn." Nevertheless, some felt its climax genuinely exciting: "The music rolls like thunder," wrote A.E. Twysden, "the stage slowly darkens, and one of Icarus's wings falls from the skies. Where and how will Icarus himself fall? The audience is tense with expectation, until he comes hurtling down a rocky slope and dies, shoulder on the ground, remaining wing and feet up, in an attitude not unlike a crashed aeroplane."[4]

Other productions new to London included Massine's *Gaîté Parisienne* and *Seventh Symphony*, and the world premiere, 21 July 1938, of his *Nobilissima Visione* (known in America as *St. Francis*), with décor by Pavel Tchelitchev and a commissioned score by Paul Hindemith. Here, in austere movements derived from studies of early Italian painting, Massine told the story of how St. Francis, after first desiring military glory, consecrates himself to the religious life when he discovers that war is base and ignoble. Incorporating many legends of St. Francis—including the legend of his taming a rapacious wolf—the ballet also depicts the young monk's visions of allegorical figures of Poverty, Chastity, and Obedience, and concludes with his spiritual union with Lady Poverty.

In 1929 Diaghilev had commissioned Hindemith to write a ballet of a mystical character, a project interrupted by Diaghilev's own death. Some years later, Hindemith took Massine to see some of his favorite works of art: Giotto's frescoes depicting the life of St. Francis in the church of Santa Croce in Florence. Massine, too, was impressed by them and wondered whether a ballet could be based upon them, yet at the same time he had doubts about the fitness of the story of St. Francis as a subject for choreography. He discussed the matter with theologian François Mauriac. Though Mauriac cautioned Massine, the choreographer had become excited by the idea. The resultant ballet delighted Mauriac, who, says Massine, pronounced it a successful expression of "what is most beautiful and sacred in this world: the love of God taking possession of the soul of a young man."

Disdaining pointe work, Massine's terre-à-terre choreography suggested modern dance to some viewers; Nini Theilade, the strikingly beautiful Javanese-born Danish dancer who played Lady Poverty, had even toured as a "concert" dancer before joining the ballet company. Though unusual, her duet with St. Francis did have a precedent in Massine's choreographic canon, for it was reminiscent of the dances for the Ragged Couple, the most striking characters in the otherwise undistinguished *Jardin Public*, which Massine had choreographed for de Basil in 1935. Tchelitchev's scenery had its own peculiarities. In the heavens of the backdrop for the final scene appeared six hands with fingers held in various apparently symbolic positions. Together, they spelled G-L-O-R-I-A in the sign language for the deaf.[5]

For Arnold L. Haskell, the ballet was a thoroughgoing disappointment: "The music by Hindemith may be extraordinarily fine technically . . . but to my ear it sounds, but for brief interludes, like so much unpleasant noise signifying nothing." As a whole, he said, the ballet "suffers from the unforgivable sin: it is dull." Likewise, the American composer and critic Herbert Elwell complained, "When a stage full of monks and white-headed sisters get together and wiggle their hands at the audience like a class in prestidigitation it may denote religious ecstacy, or it may be just extravagant nonsense. But it is certainly not dancing." Finally, there were those who, just as Massine had feared, thought the subject inappropriate for choreography. Believing ballet to be one of the worldly pleasures a St. Francis would renounce, Francis Toye wondered, "How and why anyone should think it possible to make a satisfactory presentation of a subject in a medium fundamentally unsuited to that subject?" He added, "I have no desire to see Massine impersonate St. Francis, who after all is one of the major saints in the calendar. It would be a pity if he were now encouraged to try his hand at St. Paul or one of the Apostles. . . ."

A few dissenters aside, American critics tended to praise *St. Francis*, objecting neither to its theme nor to that theme's choreographic treatment. Possibly, intellectual dancegoers in one of the strongholds of modern dance were accustomed to unconventional choreography. In any case, John Martin, the champion of modern dance, championed *St. Francis*:

> Massine has achieved one of the most memorable and beautiful dance works of our time. Unorthodox in subject matter, elevated in tone, and revolutionary in its choreographic procedure, it is one of those creations which, like Bronislava Nijinska's *Les Noces*, grow out of boldness of conception without regard for precedent or consequences. . . . [Massine] has evoked a masterly picture of the Middle Ages . . . its sumptuousness and its misery, its cruelty and its vision, and above all its violence and intensity. . . .

Nevertheless, the ballet was dropped after a few seasons. Robert Lawrence blames this on managerial shortsightedness:

> *St. Francis* . . . needs repeated performances by a company that believes in it so that a general public might be created and retained. The customary Ballet Russe audience, attuned to romantic stage design and rich orchestral harmonies, was puzzled by *St. Francis* at the outset; the management took no long-range steps to repeat the work until its style would have become more familiar. . . .[6]

While the two Ballets Russes danced out their war, their managements made a final attempt to call a truce. When efforts failed, Hurok, representing Universal Art, approached Educational Ballets to suggest that, if the companies could not reunite, they might amicably divide up the ballet world among themselves. He recommended that Educational Ballets allow Universal Art to stage certain de Basil productions in America. Educational Ballets would then undertake a lengthy tour of Australasia, without competition, during which time the Ballet Russe de Monte Carlo would tour America.[7] Universal Art never did acquire de Basil productions, yet de Basil's company did tour Australia and remained away from North America until 1940.

On 5 September the Ballet Russe reopened in London for a three-week season, unopposed, at Covent Garden, during which *Coppélia* was presented in its entirety. In those days, companies often lopped off the last act. While some people claimed that the third act was superfluous because it was a divertissement, Edwin Denby, seeing the production in America, pointed out that this suite of dances was justified because, until then, the hero and heroine had never had a chance to dance together. Although frequently relegated to children's matinees, *Coppélia* over the years had defenders who took it seriously as adult entertainment, Denby thinking that in its thematic content *Coppélia* was a study of "the basis for a good marriage." Even the ballet's detractors capitulated, like Denby, to Alexandra Danilova, who (partnered that first season by Michel Panaieff, and later by Frederic Franklin) made a Swanilda "incomparably brilliant in coquetry, wit, warm feminine graces and warm intelligence. . . ."[8]

On 12 October 1938 the Ballet Russe de Monte Carlo opened at New York's Metropolitan Opera House with a program consisting of *Giselle* and *Gaîté Parisienne*. The audience was fashionable and dressy, for the company had been adopted by café society. *Gaîté* took New York by storm, and *Giselle* was danced by a cast headed by Alicia Markova (Giselle), Serge Lifar (Albrecht), and Alexandra Danilova (Myrtha). (At other performances that season Nathalie Krassovska appeared as Myrtha.)

Giselle, as it turned out, caused trouble. Massine, as artistic director, had promised the first *Giselle* of the season to Markova. But Lifar (in no way a director of the company) had promised it to Toumanova. When Massine remained adamant, Lifar grew so angry he declared he would not dance at all. He eventually went on with Markova, but Toumanova resigned from the company. The intrigues surrounding the casting of *Giselle* assumed sinister proportions. One day a man leaped out of a crowd on the street and thrust into Markova's hand a paper bearing the message, "Don't dance tomorrow night, or . . ." Massine advised Markova not to be alone. So she spent the evening before her first American *Giselle* with Alexandra Danilova and Igor Youskevitch at Madison Square Garden watching the rodeo. Taking every precaution, Hurok posted detectives disguised as stagehands backstage at the Met, and the use of trapdoors was eliminated entirely.

John Martin acclaimed Markova's *Giselle* and some months later wrote an article examining her dancing in detail:

> Certainly, the first quality in her movement that meets the eye is its incredible lightness. If there was ever a dancer for whom rising upon the points were merely the preliminary step toward floating off into the air, she is it . . . even when she is at her most extended she is without rigidity and strain. The extension seems to originate in the trunk rather than in the extremities, and the result is a continuous sequence, an ebb and flow of movement that is extraordinary in the ballet.

Extraordinary she may have been, but New Yorkers were to see little of her. Scheduled to dance the second night, as well as the opening *Giselle*, Markova met with an accident at that performance. At the end of the vinegatherers' dance in the first act where Giselle sits on Albrecht's knee, Lifar lost his balance and Markova fell, Lifar in the tumble rolling onto her feet. She finished the act in pain, then fainted. The injury was diagnosed as a fractured foot and she was unable to continue the ballet, Mia Slavenska going on for her in the second act. Markova was out for the rest of the New York season. Even after she recovered, bad luck plagued her. In Boston, at one performance of *Giselle*, when Markova was ready to change into her second-act costume, she discovered that only the bodice and a thin layer of tulle remained of it, some unknown person having ripped away the whole of the inside skirt. Again, she fell back upon her old costume from the Markova-Dolin Ballet. The remains of the Ballet Russe costume were later found stuffed in a corner of one of the theatre's rest rooms.[9]

Giselle was not the only production plagued with intrigue. The company's version of the second act of *Swan Lake* included the first act pas de trois, given to Benno and two swan maidens, the Benno being the well-regarded American dancer Roland Guerard. Lifar demanded that Benno's variation be cut. Massine refused. Thereupon, after further complaining that he had been given insufficient rehearsal time for *Icare*, Lifar challenged Massine to a duel in Central Park. Massine replied, "Go take an aspirin, Serge."[10] Lifar left the company before the season's end.

The New York repertoire offered Massine's new ballets in their American premieres and the world premiere of his *Bogatyri,* set to Borodin's B-Minor Symphony, the unfinished A-Minor Symphony (arranged by Glazounov), and the nocturne from the Second String Quartet (orchestrated by Nicolas Tcherepnin). The complicated story, taken from legends of the knights of Vladimir, first Christian Prince of Russia, dealt with battles between the Bogatyri and the Tartars and the rescue of a princess from a monster. Whatever emotions this scenario might have stirred in Russian audiences, to Americans it meant little and only Nathalie Gontcharova's opulent designs won praise. In 1941 Massine revised *Bogatyri*, simplifying the plot, eliminating characters, and using only the B-Minor Symphony. Nonetheless, John Martin still thought it "obscure in story, unimaginative in choreography and swallowed up in scenery."[11]

Bogatryi aside, the New York engagement was highly successful. The final week was entirely SRO, average box office takings were $3,000 nightly, and gross earnings were estimated at $83,000. There were many plans for the future, including a new ballet, which Charles Ives would compose, about a New England Fourth of July; Marc Platoff would "assist" with the choreography.[12] Awareness of Ives at a time when this reclusive composer was little known suggests that someone involved with the company possessed considerable musical sophistication. Yet Ives's chronic ill health would have made the completion of a score unlikely. In any case, no such ballet resulted, although the production of American ballets was to be a matter with which the company would be increasingly concerned.

Critical response was largely favorable. John Martin thought the company's chief virtue was "freshness. There is a far breezier, less self-consciously exotic air about the present group of young people than there was about their predecessors, and to the taste of this department such straightforward likeableness is worth any amount of Olympian glamour." Not all reviewers were so pleased, however. It was perhaps only to be expected that *Dance Observer*, that spokesman for modern dance, should find "old forms and old conceptions staggering on the stage," since its critic believed that "To dance to the music of other ages is . . . to limit the movement of the dance to the tempo of other times" and regarded ballet itself as "singularly sterile and unrewarding." Nor could one expect sympathy from *The Daily Worker*, which sneered, "This company presents ballets with settings in France, Russia, Greece, Italy, Germany. But all the audience gets is sugary anecdotes about Princess loves pauper, warrior gets girl, brave Prince slays ogre, man loves doll, bohemian life is the gay life, we'll die for good King Gargoyle, etc., etc., from all and sundry of these settings."

Lincoln Kirstein, however, raised some genuinely provocative objections. He maintained that "great dancing does not consist merely of great personal performances. If it did, we might have just seen some. But great dancing is inseparable from a grand theatrical design, the formula Diaghilev familiarized, of collaboration on a large *Idea,* by artists capable of great painting, music or choreography." He then asked, "What is Serge Denham's idea? What is his one idea?"[13]

Following an American tour, the company returned to the Met, 13-16 March and 20-23 March 1939, the gap being filled by a visit to Cincinnati. Although there were no premieres, the season included the first New York performances in many years of Fokine's *Les Elfes* (to Mendelssohn's overture to *A Midsummer Night's Dream* and the last two movements of the violin concerto), created for Fokine's own company in 1924 and revived by René Blum's company. Costumed by Christian Bérard, the ballet figured intermittently in the repertoire, receiving favorable yet guarded notices. Thus Ann Barzel commented that the ballet "has lovely patterns and groupings and some of the best plastic designs of Fokine's early Greek-influence period. It lacks the sharp architectural beauty of *Les Sylphides* and has an irreparable raggedness due to the setting of very definite steps to dreamy indefinite music." Possibly its recalling of *Les Sylphides* prevented this airy abstraction from receiving unreserved praise, for, as a South American critic acknowledged, "As long as there is 'Sylphides,' anything else along the same lines is sandy spinach." Bérard's blue-green costumes with little wings also reminded some observers of "Psyche in the White Rock beverage ads."[14]

Things were going well for the company. On 23 March 1939 Massine signed a new contract with Universal Art making him artistic director and choreographer until 30 April 1948, during which time he would devote himself to that company exclusively at a salary of $22,000 annually plus $1500 annually for expenses. Royalty payments for his ballets would be $25 a performance, royalties ceasing after a ballet was twenty years old.[15]

On 4 April 1939 the company opened its annual Monte Carlo season. As in the previous year, there were two new Massine ballets—one frivolous, one serious. The frivolous came first on 4 May: *Capriccio Espagnol,* a choreographic collaboration with

Argentinita (who also danced the Miller's Wife in *Three-Cornered Hat*) to the Rimsky-Korsakov score, utilizing the décor Mariano Andreù had designed for Fokine's *Jota Aragonesa*. Massine's *Capriccio* received comparatively little serious criticism, not even that awarded such other frolics as *Beau Danube* and *Gaîté Parisienne*. Yet if only a trifle, its admirers, among them Robert Lawrence, considered it expertly crafted:

> . . . the entrance of Slavenska—vivid, and spectacularly blond in the midst of a swarthy ensemble—made a deep impression. But even more compelling, as this ballet moved masterfully from one pictorial climax to another, was the first appearance of her partner, Massine. Soft strokes of the tympani, imperceptible throbs of the cymbals, faintly reiterated rustlings of the tambourine; and, from the wings, insistent tapping of the heels, flamenco style. At last Massine emerged: slim, dark, slightly sinister with his broad-brimmed hat pulled down over his face, whip in hand. From the moment of his entrance until the fall of the curtain, it was he who dominated the ballet. . . . In a surprising touch of theatre, two new leading characters are brought on stage at the moment that the gypsy dance plunges into the closing fandango.[16]

The other creation, *Rouge et Noir* (premiered 11 May 1939), was a symphonic ballet to Shostakovitch's First Symphony with settings and costumes by Henri Matisse. In Paris that June the title was changed to *L'Etrange Farandole*, reportedly to acknowledge that Matisse was known to sing a farandole as he painted, but the original title was permanently restored when the company reached America. Massine had wanted to collaborate with Matisse as early as 1937, Massine proposing a "vast mural in motion." Matisse had the idea of interpreting Shostakovitch in terms of five colors to which Massine assigned allegorical significance: white (man and woman), yellow (wickedness), blue (nature), red (materialism), and black (violence).[17] The designs consisted of a space dominated by an arch, while the dancers wore colored all-over tights. Grace Robert pronounced the results "extraordinarily effective scenically. . . . The groups formed and came apart, making wonderful blocks of color like an abstract painting set in motion." But Robert Sabin was reminded only of a "Walpurgis night in winter underwear."

Whereas George Beiswanger unhesitatingly called *Rouge et Noir* Massine's "best constructed and most poetic symphonic ballet," John Martin stated the case against it: ". . . reservations must be made on several scores. One is on the grounds

that the work is partly abstract, partly programmatic, partly dominated by a color symbolism that is far from clear. Another is on the
ground of the willful mysticism of the theme."[18] What Martin objected to is that the ballet was both a near-abstraction emphasizing
the shifting patterns of groups of dancers and an allegory in which
those patterns represented forces of destiny shaping man's life.
Massine's earlier symphonic ballet, *Les Présages,* had also concerned destiny; but whereas in *Présages* a hero finally brought
concord out of discord, *Rouge et Noir* consistently resolved itself
on a discordant note. It was, perhaps, *Les Présages* with an unhappy ending. It may also have represented Massine's reponse to
the worsening international situation. One of its most effective
moments, a solo of lamentation for Markova, symbolized to some
audiences the grief of Czechoslovakia overcome by Germany.[19]
When revived in 1948, *Rouge et Noir,* like *Seventh Symphony,* was
called dated, John Martin dismissing it as "a highly symbolic ballet
about nothing at all."[20]

After Monte Carlo, the company went to the Florence
May Festival (where *Cimarosiana,* a Massine piece for Diaghilev,
was briefly revived) and on to Paris.[21] Everyone was looking forward
to opening in London on 4 September 1939. But that London
season never took place. War intervened—this time not a ballet
war, but a real one. On 1 September Hitler's forces marched into
Poland. World War II had begun.

The London season canceled, attempts were made to
get the company to America for its New York season, scheduled to
open 10 October. The sets and costumes, which had been in
England when war broke out, were loaded upon a ship and sent
across the Atlantic. Transporting personnel proved more difficult.
Massine managed to arrive on 14 September. But almost all civil-
ian vessels were now canceling sailings. Many of the dancers,
being refugees or children of refugees traveling under Nansen
passports, encountered immigration difficulties. When Hurok tried
to book the company on United States Line vessels, the steamship
company ruled that priority must go to American citizens. That, at
least, permitted the Americans in the company to cross on the
Shawnee.

Back in New York, opening night had been postponed
until 26 October and Massine was training a new ensemble in case
his regular company was stranded overseas. At last, passage was
secured for them on the *Rotterdam,* which docked in New York 26
October, the very morning of opening night. As soon as they had

cleared customs and immigration, the dancers were whisked to the theatre. The season began.

Yet there still were difficulties. Nini Theilade had to spend a night on Ellis Island. Several dancers never made it to America. One of them was Marcel Fenchel, who, to recuperate from injuries, had gone home to his native Germany, even though Massine had warned him that Hitler was preparing for war. After World War II, Fenchel adopted his mother's surname and, as Marcel Luipart, achieved considerable success as a choreographer and teacher.

Some of the dancers of the Ballet Russe rehearsed in mental agony during the first years of the war, for they were worried about what might be happening to friends and family abroad. Eventually, Massine banned newspapers from the studio, since the sight of war headlines upset some dancers too much.[22] Audiences, aware of the company's travails, greeted it warmly, John Martin declaring that the very fact that the Ballet Russe weathered the crisis "speaks eloquently for its stamina and its good spirit."[23]

Wartime difficulties notwithstanding, it was an exciting season. The first novelty—Frederick Ashton's *Devil's Holiday* (to music by Vincenzo Tommasini based upon themes of Paganini, and décor by Eugène Berman)—came on the first night. That, perhaps, was unfortunate. John Martin called the ballet "thin and static, and markedly ungrateful to the dancers." Yet it had admirers, Edwin Denby recognizing the piece as a young man's ballet, "the kind of awkward and inspired dancing that young people do when they come back from their first thrilling ballet evening and dance the whole ballet they have seen in their room in a kind of trance." However, almost everyone agreed that *Devil's Holiday* needed extra rehearsals and, even more than that, tightening—tightening which, because of the war, it never received. If there had been that London season, Ashton would surely have been able to make adjustments. As it was, with the company in America, Ashton never even saw a performance of his ballet.

Devil's Holiday was what finally resulted from that often discussed plan to do a ballet about the life of Paganini. Initially, Balanchine was to choreograph it; then the project was entrusted to Ashton. But by the time he was ready to begin, Fokine was preparing his own *Paganini* for de Basil and, understandably enough, not wishing to compete with Fokine, a new, rather thin, story was concocted concerning the devil's attempts to meddle in human affairs, especially in human love affairs. Ashton's working methods intrigued the company. Used to the authoritarian Massine, the dancers were amazed when Ashton, apparently stumped for a moment, would simply ask someone, "Show me something." When Frederic Franklin was asked to "show something," all he could think of was that the music at that point—a set of variations upon the "Carnival in Venice"—vaguely resembled the "Mexican Hat Dance." Feeling foolish, he demonstrated a few steps of the hat dance: Ashton made them the basis for an ensemble. Later, Ashton asked Danilova, "Show me something old from Russia." She did—and Ashton likewise transformed it to serve his purposes.[24]

The season's scandal was *Bacchanale*, a collaboration between Massine and Salvador Dali set to Wagner's Venusberg music from *Tannhäuser*, with the Pilgrims' Chorus as finale.[25] Purporting to show the delirious visions of Ludwig II of Bavaria, it mixed mythological figures with such personages as Lola Montez and Sacher-Masoch. A Massine-Dali collaboration had been planned for several years. Early reports had it that the piece, to be called *Tristan Fou*, would employ Cole Porter songs and would model the character of Tristan upon Harpo Marx, complete with blond wig.[26] Eventually, Massine and Dali would produce a *Tristan Fou*, but that would not be until 1944 when they worked together for the Marquis de Cuevas' Ballet International. Somewhere in the process of the Ballet Russe collaboration, Mad Tristan had become Mad Ludwig.

Dali's décor was dominated by a huge swan with a hole in its breast through which dancers emerged, some in remarkable costumes. There was a woman with a rose-colored fish head. Lola Montez wore harem trousers and a hoop skirt decorated with false teeth. The Knight of Death turned out to be an immense perambulating umbrella. Later, when Ludwig died, a whole set of umbrellas opened on stage. Prudish audiences blushed to behold the male ensemble with large red lobsters (as sex symbols) on their tights, and Nini Theilade, portraying Venus, created a sensation because she seemed totally nude. In actuality, she wore flesh-colored tights from her neck to her toes. During much of the action, a satyr sat knitting in one corner of the stage, a midget clinging to his side. That posed a casting problem on tour, since a real midget had to be found in each city along the way.

The program called the opening night, 9 November 1939, the "first paranoiac performance." This, Grace Robert recalled, "was no more paranoiac than subsequent performances, though possibly more hysterical." The hysteria was induced because the costumes not only had been unready for dress rehearsal, they were not even ready when the curtain went up on the first ballet that night. They arrived in fleets of taxis during the intermission. When they saw them, the dancers were flabbergasted. Some were so bewildered that they had no idea how to put them on. A few were shocked, because Dali had adorned some of the women's costumes with outsized breasts. At last, after a forty-five minute intermission, *Bacchanale* began.[27]

Many critics regarded *Bacchanale* as Dali's show, John Martin finding Dali's designs well suited to the theatre because "His fantasies benefit greatly by the addition of the time element, for they can develop to climaxes with a degree of shock and surprise that static presentation . . . cannot hope to approximate." Yet "To take such a ballet as a serious piece of psychoanalysis or as an important work of art would be a grave mistake." It disappointed Albertina Vitak that, despite *Bacchanale's* visual strangeness, it was not choreographically strange enough. She expected Massine to "have invented some distinctly peculiar style of movements, whether serious or frivolous, for this psychoanalytic Ballet instead of clearly recognizable academic dancing such as *tour jetés, pirouettes* etc., most of which could be just as appropriate in any other classical Ballet." In fairness to Massine, it should be noted that, judging from a film in the New York Public Library Dance Collection, parts of *Bacchanale* appear genuinely distinctive. For example, Sacher-Masoch and his Wife constitute a truly peculiar couple, she forcing him to the floor and kicking him while he cringes with delight in degradation. Death as a dancing umbrella is another remarkable conception. His mincing, fidgety steps are ludicrous, yet unsettling. A macabre descendant of the Managers in *Parade*, the dancing unbrella attests to Massine's longstanding interest in the grotesque.

At least two critics considered *Bacchanale* genuinely valid. Surely aware that Freud found significance in jokes and puns, Hilmar Grondahl concluded that "this endeavor is the most amusing example of visual punning before the public today. If you define dryad as a wood nymph, isn't it logical that a tree should sprout from the head and upper limbs? If a man has a chest, wouldn't there be drawers in it? And so forth." Alfred Frankenstein thought *Bacchanale* an ingenious visualization of Wagner, because the score

> for all the grandeur of its architecture, belongs in the same
> bracket with the nymphs of Bouguereau and other Victorian

purveyors of sweetness and light. It also extols that hefty, Germanic, cymbal-and-drum vulgarity of which Wagner was sometimes guilty. . . .

Dali, it seems to me, thoroughly appreciates this, and embodies it in his figure of the mad King Ludwig, whose attitudinizing is almost the ultimate satire on inflated, rhetorical grandiosity. At the opposite pole to Ludwig are the two imps soberly tending to their knitting. These are the imperturbable answer of common sense to Ludwig's soaring, Olympian ambitions. . . . They are a kind of choreographic Bronx cheer.[28]

For all its calculated surrealism, nothing about *Bacchanale* was quite as surrealistic as something that happened by accident at a Chicago performance. The Yugoslavian consul was backstage chatting with Yugoslavian dancer Mia Slavenska. Their visit ended, he headed for what he thought was the exit. Instead, he found himself on stage. Slow to realize that the curtain was up, he strolled leisurely across the stage in top hat and tails just as Nini Theilade, seemingly nude, emerged from the swan. Now aware that some kind of commotion was going on, he turned, doffed his hat, bowed to the naked damsel, and continued his passage into the wings. The stage manager was aghast, but Massine was ecstatic. "That was magnificent!" he cried. "I wish we could have it in at every performance!"[29]

The autumn season's other premiere, though no scandal, was nonetheless of importance. *Ghost Town,* the choreographic debut of American dancer Marc Platoff (born Marcel LePlat and later known in musical comedy as Marc Platt), was the first of several attempts by the Ballet Russe to satisfy demands for ballets on American themes. Platoff's ballet (premiered 12 November 1939), to a commissioned score by Richard Rodgers, showed present-day hikers in a ghost town meeting an old prospector who told them the town's story, that story constituting the bulk of the ballet. Though Platoff was the great-grandson of Frederick Stork, a California pioneer who built the original mills for Comstock's miners, some critics charged that the ballet did not capture a genuine American atmosphere. For Edward Downes it was "about as American as a Russian Grand Duchess in dude ranch clothes." Edwin Denby, however, though he disliked *Ghost Town's* "awkward spacing, and operatic arm-waving," detected "an exuberant energy in it."[30]

The season included a revival of Fokine's *Igrouchki,* a peasant comedy originally devised as a nightclub act for Gilda Gray, inventor of the shimmy, though no one had to shimmy in it.

There were also a number of outstanding performances. *Dance* called Mia Slavenska the company's "technically . . . strongest dancer. . . . With an exceptional aplomb, fine beats and turns, Slavenska is a dramatic dancer who delights any audience. . . ."[31] John Martin singled out newcomer André Eglevsky: "He has fine elevation, his pirouettes have already become famous, and perhaps almost more important than any such matters, his manner on the stage is simple and gracious." Yet in later seasons other critics found Eglevsky's manner tending toward mannerism. In 1941 Walter Terry pointed out the anomaly that Eglevsky "is a husky man, but he is inclined to move like one of delicate cast and winds up making himself appear heavier than he really is."[32]

After breaking ballet box office records at the Met, the company toured, with Vincenzo Celli traveling along as guest teacher, just as his own teacher, Enrico Cecchetti, had once traveled with Diaghilev.[33] In New York, steps were taken to guarantee company stability through the formation of the Ballet Foundation, with William L. Chadbourne as chairman of the board and Julius Fleischmann, Edward R. Wardwell, and Watson Washburn as trustees. The foundation hoped to establish a fund which would aid the company and take part of the burden of supporting it off the shoulders of Fleischmann.[34]

Working in cooperation with the Ballet Foundation, the Ballet Guild (which had helped finance *Ghost Town*) started to get one of its often announced contests for new ballets underway. It offered a $500 prize for the best score, $300 for the best designs, and $200 for the best scenario. The new ballet's subject matter was to be American ("American Indian themes or characters excepted"), and it was to require no more than forty-five dancers and to run no longer than twenty-five minutes. Philip Barry, William Rose Benét, John Erskine, and Léonide Massine were to judge the scenario contest.

But nothing happened. Deadlines came and went. Yet the Ballet Guild remained silent, so silent that John Martin felt obliged to ask, "By the way, what ever happened to that contest. . . ?" Finally, on 28 July 1940, the guild awarded the scenario prize to novelist Glenway Westcott for *The Dream of Audubon*, which, strictly speaking, was not new since, three years before, it had been written for the American Ballet to be choreographed by Balanchine, with Lew Christensen as Audubon. Based upon the legend that Audubon was the lost Dauphin (the son of Louis XVI and Marie Antoinette), it contrasted Audubon's life as a painter in the American wilderness with his memories of the French court. A music committee consisting of Hugh Ross, Nicholas Nabokov, and Walter Piston in 1941 awarded David Diamond the commission for composing the score. But the Ballet Russe made no further efforts to stage the work. Even to this day, however, it has not been totally abandoned. For *The Dream of Audubon* is the basis for *Birds of America*, a work with choreography by Balanchine and music by Morton Gould which the New York City Ballet has several times announced but never produced.[35]

Another project which came to nothing was to make Montalvo, the estate of the late California Senator James Phelan, an art center which would replace Monte Carlo as the company's spring and summer home.[36] What did eventuate was a spring season at the Metropolitan Opera House. Not only was the announced season, 26 March-7 April 1940, the longest season of any ballet company at the Met since the Diaghilev Ballets Russes in 1916, but the season was extended an extra week.[37]

It very nearly never took place. For years the American Guild of Musical Artists had been trying to unionize ballet companies. Other companies (Ballet Caravan, the Littlefield Ballet, and the newly formed Ballet Theatre) had signed union contracts. Only the Ballet Russe delayed. Now, as negotiations resumed just before a major season, a two-thirds majority of Ballet Russe dancers voted to strike if the contract remained unsigned. They were supported by Ballet Theatre founder Richard Pleasant, who charged that the Ballet Russe was unfair competition, since it could present elaborate productions at less expense than unionized American companies could. Dancers from Ballet Caravan and Ballet Theatre indicated their willingness to picket the Met. So did Lincoln Kirstein, who said he would march on the picket line "in white tights, if necessary." On 23 March 1940 the Ballet Russe was unionized.[38]

The spring season featured guest appearances by Argentinita (in *Capriccio Espagnol*), Anton Dolin (partnering Markova in *Giselle*) and, in various roles, Irina Baronova. Baronova, a much loved member of de Basil's company, was eagerly awaited. To Anatole Chujoy, she was "Authoritative, mature, more beautiful than ever," yet stylistically dismaying. Previously, said Chujoy, "Baronova was one of the few dancers to understand that the classic dance is an abstraction. . . . Baronova today is disposed to introduce into her dancing a dramatic quality. . . . The change in her, however, is disturbing to those, perhaps not so many people, who want to see the classic ballet as much preserved in its pure form, as is possible under contemporary conditions."[39]

There were two new productions. On 9 April 1940 Nini Theilade offered *Nuages*, which, to Debussy's tone poem, showed Night eternally pursuing Day, meeting only for fleeting embraces at dawn and twilight. Walter Terry called the costumes by painter Willem de Kooning "delicate of hue" but, like most of his colleagues, thought the ballet "pretty wispy."[40] The following night, 10 April 1940, the company presented Balanchine's *Le Baiser de la Fée*, originally choreographed for the American Ballet's Stravinsky Festival in 1937. Based upon a fairy tale by Hans Christian Andersen, the work concerns a young man marked with a mysterious kiss by a fairy when he is still a child; on his wedding day, the fairy returns and claims him. The story has been treated by some critics as an allegory of the essential loneliness of the creative artist. Very much a fairy tale for adults, *Baiser* was performed by a Ballet Russe cast headed by Danilova as the Bride, Eglevsky as the Bridegroom, and Slavenska as the Fairy.

Though the season was a popular success, the company encountered critical sniping. One reason may have been that the Ballet Russe was no longer the sole major ballet company in America. It had competition in the form of Ballet Theatre, which had opened its first season that January. Ballet Theatre's unusually fine corps de ballet prompted Walter Terry to snap, "I know of a good many people who have lost interest in the Russian ballets because they feel that they can see better spectacle and better teamwork at the Radio City Music Hall." Whereas Ballet Theatre prided itself on its American dancers, the Ballet Russe was—well, "Russe." The very month of Ballet Theatre's opening, Albertina Vitak issued a challenge to the Ballet Russe: "I believe the time has come for the Americans in the company to drop their assumed Russian names. Each season has had a few souls brave enough to use their own names, now let *all* do so proudly." A further sour note was sounded by René Blum, who, in an open letter to *Dance*, complained that his role in establishing the Ballet Russe was being deliberately minimized by Massine.[41]

Unfazed, the troupe spent the summer touring South America (where Nini Theilade left the company to get married). When it returned, it found that Colonel de Basil's organization, now named the Original Ballet Russe, had also returned. For 1940-41 there were to be two Ballets Russes in America, both managed by Hurok.

This development was not entirely a surprise. Talk of de Basil's return had been floating about for some time and Hurok had repeatedly asked Denham to release him from having to manage the Monte Carlo exclusively. He claimed that, by handling both companies, he would be able "to eliminate any possible competition or clashes."[42] Once the release was granted, Hurok's plan to "eliminate" competition may not have been to Denham's liking: Hurok canceled the Monte Carlo's customary fall season. Instead, that company would tour while de Basil's played New York.[43]

Then Hurok changed his plans, announcing a three-week season by the Monte Carlo beginning 14 October, followed immediately by a season by the Original Ballet Russe. Among the novelties of casting would be guest appearances by an American ballerina, Marie-Jeanne, who had been a principal dancer of Lincoln Kirstein's touring Ballet Caravan from 1937 to 1940. Unfortunately, all performances by both companies would be in the 51st Street Theatre (today the Mark Hellinger) because the Metropolitan Opera House was closed for renovations.[44]

The Monte Carlo led off with two new productions on opening night. One, the Balanchine-Stravinsky *Jeu de Cartes* (renamed *Poker Game* by the Monte Carlo), came from the repertoire of the American Ballet, the company Balanchine had founded in 1934 and which had been inactive since 1938. Although Edwin Denby said that *Poker Game* "makes you feel as if you were for a while in the best of company," Albertina Vitak thought "Many of the steps . . . are almost distortions and certainly not pretty."[45]

At least, *Poker Game* elicited definite responses of some kind. Massine's *Vienna—1814*, premiered the same night, made virtually no impression, though the cast included most of the company's best dancers. The previous year, Comte Etienne de Beaumont had expressed interest in devising a ballet to themes by Carl Maria von Weber that would be orchestrated by Hindemith. Denham urged his Paris representative, "Please impress upon de Beaumont that it must be a gay lively ballet."[46] The resultant ballet, based upon Weber's *Turandot* overture and four-hand piano pieces,[47] was orchestrated not by Hindemith but by Broadway arranger Robert Russell Bennett. In 1943 Hindemith completed his "Symphonic Metamorphosis of Themes of Carl Maria von Weber," a glittering orchestral piece. Yet if this work suggests the approach to Weber he proposed for the ballet, it certainly would not have satisfied Denham's demand for a "gay lively ballet." *Vienna—1814* showed delegates from many nations dancing at a ball given by Prince Metternich, their joyousness interrupted when the news comes of Napoleon's escape from Elba.

Vienna—1814 had one articulate defender, St. Louis

critic Harry R. Burke, who was consistently one of Massine's admirers. According to Burke, *Vienna—1814* was, at heart, serious,
even topical: "A divertissement in surface aspect, it is Massine's
bitter denunciation of the pomp and panoplies of war and the
luxuries of war-makers; a caustic satire upon the ironies of con-
quest."[48] Nonetheless, *Vienna—1814* is generally regarded as a
failure—the first in a series of ballets that would severely damage
Massine's reputation.

On 17 October 1940 two other productions received
first performances. Balanchine's *Serenade* was taken over from
the American Ballet repertoire. This haunting work, in which (as
Edwin Denby said) "the sequences suggest a romantic personal
grief but the dancers themselves remain clear and open as in the
morning classroom," was presented in a version both like and
unlike that danced by the New York City Ballet today. For the first
time, Balanchine choreographed all movements of Tchaikovsky's
score (although with internal cuts), his original staging for the
American Ballet having utilized only three of the four movements.
The new choreography for what is the score's fourth movement
came as the ballet's third movement, Balanchine reversing their
concert order. In the American Ballet production solo passages
were shared by all the women, with nine given prominence; current
productions divide the solo parts among three to five women. For
the Ballet Russe all female solos were danced by a single ballerina
(originally Marie-Jeanne; later Alexandra Danilova), with a second
female soloist briefly appearing in the "Elegy" movement. This
distribution of roles made the Ballet Russe *Serenade* more overtly
dramatic than other productions usually are.[49]

Also premiered on 17 October was another Tchaikovsky
ballet, Ivanov's *Nutcracker,* staged by Alexandra Fedorova (a former Maryinsky dancer who married Fokine's brother) with designs
by Alexandre Benois. Getting the sketches for those designs to
America assumed the dimensions of an espionage adventure.
Benois, living at the time in occupied Paris, entrusted the sketches
to a friend who, possibly because wartime conditions disrupted
public transportation systems, walked all the way from Paris to
Lyon with them, where he entrusted them to another person who
got them to Lisbon and, via clipper, to Bermuda. But they were not
safe yet. Inspectors seized them as suspect materials, and the
British Embassy had to guarantee their harmlessness before they
could enter America.

By current standards, the Ballet Russe *Nutcracker* was a
truncated version capable of serving as one item on a mixed bill. A

brief first scene showed the Christmas party, after which Clara fell asleep and—there being no battle with the mice (although Benois made sketches for it)—journeyed immediately in her dreams to the snow country and the land of sweets. Yet this was the first *Nutcracker* most American balletgoers had ever seen and it was extremely popular on tour, so popular that, in time, the production grew battered and scenes (particularly the party and snow scenes) were further condensed or omitted entirely. This shopworn version was surely one of the stagings to which Robert Lawrence alluded when he sighed that "In the drabness of certain current productions of *The Nutcracker*, seasonal festivities at a Bowery mission are suggested."

Children's roles were played by regular company members, the role of Clara being an occasional exception. While a short adult dancer always played her in the party scene, sometimes an actual child was used for Clara's entrance into the land of sweets. At a few performances, that child was the daughter of company member Nicholas Beriozoff. She grew up to become Svetlana Beriosova, one of the best-loved ballerinas of the Royal Ballet. The casting of a child in *Nutcracker* could have considerable publicity value on tour. In some cities contests were held to select a Clara, or the Clara would be the daughter of some prominent local citizen. Once in Hollywood, the Clara was Maureen Reagan, daughter of actors Ronald Reagan and Jane Wyman.[50]

Massine premiered a second "gay lively ballet" on 18 October 1940—and had his second failure. This was *The New Yorker*, to Gershwin songs and bits of his concert music, arranged by David Raksin. Inspired by *New Yorker* magazine cartoons of Peter Arno, Helen E. Hokinson, William Steig, and Otto Soglow, the ballet was a comic portrait gallery of people one might see in and about a Manhattan nightclub. Massine modeled his choreography upon his observations of the chauffeurs, doormen, dowagers, socialites, and peddlers he encountered on the Upper East Side. Ever insistent that dancers achieve the proper style for a ballet, Massine even made Nathalie Krassovska take tap lessons to prepare her for her role as a debutante. Shortly after the premiere, Massine revised his own part, finally creating a solo, as a Timid Man let loose on the town, which John Martin praised as "funny, inventive and completely off the beaten track."

Nevertheless, while Massine may have hoped that *The New Yorker* would be an American *Gaîté Parisienne*, critics were disappointed. Some of their adverse reactions have curiously chauvinistic undertones. For years critics had been chiding Massine's company for not doing American works. Now that Massine actually tried to do one, they chided him because he was foreign-born. Thus Irving Kolodin claimed that "all of Massine's good intentions and wit did not compensate for the orientation that might have been supplied by an American choreographer." On the road, where Massine's reputation remained undimmed, *The New Yorker* enjoyed moderate popularity. Typical reactions are those of Boston's Elinor Hughes, who said that "Massine's choreography has caught not a little of the goofier side of Americans in their pursuit of pleasure."

There may be another reason why *The New Yorker* was troublesome. Neither subject nor score permitted easy styliza-tion. As choreographer, Massine could view the Paris and Vienna of nearly a century ago with sufficient aesthetic dis-tance to enable him to select those aspects of their life that he wished to stylize in *Gaîté Parisienne* and *Beau Danube*. But the Gershwin era was an awkward age. It was recent enough for most people of 1940 to have lived through it; therefore they would have their own personal interpretations of it. Yet that period was also just distant enough to seem old hat to those who fancied them-selves trend setters. Massine himself recognized this difficulty at the time when he said, "The Gershwin music which has real melodic quality is really either too close to some of us or too outdated for present swing enthusiasts. In a hundred years such a ballet would be very easy to formulate."[51]

Of the two Ballets Russes he now managed, Hurok ap-parently favored de Basil's, for immediately after the Monte Carlo's season ended, the Original followed it into the 51st Street Theatre, remaining there until 12 January 1941 in what then constituted the longest consecutive engagement by any ballet company in New York. It returned for seven additional performances, 22 January. At the outset, John Martin thought

> the auspices are perhaps unusually fortunate for the success of the Original Ballet Russe, not only because it has been absent for a time but also because it comes on the heels of what is undoubtedly the least distinguished season Massine's company has given. Just what the trouble has been it would be hard to say. Its first season had shortcomings which were easily forgiven because it was a first season; its second season was seriously handicapped by the outbreak of the war just at sailing time. This year it was apparently plain bad luck.

Later, he compared the companies, finding that the Monte Carlo had the better style, orchestra, and male roster, while the Original had the better staging, lighting, and repertoire (though he acknowledged that much of that repertoire was inherited from Diaghilev): "As far as ensemble dancing and playing are concerned there is not much choice between the two organizations. Apparently, canon is the favorite form of all current Ballet Russe ensembles. . . ."[52]

Critical demurs notwithstanding, the Monte Carlo's tour (during which Danilova married Casimir Kokitch and Markova left the company, while Toumanova rejoined it) was its most successful thus far. The company also signed a contract with Warner Brothers to film *Gaîté Parisienne* and *Capriccio Espagnol*.[53] Yet affairs were not going quite right. Looking back, Hurok said that he felt the 1940-41 season had shown signs of deterioration and that Massine was exhausted.

There were other signs of changing tastes and allegiances. The Ballet Guild, which had theretofore been closely associated with the Monte Carlo, was reorganized in 1941 (again with Parmenia Ekstrom as president) to assist all worthy companies. Rumors circulated that Balanchine might replace Massine at the Monte Carlo. As for the other Ballet Russe—de Basil's—that company during the 1941-42 season embarked for South America and remained away from the United States until 1946. Yet Hurok announced that for 1941-42 he would again manage two companies. One, as usual, would be the Ballet Russe de Monte Carlo. But, this time, the other would be Ballet Theatre.[54]

Hurok booked the Monte Carlo into the Metropolitan Opera House 8 October-2 November 1941, the first premiere occurring on the first night. *Labyrinth,* to Schubert's Ninth Symphony, reunited Massine and Dali in a work which, unlike *Bacchanale,* was intended to be no mad delirium, but a sober allegory using the myth of Theseus and the Minotaur to symbolize the finding of a way out of the labyrinth of modern life by means of the guiding thread of classicism. Among Massine's most praised choreographic touches were the use of the massed corps de ballet to suggest a great wave of the sea (and, allegorically, the march of history) and a cockfight danced by two men in costumes worn backward to make the bend of the knee recall the actual movements of roosters.

Massine confessed to being "both amused and revolted" by some of Dali's production ideas, vetoing at the outset Dali's proposal to smash a grand piano on stage. For the scene in which Theseus slays the Minotaur, Dali wanted to use a real calf's head which the dancers would cut apart and eat. Massine accompanied Dali from one restaurant to another in search of such a head. Waiters, though stunned by Dali's request, remained ever polite; one, having no head to proffer, suggested a veal sandwich instead.

Reviews of *Labyrinth* are even more contradictory than those of *Bacchanale*. But seldom are they favorable. Scorning the choreography as being "on a par with the activities captured in the annual Greek play by a girls' finishing school," Walter Terry praised Dali's settings as "more magnificent than any that ballet has disclosed before. Strangely enough, they are not silly, and although the opening scene reveals a tremendous cracked skull and a chest with a doorway in it, the effect is one of archaic grandeur." For Edwin Denby, their monumentality was their defect: "Dali hogs the show so completely he won't let you see Massine's part of it. . . . He focuses your eye at a spot so high on the drop, that every time you pull it down to look at the dancers below you feel uncomfortable." Not so, claimed John Martin, for whom *Labyrinth* "is classifiable less as Dalian delirium than as another of Massine's symphonic ballets, and far from the best one." The production's happiest surprise was that it did not seem a betrayal of Schubert. "One is accustomed to thinking of this symphony as architectural rather than dynamic," wrote Robert Lawrence, "but certain passages last night, when heard merely with lights beating down upon a decorated stage, assumed new significance."[55]

Under the title of *The Magic Swan,* New Yorkers had their first glimpse of the third act of *Swan Lake* (staged by Alexandra Fedorova) on 13 October 1941. Many balletgoers, unfamiliar with Petipa's episodic structure, belittled these divertissements. Even the knowledgeable Walter Terry called the choreography "not worthy of a dancing school's annual recital." For him, the work's sole redeeming feature was the electrifying performance by Tamara Toumanova and Igor Youskevitch in the Black Swan pas de deux. Famed for balance and turns, Toumanova was sensational in the fouettés. James Starbuck remembers how before each performance the ballerina and her mother minutely inspected the stage until they found the precise spot where they thought the fouettés should be that night. Then they would pray over the spot. That night, the fouettés were invariably there—and perfect.

It was a critic for a modern dance publication, *Dance Observer's* Gervase N. Butler, who recognized the difficulty of presenting *Swan Lake*'s third act independently. Whereas the second is self-contained, the third is obviously "a section from a longer composition and suffers as a consequence."[56] Since the second act had been in the repertoire for years, it might seem that by pairing the two acts the company could have had an attractive *Swan Lake* in miniature. Inexplicably, such a pairing never occurred.

On 19 October 1941 came Massine's truly disastrous *Saratoga,* a would-be comedy about love and horseracing at a New York spa, with commissioned music by Jaromir Weinberger and designs by Oliver Smith and Alvin Colt. In his memoirs Massine claims he knew at the outset it would be disastrous, that the ballet's subject was offered him as the first project under a new policy whereby the company's business staff "had decided in future to produce only ballets directly sponsored by individual backers. I sensed that this would mean lowering our standards. . . ." Reviews were scathing. Robert Sabin: "an all time low"; Edwin Denby: "inept"; Walter Terry: "pretty tragic"—and so on.[57]

As always, seasonal highlights included noteworthy performances. In a company remarkable for its male dancing, George Zoritch attracted increased attention, Walter Terry saying, "It is impossible for him to make a bad line, to move unrhythmically, for there is a catlike smoothness about everything he does."[58] Also, during 1941-42, Warner Brothers released the films the Ballet Russe had made in Hollywood: *Spanish Fiesta* and *The Gay Parisian* (as *Capriccio Espagnol* and *Gaîté Parisienne* had become), both directed by Jean Negulesco. Terry preferred the former because of its "direct and unpretentious" camerawork, whereas *Gay Parisian* was "pretentious and far from direct."[59] For balletomanes, that film's greatest weakness was the absence of Danilova as the Glove Seller. Hollywood authorities considered her unglamorous and she failed her screen test, her role going to Milada Mladova. Thus the opportunity to preserve a great comic performance was irreparably lost.

The fact that Hurok now managed both Ballet Russe and Ballet Theatre became conspicuously apparent in 1942 when he sponsored a spring ballet season at the Met consisting of a week of Ballet Theatre, beginning 6 April, followed by a week of Ballet Russe, and concluding with a third week divided between the two groups. While it was surely laudable to show New Yorkers these companies, one can seriously question Hurok's manner of doing so. By splitting a season between two companies, he may have caused casual balletgoers to confuse them or to lump together both as one gigantic "Hurok Ballet." (There were even rumors that Hurok was trying to merge the Monte Carlo with Ballet Theatre.) Moreover, to the horror of proponents of native American ballet, Hurok billed Ballet Theatre as "the greatest in Russian ballet," a practice he defended on the grounds that Americans were "conditioned" to Russian ballet.[60]

While promoting "Russian ballet," Hurok may have been losing interest in Ballet Russe. When the schedules of the two companies are compared, it seems that programming obviously favors Ballet Theatre. Ballet Russe offered no premieres. Ballet Theatre gave Fokine's *Russian Soldier* and made history with Tudor's *Pillar of Fire*. Worse, Ballet Russe opened with a program which can only be termed an aberration. Though it concluded with the surefire *Gaîté Parisienne*, before it came *Labyrinth*, never anybody's favorite, while the first ballet was *Saratoga*, by consensus Massine's worst effort in years. Who approved such a program—and why?

That question sent flurries of memorandums back and forth from one Ballet Russe staff member to another. Conductor Franz Allers wrote Denham that he had suggested *Serenade* as an opener, but Massine rejected it because of its allegedly "poor decor." Nor did Massine warm to *Capriccio Espagnol*.[61] Denham, in a draft of a letter (which, though never sent, was preserved in company files), states that the choice of repertoire "was made by Mr. Hurok" but with Massine's approval.[62] Allers told Denham that when the selections for opening night were made, Massine and musical director Efrem Kurtz thought that the ballets, "though none too fortunate, were under the circumstances chosen adequately."[63] A month before the opening Massine telegraphed Denham:

> IN VIEW VARIOUS IMPROVMENTS [sic] AND NEW NUMBER MADE IN SARATOGA AND LABYRINTH BEING MOST SPECTACULAR PRODUCTION THIS YEAR BELIEVE IS BEST OPENING PROGRAM FOR NEW YORK HAVE NO BETTER SUGGESTIONS[64]

Whoever approved the programming, it pleased nobody. Critics were quick to compare Ballet Russe with Ballet Theatre, and always to the detriment of the Ballet Russe, Walter Terry reaching the devastating conclusion, "The current weakness of the Ballet Russe de Monte Carlo is not a sudden occurrence. The process of enervation commenced months, perhaps years ago, and a good share of the blame must be laid to its artistic director, Leonide Massine. . . . Every creator needs a rest, and Massine has needed one for two years."[65]

Serious trouble now existed within the Ballet Russe. As may happen in any company, there was occasional petty squabbling. During the 1941 season several dancers were angered at Massine's decision to cast his new wife, Tatiana Orlova, in roles for which they and some critics thought her unsuited. (As Zobeide in *Scheherazade,* wrote Walter Terry, Orlova's "characterization seems to be limited to unfortunate posturings and her supposedly enticing walk is dangerously reminiscent of an American Indian stalking his prey."[66]) These dancers threatened to strike if such casting continued. Today, Igor Youskevitch thinks he would not have been so unbudging on the issue if he had realized the severity of the tension which then existed between Massine and Denham. Both Youskevitch and Frederic Franklin believe that Massine was making the businessmen who supported the company uneasy. "To them," says Youskevitch, "Massine was no longer an asset. His last ballets had been flops. For purely economic reasons, Denham may have wondered, do we still need Massine?" As for Massine, he had grievances of his own. He protested that his name, as artistic director, was being omitted from posters, that his salary was reaching him only after long delays, and that he was receiving neither royalties nor traveling expenses.[67]

Massine also had to counter the charges that he had exhausted himself artistically. Therefore he submitted a list of twenty projects he felt able to undertake over the next few years. These proposals, complete in many cases with suggested literary sources, composers, and designers, were as follows: *Duly Griet* (based upon Brueghel, décor by Dali); *The Dream of Audubon; Don Pasquale* (Donizetti/Chirico); Brazilian ballet (Villa-Lobos/ Portinari); *Lieutenant Kije* (Prokofiev) [this score was about to be used by Fokine for *Russian Soldier*]; *Johnny Goes to Town* (new score by Roy Harris to an Archibald MacLeish scenario); Mayan ballet (Chavez/Diego Rivera); *Sacrifice* (Spanish ballet with Dali décor); English ballet (Gilbert and Sullivan/Oliver Smith and Alvin Colt); *The Gypsies* (Pushkin/Tchaikovsky) [this eventually materialized as Ballet Theatre's *Aleko*]; *The Golden Age* (Shostakovitch/Alexander Calder); *Golden Wife,* a Finnish legend (Sibelius/Tchelitchev); *Le Mariage Forcé* (Molière); *Elegie* (Chopin); *Hungarian Rhapsody* (Liszt); *Le Roi Valet* (Derain libretto, Françaix music, Tchelitchev or Derain décor); and revivals of *Astuzzi Femminili, Soleil de Nuit, Pulcinella,* and *Sacre du Printemps.*[68]

In the face of criticism, Massine opposed policies which might undermine his authority. He spoke against further attempts to acquire repertoire or personnel from the defunct American Ballet. Yet he did not oppose guest choreographers in principle. He suggested that forthcoming seasons offer two new productions by himself and two by someone else: Fokine, Balanchine, or any other appropriate choreographer.[69]

Backstage, the atmosphere was tense. One night, Massine startled a dancer by telling her that he was leaving the company and that with his departure the company would perish. The dancer did not calm down until a management spokesman convinced her "it was only Mr. Massine's imagination and his desire to spread alarming news."[70]

No, it was not just his imagination. He was receiving offers from other sources and, given his uncertain position within his own company, he was willing to consider them. Hurok, now enamored of Ballet Theatre, wanted him to join that company, and Universal Art ultimately permitted him to choreograph for Ballet Theatre during the summer of 1942.[71] Lincoln Kirstein invited Massine to teach at the School of American Ballet and to participate in a never realized scheme which sounds like the prototype for the postwar Ballet Society: Massine, Balanchine, and American-born choreographers would stage experimental evenings of ballet at Hunter College which would be open to subscription audiences only, thereby making it possible to collaborate with easel painters who were not members of the stage designers' union.[72]

While receiving offers to choreograph elsewhere, Massine was experiencing difficulties in choreographing for the Ballet Russe. Desiring to collaborate with Dali on a Bach ballet, he accused management of "sabotaging" his efforts.[73] Denham replied that Massine, always a painstaking worker, was demanding inordinate rehearsal time. He reminded Massine that Balanchine's *Poker Game* had been produced in only ten days[74]—conveniently forgetting that that ballet had been not a piece of new choreography, but a revival of an extant work.

By the autumn of 1942 reconciliation was impossible. Massine, after choreographing *Aleko* and *Don Domingo* for Ballet Theatre, returned to the Ballet Russe. But he was no longer in power. Although his contract made him artistic director until 1948, on 6 November 1942 he signed a new agreement with Universal Art whereby Universal assigned to him rights to *Boutique Fantasque, Three-Cornered Hat,* and *Capriccio Espagnol,* while retaining its own right to produce them upon paying royalties of $25 per performance. Massine, in turn, granted Universal "a non-exclusive license" to all works created for the Ballet Russe de Monte Carlo since 1938, royalties to Massine ceasing thirty-four years after the premiere of each ballet.[75]

On 10 November 1942 Massine joined Ballet Theatre.[76] The Massine era of the Ballet Russe was over.

NOTES FOR CHAPTER 2

1. Conversation with Roman Jasinski. Henceforth, all statements for which no printed source is given were made in conversation with the author.
2. Michel Katcharoff, unpublished autobiography, p. 40.
3. Alicia Markova, *Giselle and I*, pp. 60-67, 86-87; and S. Hurok, *Impresario*, pp. 210-211.
4. Fernau Hall, *An Anatomy of Ballet*, p. 180; and A.E. Twysden, *Alexandra Danilova*, p. 82.
5. *Nobilissima Visione* origins—Cyril W. Beaumont, *Supplement to Complete Book of Ballets*, p. 50; Léonide Massine, *My Life in Ballet*, pp. 207-210; Ann Barzel, "Ballets Down the Drain," *Ballet Annual #17*, p. 79; "Hands Seen on Ballet Scenery Spelled Out Words—'Gloria!' " *Hartford Times*, 9 December 1938.
6. *Nobilissima Visione* reviews—Arnold L. Haskell, "Ballet Extremes," *The Bystander*, 10 August 1938, p. 214; Herbert Elwell, "Drama Is Accented by Ballet Dancers," *Cleveland Plain Dealer*, 4 December 1938; Francis Toye, "Ballet on Life of St. Francis," London *Daily Telegraph and Morning Post*, 22 July 1938; John Martin, "The Dance: Massine's St. Francis," *New York Times*, 23 October 1938; Robert Lawrence, *The Victor Book of Ballets and Ballet Music*, p. 388.
7. "Ballet Accord Sought," *New York Times*, 10 July 1938.
8. "The Sitter Out," *The Dancing Times*, September 1938, p. 623, and October 1938, p. 6; and Edwin Denby, *Looking at the Dance*, pp. 85-86, 117.
9. New York and Boston *Giselle*—"Tempo!" *Dance*, December 1938, p. 8; Walter Ware, "Foot-Notes," *The American Dancer*, February 1939, p. 16; Alicia Markova, *Giselle and I*, pp. 72-77; S. Hurok, *S. Hurok Presents*, p. 134; John Martin, "The Dance: A Ballerina," *New York Times*, 19 March 1939.
10. Lifar quarrels—S. Hurok, *Impresario*, pp. 212-215; Russell Rhodes, "New York Letter," *The Dancing Times*, December 1938, pp. 318-320; "Backstage Intrigue at the Ballet," *Pic*, 13 December 1938, p. 23.
11. John Martin, "Ballet Russe Returns," *New York Times*, 24 October 1941.
12. Seasonal plans—Russell Rhodes, "New York Letter," *The Dancing Times*, December 1938, pp. 318-320; "Tempo!" *Dance*, January 1939, p. 36.
13. Seasonal reviews—John Martin, "The Dance: Summing Up," *New York Times*, 30 October 1938; Elizabeth McCausland, "The Ballet Russe Packs 'em In," *Dance Observer*, November 1938, p. 128; Margery Dana, "Ballet Russe de Monte Carlo—Variety of 'Sugary Anecdotes,' " *Daily Worker*, 26 October 1938; Lincoln Kirstein, "Let's Go Native," *Town and Country*, January 1939, pp. 50, 70.
14. *Les Elfes*—Walter Terry, *Ballet: A New Guide to the Liveliest Art*, pp. 121-122; Ann Barzel, "Dance in Review," *Dance*, March 1939, p. 46; H.M.C., "Ballet Russe," *Buenos Aires Herald*, 17 June 1940; Doris Hering, "The Season in Review," *Dance Magazine*, June 1950, p. 42.
15. Contract with Léonide Massine dated 23 March 1939.

16. A.E. Twysden, "The Monte Carlo Ballet," *The Dancing Times*, May 1939, p. 156; Cyril W. Beaumont, *Supplement to Complete Book of Ballets*, p. 55; Robert Lawrence, *The Victor Book of Ballets and Ballet Music*, p. 91.

17. *Rouge et Noir* origin—Cyril W. Beaumont, *Supplement to Complete Book of Ballets*, p. 56; Eleanor Page, "Massine Tells How He Charts a New Ballet," *Chicago Tribune*, 23 December 1937; John Martin, "The Dance: New Ballets," *New York Times*, 16 July 1939; Léonide Massine, *My Life in Ballet*, pp. 211-212.

18. *Rouge et Noir* reviews—Grace Robert, *The Borzoi Book of Ballets*, pp. 257-258; Robert Sabin, "Reviews of the Month," *Dance Observer*, November 1941, p. 124; George Beiswanger, "Dance Highlights," *Theatre Arts*, July 1940, p. 26; John Martin, "The Dance: Ballet Russe Premieres," *New York Times*, 5 November 1939.

19. Mack More, "Diaghilev Protegee—Gives Ballet World New Classic Role," *The Music News*, 21 March 1940, p. 35.

20. John Martin, "Markova Dances in 'Rouge et Noir,' " *New York Times*, 4 March 1949.

21. A.E. Twysden, "Massine's New Ballets," *The Dancing Times*, July 1939, p. 388.

22. Wartime—Louis Biancolli, "Ballet Their Escape from War Jitters," *New York World Telegram*, 14 September 1940; John Martin, "The Dance: New Season," *New York Times*, 17 September 1939; John Martin, "The Dance: Ballet and the War," *New York Times*, 1 October 1939; Léonide Massine, *My Life in Ballet*, p. 213; Lillian Moore, "War-Time Adventures of a Company," *The Dancing Times*, December 1939, pp. 131-133; "Rotterdam Here with 1,123 Aboard," *New York Times*, 27 October 1939; Conversation with Marcel Fenchel.

23. John Martin, "The Dance: Ballet Russe Premieres," *New York Times*, 5 November 1939.

24. *Devil's Holiday*—John Martin, "The Dance: Ballet Russe Premieres," *New York Times*, 5 November 1939; Edwin Denby, *Looking at the Dance*, pp. 215-216; Ann Barzel, "Ballets Down the Drain," *Ballet Annual* #17, p. 80; David Vaughan, *Frederick Ashton and His Ballets*, pp. 170-172; Conversation with Frederic Franklin.

25. Robert Lawrence, *The Victor Book of Ballets and Ballet Music*, p. 48.

26. *Tristan Fou*—Russell Rhodes, "New York Letter," *The Dancing Times*, December 1938, p. 320; Walter Ware, "Foot-Notes," *The American Dancer*, April 1938, p. 22.

27. *Bacchanale* production and premiere—"Ballet Russe to Give Three New Dances in Program Thursday," *Atlanta Journal*, 25 February 1940; Michel Katcharoff, unpublished autobiography, p. 43; Grace Robert, *The Borzoi Book of Ballets*, pp. 33-34; S. Hurok, *Impresario*, p. 220; Conversations with Alexandra Danilova, Milada Mladova, James Starbuck.

28. *Bacchanale* reviews—John Martin, "The Dance: Surrealism and Americana," *New York Times*, 19 November 1939; Albertina Vitak, "Dance Events Reviewed," *The American Dancer*, January 1940, p. 19; Hilmar Grondahl, "Ballet Russe Ends Booking," *Portland Sunday Oregonian*, 28 January 1940; Alfred Frankenstein," "Bacchanale, an Amazing Work," *San Francisco Chronicle*, 3 February 1940.

29. Conversation with James Starbuck and Milada Mladova.

30. *Ghost Town*—Alfred Frankenstein, "Ballet Resurrects Uproarious Rivalries of the Old West," *San Francisco Chronicle*, 2 February 1940; Edward Downes, "Ballet Premieres," *Boston Transcript*, 19 April 1940; Edwin Denby, *Looking at the Dance*, p. 218.

31. "The Ballet That Massine Built," *Dance,* February 1940, p. 54.

32. John Martin, "The Ballet Russe Hailed at Opening," *New York Times,* 27 October 1939; Walter Terry, "Dancing Gentlemen," *New York Herald-Tribune,* 2 November 1941.

33. John Martin, "The Dance: Surrealism and Americana," *New York Times,* 19 November 1939; "Barnstorming with Ballet Russe," *Los Angeles Herald-Express,* 8 February 1940.

34. "Tempo!" *Dance,* December 1939, p. 7.

35. Contest—Walter Terry, "Dance: "Hard Work," *New York Herald-Tribune,* 25 February 1940; John Martin, "The Dance: Miscellany," *New York Times,* 14 July 1940; Glenway Westcott, "The Dream of Audubon," *Dance,* December 1940, pp. 18, 30-32, and January 1941, pp. 30-31; Gervase N. Butler, "Choreographics," *Dance Observer,* December 1940, p. 146; "Dance Notes," *New York Herald-Tribune,* 6 October 1940; and 23 March 1941; Letter from Lincoln Kirstein to Jack Anderson, 4 January 1978.

36. "Phelan Estate Pushed Home for Ballet Russe," *San Francisco Examiner,* 24 March 1940.

37. John Martin, "The Dance: Miscellany," *New York Times,* 3 March and 31 March 1940.

38. "Ballet Theatre Can't Compete, Wants Ballet Russe Unionized," *New York Herald-Tribune,* 22 March 1940; "Tempo!," *Dance,* April 1940, p. 6.

39. Guests—"Argentinita at Metropolitan," *New York Times,* 5 April 1940; "Dolin to Dance with Ballet Russe," *New York Post,* 11 April 1940; John Martin, "The Dance: Ballet et Al," *New York Times,* 17 March 1940; Anatole Chujoy, "Dance in Review," *Dance,* April 1940.

40. Walter Terry, "Theilade Work, 'Clouds,' Staged by Ballet Russe," *New York Herald-Tribune,* 11 April 1940.

41. Complaints—Walter Terry, "The State of Ballet," *New York Herald-Tribune,* 21 July 1940; Albertina Vitak, "Dance Events Reviewed," *The American Dancer,* January 1940, p. 30; "René Blum Writes a Letter of Protest," *Dance,* April 1940, p. 31.

42. Letter from S.J. Denham to Jacques Rubinstein, 14 December 1939.

43. John Martin, "The Dance: Ballet Russe," *New York Times,* 8 September 1940.

44. John Martin, "The Dance: Many Ballets," *New York Times,* 15 September 1940; "The Monte Carlo Ballet: American Girl Is One of Stars of the Russian Troupe," *Newsweek,* 28 October 1940, p. 56.

45. Edwin Denby, *Looking at the Dance,* p. 219; Albertina Vitak, "Dance Events Reviewed," *The American Dancer,* December 1940, p. 12.

46. Letter from S.J. Denham to Jacques Rubinstein, 19 December 1939; Letter from Jacques Rubinstein to S.J. Denham, 27 December 1939.

47. Rosalyn Krokover, *The New Borzoi Book of Ballets,* p. 320.

48. Harry R. Burke, "Ballet's 'Vienna—1814' Earns Calls of 'Bravo,'" *St. Louis Globe-Democrat,* 13 January 1941.

49. *Serenade*—Edwin Denby, "Monte Carlo Company," *New York Herald-Tribune,* 18 February 1945; Nancy Reynolds, *Repertory in Review,* pp. 36-37; Conversation with Alexandra Danilova.

50. *Nutcracker*—"Ballet Russe de Monte Carlo," *Dance,* August-October 1940, p. 40; Robert Lawrence, *The Victor Book of Ballets and Ballet Music,* p. 268; "Judges Swamped with Beauty in Contest to Pick Junior Ballet Russe Talent," *Houston Post,* 18 December 1947; Conversations with Robert Lindgren and Ann Barzel.

51. *The New Yorker*—Léonide Massine, *My Life in Ballet,* pp. 216-217; John Martin, "Massine Appears in 2 Ballet Roles," *New York Times,* 30 October 1940;

Irving Kolodin, " 'New Yorker' Given to Gershwin Music," *New York Sun*, 19 October 1940; Elinor Hughes, "The Ballet," *Boston Herald*, 8 November 1940; "Massine's New Ballets," *Dance*, November 1940, p. 9.

52. Original Ballet Russe—Schedules: John Martin, "The Dance: Events Ahead," *New York Times*, 5 January 1941; "The Dance: Premieres," *New York Times*, 19 January 1941. Reviews: John Martin, "The Dance: Vale et Ave," *New York Times*, 3 November 1940; "Ballet No. 2," *New York Times*, 17 November 1940.

53. Tours—A.E. Twysden, *Alexandra Danilova*, p. 124; "The Ballet in America," *The Dancing Times*, October 1941, p. 7; "Dance Notes," *New York Herald-Tribune*, 30 March 1941.

54. Troubles—S. Hurok, *S. Hurok Presents*, p. 137; "Notes from the Field," *New York Times*, 16 March 1941; Auricle, "Entr'acte," *Dance*, December 1940, p. 6.

55. *Labyrinth* production—Robert Lawrence, *The Victor Book of Ballets and Ballet Music*, p. 255; Grace Robert, *The Borzoi Book of Ballets*, pp. 35-36; Léonide Massine, *My Life in Ballet*, pp. 218-219. Reviews: Walter Terry, "Ballets and Books," *New York Herald-Tribune*, 19 October 1941; Edwin Denby, *Looking at the Dance*, pp. 257-258; John Martin, "Season Is Opened by Ballet Russe," *New York Times*, 9 October 1941; Robert Lawrence, "Music of the Ballet," *New York Herald-Tribune*, 9 October 1941.

56. *Magic Swan*—Walter Terry, "Ballets and Books," *New York Herald-Tribune*, 19 October 1941; Gervase N. Butler, "Reviews of the Month," *Dance Observer*, November 1941, p. 123.

57. *Saratoga*—Léonide Massine, *My Life in Ballet*, pp. 220-221; Robert Sabin, "Reviews of the Month," *Dance Observer*, November 1941, p. 124; Edwin Denby, *Looking at the Dance*, p. 259; Walter Terry, "The Week's Dance," *New York Herald-Tribune*, 26 October 1941.

58. Walter Terry, "Dancing Gentlemen," *New York Herald-Tribune*, 2 November 1941.

59. Walter Terry, "Screen Ballet," *New York Herald-Tribune*, 11 January 1942.

60. S. Hurok, *Impresario*, p. 228.

61. Letter from Franz Allers to S.J. Denham, 21 April 1942.

62. Letter from S.J. Denham to Sidney Cohn, 16 April 1942.

63. Letter from Franz Allers to S.J. Denham, 21 April 1942.

64. Telegram from Léonide Massine to S.J. Denham, 15 March 1942.

65. Walter Terry, "Monte Carlo Case," *New York Herald-Tribune*, 19 April 1942.

66. Walter Terry, " 'Magic Swan' on Stadium's Ballet Program," *New York Herald-Tribune*, 25 June 1942.

67. Letter from David Libidins to Hurok Attractions Inc., 17 March 1942; letter from Léonide Massine to S.J. Denham, 28 March 1942.

68. "Léonide Massine's Production Project," dated 5 January 1942.

69. Letter from Léonide Massine to S.J. Denham, 20 February 1942.

70. S.J. Denham memorandum dated 17 April 1942.

71. Letter from Watson Washburn to Sidney E. Cohn, 30 April 1942.

72. Letter from Lincoln Kirstein to Sidney E. Cohn, 4 May 1942.

73. Letter from Sidney E. Cohn to S.J. Denham, 14 September 1942.

74. Letter from S.J. Denham to Léonide Massine, 30 June 1942.

75. Contract with Léonide Massine dated 6 November 1942.

76. "Léonide Massine Joins Ballet Theatre on Tour," *New York Herald-Tribune*, 11 November 1942.

3 MASSINE AND HIS BALLETS

ADMIRED as a choreographer since World War I, Léonide Massine was virtually worshipped by balletgoers during the 1930s. From the 1940s onward, however, his reputation began to plummet. Many of his new ballets were unsuccessful, while his old failed to interest a younger generation of critics and audiences; Massine came close to being relegated to the history books. Yet since the early 1970s there has been renewed interest in Massine, and revivals of his ballets have received genuine, if occasionally hesitant, praise. Few choreographic reputations have fluctuated so strangely.

During all these shifts of taste, Massine's staunchest supporters were his dancers. Typically, with near unanimity, Ballet Russe dancers will claim that not only was such a work as *Bacchanale* fun to dance but, far from being a muddle or a prank, it was a meritorious piece of choreography which received mixed notices only because it was ahead of its time. Massine inspired loyalty. Yet in terms of personality he could not in any simple sense be called affable or congenial.

Again with near unanimity, Ballet Russe dancers employ such words as "reserved," "cool," "pedantic," and "aloof" when describing Massine.[1] Even when the Ballet Russe toured, Massine usually kept apart from the rest of the company. Though known to possess a dry wit, he was not genial in the rehearsal studio. "You

57

could always joke with Balanchine," says Michel Katcharoff, the company's former régisseur, "but you never joked with Massine." Some observers feel this aloofness was armor donned by a man who was basically shy. Others feel it was a concomitant of Massine's highly developed powers of cerebration. "Massine's poise and sense of order never leave him," Sol Hurok writes. "There is a meticulousness about him and a neatness that indicate the possession of an orderly mind."[2]

Massine's meticulousness revealed itself in several crotchets. One was a very real and practical concern for money. He expected—and received—high salaries, and he was known to drive employers into awkward financial corners. He never forgot about royalty payments, and the Ballet Russe files contain innumerable notes from Massine reminding the company that his royalties were due. Massine was also quick to appeal to the law courts when he suspected he had been ill-used. Yet if such legalism seems annoying, or even comic, Massine's motives are defensible. Believing himself to be an artist, Massine also believed that he should be paid—and paid well—for his art. During his long career he must have had many unpleasant dealings with inept or downright unscrupulous agents and managers to justify his financial fussing.

Massine's reserve often struck casual observers as secretiveness, and some balletomanes grew angry because, unlike Balanchine, who can choreograph with outsiders present, Massine barred visitors from his rehearsal room. Yet why should this have seemed surprising or odd? Few practitioners of the other arts create in public. As British critic A. H. Franks points out, "Stravinsky does not compose amid guests, however amiable. . . ."[3]

What dancers have responded to in Massine is that beneath the aloofness one sensed an underlying passion, a single-minded devotion to the art of ballet which he communicated to his associates. Therefore they were willing to work—to slave—for him. Once when James Starbuck was new to the company, Massine took him aside and said, "I hired you, so you must be a good dancer." At that, Starbuck felt willing to work like a dog to justify Massine's faith in him. When one worked hard, there were rewards. Eagle-eyed, Massine could spot a dancer in the last row of an ensemble, and if that dancer had been unusually good, Massine might tell him so. Sometimes the rewards were tangible. When Tamara Toumanova unexpectedly resigned from the company, Nathalie Krassovska had to learn several Massine ballets virtually overnight. In gratitude, Massine bought her two evening gowns.

But one did have to work hard for Massine. There was no

stopping him once he decided to rehearse. And he rehearsed everywhere. He rehearsed in the corridors of moving trains. He rehearsed on tour in theatres after the evening performance. Shooed from a theatre by crews wishing to lock up for the night, Massine resumed rehearsals in the ballroom of whatever hotel the company was staying at, the walls shaking with the piano playing of Rachel Chapman, the company's indefatigable pianist, until the night manager, aghast at the noise, called a halt. Sometimes during these marathons Massine would order sandwiches for the company, or would fortify a flagging soloist by making him down a shot of gin. But dancers were known to faint under the strain. Today, Frederic Franklin can joke—but it was no joke then—that one reason why the dancers joined the union was in self-defense against Massine's rehearsal schedules.

Massine's manner in rehearsals apparently varied according to circumstances. Roman Jasinski recalls that, in the de Basil company, Massine could get "hysterical," and some of the dancers who worked with him when he returned as guest choreographer in the late days of the Ballet Russe de Monte Carlo found him, as one put it, "very manic." But that dancer, a brash youngster then, also thought Massine at the time to be "someone out of another age." So, perhaps, his ferocity constituted an attempt to impress dancers who might otherwise have regarded him as passé. On the other hand, Charles Dickson, a member of Massine's company at its Monte Carlo debut, remembers Massine as being "cool but kind, and almost always very quiet. He seldom raised his voice. If he grew annoyed, he'd sometimes deliver a devastating remark, but even then it was always in low tones." The reason for this absence of tempestuousness, Dickson speculates, is that in 1938 Massine was a happy man. He had a company all his own and was engaged in rewarding creative work. There was no need to be stormy.

Whatever his manner, Massine's work methods remained largely the same over the years. Unlike Balanchine or Ashton, who compose on the spot, Massine liked to give the impression when he entered the studio that he had thought out his choreography in advance. Usually at his side was an immense book which he would occasionally consult, presumably a book containing the steps of his ballet written down in his adaptation of the Stepanov notation system. But since he never permitted anyone to peek into the book, it always remained something of a mystery. Despite his conscious planning, a choreographic session with Massine was not simply a matter of being told, "Now do this

. . . now do that," from the first minute of the piece to the last. Massine seldom choreographed scenes of his ballets in their consecutive order. He might begin with the last first, or with some intermediate scene—more than that, he might begin with a bit from a scene, then choreograph a bit from a totally different scene, the eventual pulling together of the ballet resembling the editing of a film. Apparently, he was especially prone to working in this manner during the 1930s. But when he created *Harold in Italy* in 1954, dancers remember that he choreographed events more or less in their proper theatrical order.

Massine liked to explore all the variants of a step, particularly if that step happened to be one of the movements which he hoped would give his new ballet its special flavor. Each step or phrase was assigned a number, and Massine would have his dancers perform them in multititudinous re-arrangements by calling out the numbers in various combinations. Remembering these combinations grew taxing. Once, at wit's end, James Starbuck dared to complain about having to learn so many versions of a ballet. Massine's reply was icy and chastening: "My ballets do not have *versions.* There is *only one* version to any of my ballets: that version which exists when I have finished choreographing it and am totally satisfied."

Massine taught steps, but seldom explained them, apparently believing that if a dancer knew too much about a ballet, individual interpretations might vary more than he was willing to countenance. In this, Massine resembled Balanchine and Tudor, who have also been known to assign movements to dancers without explaining them, believing that, if properly executed, the movements will be automatically expressive. Nevertheless, once a role was learned, one might then find within it opportunities for legitimate individual interpretations: for instance, both James Starbuck and Leon Danielian were successful in Massine's own role of the Peruvian in *Gaîté Parisienne,* yet each was unlike the other; and while critics thought Nina Tarakanova charming as the original Glove Seller, it was only when Alexandra Danilova assumed the role that it received its definitive interpretation.

Sometimes, though, it was difficult to discern just what role it was that one had been assigned. At most, Massine might say, "You are a slave," but whether that slave was a slave in Alabama or in the court of an Oriental potentate was a matter the dancer had to decide for himself.

To complicate matters further, one could never be sure whether the steps one learned in rehearsal would be the steps one would dance in the actual ballet. Massine liked to use dancers as guinea pigs, trying out on responsive bodies steps which might ultimately be assigned to someone else. Men were even known to have learned passages later given to women, and more than one dancer was disappointed to find that that virtuoso sequence he had worked so hard to master—and of which he was so proud—was not really his at all. Frederic Franklin was a favorite guinea pig because of his good memory. During the creation of *Gaîté Parisienne* Franklin learned every male role. Massine was so proud of him that one day he asked, "Now that you know all the parts, which do you want for yourself?" At these unexpected words, the young Franklin gulped and, for a moment, did not know what to reply, afraid that any preference of role would displease the master. Finally, he ventured, "I think I like the Baron best." "Good," smiled Massine, "the Baron was meant for you from the beginning."

Other dancers might have been surprised to hear that. Massine had made Franklin learn the choreography for the Peruvian and Franklin was still doing the Peruvian so late in rehearsals that there was speculation that he would be the Peruvian, while Massine would portray the Baron. Massine habitually worked out his own roles on other bodies. That way he could see the choreography, perfect it, then do it himself. And some dancers think that the fact that he used other people—and, inevitably, other body types—in the creation of the roles he himself danced, helps explain why these roles were unusually varied, ranging from the ascetic St. Francis to the ebullient Peruvian.

Though he had a keen sense of style, Massine's literal memory was occasionally faulty; hence his interest in notation and archival films. Massine tried to film all his ballets, and when reviving a work he would come to rehearsal bearing his films ("Massine's Looney Tunes," irreverent dancers called them). But the films were no guarantee that the revival would proceed smoothly. Because the camerawork was usually amateurish, some passages were indistinct, and in the midst of a contrapuntal ensemble it was difficult to sort out all the dancers. The mechanical nature of the film medium also posed problems. Reviving *Seventh Symphony* in 1948, Massine wanted a certain dancer to take over the role originally portrayed by a dancer no longer in the company. The dancer sat down with projector and film, saw a bit of choreography, and was stumped. Speaking of his predecessor, he said, "I knew he was a great dancer, but how could anyone ever do a step like that?" Then it was pointed out that he had been running the film backward.

The 1948 season also saw the revival of *Rouge et Noir*. To expedite the reconstruction of this complex work, the company was divided into groups which rehearsed simultaneously. One day, some dancers studied the films of a passage while others were coached in the same passage by a member of the original cast. Massine was attending to yet a third group elsewhere. At the end of the session the groups rejoined to perform the sequences they had just learned. There came one of the monumental architectural formations typical of Massine's symphonic style—except, here, chaos reigned. The group which had studied the film was turned one way, the group which the dancer from the original cast had coached was turned another. "Let's try it again," said Massine. They did. Again there was chaos. Now arguments flared up. "That's the way it is on film," said some of the dancers. Nevertheless, the original cast member insisted that she had taught her charges the scene as she had always danced it during her years with the Ballet Russe. To settle the quarrel, Massine asked to see the films himself. The films were shown. The moment for the architectural formation occurred. In the film there was complete ensemble unanimity, except for one lone mistaken dancer—the very dancer who was now coaching the company and who had indeed taught *Rouge et Noir* "as she had always danced it."

Diaghilev reportedly said, "Massine is the only dancer who ranks as my intellectual equal,"[4] and Massine was possibly the purest product of the cultural education Diaghilev liked to give his protégés. When Fokine, Nijinska, and Balanchine came to Diaghilev, they already had had choreographic experience, while Nijinsky's course of choreographic study was interrupted by his marriage. Aesthetically, Massine was shaped by Diaghilev, Diaghilev taking him to galleries and concerts and introducing him to the cultural leaders of the day. One result of this is that Massine became an unusually cosmopolitan choreographer, though one who, for some commentators, remained Russian at heart.[5]

Circumstances helped foster Massine's cosmopolitanism. For much of his life he was an itinerant. The Russian Revolution and the touring schedule of the Diaghilev Ballet severed him from his native land at an early age. After that, he was "on the road" for much of the time; while home, for Massine, was a solitary island off the Italian coast. An essentially private person, the home he preferred was a place apart.

His ballets about public places—his ballets about Paris and Vienna, Italy and Spain—might be called traveler's impressions, scenes glimpsed by unusually sharp eyes. But the eyes are those of an outsider. This proved insufficient when Massine attempted American ballets. Serious American balletgoers of the early 1940s did not want travelogues or pastiche. At a time when it was an urgent matter to prove that, far from being exclusively European, ballet was an art that could flourish in America, our balletic intelligentsia demanded creations which not only would depict the foibles and manners of Americans, but would convey a sense of what it actually felt like to be an American. That Massine could not quite do this is a sign, not necessarily of lack of interest in America, but of a choreographic talent which was essentially of another sort than that which the propagandists for American ballet were prizing. One has only to ponder *Beau Danube* and *Gaîté Parisienne* to realize this.

In these comedies, Massine the cosmopolitan world traveler was a choreographic caricaturist. Looking at a place, he isolated, then exaggerated, its key elements just as, looking at a person, he isolated, then exaggerated, key elements of the way that person looked in motion or repose. When Massine knew precisely what particular elements were worth isolating, his ballets became convincing in atmosphere. A number of critics have observed that *Three-Cornered Hat* has dances from several Spanish provinces performed in one single town. No matter. *Three-Cornered Hat* seems essentially and convincingly Spanish. So *Le Beau Danube*, in Grace Robert's words, conveys "the very essence of youth, gaiety, and the glamour of a romantic uniform. It evokes nostalgia for a Vienna that never existed except in some exile's dream."[6]

Character development in Massine's comedies is slight. Character traits are simply reiterated and reinforced, and a ballet's internal variety derives from the way contrasting characters are juxtaposed. *Gaîté Parisienne* exploits the contrasts between the chic Glove Seller and the attractive but less assertive Flower Girl; between the dashingly romantic Baron and the frenetic but bumbling Peruvian. *Beau Danube* contrasts the demure young girl and the worldlywise Street Dancer, the aristocratically elegant Hussar and the merely snobbish Dandy. While Massine often contrasted innocence and sophistication, gaucherie and suavity, the parts he conceived which fit these categories are far from alike. Alexandra Danilova points out that even such superficially similar women as the Glove Seller and the Street Dancer are fundamentally different: "The Glove Seller is pure champagne, she is simply Paris, the Paris that is very chic, yet she has no depth of character.

The Street Dancer, now she has depth: she has pride and passion, and is finally able to let an old love go."

The fact that Massine's comic characters are apt to be, in the best sense of the term, caricatures by no means makes them easy to dance. Quite the contrary. This is one reason why young dancers unfamiliar with the unabashedly presentational style of character dancing required for Massine are often ineffectual in his ballets. Igor Youskevitch maintains that Massine based both his comic and many of his serious works upon the grotesque style which in his day was, along with classical and national character dance, recognized as a legitimate form of ballet: "The grotesque was a free-form, endlessly inventive, style which had previously been used sparingly as a kind of spice or special coloration in ballet. Massine, though, made it the very basis for much of his choreography."

The dancers who came to specialize in Massine roles were dancer-performers of a sort that is rare today. Youskevitch thinks that today's dancers usually excel either in the neo-classicism of abstract ballets or in introspective ballets hinting at psychological nuances. What they are unable to do is to externalize character so that, in a mere instant, they can present before an audience the distinctive gestures which epitomize a certain human being. Their inability to do this also affects their attitude toward their roles. Michel Katcharoff recalls that, formerly, such minor figures as the waiters in *Gaîté* offered opportunities for little jewels of characterization, whereas, currently, dancers seem to regard them only as bit parts—and it shows on stage.

Whether comic or serious, Massine's ballets are apt to be bustling. Dancegoers used to the long classical phrases of Balanchine or the sustained moodiness of Tudor may find them fussy, short-breathed, and frantic. So much happens in such little time. As many quirky steps are crammed into a measure of music as that measure will hold. Possibly no more fidgety style was seen in ballet until Twyla Tharp started choreographing for ballet companies. A.H. Franks even describes Massine's restlessness in terms that might also apply to Tharp:

> Adept in the organization of large groups, whether for pure dance or decorative effect, he frequently displays his invention to such an extent as to have two or three focal points of interest occurring simultaneously. Occasionally one of these focal points dominates the stage, with various contrapuntal features of secondary interest in different corners.[7]

Massine's ability to keep things moving has meant that the finales of his ballets are often elaborate. At worst, they can be scrambles in which Massine tries to bring together and resolve all the dramatic, thematic, or allegorical matters he had introduced earlier. At best, they can be so exhilarating that they set audiences cheering. Sonja Taanila says that she considers herself fortunate to have been able to dance in ballets by three masters of the finale: Fokine, Balanchine, and Massine, and "of the three I sometimes think the Massine finale the greatest of them all. The momentum and excitement of his movements are remarkable. Sometimes the choreography is nothing but kick-steps, but if they are done with gusto the effect is overwhelming." Examples of simple but memorable finales include the giddy swoop of the chain-dance in *Beau Danube* and, in *St. Francis*, the solemn procession of monks and nuns, their arms crossed above their heads, the rhythmic opening and closing of their hands suggesting a flicker of Pentecostal flames.

A tendency toward complexity of stage action is present from the very start of Massine's choreographic career. In choreographing *The Good-Humoured Ladies* for Diaghilev in 1917, Massine said he

> learned the value of concentrating on detail, and giving full significance to even the most minute gesture. I also discovered that the body includes various more or less independent structural systems, each answerable only to itself, which must be co-ordinated according to choreographic harmony. This led me to invent broken, angular movements for the upper part of the body while the lower limbs continued to move in the usual harmonic academic style. Such an opposition of style is, in my opinion, possible, and creates an interesting contrast.[8]

Massine's ballets of the 1930s and early 1940s are often divided into two categories: the comic and the symphonic. Such categorization might seem to ignore the dramatic *St. Francis*. Yet the peculiar kind of dramatic ballet which *St. Francis* is really allies it to the symphonic mode. Massine's emphasis upon character traits suggests a predisposition toward allegory, since allegory can involve the presentation of universalized or impersonal qualities in terms of individual idiosyncrasies. It also suggests why Massine could work congenially with Salvador Dali in *Bacchanale* and *Labyrinth* since, with their elaborate symbolism, Dali's paintings often appear to be allegorical guessing games.

St. Francis is allegorical drama. Some of its characters,

including Poverty, Chastity, and Obedience, are not real people at all, but abstractions given human flesh, while another—the Wolf—is no wolf a naturalist would recognize, but an incarnation of vice. All the characters in *St. Francis* are somehow emblematic of virtue or vice, of worldliness or spirituality. Judging from reviews and from the rehearsal film in the New York Public Library's Dance Collection, *St. Francis* must have been a ballet of genuine consequence. Even when performed on film in practice dress, it has a distinctive look owing to the way Massine's angular movements for his dancers' upper bodies, including the gesture of hands raised in prayer, resemble the angles of Gothic arches and, like Gothic arches, suggest aspiration heavenward. One exception is the choreography for the Wolf, where the impulse is downward (the Wolf even holds his victims by their heels). Here, Massine may be agreeing with those moralists who maintain that vice derives from misdirection, from turning energies and powers away from the source of virtue, Satan himself having been one of the good angels before he turned away from God.

That Wolf bothered some critics. Herbert Elwell complained that "the spectacle of a big bad wolf dragging off helpless victims" did not add "a very homogeneous note to the development of a metaphysical and symbolic theme." One wonders whether someone from the Middle Ages would feel the same way. For though medieval art and literature were certainly metaphysical and symbolic, they were not always unremittingly solemn, medieval mystery plays mixing the pious with the bawdy. Massine's seriocomic Wolf may have been one of his ballet's genuinely medieval touches.

Another aspect of *St. Francis* to which critics took exception might also be defended as authentic. It worried the London *Observer* that "poverty translated into the figure of a beautiful girl merges miraculously into sensuality, and, in accepting poverty, St. Francis seems, in fact, to be accepting the finest of Bacchanalian feasts."[9] Again, one wonders whether St. John of the Cross or any of the other saints who described mystical experiences in terms evocative of sexual rapture would object to such a translation. The way Massine invests St. Francis's mystical marriage with the ecstasy of a marriage in the flesh suggests an awareness, not only of medieval thought, but of human psychology, and it prefigures such symbolic dualisms as those of Martha Graham's Joan of Arc ballet, *Seraphic Dialogue,* in which, for example, Joan's sword is simultaneously a weapon of battle and a phallic symbol.

In his ballets to actual symphonies Massine sometimes became totally allegorical. This bothered people at the time, and the notion continues to bother people. Some of the issues the symphonic ballets raised, however, are purely academic today. Surely, no one now would categorically deny a choreographer the right to employ symphonic music. One might point out certain inherent risks—such music may be too long to sustain choreography and, if familiar, may have personal meanings for each individual auditor which may not coincide with those of the choreographer—but few contemporary music critics would shriek the way Massine's opponents did in the 1930s. Yet Massine's allegories might still disconcert.

For one thing, they are arbitrary. Of course, setting steps of any kind, dramatic or abstract, to concert music is inevitably arbitrary. Concert music, being self-sufficient, demands no choreographic embellishments. Still, talented choreographers have found no difficulty in employing concert music. Their successful usages are apt to be of two kinds. In totally plotless pieces, the music serves, to borrow one of Balanchine's phrases, as "a floor for dancing" upon which the choreographer builds a kinetic structure which rises from that floor as an object of interest in and of itself, and yet still needs that floor as a basis upon which to stand. In successful dance-dramas a piece of concert music, through its mood and coloration, can help establish an emotional climate, Schoenberg's brooding "Transfigured Night" being a sonic equivalent of Hagar's brooding in Tudor's *Pillar of Fire,* the buzzings of Stravinsky's Concerto in D generating nervous tension appropriate for the macabre insect world of Robbins' *The Cage.*

Massine's allegorical ballets are scarcely personalized dance-dramas. Yet seldom are they fully abstract. Rather, they convey the grandiose messages and visions which, presumably, Massine has extracted from the music. But are these messages, if meaningful to Massine, meaningful to others? For some critics they are not. Francis Toye complained of *Seventh Symphony* that "the result in general seemed indeterminate, inchoate . . . there appeared no particular reason why anything should happen at any particular time or place." Surveying the symphonic ballets in general, Robert Sabin noted that Massine "seems to compose a series of static episodes (some of them admittedly magnificent) and then to set them going, so to speak." Edwin Denby found these episodes peculiarly monotonous, saying of *Seventh Symphony,* "Every gesture is unusually clear, but every gesture is at the same pitch, hit equally hard. The picture changes, but the tension remains the same."[10]

Massine has written of how he and Henri Matisse conceived *Rouge et Noir* in terms of shifting blocks of color and how they assigned allegorical significance to those colors. He has also described the genesis of *Seventh Symphony*. He envisioned the scheme of the ballet one afternoon when, at his island home of Galli, he watched waves pound against rocks during a storm. When planning the finale, in which the world is consumed by fire, he had his caretaker light a bonfire so he could study the motion of flames. To Massine, the powerful opening chords of Beethoven's first movement

> suggested the formation of the earth, with moving masses of soil and water creating rivers, hills and valleys. The clarinet theme which follows seemed to me to represent the evolution of plant life, while the chords of the next passage conjured up in my mind the flight of birds and the running of small animals through the forest.[11]

No clearer indication of Massine's cast of mind could be found. Massine analyzed symphonies programmatically; he let them tell stories or paint pictures, a practice which is anathema to present-day lecturers on music appreciation, who insist that a score must be treated as an autonomous entity apart from painting, literature, or daydreaming. Nevertheless, despite these strictures, many people still listen to music as Massine did. Whether or not this is the best, or even a good, way to listen to music is perhaps beside the point here. It was Massine's way, and as a result of it he derived his visions and messages. The problem now becomes, does he effectively present these visions, or are his symphonic ballets essentially static, as his detractors allege?

The curious thing is, judging from a rehearsal film, *Seventh Symphony*, though allegorically arbitrary, is far from static. Provided one does not object to its references to the Descent from the Cross, the second movement constitutes a remarkable kinetic crescendo as, with a rhythmic insistence of movement presumably matching the score's rhythmic insistence (the film is silent), the stage gradually fills with mourners, all repeating a choreographic motif involving reaching upward and sinking heavily downward until, at last, the dead youth is carried in. The tread of the scene is inexorable. The opening movement is equally impressive. First, with great wide summoning gestures, the Spirit of

Creation pulls forth life from inert matter. Then the stage grows vibrant with energy, Massine contrasting blocklike masses with rapid, leaping, bounding traversals of the stage by smaller groups of soloists representing the beings which have just been created. Everything is airy and joyous, except for the Serpent, who crawls laboriously from one side of the stage to another. In the midst of exuberance, this thick heavy movement serves as a premonitory hint of tragedy to come.

It may be fortunate that in the film *Seventh Symphony* is danced in practice dress. For today's balletgoer used to the abstractions of Balanchine, the sight of costumes supposedly representing plants, birds, and animals might be both excessively allegorical and excessively literal. Massine's choreography speaks for itself. It is enough that some dancers, through fleetness coupled with shyness, suggest deer, while other dancers seem birdlike. There may be no need to see them costumed as either deer or birds. After viewing the film it is fascinating to remember that Albertina Vitak thought that *Seventh Symphony* "has more straight dancing with less theatricalities than Massine's previous symphonic works. So Massine is really progressing. . . ."[12]

Many of the same critics who objected to the Crucifixion references in the second movement opposed the way Massine mixed mythological references throughout the ballet. They maintained, along with Robert Lawrence, that "Massine's superimposition of a Christian experience on an early Greek background is wild."[13] However, two dancers, Sonja Taanila and Robert Lindgren, feel that this mythological mixing was one of the ballet's distinctive features. As they see it, Massine was attempting a synthesis of the great Western myths. If that is so, then *Seventh Symphony* might be viewed as a dance equivalent of such T.S. Eliot poems as *The Waste Land* and *Four Quartets* where, in the course of a single work, Eliot may combine Christian, Greek, and Hindu religious references. So viewed, an oft-noted pecularity about Christian Bérard's décor becomes explicable: the fact that, even in the scenes before the world is fully created, the settings consist entirely of ruins. Conceivably, Bérard and Massine were trying to say, along with T.S. Eliot, that "Time present and time past / Are both perhaps present in time future, / And time future contained in time past," and "In my end is my beginning."

Whatever one may think of theme and movement, in *Seventh Symphony* theme and movement are meshed. *Rouge et Noir* was problematical because it seemed partly programmatic and partly abstract. While the ballet may have resulted from Massine's genuine dismay at the prospect of international war, "As *philosophie dansé* it is pretentious and believed by no one" (to quote Lincoln Kirstein). Here Massine may have done balletgoers a disservice by providing an explicit scenario, for (or so Robert Lawrence thought) "the printed synopsis . . . belies—in its elaborate prose—the simplicity of the ballet itself."

The admirers of *Rouge et Noir* recommended that audiences devote their energies to watching the ballet, rather than to pondering the program notes. Then they might be able to see, as Robert Lawrence saw, that "*Rouge et Noir* is—as its title implies—an abstract play of color and line which may be enjoyed without recourse to a deeper meaning. Massine's patterns are self-sufficient; and in few other ballets by any master is emotional content so compellingly wedded to formal design." Similarly, George Beiswanger, who thought it the finest of Massine's symphonic ballets, admired it, not for its messages, but for its masterful deployment of figures in space and time: "Dancers by twos and threes, and fives and sevens, severely sculptured against the columns of a monumental set, flow into the asymmetrical area formed by a towering Gothic arch . . . coalesce into nuclear groups, and dissolve again into space. Only at the half-way point and at the close does the stage build to impassioned tableaux."[14]

Harold in Italy, Massine's last symphonic ballet for the Ballet Russe, came in 1954 when his reputation was at a particularly low ebb. He had not had an American success since his *Aleko* of 1942 for Ballet Theatre. Encountering Massine as guest choreographer, some of the young dancers found his grandiloquent style so alien that they could never decide whether the ballet was good or not. Nor could some of the critics. One, at its Boston premiere, saw nothing but "a kaleidoscopic succession of mass movement going nowhere." Five days later, a Pittsburgh critic rhapsodized, "I can think of few, if any, contemporary ballets that approach 'Harold in Italy' in originality of choreography, clarity of expression or affinity between music and dance." Two eminent New York critics likewise had contradictory impressions, Doris Hering characterizing *Harold* as "a hopelessly outdated ordeal of plushy plastique," P.W. Manchester praising the work "as one by a master choreographer who has not lost his touch."[15]

If Massine's approach is again programmatic, that approach can be defended because he follows the programmatic suggestions made by Berlioz himself. In the first movement

Harold, the contemplative poet, observes the swirl of life around him; the second is a pilgrims' march (Massine achieving grotesque effects by contrasting the grave pilgrims with the antics of a capering Simpleton); the third, a country idyll; and the last, by universal agreement the weakest choreographically, an attack by a band of brigands. The rehearsal film in the collection of the Ballet Foundation reveals impressive ensemble movement. But, on first viewing, the principal trouble seems Harold himself. Not only does he appear to be the stock Romantic poet, and a rather droopy, soggy one at that; choreographically speaking, he has little to do except make overblown gestures. However, if one adjusts to such attitudinizing, then the presence of Harold becomes not only dramatically, but kinetically interesting. For with his slow, steady, meditative gestures and his periods of immobility, he becomes the ballet's focal point, the weight of his presence serving as a contrast to the ensemble's restlessness. Whatever excellence it may have possessed, *Harold in Italy* was unable to save Massine's dwindling reputation. And since the Ballet Russe was a touring organization which seldom stayed long in any one place, audiences never saw *Harold in Italy* often enough to get used to it.

Massine's popularity may have waned, in part, because so many of his ballets were semi-abstract, semi-allegorical at a time when those of other choreographers were becoming either totally dramatic or totally abstract. As Frederic Franklin has said, "It was the advent of Tudor and we were finally getting ready to appreciate Balanchine." As interest in Massine's ballets faded, most were dropped from the repertoire. Because young dancers had few opportunities to familiarize themselves with the style necessary to perform them—classes in character dance were not even emphasized at some American schools—Massine's ballets often failed to impress when they were revived.

Massine may also have been used as a pawn in an ideological battle. He found himself domiciled because of war in America during a period when it was necessary to demonstrate the viability of American ballet. Because he failed to produce the kind of American ballet certain advocates demanded, Massine, the personification of Ballet Russe, was open to attack, and some critics attacked ferociously.

It is undeniable that, beginning with *Vienna—1814* in 1940, Massine choreographed a number of failures. It is likewise undeniable that his creations of the 1940s and 1950s were, by and large, not as important as those of earlier decades. (But to know this in 1940 a critic would have had to be clairvoyant.) When Walter Terry thundered in 1942 that, because of his failures, Massine needed a rest, the severity of his tone might suggest that Massine had perpetrated a whole string of disasters. Actually, there were but four: *Vienna – 1814*, *The New Yorker*, *Labyrinth*, and *Saratoga*. If this is scarcely an enviable record, neither is it catastrophic, especially considering that the ballets before *Vienna – 1814*, with the exception of *Bogatyri*, were successes of one kind or another. *Gaîté Parisienne* and *Capriccio Espagnol* were outright hits. *St. Francis* and *Rouge et Noir* were admired by critics of recognized sensitivity. *Seventh Symphony*, if flawed, was nevertheless taken seriously, while *Bacchanale* was an experiment as trendy in its day as, say, Robert Joffrey's *Astarte* was to be three decades later.

Time passes. Fame is fleeting. The vagaries of taste are unpredictable. Yesterday's burning question suddenly seems inexplicable. Or irrelevant. The ballet battles of 1940 have been won. America has become one of the great nations of the ballet world. The abstract ballet has demonstrated its validity. So has the psychological dance-drama. These issues settled, one may be able to look at Massine with unclouded eyes.

Massine's admirers had reasons to justify their admiration and found genuine virtues in his ballets. We today may not value those virtues as highly as they did. Then again, we just might. Or we might find other, unexpected virtues. Perhaps now is the time for a fresh appraisal of the ballets of Léonide Massine.

NOTES FOR CHAPTER 3

1. All statements not attributed to a printed source were made in conversation with the author. I am particularly grateful to have had the opportunity to speak with Ruthanna Boris, Yvonne Chouteau, Alexandra Danilova, Eugénie Delarova, Charles Dickson, Marcel Fenchel, Frederic Franklin, Roman Jasinski, Michel Katcharoff, Nathalie Krassovska, Moscelyne Larkin, Robert Lindgren, Gilbert Reed, Eugene Slavin, James Starbuck, Sonja Taanila, Igor Youskevitch, and Rochelle Zide.
2. S. Hurok, *S. Hurok Presents*, p. 118.
3. A.H. Franks, *Twentieth Century Ballet*, p. 31.
4. A.H. Franks, *Twentieth Century Ballet*, p. 27.
5. S. Hurok, *S. Hurok Presents*, p. 118.
6. Grace Robert, *The Borzoi Book of Ballets*, p. 51.
7. A.H. Franks, *Twentieth Century Ballet*, p. 27.
8. Léonide Massine, *My Life in Ballet*, p. 95.
9. *St. Francis* Reviews—Herbert Elwell, "Drama Is Accented by Ballet Dancers," *Cleveland Plain Dealer*, 4 December 1938; H.M., "Nobilissima Visione," *The Observer*, 24 July 1938.

10. Symphonic ballet criticisms—Francis Toye, "Ovation for Massine," London *Daily Telegraph and Morning Post,* 13 July 1938; Robert Sabin, "Gilding the Symphonies," *Dance Observer,* January 1940, p. 4; Edwin Denby, *Looking at the Dance,* p. 214.
11. Léonide Massine, *My Life in Ballet,* pp. 206-207.
12. Albertina Vitak, "Dance Events Reviewed," *The American Dancer,* January 1940, p. 30.
13. Robert Lawrence, *The Victor Book of Ballets and Ballet Music,* p. 414.
14. *Rouge et Noir*—Lincoln Kirstein, "Dance in Review," *Dance,* November 1940, p. 5; Robert Lawrence, *The Victor Book of Ballets and Ballet Music,* pp. 374-378; George Beiswanger, "Dance Highlights," *Theatre Arts,* January 1940, p. 28.
15. *Harold in Italy*—Cameron Dewar, "Massine's 'Harold in Italy' Premiere Danced Here," *Boston Traveler,* 15 October 1954; Donald Steinfirst, "Massine Work Wins 'Bravos' from Audience and Critics," *Pittsburgh Post-Gazette,* 20 October 1954; Doris Hering, "Ballet Russe de Monte Carlo," *Dance Magazine,* December 1954, p. 57; P.W. Manchester, "Ballet Russe de Monte Carlo," *Dance News,* November 1954, p. 7.

4 INTERIM: RUSSIANS AND 'RODEO' (1942-1944)

THE souvenir program for 1942-43 rejoices. "This season is especially significant in the life of the Ballet Russe de Monte Carlo," it asserts, "since, for the first time in its history, it takes on the full and individual responsibility for both its artistic and business activities."

There is a touch of bravado to these words, however, since the situation in which the Ballet Russe found itself did not readily inspire rejoicing. Although Hurok would again sponsor a New York season by both the Ballet Russe and the Ballet Theatre, at the end of autumn he would no longer manage the Ballet Russe and would instead devote himself entirely to Ballet Theatre. The Ballet Russe had to find itself other management—and quickly. When it thought it found such management—Columbia Concerts, which signed the company for a nationwide tour—the association proved short-lived, for Columbia announced that for 1943-44 it would join forces with Hurok to present Ballet Theatre.[1] The Ballet Russe was being dropped.

Within the company, people were preparing to drop out. Efrem Kurtz, who had been associated with one or another Ballet Russe for nine years, resigned as musical director to devote himself to a concert career. He was succeeded by Franz Allers, who had previously been on the company's conducting staff. Also resigning was administrative director David Libidins. While Libidins had de-

75

clared that he would open his own managerial offices in order to book the company's tours, almost immediately thereafter he accepted the post of administrative director of Ballet Theatre. His tenure at Ballet Theatre was brief, Libidins in 1944 becoming an independent concert manager with the Ballet Russe among his clients.[2] But in 1942 his departure must have seemed serious indeed.

The most crucial loss was that of Massine, who remained with the company for the fall season in New York, then left for Ballet Theatre, proclaiming, "The greatest opportunities for perpetuating the traditions and standard of Russian ballet can now be found in the Ballet Theatre."[3] The acquisition of so famous a name was of the utmost commercial importance for Ballet Theatre. As *Dance News* observed, local managers on the road, who knew nothing else about ballet, knew (or thought they knew), as a result of the squabbles of the 1930s, that there were only two important ballet companies: "de Basil's" and "Massine's." Now Ballet Theatre in their eyes could become "Massine's."[4]

Massine's loss was potentially devastating. Although his last ballets were failures, he was a choreographer of recognized importance. Without him, Sergei J. Denham, who in the reshuffling of forces gained the title of Director of the Ballet, found himself a director without a choreographer. Speaking optimistically, one could say, as a British writer did say some years later, that the Monte Carlo's "strength is that it is under Sergei Denham's sole direction." But a shrewder appraisal of the company's predicament was that of George Amberg, for whom Massine's departure "indicated that the company would henceforth be run by a businessman with artistic responsibilities, instead of by an artist with business responsibilities."[5] From 1942 onward, the fate of the Ballet Russe would be determined by Denham's taste as well as by his business acumen.

Lacking a resident choreographer, Denham was determined that the Ballet Russe would nonetheless have new productions. Therefore he invited outside choreographers and tried to develop a new choreographer within the company's ranks. That choreographer was ballerina Mia Slavenska, who proposed to set a work to Bruch's G-minor violin concerto. As Slavenska describes it, her ballet resembled a "music visualization," Slavenska wanting each instrument to be portrayed by a separate dancer or group of dancers. During rehearsals, Slavenska found her cast uncooperative. A choreographic novice, she roused anger by putting "hardworking Americans, rather than certain lazy Russians I could name" at the front of ensembles, and one dancer, a soloist who had become both lazy and nasty, threw temper tantrums when he learned that he was cast as the Bassoon and would have comparatively little to do since the bassoon is seldom used in Bruch's score. Unable to cope with dissension, Slavenska abandoned her ballet.[6]

Denham announced several projects. One was *Mysteria,* the Bach ballet by Dali and Massine which had caused Denham and Massine to quarrel over rehearsal time. Not unexpectedly, given Massine's disaffection with the Ballet Russe, *Mysteria* never materialized. Other proposals included a Balanchine ballet to a Vittorio Rieti score adapted from Bellini (one of the earliest references to the ballet which eventually became *Night Shadow*); two ballets by Bronislava Nijinska, *Pan Twardowsky* (originally produced by the Polish Ballet) and *Snow Maiden,* a new work with a scenario by Denham based upon the Russian fairy tale about the winter sprite who remains on earth until she is melted by the warmth of spring; and "a Mozartian ballet" by Agnes de Mille.[7] *Snow Maiden* did get produced. And there was a ballet by Agnes de Mille. But it was most emphatically not Mozartian.

The Ballet Russe de Monte Carlo's season was supposed to begin 28 September 1942 in Toronto, but the opening had to be postponed two days because of wartime immigration laws. Whereas in previous years the company passed easily across the Canadian border, now several dancers traveling on Nansen passports found it impossible to obtain exit visas from the United States.[8] Therefore the Ballet Russe took to Canada several young Americans—among them Maria Tallchief—who had previously been unable to join the company because its ranks were filled.

Like the previous spring season, Hurok's fall "Season of Ballet" at the Met was shared by Ballet Russe and Ballet Theatre. Ballet Theatre opened it 6 October. Ballet Russe appeared 12-21 October, then Ballet Theatre was in residence until 1 November. Hurok sanguinely recalls that in those days of shared seasons "I doubt whether the public knew or cared . . . which company they were seeing." The dancers took things much more cholerically. Agnes de Mille writes that the members of the two companies used to glare at one another as they passed in the halls at the Met. Certainly, the Ballet Russe dancers had legitimate reasons for anger. As he himself puts it, Hurok was preparing to kiss "the Monte Carlo and Universal Art goodbye" and to gain the Monte Carlo's principal choreographer in the process.[9]

The bill for the Monte Carlo's first night featured two new

Nijinska productions, *Chopin Concerto* and *Snow Maiden*. Seeking a choreographer in the Diaghilev tradition to replace Massine, Denham turned to Nijinska. Like Massine, she was a skilled and sensitive artist whose ballets ranged in scale from bold experiments to frothy confections. Also like Massine, she could be a tyrant in the studio. And her tyranny, like Massine's, was the outward sign of a creative passion. It could also be a sign that she liked a dancer. One Ballet Russe dancer remembers, "The better she liked you, the more she fussed, the more she nagged."

Diaghilev's choreographers were acutely aware of how they had changed the course of ballet. But while they may have respected each other's artistry, they did not necessarily get along well personally. Moreover, each demanded absolute loyalty from dancers. Frederic Franklin puts it this way: "Nijinska hated Balanchine and Balanchine hated her, and Balanchine hated Massine and Massine hated them both, and Fokine you couldn't get near. I just hope all this will be said, because this was how it was. And we young artists were in the middle of this."

In one other respect did Nijinska resemble Massine. By 1942 both had created most of the choreography upon which their reputations now rest. Thus Alexandra Danilova says of Nijinska's works for the Ballet Russe, "The late ballets of Nijinska did not turn the pages of history. Yet they were very nice, very charming."

Chopin Concerto is generally considered the finest of these late ballets. Set to the E-minor piano concerto, it was a revision of a piece she had choreographed in 1937 for the Polish Ballet and which that company had brought to the New York World's Fair in 1939. Whereas the Polish production employed a corps of sixteen women and ten men, the Ballet Russe version utilized eighteen women and six men. Edwin Denby thought the ballet "oddly beautiful . . . because it is clear and classic to the eye but tense and romantic in its emotion." Because it was set to Chopin, it was inevitably compared with *Les Sylphides*. Yet Nijinska's ballet possessed a quirky individuality because of the way Nijinska contrasted (as Denby said) "rigid impersonal groups or clusters . . . that seem to have the weight of statues" with "rapid arrowy flights performed by individual soloists." George Amberg also praised *Chopin Concerto*, yet thought that it—indeed, all of Nijinska's Ballet Russe creations—harked back to an earlier period without furthering the development of a fresh classicism. For Amberg, *Chopin Concerto* "carried with it the climate of Paris and the suggestive beauty of a vanishing era. It marked a moment of creative culmination, rather than of a new departure. It was the absolute ballet in retrospect."[10]

Similarly, *The Snow Maiden* (to Glazounov's *Seasons*) did not open any new avenues of artistic exploration. Denby thought it "rather like a fairy tale told by a poetical maiden aunt, who doesn't care to be hurried. But she is a well educated and an intelligent lady, and she has a curious urban grace in her affectation of sweetness." So, while the ballet "flirts with greeting-card effects and sentiments . . . the groupings and the dance phrases often develop very interestingly and by preserving just enough independence of rhythm in relation to the sugary Glazounoff score they keep a certain acid edge."[11]

It was not Nijinska but another woman—an American—who revitalized the Ballet Russe in 1942. Agnes de Mille accomplished this with the premiere of *Rodeo*, on 16 October. Set on a ranch, the ballet concerns a gawky but lovable tomboy Cowgirl (originally danced by de Mille herself) who, though she rides and ropes with the male ranch hands, fails to attract their attention romantically. It is only when she puts on feminine airs and graces—and a dress—that she manages to get herself a man. Edwin Denby characterized *Rodeo* as "a pleasant comic strip." Yet in the context of its time it was more than that. It was an attempt to make a statement about ballet and America, and about ballet in America, de Mille succeeding where others had failed. George Amberg lists the reasons for *Rodeo's* importance:

> First, it was evidence of a deliberate change of policy in the Ballet Russe; second, it showed that the Russian company had developed into an American one; third, it proved the artistic validity of a genre which heretofore had been tolerated rather than furthered.[12]

De Mille often develops ballets from sketches or other choreographic materials she has used on previous occasions. *Rodeo* was no exception. A sketch called "Rodeo" turned up on a program given in London 26 May 1938 at the Fortune Theatre by de Mille and a group with Hugh Laing, Peggy van Praagh, and Charlotte Bidmead as soloists. The concert was so successful that it was repeated 8 June at the Arts Theatre Club. British critic Fernau Hall remembers that the "Rodeo" sketch required dancers to imitate bucking broncos, thereby substantiating de Mille's contention that the equine movement that figures so prominently in *Rodeo* and in Eugene Loring's *Billy the Kid* (premiered in Chicago in 1938) was developed independently by the two choreographers. When she returned to New York from London de Mille assembled a group, including Ruthanna Boris and Joseph Anthony, which danced 15 January 1939 at the 92nd Street YMHA. "Rodeo," again programmed, was singled out by *Dance* for having "substance."[13]

In her autobiography, *Dance to the Piper,* de Mille said it was the wife of dance writer Irving Deakin who first told her that the Ballet Russe was looking for a new work and that Deakin was trying to persuade Denham that it should be by an American. De Mille had nothing ready. Yet neither did she have a job. She therefore devised a scenario based upon her concert sketches which greatly pleased David Libidins, who became her champion in the Ballet Russe office. Ever cautious about finances, Denham seldom drew up extravagant contracts, the one de Mille signed offering her $500 as fee for *Rodeo,* with $12.50 royalties for the first ten performances of each season, $10 for the next ten, and $7.50 thereafter. Since she would be rehearsing the ballet on tour, de Mille received an additional $3 a day as travel expenses. That was just not enough, and she recalls scrimping along by exchanging her first-class ticket for coach accommodations, by carrying her entire wardrobe in one wicker basket to avoid the expense of porters, and by living on a diet of sandwiches and coffee.

One clause in her contract gave de Mille the right to retain the final word on artistic matters pertaining to *Rodeo.* She was grateful for this provision because there was repeated wrangling over *Rodeo,* some of it owing to Denham's desire to economize and to his lack of firsthand knowledge of life in the Southwest. Thus he decided that in the party scene barns should figure in the décor. He was surprised to learn that there are few barns in the Southwest because ranchers usually have so many cattle that they cannot be fitted into a barn. Denham regretted to hear that: he thought barns picturesque. Later, wishing to cut expenses, he wondered whether anything could be salvaged from the designs for Fokine's Russian peasant ballet *Igrouchki,* perhaps basing this speculation upon the fact that both *Igrouchki* and *Rodeo* did, after all, concern rural life.

Aaron Copland was chosen as composer. For scenic advice, de Mille and Denham consulted Pavel Tchelitchew, who took a perverse delight in startling the young American unfamiliar with the ways of Russian ballet and the suave Russian unfamiliar with American ranches. Whimsically, he suggested the eccentric American painter, Florine Stettheimer, as designer. "She would paint things you have never seen in your life," Tchelitchew promised. But this was not what either Denham or de Mille was after. Then Tchelitchew professed to be bored with the project, saying, "I think it would be less banal if Nijinska did the cowboy ballet and you did the Russian fairytale." Finally, tired of teasing, he recommended Oliver Smith. One wonders whether the suggestion was worth the rigmarole, Smith hardly being an unknown name at the Ballet Russe, since he had designed *Saratoga* the previous season.

De Mille has made much about how confused the Russian dancers were by her choreography, how she had to spend hours just to get them to walk like saddle-sore cowboys. As rehearsals proceeded, she dropped most of the Russians from the cast. Her memoirs describe these rehearsals with such wit and passion that one could even suspect de Mille of exaggerating for literary effect. Michel Katcharoff, one of the Russians de Mille retained in the cast, says that he did indeed find cowboy movements difficult. But de Mille was difficult too. At times, he insists, she was downright rude. Perhaps de Mille adopted this rehearsal manner after Martha Graham recommended that she be arrogant among the Russians because arrogance was something the Russians respected.

However, American dancer James Starbuck believes that de Mille's account does not seriously exaggerate. A member of the Ballet Russe since 1939 and accepted by both the American and Russian contingents of the company, Starbuck acted as a rehearsal assistant for de Mille. One of his daily jobs was to get the Russians to rehearse at all. They loathed *Rodeo*. Instead of assembling in the studio, they would smoke outside in the hallway while Starbuck tried to cajole them into rehearsing. If de Mille was rude and arrogant, so were many of them, one soloist muttering the Russian word for "shit" throughout rehearsals. Some of the Russians complained so much that Denham, feeling uneasy, summoned Starbuck for a private conference about *Rodeo*. "Is it any good?" he asked. Starbuck replied, "It's not only a true American ballet, it will be a smash hit."[14]

He was right. A smash hit it was, gaining cheers from audiences and tributes from critics. From most critics, at any rate. Composer-critic Virgil Thomson had doubts about the music: "Miss de Mille's work appeared to me as fresh and abundant, Mr. Copland's as stale and a bit skimpy. It is 'Billy the Kid' all over again, only not so full of invention as the first time." There also existed dancegoers who considered ranch life an inappropriate subject for ballet. As late as 1948, when *Rodeo* had established itself as a favorite almost everywhere, Montreal balletomanes were so incensed at the inclusion of *Rodeo* in the repertoire for the company's engagement in their city that they protested until the theatre management requested Denham to schedule *Beau Danube* in place of de Mille's ballet. A local critic, the powerful, knowledgeable, but aesthetically conservative S. Morgan-Powell, congratulated the protestors, considering their objections to be a sign of the good taste of the Montreal public:

> When "Rodeo" was first presented here the impression it made was not a favourable one. The subject of a rodeo is about as suitable for expression in ballet form as a herd of elephants in flight through the African jungle would be; or a battle between strikers and police; or a barnyard struck by a cyclone. These things may be excellent subjects for artists to attempt to transfer to canvass [sic], but they have nothing whatever to do with ballet, nor has sheep-shearing nor an Australian sheep-dipping, nor any other mass incident remotely connected with any industry. It is about time that we had some sense of proportion and fitness in connection with ballet. It should not be subject to the fantastic vagaries of eccentrics of the de Mille brand.
>
> The Montreal public which enjoys ballet and can appreciate it knows now how to secure the elimination of those spectacles which it does not wish to see.

By and large, however, critics were jubilant—and jubilant after a particular fashion. *Rodeo* made Alfred Frankenstein declare that "the era of Russian ballet is about over, and the art reaffirms its universality." Other critics were more specific still: for them, *Rodeo* symbolized the opening of the era of American ballet. Dancers agreed, and some of the Americans who had adopted Russian names were encouraged to revert to American names. The man who played the Caller in the square dance changed his name from Anton Vlassoff (which was not his real name) to Robert Pagent. That was not his real name either (his name was Robert Weisser). But Pagent sounded American, and he was an American dancer. *Rodeo* satisfied those ideologists who had demanded a native American ballet. John Martin certainly found it so: ". . . its point of view and its very stuff grow out of the American mind and the American landscape." Months later he selected *Rodeo, Chopin Concerto,* and Balanchine's *Ballet Imperial* (produced by the dance ensemble of the New Opera Company) as the three best new ballets of 1942-43. Of them, he preferred *Rodeo,* partly because the music of the other two

> is inferior—and if there are those who choose to leave the room at this point, the exit is at the rear. . . . unless one thinks automatically in terms of Love, Death, Passion and the

Eternal Verities, it is difficult to believe that the nineteenth-century Continental aroma of these two delightful romantics [Chopin and Tchaikovsky] touches into life the emotional realities of contemporary-minded America the way Mr. Copland's lean and hearty, tough and tender, measures do. Nijinska and Balanchine, for all the sheer brilliance of their choreographic invention, have necessarily entered a twilit world.[15]

Chopin Concerto has vanished. But companies still perform *Rodeo* and *Ballet Imperial,* and the question of which is better might still inspire lively arguments among balletgoers representing divergent aesthetic viewpoints.

Despite *Rodeo's* success, de Mille never worked for the Ballet Russe again, having become—largely as a result of *Rodeo*—a much sought-after choreographer. The Ballet Russe did occasionally announce that she would return to choreograph *Ballet Class,* an expansion of her concert sketches based upon Degas. But she never found time.

What happened to *Rodeo* at the Ballet Russe is that it gradually deteriorated. Scarcely more than six months after its premiere, Robert Lawrence found reason to chide Lubov Roudenko, who succeeded de Mille as the Cowgirl: "Last night Miss Roudenko danced well but looked tawdry and utterly unknowing in her approach to the role. This cowgirl, who should be devoid of any feminine allure until she discards her trousers at the end of the ballet . . . appeared with heavy makeup, red fingernails, and a hippy swagger at the outset." De Mille attributes the decline to the strains of touring. Also, she feels that Denham, like all too many ballet directors everywhere, seemed "to think comedy a lesser form than serious ballet. Not only in the Ballet Russe but in other companies, a director will put a girl into *Rodeo* simply because she can't quite do *Swan Lake.* That girl may be pretty and charming and she may have a fair technique, but she's usually someone who can't act. Comedy isn't easy! Few people recognize the importance of timing in comic ballet. Without split-second timing *Rodeo* degenerates into bad slapstick. I can chart for you exactly where each potential laugh in the ballet comes—nobody gets them all today."

De Mille's contract gave her the right to approve the casting of principals, a right she has insisted upon in all her ballets. Usually, granting approval was a mere formality. When Dorothy Etheridge or Vida Brown danced the Cowgirl for the Ballet Russe, there was no cause for complaint. By the 1948-49 season, however, de Mille was complaining bitterly. Denham cast Nina Novak as the Cowgirl. Novak, a Polish-born dancer, was increasingly being cast in contemporary and classic roles. De Mille thought her "shocking" as the Cowgirl: "She could jump and she was pretty, but she couldn't act." (John Martin, it should be noted, was much kinder to Novak, saying she "has not begun to get under the skin of the character and there is a minimum of that pathos that belongs to Agnes de Mille's creation, but she is an excellent performer with a good sense of theatre.") Finally, de Mille categorically withheld approval of casting, which meant, in effect, that the Ballet Russe no longer could present *Rodeo*. In 1950 it entered the Ballet Theatre repertoire.[16]

With *Rodeo* a hit and *Chopin Concerto* and *Snow Maiden* recognized as honorable efforts, the season the Ballet Russe shared with Ballet Theatre in the fall of 1942 did not make the older group seem obsolescent. John Martin even detected "a notable strengthening of morale."[17]

The company returned to Manhattan the following spring, after a tour during which Alexandra Danilova, theretofore a much praised Myrtha in *Giselle*, essayed the title role for the first time on 24 November 1942 in San Francisco.[18] The company was obviously in some sort of transitional state. Its New York season (which began 19 May 1943 at the Broadway Theatre) was the first under auspices other than those of Hurok. Its future development remained uncertain, and two ballerinas resigned: Nathalie Krassovska and Mia Slavenska. Krassovska, who had quarreled with Denham about casting, returned the next season, but it would be several years before Slavenska danced again with the Ballet Russe. To complicate matters, the Ballet Russe found itself unwittingly in direct competition with Hurok's Ballet Theatre. It had been having a spring season at the Met, a season so popular it was extended until 23 May, thus making the first week of Ballet Russe coincide with the last week of Ballet Theatre.

Scheduling no premieres, the Ballet Russe called its engagement a "season of favorite ballets." A look at what the management considered "favorites" indicates how the company's emphasis had shifted. In 1938 it had a large Fokine repertoire acquired from René Blum, and one of its intentions was to serve as the showcase for Massine's new ballets. Now only two Massine ballets—*Beau Danube* and *Gaîté Parisienne*—survived, while all but six of the twenty-two programs contained at least one ballet by Fokine. There were few complaints about this. Indeed, the "favorites" so delighted New Yorkers that the engagement, scheduled to end 29 May, was prolonged until 5 June.[19] John Martin thought the season "pleasant and restful and definitely homey." If that sounds slightly patronizing, he unreservedly praised the dancers, finding the company "in unusually attractive form." He was particularly enthusiastic about two young North Americans: Maria Tallchief, blessed with "lovely simplicity of style and ease," and Anna Istomina (born Audrée Thomas in Vancouver, British Columbia, Canada), notable for her "charm and her highly respectable technical ability."[20]

If the Ballet Russe had regained critical good will, there was fierce competition with the Hurok forces, and Universal Art charged that Hurok "through defamatory publicity had sought to ruin Monte Carlo's reputation. . . ." These were indeed the days when members of the Ballet Russe and Ballet Theatre could be seen at the Russian Tea Room giving each other daggerlike glances from opposite tables.[21]

The situation worsened. For the first time there was no New York theatre available for a fall engagement. It was feared that the company might have to spend the entire 1943-44 season on the road. Also for the first time the company would be touring without a booking management. While Libidins had arranged some touring dates, he had then left to join Ballet Theatre. Forgoing the prestige of a New York season, the company nevertheless rehearsed new ballets, appointed Edward Caton as guest teacher, announced its intention to develop young American artists (including Ruthanna Boris and Mary Ellen Moylan), and set its opening for 8 October 1943 in Cleveland.[22]

One problem remained. The company was not certain it had sufficient funds to get itself to Cleveland. Frederic Franklin remembers that, shortly before the Cleveland opening, the dancers were still in New York rehearsing in a Carnegie Hall studio, but with their suitcases in one corner of the room in the event that, through some miracle, funds might arrive which would enable them to leave for Cleveland. Denham said, "I'm going out to make one last attempt to find the money. Don't stop rehearsing." A short time later he returned, shouting, "Stop! Change! Pack! Go to the station immediately. I've got the money. We're going to Cleveland." There the performances were sold out. "Good," said Denham. "We've made money. Now we can move on to Chicago." Because the Chicago performances were also sold out, the company could proceed further. And that was how the company toured the country that season.

Four works, which ordinarily would have been premiered in New York, received first performances at the Cleveland Music Hall. Theoretically they represented a variety of styles and themes. Not one, however, was to prove significant. Neoclassicism was represented by Bronislava Nijinska's *Etude*, the latest incarnation of a ballet to excerpts from Bach's Brandenburg concertos and orchestral suites which, in one form or another, Nijinska had been staging since the 1920s. With dancers costumed to resemble angelic figures moving in patterns suggesting the harmony of stars and planets, *Etude* had deep personal significance for Nijinska. But audiences never warmed to it—partly, some dancers think, because of the look of it, particularly the look of Boris Belinsky's costumes. Apparently taking seriously the theological speculation that angels are sexless, he dressed male and female dancers identically in halolike headpieces and tunics which gave rise to jokes about not being able "to tell the girls from the boys." Nevertheless, Ann Barzel believed that if one took it seriously one would discover that *Etude* was "a beautiful ballet with a great deal of beautiful dancing. . . ." After seeing a New York performance, Edwin Denby thought *Etude* looked "like evolutions by a recently demilitarized heavenly host." Analyzing the ballet, he concluded that its movements, though obviously angelic in intention, were insufficiently angelic in effect:

> The palms facing forward, wrists crossed above the head, suggest wing-tips of icon angels; and the legs extended in arabesque sometimes hint at the line of the wing below. Because the movement is wilfully stylized, it is difficult to give it sweep and vitality. . . . As a result one did not have the impression that these angels were controlling an immense power in their reserve, as I think had been the choreographer's intention. They seemed mostly stiffly regimental where they might have been magnificently lawful.[23]

If nothing else, *The Cuckold's Fair*, by Pilar Lopez (sister of Argentinita), promised to be exotic, even risqué. With a scenario adapted from Lorca, it treated a Spanish peasant custom of sending barren wives to the forest to search for verbena, accompanied by unmarried youths. She who finds verbena will bear a child—or so goes the legend. With a score by Gustavo Pittaluga and designs by Spanish artist Joan Junyer, *The Cuckold's Fair* struck John Martin (when he saw it later in New York) as "one of those ballets in which all the action takes place off-stage, and in this case, that is perhaps just as well." And Robert Sabin sighed, "The Cuckold's Fair accomplished the well-nigh incredible feat of making adultery seem boring."[24]

The season's closest thing to a hit was Igor Schwezoff's one-act adaptation of The Red Poppy, the evening-long ballet with music by Reinhold Glière which at its Moscow premiere in 1927 was acclaimed as a triumph of Soviet revolutionary choreography. Like its Moscow predecessor, this Red Poppy told a story about a dancing-girl, Taia-Hoa, who is oppressed by a villainous capitalist. However, in response to wartime political conditions, Schwezoff made the capitalist a Japanese bar owner, while Taia-Hoa's friends included not only the Russian sailors of the original, but British and American sailors as well. When the company brought The Red Poppy to New York, John Martin expressed the prevailing critical opinion by saying, "It is timely and topical, and, as you may suspect, very corny indeed."

Although the United States and the Soviet Union were allies during World War II, it disturbed some balletgoers that the Ballet Russe should be presenting a ballet which had once been considered a vehicle for Soviet ideology. Critic Robert Garland predicted, "When World War II is over, when Russia is Russia, Britain is Britain, and America is America, 'The Red Poppy' may not seem so right, so rapturous, so one-for-all-and-all-for-one as it seems today." Most audiences, though, forgot about politics and enjoyed The Red Poppy for such things as the sight of Alexandra Danilova in a big dramatic role, the perennially popular "Russian Sailors' Dance," and a set of divertissements which included a ribbon dance for Igor Youskevitch and a number in which Ruthanna Boris was carried in on a platter. Even The Daily Worker minimized the ballet's propaganda content: "The idea, of course, is the unity of the four nations against rapacious Japan though the political analogy should not be carried too far." Perhaps to press political analogies further might have embarrassed the Worker, since in 1943 Russia had not yet officially declared war on Japan.[25]

The last of the Cleveland premieres, 11 October 1943, was Bronislava Nijinska's Ancient Russia. It probably would not have existed if it had not been for some scenery. In 1938 Nathalie Gontcharova's designs for Massine's Bogatyri had been the best-liked feature of that ill-fated ballet. Not wishing them to moulder in a warehouse, Denham commissioned Nijinska to choreograph a new ballet making use of them. The result, to Tchaikovsky's first piano concerto, dealt with the rescue of Russian women from

Tartar captors. Unfortunately, *Ancient Russia* was no more successful than *Bogatyri* had been.

Once underway, the 1943-44 tour was highly successful. It was also one which saw some changes in personnel. Eugénie Delarova and Lubov Rostova left to open a flower shop on New York City's Madison Avenue, and on 5 January 1944 Igor Youskevitch was inducted into the Navy. The company was beginning to feel the wartime shortage of male dancers, and often women, even such principals as Ruthanna Boris and Alexandra Danilova, were drafted to appear with moustaches painted on their faces as warriors in *Prince Igor*.[26]

Denied an autumn season in New York, the company was given the opportunity to present a spring season there. The Ballet Russe was invited to be the first ballet company to appear at the City Center of Music and Drama, a former Shriners' auditorium on West 55th Street which had been acquired by the City of New York to serve as a theatre offering popularly priced cultural attractions. There was even talk of making Ballet Russe seasons regular attractions at City Center.

That spring season of 1944 was to plunge New York into a ballet war waged with such ferocity that the London ballet war of 1938 seemed gentlemanly dueling in comparison. The Ballet Russe engagement coincided exactly with a Hurok-managed Ballet Theatre engagement at the Met, both companies opening on Easter Sunday (9 April), Ballet Russe presenting *Les Sylphides*, the New York premiere of *Red Poppy*, and *Gaîté Parisienne*, Ballet Theatre luring audiences with *Giselle* (starring Markova), *Princess Aurora*, and *Dim Lustre*. Subsequent performances also found both companies offering premieres on the same night. On 10 April the Monte Carlo introduced *Etude* and *Cuckold's Fair* to Manhattan, while Ballet Theatre premiered Argentinita's *El Amor Brujo*, thereby preventing Pilar Lopez from seeing the first New York performance of her own ballet, since she was cast in her sister's work at the Met. On 11 April audiences had the choice of acquainting themselves with either *Ancient Russia* at City Center or Agnes de Mille's *Tally-Ho* at the Met.

Because City Center could offer popular prices ranging from 85¢ to $2.20 (while Ballet Theatre prices, though also starting at 85¢, went to $4.20), some critics thought that the Ballet Russe season constituted a threat to free enterprise. Thus Robert Garland: "I'm both disappointed and surprised not to have heard a great big squawk out of Impressario [sic] Hurok of the Ballet Theatre. Frankly, I think Impressario Hurok has a great big squawk coming to him. If the City of New York, with its comparative lack of taxes, rents and regulations, going into the ballet business isn't unfair competition, I just don't know what unfair competition is." That charge was also raised by *Dance News* in a violent editorial which placed the blame for the ballet war squarely on the Ballet Russe. Since a Hurok-sponsored spring ballet season "has been an institution for eight years," the magazine contended, the Ballet Russe ought to have been wary about scheduling its own spring ballet season. The editorial grew so intemperate that in its next issue *Dance News* felt obliged to apologize for any remarks that might have cast aspersions upon company ethics, the apology humbly stating that "no ballet company in the world has shown higher business ethics throughout its career than the Ballet Russe de Monte Carlo."[27]

Though critics denounced the ballet war, New York had never before been so ballet-conscious. Shop windows were adorned with ballet photographs, paintings, and souvenirs; War Bond rallies featured ballet sketches as prizes, and Anatole Chujoy, editor and chief critic of *Dance News,* even hosted a ballet quiz program on the radio. Skeptics who feared that two companies performing simultaneously would so divide the ballet audience that neither would be a success were refuted. Ballet Theatre did well at the Met. And the Ballet Russe did well at City Center, the three-week season taking in $90,000 from ticket sales.[28]

While the City Center season was still in progress, Edwin Denby termed the Monte Carlo "a company of first-rate dancers, who are handicapped by two disadvantages: In the first place, the stars are overworked; in the second place, the Center was not built for ballet." Denby criticized its shallow stage and the way seats were either under a deep balcony or too close to the stage for ideal viewing. Still, "the Monte Carlo seems to me a fine ballet company at any price." Later, after both companies' seasons had ended, he compared them and found both wanting:

> The April "war" between Ballet Theatre and the Monte Carlo would have been more exciting to watch if it had been a competition between artistic directions instead of a competition for customers. There were plenty of customers everywhere, so both companies won. . . . [But] neither company can boast of a new production an intelligent citizen can get excited over; with all their rich resources neither company produced anything as remarkable as Martha Graham's *Deaths and Entrances.* . . . Both companies underestimate the intelligence, the sensibility and the curiosity of the public.

John Martin was troubled because City Center spokesmen were priding themselves upon the financial success which, so they argued, had also introduced a whole new audience to ballet. What bothered Martin was the quality of that ballet. Though he had praised the Ballet Russe the previous spring, he now said, "The repertory is overweighted with old works in shabby condition choreographically as well as scenically," and the general atmosphere is "very much that of a road show." As for developing new audiences, that worried Martin most of all, for it seemed to him that the City Center was proceeding on the theory that "by showing them mediocrity first their taste for the best will be cultivated. It is an extremely dubious thesis, however, and nothing at all to go around chanting paeans to one's self about."[29]

Summertimes were usually quiet times for dancers in the 1940s. Except for occasional outdoor performances at Hollywood Bowl or Red Rocks near Denver, there was nothing that could be called a summer ballet season. In 1944 Frederic Franklin received an offer to appear in a summer musical. His friends Robert Wright and George Forrest were adapting the music of Edvard Grieg for a show based upon Grieg's life to be called *Song of Norway*. They had written a novelty number, "Freddie and His Fiddle," especially for Franklin. Would Denham allow Franklin to appear?

Franklin asked that question one day, and after mulling over the project Denham decided, "I will not only let them have you, I'll let them have the entire Ballet Russe." With Danilova, Franklin, and Krassovska as stars, the company became the dance ensemble for *Song of Norway* which, presented by Edwin Lester as part of his annual Civic Light Opera series, opened 12 June 1944 in Los Angeles, moved to San Francisco on 3 July, and settled down for a Broadway run at the Imperial Theatre on 21 August. Initially there had been talk of hiring David Lichine as choreographer, but Alexandra Danilova persuaded Denham that "the only man who could choreograph that show was George Balanchine." Balanchine's contributions included Norwegian folk dances, a satire on ballet mannerisms to the *Peer Gynt* music and, as finale, an ambitious and serious classical ballet to an abridgment of the piano concerto. A danced finale—a classically danced finale, at that—was considered experimental on Broadway at the time. John Martin happily found it "a distinctly successful experiment. Instead of letting the dramatic action down, as might be feared, it brings the evening to a close on a broad and spacious note. . . ."

Olin Downes, chief music critic of the *Times,* disagreed. He attacked *Song of Norway* in an essay which not only reveals his personal taste, but also indicates the lack of understanding of ballet which still prevailed among certain music critics in the 1940s. He termed the choreographic concerto "far-fetched and incongruous." Since the show concerned Grieg's awareness of his destiny to be a Norwegian composer, the finale ought to show not ballet but, in Downes's opinion, Norway's "rejoicing people, dancing their own folk dances . . . in their native costumes, in their peasant ways." Balanchine's concerto amply confirmed Downes's theory "that the average virtuoso dancer is somewhat lower in musical intelligence and sense of fitness than the average virtuoso singer, which is saying a great deal."

Fortunately, audiences did not share Downes's views, and *Song of Norway* became such a success in New York that in order to prepare for its own fall season, the Ballet Russe had to superintend the formation of a new dance ensemble to appear in the show while the main company worked at City Center. Danilova's replacements included Olga Suarez and Dorothie Littlefield, while James Starbuck and Roland Guerard took over Franklin's duties.[30]

Enjoying popular success, the Ballet Russe had many reasons to look forward to 1944-45. There was a sense of new life about the company. Although régisseur Jean Yazvinsky had resigned, Frederic Franklin, at Balanchine's recommendation, was appointed to the new post of *maître de ballet.* Balanchine himself was not to sever connections with the Ballet Russe after *Song of Norway,* but would continue choreographing for it. Assuming control of an organization facing possible collapse, Sergei Denham had for two seasons valiantly struggled to give that company stability. Now the Ballet Russe was on the verge of a renaissance.

NOTES FOR CHAPTER 4

1. Management—John Martin, "The Dance: Ballet Plans," *New York Times,* 28 June 1942; "Tempo!" *Dance,* January 1942, p 5; "Hurok and Columbia Combine—Back Ballet Theatre Next Fall," *Dance News,* March 1943, p. 1.
2. Personnel—"Kurtz Leaves Ballet Russe," *New York Herald-Tribune,* 28 June 1942; "David Libidins Dies in New York," *Dance News,* January 1959, p. 5.
3. "Notes," *Dance Observer,* December 1942, p. 134.
4. "Léonide Massine," *Dance News,* December 1942, p. 2.
5. Denham—Jossleyn Hennessy, "Ballet Russe in America," *The Ballet Annual* (first issue), p. 45; George Amberg, *Ballet,* p. 52.

6. Conversation with Mia Slavenska. Henceforth, all statements for which no printed source is given were made in conversation with the author.

7. Plans—Souvenir program 1942-43; "Dance Notes," *New York Herald-Tribune,* 21 June 1942; "Ballet Russe Announces Works in Preparation," *New York Sun,* 27 June 1942.

8. "Inability to Get Exit Visas Will Delay Opening of Ballet," *Toronto Globe and Mail,* 28 September 1942.

9. Shared season—John Martin, "The Dance: An Old Series," *New York Times,* 20 September 1942, "The Dance: Events Ahead," *New York Times,* 27 September 1942; S. Hurok, *Impresario,* pp. 229-230; Agnes de Mille, *Dance to the Piper,* p. 298.

10. *Chopin Concerto*—Edwin Denby, *Looking at the Dance,* p. 69; George Amberg, *Ballet,* p. 58.

11. Edwin Denby, *Looking at the Dance,* pp. 105, 73.

12. *Rodeo* comments—Edwin Denby, *Looking at the Dance,* p. 235; George Amberg, *Ballet,* p. 55.

13. *Rodeo* origins—"The Sitter Out," *The Dancing Times,* July 1938, pp. 389-390; Fernau Hall, *An Anatomy of Ballet,* p. 233-235; Joseph Arnold Kaye, "Dance in Review," *Dance,* March 1939, p. 29.

14. *Rodeo* negotiations and rehearsals—Agnes de Mille, *Dance to the Piper,* pp. 267-286; Michel Katcharoff, unpublished autobiography, p. 50; conversations with Agnes de Mille, Michel Katcharoff, James Starbuck.

15. *Rodeo* reactions—Virgil Thomson, "Two Ballets," *New York Herald-Tribune,* 25 October 1942; S. Morgan-Powell, "Montrealers Succeed in Having Ballet Russe Drop 'Rodeo,' " *Montreal Daily Star,* 21 February 1948; Alfred Frankenstein, quoted by John Martin in "The Dance: Travel Notes," *New York Times,* 3 January 1943; "Attitudes and Arabesques," *Dance News,* May 1943, p. 2; John Martin, "The Dance: A New Period," *New York Times,* 1 November 1942; John Martin, "The Dance: Laurels—Award No. 1," *New York Times,* 18 July 1943.

16. *Rodeo* decline—Robert Lawrence, "Carbohydrate Cuisine," *New York Herald-Tribune,* 20 May 1943; John Martin, "De Mille's 'Rodeo' Offered by Ballet," *New York Times,* 23 February 1949; Conversation with Agnes de Mille.

17. John Martin, "The Dance: A New Period," *New York Times,* 1 November 1942.

18. "Danilova's Giselle a Hit," *Dance News,* January 1943, p. 1.

19. Spring schedules— John Martin, "The Dance: Competing Ballets," *New York Times,* 16 May 1943; John Martin, "The Dance: Ballet Russe," *New York Times,* 30 May 1943; "Ballet Russe Needs Ballerina," *Dance News,* June 1943, p. 1.

20. John Martin—on season and Tallchief: "The Dance: Ballet Russe," *New York Times,* 30 May 1943; on Istomina: "The Dance: Honor Roll," *New York Times,* 29 August 1943.

21. "Attitudes and Arabesques," *Dance News,* June 1943, p. 2.

22. John Martin, "The Dance: Ballet Russe," *New York Times,* 22 August 1943, and "Ballet Russe to Open Out-of-Town," *Dance News,* September 1943, p. 1.

23. *Etude*—Ann Barzel, "Ballet Season in Review," *Dance News,* November 1943, p. 3; Edwin Denby, "Angels and Gypsies," *New York Herald-Tribune,* 11 April 1944; Conversation with Alexandra Danilova.

24. *Cuckold's Fair*—John Martin, "The Dance: A Flock of Premieres," *New York Times,* 11 April 1944; Robert Sabin, "Ballet Seasons," *Dance Observer,* May 1944, p. 51.

25. *Red Poppy*—John Martin, "2 Ballet Groups in Rival Opening," *New York Times,*

10 April 1944; Robert Garland, "Ballet Russe Offers 'Red Poppy' as Sub," *New York Journal-American,* 14 April 1944; M.M., "The Ballet Russe," *Daily Worker,* 12 April 1944.

26. Changes—John Martin, "The Dance: Events Ahead," *New York Times,* 27 February 1944; "Youskevitch Now in Navy," *Dance News,* February 1944; p. 1; conversation with Ruthanna Boris.

27. Ballet war—*New York Herald-Tribune* dance calendars 5 March, 12 March, 23 April 1944; *New York Times* dance calendar, 19 March 1944; Robert Garland, "Sol and Butch to Vie for Battle of Ballets," *New York Journal-American,* 27 March 1944; "A Deplorable Situation," *Dance News,* April 1944, p. 2; "Apology to Ballet Russe de Monte Carlo," *Dance News,* May 1944, p. 1; conversations with Frederic Franklin, M. Hornyak.

28. Success—Lillian Moore, "The Ballet Theatre Season," *The Dancing Times,* July 1944, p. 452; Rudolf Orthwine, "Bombardment of Ballet in New York," *Dance,* May 1944, p. 2; John Martin, "The Dance: More in Sorrow," *New York Times,* 7 May 1944.

29. Reviews—Edwin Denby, "The Monte Carlo at the Center," *New York Herald-Tribune,* 16 April 1944; Edwin Denby, *Looking at the Dance,* p. 179; John Martin, "More in Sorrow," *New York Times,* 7 May 1944.

30. *Song of Norway* —Preparations and premiere: Isabel Morse Jones, "Grieg's Immortal Music Heard in New Operetta," *Los Angeles Times,* 13 June 1944; Hazel Bruce, "Rare Music, Color, Fine Cast in 'The Song of Norway' " *San Francisco Chronicle,* 5 July 1944; Burton Rascoe, "Song of Norway Is Tops as Operetta," *New York World-Telegram,* 22 August 1944; conversations with Alexandra Danilova, Frederic Franklin. Reviews: John Martin, "Ballet de Norway," *New York Times,* 9 September 1944; Olin Downes, "The Dance vs. Grieg," *New York Times,* 29 October 1944.

Sergei J. Denham. Photo: Maria Martel.

Top left: Alexandra Danilova and Léonide Massine in Massine's *Boutique Fantasque.* Photo: Alfredo Valente.

Bottom left: The death of Don Juan from Fokine's *Don Juan.*

Top right: Nathalie Krassovska as Chung-Yang and Jean Yazvinsky as her father, the Mandarin, in Fokine's *L'Épreuve d'Amour,* 1938.

Bottom right: Alicia Markova. Photo: Cannons of Hollywood.

Top left: Group from
Massine's *Seventh
Symphony*, 1938.
Photo: Raoul Barbà.

Bottom left: Mia Slavenska
and Igor Youskevitch
in Fokine's *Carnaval.*

Top right: Massine
rehearsing *Gaîté Parisienne,*
Monte Carlo, 1938.
From left: Massine, Nesta
Williams, Frederic Franklin,
Marina Franca, Adda
Pourmel, Michel Panaieff,
Lubov Roudenko, Tatiana
Flotat, Roland Guerard,
and an unidentified dancer.
Photo: Raoul Barbà.

Bottom right: Alexandra
Danilova and Frederic
Franklin in Massine's *Gaîté
Parisienne.*

Left: Léonide Massine as St. Francis.

Below: Massine (center) in the title role of *St. Francis,* 1938, with (from left) Marcel Fenchel, Michel Panaieff, and Roland Guerard as the Three Companions.

Mia Slavenska in Fokine's *Les Elfes.*

Above: Alexandra
Danilova and
André Eglevsky in
Massine's
*Capriccio
Espagnol.*

Left: Roland
Guerard as Orson
Hyde, the
Mormon Apostle,
and his five wives
in Marc Platoff's
Ghost Town.

Alicia Markova and George Zoritch in Fokine's *Les Sylphides*.
Photo: Maurice Seymour.

Above: Group from Massine's *Rouge et Noir* in its 1948 revival.

Left: Alexandra Danilova as the Daughter and Marc Platoff as the Devil in Ashton's *Devil's Holiday*, 1939.

Left: Nini Theilade as Venus in Massine's *Bacchanale*.

Below: Group from *Bacchanale*, 1939.

Above: Scene from Massine's *Saratoga,* 1941, with (from left) Nicholas Beriozoff, Vladimir Kostenko, Roland Guerard, Frederic Franklin, Alexandra Danilova, Tatiana Chamié, and Sviatoslav Toumine. Photo: Maurice Seymour.

Bottom left: Lubov Roudenko and Ian Gibson as characters based on William Steig's "Small Fry" cartoons in Massine's *The New Yorker,* 1940. Photo: Maurice Seymour.

Michel Katcharoff as Dr. Coppelius. Photo: Maurice Seymour.

Above: Nijinska's *Chopin Concerto* with soloists Maria Tallchief (far right) and Nathalie Krassovska (downstage center in group of women). Others in photo include Ruthanna Boris (left of Krassovska) and Gertrude Tyven (left of Tallchief).

Below: Alexandra Danilova and group in Nijinska's *Snow Maiden*. Photo: Fred Fehl.

Above: Group from Nijinska's *Etude* wearing the controversial unisex costumes. Photo: Ted O'Brien.

Below: The Russian Sailors' Dance in Schwezoff's *The Red Poppy* with (from left) George Verdak, Herbert Bliss, Alan Banks, Alexander Goudovitch, Nikita Talin, and Alfredo Corvino.

5 THE BALANCHINE YEARS (1944-1946)

THERE was much ballet in New York during the autumn of 1944. Ballet Theatre scheduled an engagement beginning 8 October at the Metropolitan Opera House, and the Marquis de Cuevas's new Ballet International opened its first—and, as it proved, only—season 30 October at the old Park Theatre, which had been renamed the International, on Columbus Circle.[1] But the Ballet Russe de Monte Carlo came first with a 10-24 September season at City Center. The Monte Carlo had just acquired George Balanchine as resident choreographer, and although his association with the company would last scarcely more than two years, he would bring it to the highest level of distinction it had known since its first seasons under Massine's guidance.

The company made news by offering on its opening night, 10 September 1944, the premiere of a ballet which Maria Tallchief remembers being "as perfectly and as intricately constructed as a tiny Swiss watch."[2] This was *Danses Concertantes*, choreographed by Balanchine to a piece of concert music that Igor Stravinsky had composed two years earlier. Although not in the literal sense a collaboration between Balanchine and Stravinsky, Balanchine found himself in such sympathy with the score that it might as well have been commissioned at his request. The ballet was a gift by Balanchine to dancers he loved, dancers who, in turn, loved working with him. The cast of fourteen was headed by two principals, Alexandra Danilova and Leon Danielian (at later performances, Frederic Franklin). In the ensemble were some of the company's most talented young dancers, several of whom went on to achieve stardom in later years: Gertrude Svobodina (Tyven), Nikita Talin, Nora White, Ruthanna Boris, Alexander Goudovitch, Dorothy Etheridge, Elena Kramarr, Herbert Bliss, Pauline Goddard, Maria Tallchief, Nicholas Magallanes, and Mary Ellen Moylan.[5]

The ballet began with a prelude. Before an inner curtain designed by Eugène Berman, the dancers paraded in twos and threes across the stage, "looking as brilliant as scarabs, if scarabs came in several colors" (said Edwin Denby). Then the curtain rose upon a black drop, which made the jewel-like costumes glitter all the more by contrast. What followed were pas de trois for the ensemble members and a witty, slightly flirtatious pas de deux for the principals.[4]

The reviews of *Danses Concertantes* in New York's two leading newspapers constitute early examples of a critical dichotomy which was to remain more or less constant throughout Balanchine's tenure with the Ballet Russe. The representatives of the *Times* and the *Herald-Tribune*, though both sensitive and articulate, had radically different opinions about the merits of Balanchine. Readers of the *Times* learned this from John Martin:

> Stravinsky's music is gravely démodé, belonging to that avant-gardism of about 1925 which is now as quaint as grandmother's antimacassar. It may or may not be "concertante" but it is assuredly not "théâtrale". . . . It is also as antagonistic to movement as any score within memory, lacking the sustained dynamics which are the very basis of dance.
>
> Mr. Balanchine has done a clever, somewhat mathematical, job of choreography, almost totally devoid of dancing. It is extremely difficult, especially from the rhythmical standpoint, and most ungrateful to dance.

Seeing it again several months later, Martin called *Danses Concertantes* a work "for the ultra-refined," and grudgingly conceded, "if you can be intoxicated by a bit of vacuum and soda, vintage 1925, it is definitely your drink."

Danses Concertantes captivated Edwin Denby of the *Herald-Tribune.* He was enthralled by Balanchine's rhythmic vitality and by his ability to devise steps which, though classically correct, yet were arranged

> in surprising sequences that contrast sharply and have a quick

effervescent invention. The changes from staccato movements to continuous ones, from rapid leaps and displacements to standing still, from one dancer solo to several all at once follow hard on one another. The rhythm is unexpected. But the shift of the figures and the order of the steps is miraculously logical and light, and so even fitful changes have a grave and a spontaneous impetus. What had first seemed separate spurts, stops and clipped stalkings turn out to be a single long phrase or impulse that has risen and subsided in a group of dancers simultaneously. . . .

[The dancers] are like characters in a garden, individuals who communicate, respond, who modify and return without losing their distinctness. The dance is like a conversation in Henry James, as surprising, as sensitive, as forbearing, as full of slyness and fancy. The joyousness of it is the pleasure of being civilized.

Balanchine was controversial in 1944, and ballets such as *Danses Concertantes* prompted many critics to take extreme stands of one kind or another. There were those who could say, along with Lillian Moore, that "Balanchine's witty and beautiful acrobatics, his clever dance-counterpoint, and his original use of a basic classicism are in precisely the right vein for Stravinsky's sharp, dry rhythmic intricacies." But that, according to the ballet's opponents, was precisely the trouble. Those who disliked the ballet could echo Robert Sabin, who complained, "It is high time that Mr. Balanchine delved a little deeper into his wells of inspiration and gave us a really memorable work. He has been lingering too long in the fleshpots of Broadway, figuratively speaking."[5]

Danses Concertantes figured in the Monte Carlo repertoire for several seasons, then was dropped, a victim of the vicissitudes of touring because pickup orchestras on the road found themselves incapable of coping with Stravinsky's score. It became a legendary work remembered fondly by dancers and ranking high on many balletomanes' lists of ballets-I-wish-I-could-have-seen. In 1972 for the New York City Ballet's Stravinsky Festival Balanchine choreographed a new version of *Danses Concertantes,* using the Berman décor and the original division of the cast into a pas de deux couple and four sets of pas de trois dancers. The work was favorably received, but failed to corruscate on stage the way the first production reportedly did. Alexandra Danilova and Leon Danielian both agree that this was partly because the original had been set on a particular group of dancers whose unique abilities were choreographically taken into account and, even more important, because the original had a jazzy thrust absent in the later staging. Danielian says, "There's something of the feeling—not of the steps, but of the atmosphere—of the old *Danses Concertantes* in the 'Rubies' section of *Jewels*."

Balanchine's second premiere that season, *Le Bourgeois Gentilhomme*, occurred under unfortunate circumstances. Originally scheduled for 19 September 1944, it was postponed until 23 September because of an injury sustained by Frederic Franklin and the necessity of training Nicholas Magallanes as a substitute. With new décor by Berman, *Le Bourgeois Gentilhomme* was a revision of a ballet (to Richard Strauss's incidental music to Molière's play) originally staged by the Blum-de Basil Ballet Russe in 1932 with designs by Alexandre Benois. The action, adapted from the play, shows Monsieur Jourdain preening himself, proud to have come into a great deal of wealth, and vowing that his daughter will marry no one but a nobleman. But daughter gets her way when her lover disguises himself as a Moslem prince and asks for, and receives, her hand in marriage.[6]

Everyone agreed that the opening night was, in Edwin Denby's words, "a disheveled dress rehearsal." But subsequent performances found the *Times* and the *Herald-Tribune* again at war with each other. John Martin complained that "Mr. Balanchine has paid little or no attention to the style of the theatre or the dancing of the seventeenth century in either accurate detail or evocative flavor, nor has he followed his composer's approach to those problems. As a matter of fact, the work is less suggestive of Molière than of a thin 'Aurora's Wedding.' " But admirers of *Bourgeois Gentilhomme* considered the comparison with *Aurora's Wedding* apt and by no means derogatory. For them, Balanchine had achieved, in contemporary neoclassic terms, a civilized entertainment capable of being discussed in the same breath as Petipa's great set of divertissements. *Le Bourgeois Gentilhomme* may have been only a light comedy, and not even one of the best of Balanchine's light ballets, but Edwin Denby seized upon it as though it were a choreographic manifesto heralding the end of Massine's grotesqueries and the beginning of a new classical era:

> After thirty years of stress on detail at the expense of flow, "Le Bourgeois" marks a complete turn about in dance style. It is the opposite of "modernism," of the deformed, the stylized, the bizarre. It looks harmless and easy, and it holds the attention effortlessly by an unfailing naturalness in invention. It shows off the dancers, not the choreographer. . . . "Le Bourgeois" in type belongs with ballet farces like, say, "Beau Danube." But its sweet grace and spontaneity bring it nearer to Mozart's kind of fooling than Massine's.[7]

Dancers, who can blissfully ignore manifestos and perform works by choreographers representing several supposedly irreconcilable viewpoints, recall *Le Bourgeois Gentilhomme* as being genial, if slight. Robert Lindgren and Sonja Taanila, two admirers of Massine's fooling, also admire that of Balanchine, citing among the pleasures of *Le Bourgeois* a female pas de sept in which the dancers wore plumed headdresses which caused the variation to be nicknamed the "pineapple dance," and a mock elephant parade in which a cluster of dancers suggested an elephant (complete with a swinging arm for a trunk) with M. Jourdain riding on top as though in a howdah.

Just as the Balanchine premieres divided critics, so did the dancing of the company as a whole. Anatole Chujoy was aware of nothing more than "a mediocre, unexciting, run-of-the-mill season," and Robert Sabin complained that "what the public is seeing these days as ballet in the great tradition is as much like the real thing as a Westchester imitation of a French chateau is like one of the masterpieces of renaissance architecture." Lillian Moore, however, found much to praise. The performance level "has improved tremendously," she said. "The corps de ballet is now composed of eager and talented youngsters. Most of its productions are carefully rehearsed."[8]

As usual, the company went on tour following its New York engagement, Balanchine all the while rehearsing new productions. Morale was high. Balanchine was immersed in rewarding creative work and so sophisticated a ballet as *Danses Concertantes*, far from confusing audiences, became genuinely popular on the road. Denham, who traveled with the company, happily noted in a letter to a friend "Artistically, and here I must pay my compliments to the masses of the USA, —our new productions, especially Dances [sic] Concertantes became the most demanded ballets. Balanchine became sort of an adopted son and travels with us, sharing our hardships, fun, glory and drinks. . . ."[9]

Balanchine's *Ballet Imperial* entered the repertoire in Chicago on 4 October 1944. Created for the American Ballet and, later, briefly performed by the dance ensemble of the New Opera Company, *Ballet Imperial* —"unquestionably the most thrilling ballet in the repertoire," for Anatole Chujoy—was considered by dancers to be the greatest technical challenge of its day and to get it right the company, reverting to a practice of Massine's time (and now, supposedly, officially forbidden), rehearsed at night after the evening's regular performance. Originally intended as a vehicle for Marie-Jeanne, famous for her brilliance and speed, the principal ballerina role in the Monte Carlo production was danced (as it had been at the New Opera) by Mary Ellen Moylan, who became indelibly associated with the part. "Delicate, long, and with a lovely pose of the head and a beautiful freedom in correctness," Moylan became one of Edwin Denby's favorite young dancers. Her "graceful intrepidity and air of candor" reminded him "of those demure ballet heroines who a century ago leapt from the top of a twenty-foot scenic waterfall into the arms of a partner."[10]

Moving on to Houston, the company started preparing Balanchine's *Mozartiana* and *Concerto Barocco*, and rehearsals also began on the road for the one ballet not by Balanchine to be premiered that season, *Frankie and Johnny* by Ruth Page and Bentley Stone. It was danced for the first time by the Ballet Russe in Kansas City, 7 January 1945, with the choreographers in the title roles (roles later danced by Ruthanna Boris and Frederic Franklin).[11] *Frankie and Johnny* dated back to 1938, when it had been collaboratively choreographed by Page and Stone for their Chicago company. Page and Stone worked together on several occasions in the creation of ballets, a process which Ruth Page describes as being "quite natural. Partners who dance together get to know each other well. So why can't they also be partners who choreograph together? Frankly, I'm surprised that more don't do it." The Ballet Russe cast discovered that the dual choreography credit was more than a line of type. After Page had set the work on them, Stone, then in military service, came on leave to coach the company and was so authoritative that Ruthanna Boris was convinced that, far from being just a name listed out of courtesy on the program, Stone "had made substantial contributions to the ballet's concept and choreography."

The work retold the old gutter ballad about how, when Johnny was unfaithful to his Frankie ("he done her wrong"), she shot him in revenge. Jerome Moross composed a lusty score which Page still considers "one of the two best scores ever written for me" (the other, Darius Milhaud's *The Bells*, would also be produced by the Ballet Russe). Dancers had their own reason for liking this music, since it required vocalists wearing Salvation Army costumes to belt out the ballad. Professional singers were hired in New York, but on the road the parts were assigned to company members who could carry a tune. Because they were paid extra for singing, the roles were considered very desirable. The score's severest critic, however, was the company's staff pianist, Rachel Chapman. Ruth Page recalls that Chapman disliked the music and was sometimes loath to play it at rehearsals, a situation which led on at least one occasion to Balanchine's filling in as rehearsal accompanist.

When the Monte Carlo *Frankie and Johnny* reached New York the two major dance critics found themselves in total disagreement, just as they had been over the Balanchine ballets— except, in this case, the roles of defender and detractor were reversed. John Martin slyly noted that "Balletomanes will definitely not like the work. It contains no 'pointes,' no 'fouettés,' and certainly no elegance. Its tone is broad, deliberately coarse and raucous, with a beer-hall insensitiveness to such major elements of tragedy as love, death and honor." Nevertheless, John Martin liked it very much, finding it "a witty and sophisticated development of good, lusty folklore." That may have been true in 1938, Edwin Denby countered, but since then *Frankie and Johnny* had been overshadowed by such superior pieces of Americana as *Rodeo* and *Fancy Free*. Calling the choreography mere milling about, Denby thought the ballet "no bawdier than Nedick's orange drink."

Orange drink or not, it was heady enough to get the Ballet Russe into difficulties both on the road and in New York, where it precipitated something of a controversy during the company's engagement in February 1945. Earlier during the 1944-45 theatrical season, New York City License Commissioner Paul Moss had closed a Broadway play, *Trio*, on the ground of immorality because it dealt with lesbianism. Members of the theatrical profession grew alarmed at what they feared was a one-man censorship crusade. And, since Moss was a member of the City Center board of directors, there were rumors that he might oppose *Frankie and Johnny* which, in addition to the beer-guzzling, ballad-spouting Salvation Army lassies, contained two lesbian characters and an irreverent depiction of a funeral in which a coffin was carried in by tap dancers. Critics were poised to attack: if Moss left *Frankie* alone, was this not, then, inconsistent with his attack upon *Trio*? Yet if he did try to close *Frankie*, was this not an example of rampant censorship?

No official action was taken. Moss remained silent and the Ballet Russe, not wishing to invite trouble, performed voluntary self-censorship by toning down some of the work's saltier passages, even though they had offended no one in the supposedly straitlaced Midwest. The only place where *Frankie and Johnny* ran into additional problems was Boston, then notorious for its strict censorship board. The city censors objected to a sight gag. In the rooming house scene, whenever one of the ladies no better than she should be entertained a "visitor," her window shades were lowered. For Boston, at the censors' request, the shades were left up, even though, literally interpreted, that might make the ladies guilty of not only solicitation, but exhibitionism.[12]

The spring New York season which saw the *Frankie and Johnny* ruckus was a spring season in name only, for in a deliberate effort to avoid any possible conflict with Ballet Theatre, it began unusually early—on 20 February 1945—and lasted until 25 March.[13] In addition to the company's first Manhattan showings of *Ballet Imperial* and *Frankie and Johnny*, there were two other novelties, both by Balanchine.

Mozartiana, to Tchaikovsky's fourth orchestral suite (based upon themes of Mozart), was offered on 7 March 1945. Designed by Christian Bérard, *Mozartiana* had been premiered by Balanchine's Les Ballets 1933 and had figured in the repertoire of the American Ballet. After the Ballet Russe presentation, the morning papers were divided in their now familiar fashion. *Mozartiana*, John Martin yawned,

> follows the oh, so familiar Balanchine formula. It is cool, clean, difficult and devised. It has its ensemble movement in which everybody plays "London Bridge" like mad, its slow movement devoted to chicly lugubrious sentimentality, its adagio section in which a ballerina is assisted in the performance of odd inventions, the virtues of which lie not in expressiveness or beauty or formalism but only in differentness.

Edwin Denby thought the ballet remarkable because, using a cast of only twelve, "Balanchine recaptures the flavor of an old-style grand ballet like Petipa's *Don Quixote*, recaptures in novel terms its variety of playfulness, tenderness and virtuosity. . . ."

Essentially, *Mozartiana* was a suite of unrelated dances, each dance establishing its own, often curious, mood. A man in an abbé's costume danced by himself, as though alone in a city square, until he was joined by villagers in a little game. A mournful woman carried in by mysterious figures danced a "Prayer." And there was a theme and variations for the ensemble which culminated in a grand adagio. The most distinctive section of *Mozartiana*—merely perplexing to some viewers, hauntingly beautiful for others—was the "Prayer," in which the female soloist, in a white tutu and black veil, was brought in hanging between two men. "We never really understood that scene," Frederic Franklin confesses. "People said it was originally one of Bèrard's bright ideas." Other dancers, including Sonja Taanila, interpreted the dance as an evocation—and a very poignant one—of an Italian funeral cortège. Today, says Ruthanna Boris, "Parts of 'Emeralds' [from *Jewels*] remind me of what we did—lots of marvelous arms and beautiful pictures forming, a very delicate thing. It didn't last long; maybe it wasn't sensational enough."[14]

Another Balanchine delicacy destined to have a short life was the *Pas de Deux* (also billed as *Grand Adagio*), premiered 14 March 1945. Frederic Franklin recalls that during the 1944 tour Balanchine sat down at a piano one day in San Francisco and started to play a piece of unfamiliar but extremely lovely music. "Oh, what is that?" asked Franklin. "It's from *The Sleeping Beauty*," Balanchine replied, "but nobody ever uses it." (The music, says Franklin, was the same interlude that Sir Frederick Ashton used much later for his "Awakening" pas de deux in the Royal Ballet's *Sleeping Beauty*.) To it, Balanchine decided to choreograph an adagio, without variations, for Danilova and Franklin. Costumed by Eugène Berman, the adagio was considered an exquisite miniature by Edwin Denby, who provides a brief description of the action:

> A prince appears with a lovely princess, he holds her gently and as she flutters and turns and bends, he lets her free, and she returns to him, and they exit together. Their intimacy is that of young people in love and engaged, and their dance figures express the dewiness, the sense of trepidation in the girl and the generous strength of the man. [15]

If the spring season of 1945 occurred in winter, it was springlike in its freshness. The Monte Carlo, said Denby, "has given us a happy season, it has regained its artistic prestige, it has won deserving friends, and it has awakened great hopes for the future." John Martin, despite his reservations about Balanchine's choreography, had to agree that "the season has had style and skill and charm."[16] Young dancers were singled out, among them Leon Danielian, who was in Denby's opinion "certainly the most brilliant American in leaps and beats."[17] The one individual who was acknowledged to be responsible for all the bright changes in the Monte Carlo was George Balanchine. To commemorate his twenty-fifth anniversary as a choreographer, two evenings (16 and 22 March) were designated Balanchine Festival performances, and at the close of the 16 March program an appreciative Sergei Denham came on stage to present Balanchine with an engraved gold cigarette case containing an actual pack of cigarettes, which in those days of wartime tobacco shortages was considered almost as precious as gold.[18] Denham was proud of all his dancers and staff members that season. The Ballet Russe had not danced so well in years, and, to celebrate the end of the spring tour, Denham hosted a lavish party on 13 May 1945, at which he gave presents to many of his associates. Danilova received a gold pin in the shape of a ballerina, Krassovska and Dorothy Etheridge received gold bracelets, Franklin a gold wristwatch, Michel Katcharoff gold cuff links, and Rachel Chapman a pin set with sapphires and rubies, while executive assistant Jean Cerrone and wardrobe mistress Sophie Pourmel each received a check for $1000.[19]

During the summer of 1945 Léonide Massine formed a totally new Ballet Russe troupe, one which had no direct connection with either the Ballet Russe de Monte Carlo or with de Basil's company. This was Ballet Russe Highlights, a concert group organized to play the straw-hat circuit during the summer and small towns during the winter. Programs, resembling a revue or vaudeville show in format, consisted of a dozen or more brief numbers following each other without pause, the repertoire including such standard items as the Bluebird, Black Swan, and Nutcracker pas de deux, Spectre de la Rose, excerpts from Coppélia, Les Sylphides, Balanchine's La Concurrence (the "Vagabond Dance"), and several of Massine's own works (including the Barman's Dance from Union Pacific, the Poodles from La Boutique Fantasque, and the Farucca from Three-Cornered Hat), plus new sketches by Massine bearing such titles as Vision, The Warrior, Polish Festival, Bumble Bee (to Rimsky-Korsakov, of course), and At the Dentist. The original company consisted of Massine, Irina Baronova, André Eglevsky, Anna Istomina, Yurek Lazowski, and Kathryn Lee. Later Baronova, Eglevsky, and Lee dropped out, while newcomers included Rosella Hightower, Jean Guelis, Bettina Rosay, Ivan Demidoff (Joseph Harris), and Igor Youskevitch (following his discharge from the Navy). The company continued until March 1946 when Massine received an offer to appear in England in a dramatization of Caryl Brahms and S.J. Simon's popular novel, Bullet in the Ballet.[20]

One of the stated aims of Ballet Russe Highlights was to win new audiences for ballet. After seeing performances 30 June and 1 July 1945, at New York's Lewisohn Stadium, Ruthella Wade of Dance thought that the company was indeed "offering dance patrons across country a fine sampling of what can be done in dance. . . ." John Martin, however, was horrified. "Not even its warmest friends can find much in its favor," he said of Ballet Russe Highlights. "The trouble apparently lies in the fact that the program was not organized but merely agglomerated. . . . [The dances] bear no conceivable relation to each other, but are shot out in rapid succession, one virtually on the heels of the other in traditional vaudeville tempo. . . ." Martin divided these items into several categories: "There is the folk and national group, the department of butterflies and bees, the division of low comedy, the 'interpretive' and symphonic, and that other department which can only be described as cutie-pie." That such fare should be touted as "popular entertainment" particularly bothered Martin: "Are we, then, to accept mediocrity as our norm, propagandize it, glorify it? It is a disturbing thought."

Although most of the bits in the repertoire tended to remind people of Massine's years as dance director of the Roxy rather than of his years as artistic director of the Ballet Russe de Monte Carlo, one vignette, *Strange Sarabande*, is still spoken of with admiration by many of those who saw it. Inspired by Breughel and set to Handel, it is a dance for blind beggars who, Ann Barzel remembers, enter with clasped hands and drink from a wine jug. When they let go of each other's hands and lose contact, they feel the terror of isolation and fumble to rejoin hands, after which they exit, linked to each other again.[21]

World War II ended during the summer of 1945, and the thrill of victory caused a peacetime euphoria to sweep through all New York, including the New York ballet world. On 9 September 1945, the opening night of the Ballet Russe de Monte Carlo's fall season at City Center, Denham presented a silk dressing gown to every woman in the company. That same night, in a gesture as magnanimous as it was surprising, the members of Ballet Theatre (supposedly the Monte Carlo's greatest rival) sent good luck telegrams to their colleagues at the Ballet Russe.

All during the war, particularly during times of melancholy dispatches from the battlefields and wearying tours of one-night stands, Ballet Russe dancers had nursed the dream of returning to Monte Carlo when peace came. "Ah, when we go back to Monte Carlo, ah then . . ." a favorite fantasy began. And there would be visions of glamour, of style, of Continental sophistication. But now that the war was over, Denham indicated that he had no intention of taking the company back to Monte Carlo. Rather, he told *Newsweek*, he preferred to bring ballet to the people of America, particularly to the ordinary citizens who filled City Center. "Here there is such a democratic undercurrent," he said. "Here you have the tremendous crowds of these people who can hardly afford it, but who come anyway—from the Bronx, Flatbush, Jackson Heights, and New Jersey."

Some dancers now wonder whether, even during the war when talk of returning to Monte Carlo was at its height, Denham really wanted to go back to Europe. Robert Lindgren speculates that Denham may have been aware of the difficulties that might arise should he try to reestablish formal connections with the Monte Carlo Opéra. In the past there had been directorial and managerial quarrels involving companies based in Monte Carlo, and if the Ballet Russe de Monte Carlo became embroiled in a legal fight and lost, then conceivably the Monte Carlo Opéra might even force the company to remove that magic phrase, "de Monte Carlo," from its name. In America, however, the company was, as its publicists liked to bill it, "an American institution." And an American institution it remained.[22]

The opening night of the fall 1945 season included the company's first performance of Balanchine's *Concerto Barocco,* which, with décor by Eugène Berman, had been created for the American Ballet in 1941. Marie-Jeanne returned in her original role, with Patricia Wilde as the second ballerina and Nicholas Magallanes as the cavalier. The Berman décor, however, was unavailable, Berman having been dissatisfied by the way his designs had been executed. As a result, the Ballet Russe performed *Concerto Barocco* in black tunics against a plain backdrop, thereby inaugurating the now common practice of dancing Balanchinian abstractions in the simplest possible costumes and settings.[23]

The absence of décor, combined with the essential rigor of Balanchine's choreography to Bach's D-minor Concerto for two violins, prompted hostile attacks. The *Times* and the *Herald-Tribune,* as usual, disagreed. John Martin dismissed *Concerto Barocco* as "just one more of those workmanlike pieces of pretty mathematics in which Mr. Balanchine specializes." Edwin Denby pronounced the ballet a "masterpiece." Yet even Denby was disturbed by the "meagerness and harshness" of the physical production. For critics of the popular newspapers, *Concerto Barocco* provided plenty of opportunities for wisecracks, Robert Garland characterizing it as "a sort of Elizabeth Arden exercise class with the ensemble in black gym suits against hypnotic blue." But critics of the professional dance press were also disturbed, some finding the ballet symptomatic of trends not at all to their liking. Dismayed at the prospect of other ballets without scenery or fancy costumes, Anatole Chujoy warned that *Concerto Barocco* "is artistically successful in spite of the absence of decor, not because of it." Rudolf Orthwine, publisher of *Dance,* complained that "the piece as presented seems rather tiny and poor" and, most crucially, "fails as theater." Robert Sabin also felt it failed as choreography:

> *Concerto Barocco* is one of those neat jobs of beautifully tailored, neo-classic *chi-chi* which flatter audiences into the illusion that they are enjoying "pure" and "classic" art, at the same time that they are having a delightful time with its prettiness and glitter. The baroque qualities of Bach's music, its majesty, its long, sweeping lines, its grandiose yet emotionally convincing richness of melody and contrapuntal detail, are conspicuously absent from the choreography. Mr. Balanchine has devised nervous, brilliant movement which breaks down into segments and loses contact with the web of Bach's thought. [24]

Although it does seem peculiar that Sabin should see "prettiness and glitter" in a production which other critics castigated for its "meagerness and harshness," his remarks indicate that many New York dance intellectuals had not yet come to terms with Balanchine's compositional procedures. As to whether a Balanchine abstraction should be austerely or lavishly decorated, that is a perennial problem which not even the New York City Ballet has managed to solve.

For its second fall premiere, the Monte Carlo encouraged a young dancer to make his choreographic debut with a major company by producing Todd Bolender's *Comedia Balletica* (to Stravinsky's *Pulcinella* suite) on 17 September 1945. The ballet was a new version of a work called *Musical Chairs* which Bolender had staged the previous summer at Jacob's Pillow. It was Denham, says John Martin, who gave it the fancy new title, "without making clear what conceivable language he might be using." Many of the critics, though, thought *Musical Chairs* a more accurate title, since the ballet was a series of solos, duets, and ensembles for five dancers who changed seats at the conclusion of each variation. Edwin Denby found it promising, but not totally satisfying. Its wit reminded him "of a little clique of professionals indulging in acid gossip," but "the jokes were all pretty much alike." [25]

Regarding the fall season as a whole, the critics—no matter how they may have argued over Balanchine's choreographic abilities—nevertheless had to agree with Anatole Chujoy that Balanchine had "assembled an excellent corps de ballet and gave them something to dance." Edwin Denby also praised ballet master Frederic Franklin for having done "a remarkable job in getting a large repertory with a dozen new dancers and several new productions successfully launched in the very first week." A 79-city tour followed, which included the most successful West Coast engagements in the company's history. Several new productions were planned. Two of them, a revival of Balanchine's *The Bat* and a new ballet, *Farandole*, to Milhaud, never came about (although *Farandole* was constantly being promised in company announcements). Yet the spring 1946 season at City Center would feature two unusually ambitious new works.[26]

That spring season was again euphemistic, since it began 17 February. Lasting six weeks (until 31 March), it was also the company's longest season to date. Opening night was an impressive program consisting of *Les Sylphides*, a revival of *Baiser de la Fée*, (which Igor Stravinsky conducted), and the evergreen *Gaîté Parisienne*. Maria Tallchief assumed the role of the Fairy in *Baiser*, making it, for Walter Terry, "one of the most sinister and compelling portrayals in ballet . . . for she dances it with arrogant intensity and feral beauty as if she were presiding over an evil incantation." *Baiser's* closing scene, in which the Fairy leads the Young Man into eternity, had always posed staging problems. Terry decided that the Monte Carlo's 1946 expedient, "in which the fairy and the young man drift and droop about in an amber-lighted limbo, is decidedly weak and not nearly as effective as the original tableau . . . in which the young man climbed a huge net to reach the fairy perched near the top."[27]

It is perhaps significant that, of all Balanchine ballets, the neo-Romantic *Baiser de la Fée* should have been chosen for opening night, since this sinister fairy tale can serve as a reminder that Balanchine is capable of things other than austere abstractions. Balanchine's first novelty of the season, like *Baiser de la Fée*, exemplified his neo-Romantic tendencies. A juicy Gothic narrative—something of a horror story—with flamboyantly theatrical décor, *Night Shadow* (premiered 27 February 1946) could almost be termed the polar opposite of *Concerto Barocco*. Nevertheless, it befuddled critics as much as *Concerto Barocco* had. *Night Shadow* dealt with somnambulism, a phenomenon that greatly intrigued Romantic artists. Yet though the score by Vittorio Rieti utilized themes by Bellini, the ballet (later renamed *La Sonnambula*) has no direct connection either with Bellini's opera, *La Sonnambula*, or with any of the ballets on the subject produced during the Romantic era. Balanchine's hero is an idealistic Byronic poet who attends a ball given by a baron and his mistress, a coquette. After an idle flirtation with the coquette, the poet watches some divertissements—superficial dances to entertain aristocrats who are not only superficial themselves, but downright evil. Then the guests depart for the supper table, leaving the poet alone. Gradually, he becomes aware of a mysterious presence. It is a ghostly woman, a sleepwalker, who enters in a white nightgown carrying a lighted candle. Entranced, the poet tries to dance with her, but the somnambulist keeps eluding his grasp. The coquette, returning, spies on their encounter and summons the baron who discovers the poet and the sleepwalker (presumably the baron's wife) together. Enraged, the baron kills the poet, but the sleepwalker gathers his corpse in her arms and carries him off to her tower.

The designs by surrealist painter Dorothea Tanning included a mouldering castle and some peculiar masquerade costumes for the party guests. The headdresses particularly caused comment, Chicago critic Claudia Cassidy describing them as "all clipper ships and antlered noddings and fish scales and even a beehive housing an alarm clock."[28]

Seeing a performance some time after the premiere, Edwin Denby compared *Night Shadow* with Poe, saying, "It gives you a sense—as Poe does—of losing your bearings, the feeling of an elastic sort of time and a heaving floor." The daily critics at the premiere were not so favorably impressed. For once, the *Times* and the *Herald-Tribune* agreed about Balanchine. Following military service, Walter Terry had returned to his old post as dance critic of the *Herald-Tribune,* Edwin Denby from then on devoting himself to freelance writing. Terry discussed *Night Shadow* in culinary terms:

> Take a portion of left-over hash, garnish with bits of surrealism, add one poet and serve; the resulting dish will be called "The Night Shadow". . . . [it] has but fleeting (very fleeting) bits of Balanchine's choreographic skill, for not only does it lack cohesion in matters of mood and dance pattern but it is encumbered with a set of divertissements on a par with those of the most inferior show which the old New York Hippodrome ever produced.

Similarly, John Martin maintained, "It is a rather foolish little piece of pseudo-surrealism which is not likely to be of much interest to anybody." He thought the whole affair a sort of Halloween prank by ultrasophisticates. Even the music was, for him, what later slang would call a "put-on." Martin considered it ludicrous to set "this bizarre bit of plot" to "the most wiltingly 'corny' " operatic music. "It is but divinely incongruous! Ho-hum." Yet, a year later, Martin found more to admire in *Night Shadow:* "From a dubious beginning a season or so ago it has developed into an interesting theatre piece, overweighted with divertissements, but touching effectively on the macabre and unusual in its sense of somnambulism."[29]

The second premiere that spring was also a ballet on a grand scale—in some respects, on the grandest scale that had been seen in New York for decades. This was nothing less than a production of *Raymonda,* the three-act ballet Marius Petipa had choreographed to music by Glazounov in 1898 and which was fondly remembered by Russian dancers as one of the treasures of the Maryinsky repertoire. At first, there had been talk of inviting Pierre Vladimiroff to stage the famous divertissements of the last act. But Balanchine and Danilova, fired by the prospect of *Raymonda,* decided to stage all three acts. Although Edwin Denby says that in 1946 he was told that there was little authentic Petipa in the production except for a male pas de quatre and a smouldering solo for the ballerina which he calls a "czardas on toe," Danilova today maintains that most of the choreography was an adaptation of what she and Balanchine remembered from the Maryinsky: "The choreographic base was always Petipa."

With storybook scenery and costumes by Alexandre Benois, the Ballet Russe *Raymonda* was premiered 12 March 1946, before an audience that included just about every Russian dancer and teacher in New York. Not since Anton Dolin had staged the *Sleeping Beauty* divertissements for Ballet Theatre in 1941 under the title of *Princess Aurora* had there been such advance interest in a Russian classic. And not since then had there been so many hairsplitting arguments among the Russian ballet set, their debates continuing long into the night at the Russian Tea Room. *Raymonda* was a gala occasion, and after the first performance Denham presented Danilova with a Capehart radio-phonograph combination.

Lasting an hour and three quarters,[30] *Raymonda* was the longest single ballet that had been presented in New York in many years. Today, multi-act ballets are commonplace, but in the 1940s they were a rarity. *Coppélia* and *Giselle* were presented with at least one other ballet, and often with two. Similarly, the Ballet Russe *Raymonda,* even in its longest version, was always accompanied by another ballet. New Yorkers, unused to the leisurely panoramic productions of Petipa, were bewildered by *Raymonda.*

It could be argued that *Raymonda,* despite its brilliant dances, was not an ideal introduction to the multi-act classical form, since the thread of plot that holds its dances together—a tenuous story about how a Crusader rescues a lady from a Saracen—has never been considered one of the triumphs of ballet-ic dramaturgy. At a time when serious dancegoers were discovering the narrative works of Tudor and Graham, the *Raymonda* scenario must have seemed downright foolish. Audiences did not quite know how to take the events of the ballet. Often, City Center patrons would hiss Nikita Talin as the evil Saracen, as though he were the villain in a parody revival of a Victorian melodrama. Some of the dancers also had difficulty adjusting to *Raymonda*. Because of an injury to Frederic Franklin, at the first performance the Crusader was danced by Nicholas Magallanes, Franklin assuming the role later. Even as experienced a trouper as Franklin, however, felt a bit peculiar as the Crusader. He said, "I always feared that the armor I had to wear made me look like Ingrid Bergman in *Joan of Lorraine,*" Maxwell Anderson's play about Joan of Arc.

Critics, too, were puzzled. George Amberg, the learned art historian who wrote so incisively about contemporary trends, could only say, "It was an anachronism, like playing at Imperial Russian Ballet." Lillian Moore, though she was also a dancer and a dance historian, found it "incredibly long and boring." Perhaps the best advice about orienting one's self toward appreciating *Raymonda* came from Anatole Chujoy, who said, "Whether you stage a classic ballet, write about it, or just watch it, you must make up your mind whether you accept it as a definite art form withal [sic] its shortcomings and conventions, or reject it—approach, form, and content." If one accepts nineteenth-century Russian ballet as a form, then, within the conventions of that form *Raymonda* can be seen to be "a superlative ballet, ingenious in choreographic invention, splendid in form, absorbing to look at, pleasant to listen to." Accepting the form, Edwin Denby even found a touch of social significance in *Raymonda:* ". . . there is not a mean gesture to be seen for a whole hour. Some people find this escapism but as a conception of society it strikes me as revolutionary." Both the friends and enemies of *Raymonda,* however, tended to complain that it was too long. Within a year after its premiere, Walter Terry noted that "generous cuts" had been made, and cuts continued to be made. At last, *Raymonda* was reduced to a divertissement in one act and as such remained in the touring repertoire for many years.[31]

At the conclusion of the New York engagement, the company again went on tour, its schedule including summer appearances at the Jacob's Pillow Dance Festival.[32] Surveying the

1945-46 season, most critics were pleased with the company's development. Danilova had distinguished herself. Nathalie Krassovska had become, for Anatole Chujoy, "a romantic dancer of fine style, excellent technique and great beauty," while Maria Tallchief was attracting increasingly favorable notice. Walter Terry thought two young men sufficiently promising to analyze their dancing in detail. Terry admired the classic technique of Nicholas Magallanes, but added an important demur:

> I think he needs something as completely non-technical as a "hot-foot," for his main problem is one of lethargy and a depressing quality of heavy-footedness. In other words, his dancing lacks a sense of lift, of buoyancy. He leaps fairly high, but one is conscious of the descent, rather than the ascent.
> . . .

Of another performer he wrote,

> The dancing of Robert Lindgren has many virtues, including crispness of style, rhythmic precision and an air of authority; the flaws, which could be easily remedied, consist of a too stern facial expression and a body which is often held so tensely that body line suffers and movement flow is impaired. . . .[33]

Terry also noticed something else about the company: it was too small. Although the Ballet Russe at its New York debut in 1938 consisted of sixty-one members, by the mid-1940s it had shrunk to about forty dancers and it would remain more or less that size for the rest of its existence. Terry observed, "The leading dancers are excellent, but there are not quite enough of them, nor are there enough experienced soloists for the supporting male roles." Noting the same thing about the company, British writer Jossleyn Hennessy thought that "too much work falls on to its leading soloists and the repercussions caused if two or three members become simultaneously incapacitated place an undue physical strain on everyone." Nevertheless, the company's standards were felt to be very high, Lillian Moore unhesitatingly asserting, "The Corps de Ballet of the Monte Carlo has improved to such an extent that it is now the best in the States." Hennessy found many "important attributes which could enable it to build for the future rather than live on the past; it has a single direction with consciousness of purpose and its freedom from guest stars gives its soloists their chance to develop . . . if it could only secure a permanent home and reduce its back-breaking tours . . . it would also secure steadiness of progress in American ballet."[34]

Virtually everybody attributed much of the company's

development to the influence of Balanchine. But at the very moment when the Ballet Russe had reached new heights, Balanchine was about to leave it, partly because of the company's lack of a permanent home and its "back-breaking tours." Dancers recall Balanchine fretting about the low standards of pickup orchestras and of the demoralizing effects of constant touring.

During the 1946-47 season Balanchine was offered opportunities to create as innovatively as he wished in a sophisticated milieu free from the pressures of the commercial theatre. That subscription series of experimental ballet performances that Lincoln Kirstein had dreamed about in 1942 (and to which he had invited both Balanchine and Massine to contribute) was, with the end of the war, about to become a reality. On 20 November 1946, Ballet Society gave its first program, a double bill consisting of Ravel's opera, *The Spellbound Child*, staged and choreographed by Balanchine, and the world premiere of Balanchine's *The Four Temperaments*, to Hindemith. Also that season, Balanchine would be blessed with an opportunity to work with one of the greatest institutions in all ballet. In March 1947 Balanchine became choreographer for the Paris Opéra Ballet, replacing (temporarily, as it proved) maître de ballet Serge Lifar, then under suspicion of having collaborated with the Germans during the occupation of France.[35] These projects would take Balanchine far from the Ballet Russe, and he never came back to it.

NOTES FOR CHAPTER 5

1. John Martin, "The Dance: Events Ahead," *New York Times*, 17 September 1944.
2. Conversation with Maria Tallchief. Henceforth, all statements by dancers for which no printed source is given were made in conversation with the author.
3. John Martin, "The Dance: Ballet Russe," *New York Times*, 10 September 1944.
4. Edwin Denby, *Looking at the Dance*, p. 81.
5. *Danses Concertantes* reviews—John Martin, "City Center Opens Season of Ballet," *New York Times*, 11 September 1944; John Martin, "2 Holiday Shows by Ballet Russe," *New York Times*, 23 February 1945; Edwin Denby, *Looking at the Dance*, pp. 81-82; Lillian Moore, "Two New Balanchine Ballets," *The Dancing Times*, November 1944, p. 60; Robert Sabin, "Ballet Russe de Monte Carlo," *Dance Observer*, October 1944, p. 101.
6. *Le Bourgeois Gentilhomme*—"Ballet Revises Week's Programs," *New York Sun*, 16 September 1944; Walter Terry, *Ballet: A New Guide to the Liveliest Art*, p. 66; Robert Lawrence, *The Victor Book of Ballets and Ballet Music*, p. 82.
7. *Le Bourgeois Gentilhomme* reviews—Edwin Denby, *Looking at the Dance*, p. 83; John Martin, "Balanchine Dance at the City Center," *New York Times*, 22 February 1945; Edwin Denby, "'Le Bourgeois Transformed,'" *New York Herald-Tribune*, 25 September 1944.

8. Season survey—Anatole Chujoy, "Dance in Review," *Dance News*, October 1944, p. 7; Robert Sabin, "Ballet Russe de Monte Carlo," *Dance Observer*, October 1944, p. 101; Lillian Moore, "Two New Balanchine Ballets," *The Dancing Times*, November 1944, p. 61.

9. Letter from S.J. Denham headed "Dear Marion," 21 December 1944.

10. *Ballet Imperial*—*Chicago Stagebill*, 4 October 1944; Anatole Chujoy, "The Dance in Review," *Dance News*, October 1945, p. 7; Nancy Reynolds, *Repertory in Review*, pp. 64-65; Edwin Denby, "The New Monte Carlo Formed," *New York Herald-Tribune*, 21 February 1945; Edwin Denby, "The Monte Carlo Now," *New York Herald-Tribune*, 25 March 1945.

11. Lillian Moore, "New York Notes," *The Dancing Times*, February 1945, p. 204; "News from Chicago," *Dance*, March 1945, p. 31.

12. *Frankie and Johnny*—John Martin, " 'Frankie, Johnny' Revived by Ballet," *New York Times*, 1 March 1945; Edwin Denby, *Looking at the Dance*, p. 106; "AGMAzine Visits Sergei Denham," *AGMAzine*, December 1958, p. 6; Conversations with Ruth Page, Ruthanna Boris, Sonja Taanila. The Paul Moss controversy—Lillian Moore, "A Balanchine Anniversary," *The Dancing Times*, May 1945, p. 348; Robert Coleman, " 'Frankie & Johnny' an Empty Ballet," *New York Daily Mirror*, 1 March 1945.

13. John Martin, "The Dance: Ballet Schedule," *New York Times*, 18 February 1945.

14. *Mozartiana*—John Martin, "Balanchine Dance Is Given at Center," *New York Times*, 8 March 1945; Edwin Denby, *Looking at the Dance*, p. 108; Ruthanna Boris, in Nancy Reynolds, *Repertory in Review*, p. 44; conversations with Frederic Franklin, Sonja Taanila.

15. *Pas de Deux*—John Martin, "The Dance: Ballet Schedule," *New York Times*, 18 February 1945; Edwin Denby, "Lovely Incident," *New York Herald-Tribune*, 15 March 1945; conversation with Frederic Franklin.

16. Edwin Denby, "The Monte Carlo Now," *New York Herald-Tribune*, 25 March 1945, John Martin, "The Dance: Going and Coming," *New York Times*, 25 March 1945.

17. Edwin Denby, "The Monte Carlo Now," *New York Herald-Tribune*, 25 March 1945.

18. Lillian Moore, "A Balanchine Anniversary," *The Dancing Times*, May 1945, p. 347.

19. "Attitudes and Arabesques," *Dance News*, June-August 1945, p. 4.

20. Ballet Russe Highlights—Léonide Massine, *My Life in Ballet*, pp. 227-228; *Ballet Annual #1*, p. 154; John Martin, "The Dance: Present and Future," *New York Times*, 24 June 1945; Ann Barzel, "Dance Reviews," *Dance*, April 1946, p. 57.

21. Reviews and commentary—Ruthella Wade, "Reviews," *Dance*, August 1945, p. 34; John Martin, "The Dance: Massine's Highlights," *New York Times*, 8 July 1945; Ann Barzel, "Ballets Down the Drain," *Ballet Annual #17*, p. 79.

22. Peacetime—"Attitudes and Arabesques," *Dance News*, October 1945, p. 2; "Ballet Russe de Gotham," *Newsweek*, 24 September 1945, pp. 110-111; conversation with Robert Lindgren.

23. *Concerto Barocco*—Grace Robert, *The Borzoi Book of Ballets*, p. 45; Robert Sabin, "Reviews of the Month," *Dance Observer*, October 1945, p. 97.

24. *Concerto Barocco* reviews—John Martin, "2 Novelties Given by Ballet Russe," *New York Times*, 12 September 1945; Edwin Denby, *Looking at the Dance*, p. 124; Robert Garland, "Ballet Russe Opens 4th Season at Center," *New York Journal-American*, 10 September 1945; Anatole Chujoy, "Dance in Review,"

Dance News, October 1945, p. 2; Rudolf Orthwine, "Reviews," Dance, October 1945, p. 50; Robert Sabin, "Reviews of the Month," Dance Observer, October 1945, p. 97.

25. Comedia Balletica — Walter Terry, Ballet: A New Guide to the Liveliest Art, p. 90; John Martin, World Book of Modern Ballet, p. 117; Edwin Denby, Looking at the Dance, p. 126.

26. Season survey, tour, plans — Anatole Chujoy, "Dance in Review," Dance News, October 1945, p. 2; Edwin Denby, Looking at the dance, p. 165; John Martin, "The Dance: Miscellany," New York Times, 16 September 1945; "Monte Carlo Scores on Coasts," Dance News, December 1945, p. 1; "Monte Carlo Plans Spring Repertoire," Dance News, June-August 1945, p. 1.

27. Baiser de la Fée — "Ballet Russe de Monte Carlo in Successful N.Y. Season," Dance News, March 1946, p. 1; Walter Terry, "The Ballet," New York Herald-Tribune, 24 February 1947; Walter Terry, "A New Season of Ballet," New York Herald-Tribune, 5 September 1946.

28. Claudia Cassidy, "On the Aisle," Chicago Tribune, 27 September 1947.

29. Night Shadow reviews — Edwin Denby, Looking at the Dance, p. 199; Walter Terry, "World Premiere," New York Herald-Tribune, 28 February 1946; John Martin, "Balanchine Dance in World Premiere," New York Times, 28 February 1946; John Martin, "Ballet Russe Finds Spring Very Early," New York Times, 17 February 1947.

30. Raymonda genesis and premiere — "Canada Plays Host to Monte Carlo," Dance News, Apri, 1945, p. 1; Michel Katcharoff, unpublished autobiography, p. 54; Edwin Denby, Looking at the Dance, p. 200; "Attitudes and Arabesques," Dance News, April 1946, p. 4; John Martin, " 'Raymonda' Given by Ballet Russe," New York Times, 13 March 1946.

31. Raymonda reviews — George Amberg, Ballet, p. 65; Lillian Moore, "American Notes," The Dancing Times, November 1946, p. 69; Anatole Chujoy, "The Season in Review," Dance News, April 1946, p. 5; Edwin Denby, Looking at the Dance, p. 200; Walter Terry, "Active Holiday," New York Herald-Tribune, 24 February 1947.

32. John Martin, "The Dance: Season's Plans," New York Times, 25 August 1946.

33. Anatole Chujoy, "Dance in Review," Dance News, October 1945, p. 7; Walter Terry, "Ballet Russe's Lesser Dancers Are Little-Sung but Essential," New York Herald-Tribune, 31 March 1946.

34. Season survey — Walter Terry, "First Impressions," New York Herald-Tribune, 24 February 1946; Jossleyn Hennessy, in Ballet Annual #1, p. 45; Lillian Moore, "Notes from America," The Dancing Times, July 1946, p. 513.

35. John Martin, "The Dance: New Ballet," New York Times, 17 October 1946; "Balanchine Paris Work Begins Mar. 1," Dance News, October 1946, p. 1.

6 BALANCHINE AND HIS BALLETS

IT was George Balanchine who almost singlehandly rejuvenated the Ballet Russe de Monte Carlo, making it once again a company of genuine distinction. At the same time, it could be said that the Ballet Russe de Monte Carlo helped rejuvenate George Balanchine as a choreographer. For the Ballet Russe provided Balanchine with eager, talented, and classically trained dancers upon whom he could create serious, even experimental, new works. The stability of the Ballet Russe as an organization also made it possible for Balanchine to revive older works originally choreographed for short-lived groups and to present them in repertoire season after season.

Before associating himself with the Ballet Russe in 1944, Balanchine had reached an odd creative impasse. "His career as a Broadway choreographer was going nowhere," Frederic Franklin remembers. "And no ballet company seemed to want him."[1] His stagings of *Apollo* and *The Wanderer (Errante)* for Ballet Theatre in 1943 had little impact, and although he would again work for Ballet Theatre in 1944, choreographing *Waltz Academy* shortly after choreographing *Danses Concertantes* for the Monte Carlo, the emphasis at Ballet Theatre in the 1940s was upon a quite different sort of ballet from that which Balanchine appeared to be most interested in creating. Moreover, several influential critics—including John Martin—did not particularly like his work.

117

Balanchine needed a company sympathetic to his ideas. The Ballet Russe needed a choreographer to give it artistic purpose and direction. Therefore, for two seasons—until Balanchine was given the opportunity to have a company all his own—Balanchine and the Ballet Russe were able to work together sympathetically.

Dancers' descriptions of Balanchine seldom vary. Almost everyone agrees that Balanchine is soft-spoken and mild-mannered, capable of preserving tranquility in the midst of any emergency. This combination of confidence and courtesy impresses dancers. They feel they can trust him; they sense his authority. Nathalie Krassovska says, "Balanchine never raised his voice. Therefore there was always silence when he entered the studio." Robert Lindgren first encountered Balanchine in the Ballet Russe during the 1940s. A decade later, Lindgren danced for Balanchine again in the New York City Ballet. During all that time, Balanchine's rehearsal procedures had scarcely altered. Unlike Massine, who tried to plot everything in advance, Balanchine, when choreographing a new ballet, came to the studio with only the sketchiest idea of what he wanted his dancers to do. He might study the score for a moment, sniff slightly and wrinkle his noise in the rabbitlike fashion dancers love to imitate, then start moving dancers about until he discovered choreographic patterns that pleased him.

The presence of Balanchine significantly modified the way the Ballet Russe danced. Now that Frederic Franklin was *maître de ballet,* Balanchine insisted that dancers attend daily company class and also allowed them to study free of charge at the School of American Ballet. Balanchine brought strict classicism to the company, a classicism even purer than that of Bronislava Nijinska—who, says Maria Tallchief, was then celebrated for her neoclassical ideals. Balanchine also refused to let dancers get by on temperament, personality, and stage projection alone. By today's technical standards, Tallchief thinks, Balanchine's productions for the Monte Carlo might look gauche. Yet, when first produced, they were a revelation of the power and potentiality of classical dancing.

Throughout the Massine era the Ballet Russe had soloists of great presence and flair. Yet the corps was occasionally called ragged. Balanchine improved corps work tremendously. Yet some balletomanes mourned the loss of "individuality." Also during the Massine era, the company's male dancers were especially noteworthy. Balanchine, however, seemed most interested in devising roles for such a great ballerina as Danilova and in developing young ballerinas such as Boris, Moylan, and Tallchief. Because of this devotion to the concept that "ballet is woman," there are those who think that the company's standard of male dancing declined slightly during Balanchine's tenure as resident choreographer, although any such decline may also be attributable, in part, to the fact that military conscription during World War II may have deprived the Ballet Russe of talented males who might otherwise have been available.

At the time of Balanchine's arrival, a number of dancers who had been originally hired by Massine left the company. Some married or found careers outside the dance world. Some went on to dance on Broadway or in films. Many of these performers had been accomplished character or demi-caractère dancers. The youngsters who replaced them, particularly the former School of American Ballet students, tended to be strong classicists, although the continuing presence of works by Fokine and Massine in the repertoire insured that they would receive far more character and demi-caractère experience than most current graduates of the School of American Ballet receive when they enter the New York City Ballet. Nevertheless, Balanchine brought about a discernible shift of emphasis. He even managed to alter the styles of several dancers in significant ways. "Balanchine completely remade me," Maria Tallchief admits. "He changed me from a demi-caractère to a classical dancer."

Balanchine was respected both by the Americans and by the Russians who remained in the company. The Russians adored him because he was Russian—because, as Sergei Denham often remarked, he was "preserving the great traditions of Russian ballet." Yet in some ways, as Robert Lindgren observes, "The most American of all the people connected with the Ballet Russe around 1945 was George Balanchine." Fervently believing that the future of ballet belonged to America, Balanchine could become testy when he heard balletomanes sigh sentimentally over Russian dancers of an earlier generation. When Chicago critic Claudia Cassidy suggested that "an older, more experienced troupe, say of Diaghileff vintage" might be superior in some of his works, particularly in such a sophisticated ballet as *Danses Concertantes,* Balanchine exploded with, "Why do Americans hate Americans?" He told Cassidy that Diaghilev's corps was "made up of husbands and wives, not so young, not so small. They loved character roles and couldn't have achieved the pinpoint brilliance of 'Danses Concertantes' in a million years."[2]

With such faith in American dancers, no wonder young

people loved working with Balanchine. It was clear that Balanchine trusted his dancers absolutely. It soon became equally clear to company members that if Balanchine suspected that certain dancers in any way betrayed that trust he might never give those dancers such responsibility again. Balanchine could be capricious in his likes and dislikes. Demanding total loyalty of his dancers, he was also capable of discarding dancers when he ceased to be interested in them. Shortly after founding the New York City Ballet, he asked one dancer from the Ballet Russe to join the new company. She replied that she would very much like to do so, but she was still under contract to Denham. "Break contract," suggested Balanchine. However, the dancer pointed out that if she did something so unethical in Denham's company, how could Balanchine be sure that she would not someday behave in a similar fashion once she had joined his company? Balanchine shrugged and turned away, and the dancer toured for the rest of the season with the Ballet Russe. When her contract expired, she did not renew it and, now free of all obligations to Denham, she arrived at the New York City Ballet studios, expecting to be taken into Balanchine's company. But Balanchine simply looked at her and shook his head. "Too late," he said. "Too late."

While it now seems clear that during his years with the Ballet Russe Balanchine was creating an American classicism and a form of ballet which, though lyrical and evocative, was nonetheless devoid of narrative, his intentions and achievements were by no means clear at the time. Balanchine mystified people. And he did so no matter what sort of ballet he choreographed. He did, on occasion, attempt narratives. But such fantasies as *Baiser de la Fée* and *Night Shadow* seemed, on the one hand, morbidly introspective when compared with the robust character ballets of Massine and, on the other, too much like conventional fairy tales when compared with the psychological dance-dramas of Tudor and some of the modern dancers. As for the plotless ballets, the pieces some critics called abstractions, they seemed cold, heartless, and perverse to many balletgoers.

Yet the abstractions did have articulate champions. These enthusiasts often defended abstract ballets by comparing them with symphonic music. Just as a symphony may be enjoyed as a self-sufficient sonic experience which need not contain any direct references to anything outside itself, so, maintained some critics, a Balanchine abstraction could be enjoyed as a self-sufficient set of movement patterns in space and time. Thus Los

Angeles music critic Albert Goldberg wrote that watching a performance of *Danses Concertantes*

> is like concentrating on the convolutions of a Bach fugue;
> there is the certainty that it will straighten itself out in the end,
> but a good deal of suspense is generated in the process. The
> dancers caught well this feeling of complication in motion,
> and the brief, spirited appearances of Alexandra Danilova and
> Frederic Franklin were like the entrance of subject and counter
> subject in a fugue, lighting the way in the general involvement
> to the final happy resolution.[3]

Composer Elliott Carter exclaimed, "There is something magical
and stirring about this drawing of the invisible lines in the air."[4]

For other viewers, such "complication in motion" was
insufficient. To eyes used to the stripped-down look of certain
current New York City Ballet productions, Balanchine's Ballet Russe
offerings designed by Berman and Doboujinsky might seem ornate. Yet in the 1940s Balanchine was regularly attacked for being
untheatrical. When *Concerto Barocco* came to be staged without
any décor at all, that, far from seeming a departure, merely confirmed the impression that Balanchine was essentially untheatrical. Even Edwin Denby was taken aback by the "harshness" of
Concerto Barocco. Today, that *Concert Barocco* may be seen as an
essential step in Balanchine's development, a production demonstrating the autonomy of choreographic movement. All *Concerto Barocco* needs are simple costumes and a clear space in
which the movements of the dancers wearing those costumes may
be seen without hindrance.

To the charge that Balanchine was untheatrical was
added the charge that he was growing hermetic and inexpressive.
Anatole Chujoy, who had often defended Balanchine in the past,
was disturbed by this newest phase. He feared that in choreographing *Danses Concertantes* Balanchine had become so "absorbed by the intricate technical problems" of Stravinsky's music
that he never made the work genuinely theatrical, and when ballet
"ceases to be theatre, it ceases to be ballet, no matter how brilliant
the choreography. . . ." This sort of work shows Balanchine trying
to be "a scientist in ballet and music, rather than the true artist he
is." *Mozartiana*, like *Danses Concertantes*, made Chujoy fear that
Balanchine had chosen to sacrifice "the theatrical quality of ballet
for the musicality of the choreography, and I have my doubts
whether the sacrifice is worth while."[5] Balanchine's absorption in
technically intricate patterns, in what John Martin called "pretty

mathematics," made his new dances, for Martin, well-nigh indistinguishable. He termed *Concerto Barocco*

> still another reworking of the same material that has already provided us with . . . half a dozen other items in the repertoire, and just why it is singled out as being any more baroque than the rest of them is not evident. . . .
>
>   It is curious that Mr. Balanchine, who is said to be a gifted musician, sees no more in this particular music than these sweet and superficial formalisms interspersed with acrobatics.[6]

Martin, during the 1930s and 1940s, subscribed to the theory that there were essentially two types of theatrical dancing: spectacular (in which the attention is directed primarily toward what the movement looks like, rather than toward what it says) and expressional (in which the attention is directed entirely toward what the movement says). Modern dance epitomized expressional dance, whereas ballet was one of the forms of spectacular dance. For Martin, not only was Balanchine essentially a choreographer of spectacular dance, his works were not always even particularly vivid examples of the form. As early as the American Ballet's production of *Baiser de la Fée* in 1937, he wrote, "It is necessary always to accept the fact that for Balanchine the dance, as he has expressly stated, is purely spectacular and should strive only for the attainment of sensuous pleasure. That he believes such pleasure is best attained by tenuous rather than robust means is apparently characteristic of his personal approach."[7]

While Balanchine may have inspired the Ballet Russe dancers, their enthusiasm was by no means shared by dancers from other companies. Writing in *Dance News*, Igor Youskevitch indicated his agreement with the objections of Chujoy and Martin. Discharged from military service, Youskevitch had joined Ballet Theatre, instead of returning to the Monte Carlo. He saw the productions that Balanchine had mounted for his old company and found them wanting. He was particularly bothered by Balanchine's apparent desire to treat movement as an end in itself since, for Youskevitch, the aim of every performing art is "to transmit the human thought through the medium of the theatre." Considering the abstract ballet to be an aesthetic absurdity, he rhetorically asked, "Can one imagine an opera or a drama without a plot, or without a thought or idea?" Finally, Youskevitch declared that he believed the choreographer's task is "to select such movements that would express with great clarity the thoughts which he injected into an individual dance or the whole composition,"[8] a statement that leaves open the whole aesthetic question of just what thought is in dance terms and how movement may convey it.

In 1945 Balanchine wrote an essay in which he expressed his own feelings about ballet and choreography. Some of his statements suggest that he, like Martin, would cheerfully designate ballet a spectacular dance form. "The important thing in a ballet," he says, "is the movement itself, as it is sound which is important in a symphony. A ballet may contain a story, but the visual spectacle, not the story, is the essential element." Later, he reiterates this point: "Choreographic movement is an end in itself, and its only purpose is to create the impression of intensity and beauty." At other points in the essay, however, he clearly recognizes that ballet may have—even ought to have—significance beyond the appeal of visual beauty alone. Thus he says, "The spectator must be willing to assimilate what is shown on the stage, and possibly be disturbed by it (for the ballet has spiritual and metaphysical elements, not merely physical ones) and to retain in his memory the preceding movements which will give significance to the ones that are being performed and the ones which are to follow."[9]

Here, Balanchine indicates his awareness of a phenomenon his admirers have often noted: that though his ballets are supposedly plotless or abstract, the movements of the dancers seem rich in emotional connotations; that sometimes they even appear to unfold enigmatic dramas. It is this paradox to which George Amberg refers when he says, "While unfolding in space, the range of significant movement seems to extend beyond the field of physical vision and the moving figures thus define mysterious relationships which transcend physical contacts and connotations."[10]

A theory of why this should be exists in, of all the seemingly unlikely places, the aesthetics of John Martin. Martin believes that no human movement can occur without a definite relation to some life experience. Through the selection and arrangement of movements, a choreographer transfers an experience to a spectator by evoking empathic responses in the spectator's muscular memory, a process of transfer Martin calls metakinesis. Thus dance movement—even in plotless, abstract works—may express meanings that cannot be conveyed by verbal means. Martin's personal taste may have prevented him from enjoying Balanchine's ballets, yet he had formulated a theory which could justify them. [11]

Balanchine's defenders found the movement in his ballets significant and expressive. Minna Lederman has left us a description of the Monte Carlo's *Baiser de la Fée* which, if accurate, makes that work seem positively bloodcurdling and not in the least an attempt to achieve spectacle through tenuous rather than robust means (as Martin would have it):

> First there is the Fairy's glittering appearance with her black Shadow. She swoops over the baby in devouring benevolence and the figure beside her moves ominously through the same arc of space—a device that fills the theater with instant mystery and dread. Later she is herself her Shadow, prowling through the village. She descends on the Boy in a series of constricting rectangles to wrestle for his soul. Rough and brutal, she thrusts him from left to right until she seizes his head in triumph and forces it to the ground. Finally there is the searing encounter in the mill. She confronts him suddenly, a towering apparition and, helpless, he embraces and carries her rigid form away with him. . . . their hands locked, they move in an open-and-shut diagonal across the stage with an effect of mounting, cruel sensuality. [12]

Baiser, of course, is a choreographic narrative. What Balanchine's supporters found particularly remarkable were the instances in which essentially abstract choreography seemed rich in dramatic and emotional implications. Over the years, many dancegoers have been tempted to read stories about the pangs of love into *Serenade*, even though *Serenade* resists sustained analysis in terms of narrative structure. Sometimes the relationship between movement and music helped create some sort of emotional or dramatic effect. Writing about his own *Danses Concertantes*, Balanchine gives an example of how such interplay between sight and sound provided the ballet with its pungency:

> The ballerina dances with sweet, lyric grace, but also with humor, for the music continues to interrupt and cut short its soft melody with sharp accents in surprising places. You get the impression that you might get from reading a lyric poem whose lines are sometimes terminated in the middle of words but nevertheless flow on to graceful conclusion. [13]

Edwin Denby has written a justly famous description of some of the emotional implications of *Concerto Barocco*:

> The correspondence of eye and ear is at its most surprising in the poignant adagio movement. At the climax, for instance, against a background of chorus that suggests the look of trees

in the wind before a storm breaks, the ballerina, with limbs powerfully outspread, is lifted by her male partner, lifted repeatedly in narrowing arcs higher and higher. Then at the culminating phrase, from her greatest height he slowly lowers her. You watch her body slowly descend, her foot and leg pointing stiffly downward, till her toe reaches the floor and she rests her full weight at last on this single sharp point and pauses. It has the effect at that moment of a deliberate and powerful plunge into a wound, and the emotion of it answers strangely to the musical stress. And (as another example) the final adagio figure before the coda, the ballerina being slid upstage in two or three swoops that dip down and rise a moment into an extension in second—like a receding cry— creates another image that corresponds vividly to the weight of the musical passage.[14]

This sort of choreography that was evocative rather than explicit pleased dancegoers tired of the hortatory and the obvious in the art of the time. The social protest of the 1930s had been succeeded by the rallying cries of World War II. This was also the beginning of a time when some artists attempted to interpret all human behavior in terms of Freudian psychology. For dancegoers tired of absolutism and sermonizing, it must have been refreshing to encounter Balanchine's ballets in which mysteries were allowed to remain mysteries. Critic and composer Arthur V. Berger relished Balanchine's lack of rhetoric, at the same time admitting that this very quality might puzzle other dancegoers:

> Balanchine is regarded in the same unfortunate light as the late Stravinsky. Because the subject matter is not hammered beyond the point at which it is sufficiently perceptible, it is thought, perhaps, to be wanting. But as far as this reviewer is concerned, a choreographer with such outstanding gifts as Agnes de Mille, for example, weakens the impact of her ideas precisely because she often loses sight of the exact degree in which they can contribute to the whole.[15]

Some observers interpret the sudden upsurge in popularity of all forms of dance during the 1940s as a reaction to wartime pressures. Edwin Denby says, "Wartime, here as abroad, made everyone more eager for the civilized and peaceful excitement of ballet. . . . And in wartime the fact that no word was spoken on the stage was in itself a relief."[16]

It is customary to say of Balanchine that he is heir to the Petipa tradition and also the creator of an American style of classical ballet. But "tradition" and "classicism" are terms that can have innumerable shadings of meaning, depending upon who employs them. For Balanchine, according to George Amberg, tradition was "not simply the faithful continuation of established practices, but the perpetual rediscovery and reapplication of those basic laws, as stated and amplified in the cumulative wisdom of countless generations."[17] Tradition, then, was not static but ever evolving, a distinction that the Ballet Russe may have lost sight of in its final years. When Balanchine paid homage to Petipa in *Ballet Imperial*, the result was not simply a reproduction of a period style. Rather, it was a thoroughly contemporary work in which period style was refashioned, a work Edwin Denby describes as

> a vivacious, exacting, inexhaustibly inventive classic dance ballet, a ballet that evokes the imperial dazzle of the St. Petersburg style in all its freshness. It is no period parody. Everything is novel in its effect. But you recognize the abounding inner gayety, the touch of tenderness, the visual clarity and elegance, the bold dance impulse that exist—often in only vestigial form—in the Petipa-school classics still in our repertory. Balanchine has re-created the spirit of the style which was its glory. And you look at "Ballet Imperial" with the same happy wonder that our grandparents may have felt in the '90s, when the present classics were novelties.
>
> "Ballet Imperial" is a ballet without a plot, as luminously incomprehensible as the old classics were. It begins with a solemn, vaguely uneasy mood, groups and solos that turn into brilliant bravura; then comes a touching pantomime scene, with softer dances, a scene that suggests a meeting, a misunderstanding, a reconciliation, a loss; and then a third section succeeds, even more vertiginously brilliant than the first, in which everybody shines, individually, in clusters, the boys, the girls, the stars, and all in unison.[18]

It was also Denby, Balanchine's most eloquent apologist during the 1940s, who articulated the nature of Balanchine's classicism. Of all the qualities that could be termed classical, those with which Balanchine was most concerned were "clarity and excitement" and "human naturalness of expression."[19] By stressing these particular qualities, Denby thought, Balanchine had effected a revolution in ballet. Balanchine based his humane classicism upon "the patterns the human body makes when it dances; it is not—like romantic choreography—based on patterns the human body cannot quite force itself into."[20] The act of dancing, then, becomes of paramount importance in classical choreography, whereas the romantic choreography that prevailed from

1910 to 1940 opposed "to that act obstacles of various kinds of mimicry—pictorial, psychological, musical or social."[21] Although, because of the specialized nature of its technique, ballet might seem the most unnatural of arts, Denby was able to employ the concept of naturalness when he discussed Balanchine's ballets, because Balanchine's "steps no matter where derived are steps that a ballet dancer specifically can do and do best; steps a ballet dancer can be brilliant in. His rhythms however complex are grateful to ballet dancers."[22]

To achieve naturalness of expression, Balanchine had to be responsive to the particular dancers with whom he was working. In the case of the Ballet Russe, this meant being responsive to the talents of the foreign-born stars and to the talents of the young Americans. For the Ballet Russe, Balanchine staged a group of ballets in which all the company's dancers were able to shine, the Americans as well as the Russians. Denby considered this one of Balanchine's most important achievements: "By showing us that the young Americans, who form most of the company, can dance straight classic ballet without self-consciousness—as naturally as people speak their native tongue—he has proved that ballet can become as native an art here as it did long ago in Russia; and can develop, as it did there, a native and spontaneous brilliance."[23] Thus it was Balanchine who really transformed the Ballet Russe de Monte Carlo into an American company. Agnes de Mille's *Rodeo* may have demonstrated the validity of Americana as a balletic genre. But that was an isolated production, following which de Mille had no further connections with the company. Balanchine proved that Americans could dance classically and, what is more, began to fashion a personal classical style which was his creative response to American temperaments and physiques. This process of development, begun in the American Ballet of the 1930s, reached its culmination in the present New York City Ballet. During the 1940s, however, it was the Ballet Russe de Monte Carlo that permitted the development to continue.

NOTES FOR CHAPTER 6

1. Conversation with Frederic Franklin. Henceforth, all statements for which no printed source is given were made in conversation with the author. Particularly helpful have been conversations with Ann Barzel, Ruthanna Boris, Alexandra Danilova, Frederic Franklin, Nathalie Krassovska, Robert Lindgren, and Maria Tallchief.
2. Claudia Cassidy, "On the Aisle," *Chicago Tribune,* 8 October 1944.

3. Albert Goldberg, "Stravinsky Piece Feature of Ballet Bill," *Los Angeles Times*, 6 December 1947.
4. Quoted in George Amberg, *Ballet*, p. 62.
5. Anatole Chujoy, "Dance in Review," *Dance News*, October 1944, p. 7, and April 1945, p. 6.
6. John Martin, "2 Novelties Given by Ballet Russe," *New York Times*, 10 September 1945.
7. Quoted in Nancy Reynolds, *Repertory in Review*, p. 52.
8. Igor Youskevitch, "Ballet Is a Theatre Art," *Dance News*, June-August 1945, p. 4.
9. George Balanchine," Notes on Choreography." *Dance Index*, IV: 2-3, February-March 1945, pp. 20-31.
10. George Amberg, *Ballet*, p. 62.
11. For a summary of Martin's theories, see Jack Anderson, "Dancers' Bookshelf," *Dance Magazine*, November 1965, pp. 47-48.
12. Quoted in Nancy Reynolds, *Repertory in Review*, p. 52.
13. George Balanchine, *Balanchine's Complete Stories of the Great Ballets*, p. 112.
14. Edwin Denby, *Looking at the Dance*, pp. 125-126.
15. Arthur V. Berger, " 'Serenade' Given by Ballet Russe," *New York Sun*, 15 April 1944.
16. Edwin Denby, *Looking at the Dance*, p. 395.
17. George Amberg, *Ballet*, p. 63.
18. Edwin Denby, *Looking at the Dance*, pp. 103-104.
19. Edwin Denby, *Looking at the Dance*, p. 112.
20. Edwin Denby, *Looking at the Dance*, p. 70.
21. Edwin Denby, *Looking at the Dance*, p. 114.
22. Edwin Denby, *Looking at the Dance*, p. 221.
23. Edwin Denby, "Ballet Magician," *New York Herald-Tribune*, 17 March 1945.

7 TRIUMPH AND TWILIGHT (1946-1952)

THE 1946-47 season returned the Ballet Russe de Monte Carlo to the situation in which it had found itself after Massine's departure in 1942. It was a company without a resident choreographer. During the next few years Sergei Denham would make persistent attempts to seek out new ballets, sometimes even staging productions of an experimental nature. Yet the Ballet Russe never again acquired a resident choreographer.

One experiment during the 4-15 September 1946 engagement at City Center was Ruth Page's *The Bells*, to a commissioned score by Darius Milhaud and with décor by Isamu Noguchi. Page's own Chicago company had premiered it on 26 April 1946. Entering the Monte Carlo repertoire on 30 August, during the company's residency at Jacob's Pillow, it received its New York premiere 6 September. An interpretation of Edgar Allan Poe's familiar poem, the poetic progress from "the jingling and the tinkling of the bells" to "the moaning and the groaning of the bells" was paralleled theatrically by a macabre scenario. Because it concerned how a band of Ghouls caused a Bridegroom to abandon his Bride, *The Bells* might be interpreted as an allegory about the breakup of a marriage.

Edwin Denby had no use for it. *The Bells*, he said, "goes on for half an hour being puerile in public." Other critics thought it contained interesting ideas, yet was severely flawed. Anatole

129

Chujoy considered its basic material good, but its treatment confused. Certain aspects of *The Bells* provoked controversy. Milhaud's music was dissonant and difficult. Page remembers it as being "hard to learn and difficult sometimes to count," and though it was "very virile," it also seemed "too strenuous all the time." Nevertheless, of the scores she has commissioned, Page considers it surpassed only by Moross's *Frankie and Johnny.* Yet its complexity made it impossible for many pickup musicians to play, and Page never heard a first-rate performance of it on tour. Noguchi's décor—a sculptural construction shaped like a church that progressively crumbled as the ballet proceeded—presumably symbolized the decay of traditional moral standards. The sight shocked pious audiences who could not abide to watch a church disintegrate, even in a ballet deploring the perils of social disintegration.

A *PM* critic hinted at another troublesome aspect of *The Bells* when he accused Page of plunging "into a pool of solemn and peculiar sexual symbolism of her own devising." Since it involved a Bridegroom abducted by a male Ghoul, it was possible to regard *The Bells* as a depiction, although a somewhat inchoate one, of a marriage threatened by homosexuality.[1]

While the fall engagement may not have shown the Monte Carlo at its highest creative level, it unmistakably demonstrated the company's superiority to Colonel W. de Basil's Original Ballet Russe, which had traveled up and down South America during World War II. Absent from New York since 1941, it returned under Hurok's management to the Metropolitan Opera House for a season beginning 29 September. The once-great company now looked bedraggled and after 1947 it played no further part in the development of American ballet.

The spirit of innovation that had led to the production of *The Bells* prevailed when the company returned to dance at City Center, from 16 February to 30 March 1947. There was talk of collaboration between the company and the Ballet Society of Lincoln Kirstein and George Balanchine, the Ballet Russe taking over the successful productions that the experimental group had presented for its subscription-only audience.[2] Since the organizations were in no way really competitive in purpose or policy, such a scheme had much to be said for it. But nothing was done about it and by 1948 Ballet Society had become the New York City Ballet, with all performances open to the general public.

The Ballet Russe showed considerable daring by offering on 4 March the world premiere of Valerie Bettis's *Virginia Sampler,* the first work by a modern dancer to be produced by any American ballet company. The second such modern-dance work, Merce Cunningham's *The Seasons,* was offered by Ballet Society a few weeks later on 18 May 1947. Denham was scouting for new productions and he was enterprising enough to let his searches take him in unexpected directions.

Bettis's commission came about because she had been doing experimental television ballets in collaboration with designer James McNaughton, who knew people at the Ballet Russe and who spread the word that she might be worth encouraging. When Denham saw a television production of a piece choreographed to Bach, he was impressed and invited Bettis to submit a proposal for a ballet. She and composer Leo Smit devised a tempestuous scenario based upon Coleridge's *Rime of the Ancient Mariner,* only to discover that what Denham had in mind was a lighter piece in the nature of a divertissement. Accordingly, Bettis and Smit revised their plans and suggested *The Unidentified Lady,* as their work was first known. "We tried to keep it as dramatic as possible, though," says Bettis, "for we thought it artistically compromising to do a mere divertissement. Yet *Virginia Sampler* was essentially a divertissement, and when I revived it for the North Carolina Dance Theatre I emphasized its divertissement qualities."

Like Massine, de Mille, and Balanchine before her, Bettis choreographed on the road. Arriving in Los Angeles, where rehearsals began, she auditioned company members for roles, just as though she were casting a Broadway show, a practice that startled dancers used to being treated dictatorially by choreographers. Bettis confesses that most of the Ballet Russe dancers were total strangers to her and "frankly, at the beginning, I had trouble telling one cygnet from another."

Just as in 1942 some dancers scorned the movement de Mille invented for *Rodeo,* so in 1947 a few dancers regarded *Virginia Sampler* with hostility. "Obviously," says Bettis, "for those dancers anything that wasn't *Swan Lake* or *Les Sylphides* was inherently inferior." But what impressed her even more was that, although the dancers were initially confused by her rhythmic accents—Bettis thinks that ballet dancers tend to round out quirky movements to the nearest classical equivalent—once she had won their confidence, the freer the movement she assigned, the better they did it. This, she speculates, may have been a result of their experience in dancing Massine, who also invented movements outside the classical canon.

Virginia Sampler dealt with life in a Virginia town after the American Revolution, with the people who lived there, and with people who passed through on their way somewhere else, the strangers including a general resembling George Washington and a mysterious woman on horseback who did much to disturb the even tenor of community life. The ballet had been inspired by old samplers and primitive paintings, particularly the works of the itinerant portraitists who would come into a town with readymade portraits in which bodies were outlined and clothed, only the faces remaining blank. The blanks would then be filled in with the features of whatever local residents desired a portrait. Bettis wanted her movement to convey a sense of flatness to match the flatness of the paintings, and hoped that the static moments in her ballet would resemble little paintings in themselves.

If the meshing of classical and contemporary movement eventually proved no problem for the dancers, it apparently bothered certain critics. John Martin stated that he thought ballet and modern dance were antithetical and that therefore a choreographer from one idiom working with dancers trained in the other had better find some "neutral realm—folk dance, perhaps, or pantomime or sheer theatre improvisation." Anatole Chujoy concurred, pronouncing ballet objective and impersonal and modern dance subjective and personal. According to Martin, Bettis tried to make all the dancers replicate her personal way of moving—"with its staccato attack, its spasmodic flurries of activity, its quick and inhibited tensions, its irregular phrases"—as though it were "a deliberate style," as objective as ballet. Chujoy, on the other hand, thought that the movement resembled ballet steps consciously distorted to look "modern." Despite his reservations, Martin termed *Virginia Sampler* "a good try at a difficult assignment." It was Bettis's only work for the Ballet Russe. Bettis explains, "That I never did other ballets for the company was my fault, not the company's. If I had come in all excited, begging and screaming to do something new, I'm sure Denham would have let me. But I had other plans."[3]

The season's second premiere, *Madroños*, was also out of the ordinary. It was the work of an American, Phyllis Nahl, who adopted the stage name of Antonia Cobos. A concert dancer who blended Spanish dance with ballet, Cobos attacted wide attention in 1944 when she choreographed *The Mute Wife* for the Marquis de Cuevas's Ballet International (in 1953 she married the Marquis's son, John).[4] Ballet Russe dancers describe Cobos as brilliant and sophisticated. They also remember her as an agonizingly slow worker, rehearsals with Cobos resembling sessions at Penelope's loom because of her tendency to undo each day what she had accomplished the day before. Many of her ideas were clever, even brilliant: she simply never could decide which to retain in any ballet.

Taking its title from the Spanish word for the pompons on some of the exquisite costumes by Castillo, *Madroños* was credited with music by "Moszkowski, Yradier and others," the term "and others" being a modest way of referring to tunes by Cobos herself.[5] Scheduled for 20 March 1947, with Cobos as guest artist in the ballerina role thereafter danced by Nathalie Krassovska, the premiere was canceled because of a foot injury sustained by Cobos in rehearsal. Instead, *Madroños* received its first performance on 22 March. Critics, however, were refused admittance to that performance, company management considering the ballet still unready for appraisal by the press. The decision caused some balletomanes to wonder why, if a work was unfit to be seen by critics, it was nonetheless shown to a paying audience. The first critics' performance was 25 March.

Just as Cobos kept changing her mind in rehearsal, so *Madroños* kept changing its shape, which it could easily do, since it was a suite of dances related only by their Spanish character. Highlights of the first version consisted of a solo for Frederic Franklin in a tattered beggar's costume and a pas de deux for him and the ballerina; a dance with castanets for Ruthanna Boris, as a blackamoor on pointe (a dance introduced into the ballet after its first performance); and, perhaps best of all, a scene starring Leon Danielian as a vain toreador. Dancers recall his entrance along a diagonal of adoring girls as being one of the most striking entrances in all ballet.

In a later version, Franklin acquired a rich velvet costume and ceased to be a beggar, while still later, in 1950, Cobos substantially revised the ballet, dropping the dances originally performed by Franklin and Boris, enlarging Danielian's role, and creating a new dance for Alexandra Danilova and a group of hunchbacks. Anatole Chujoy found that *Madroños* became "more and more divertissement and less and less Spanish" as revisions continued. In any version, *Madroños* amused audiences. John Martin located its essential weakness as well as its strength when he said, "One is never quite sure just what the choreographer is trying to say—whether she is making fun of something (and if so, of what), or whether she is simply putting together half a dozen dances that amuse her. That she makes fun, however, is undeniable, and very engaging fun at that."[6]

The productions by Bettis and Cobos, as well as *The Bells* of the previous season, led Martin to say that the Monte Carlo "is rapidly establishing itself as the most experimental company in the field."[7] Yet although the company did offer varied new works, as well as a catholic assemblage of ballets extending from the Maryinsky period onward, there were also signs that the company found it easy to settle for a conventional bread-and-butter repertoire. If newspaper announcements of seasonal schedules are to be trusted, it was on 25 February 1947 that the Ballet Russe de Monte Carlo may have given the first New York presentation of the triple bill for which the company became famous: *Swan Lake, Nutcracker, Scheherazade.* These ballets had been in the repertoire for years, but had not been offered on the same program. Billed together, they proved a combination that never failed to attract audiences, particularly on tour.

The appeal of the first two works is not hard to imagine. Ivanov's choreography for *Swan Lake's* second act continues to be esteemed as a lyrical masterpiece, while *Nutcracker* contains some of the most beloved music in all ballet. That *Scheherazade* should have retained its popularity into the 1950s is genuinely perplexing, however. The purely choreographic virtues of Fokine's ballet are often evident only to the most sophisticated dancegoers, whereas by 1950 one should have thought that this tale of an orgy in a harem would no longer have seemed titillating. But apparently *Scheherazade* remained potent stuff in some quarters. In 1951 the noted Washington music critic Paul Hume could still cluck that *Scheherazade* was "nothing but organized lechery."

For purely practical reasons, many dancers loathed *Scheherazade.* It required heavy body makeup and was usually last on a bill. Therefore if a theatre lacked proper showers (as some did), cast members had to endure the discomfort of wearing street clothes over their layers of makeup. Almost because *Scheherazade* was universally recognized as an ordeal, Rimsky-Korsakov's melody for the odalisques was adopted as a sort of theme song by dancers of the time. Robert Lindgren remembers instances when dancers, finding themselves ill at ease and surrounded by strangers at social gatherings, would quietly hum the odalisque theme. If they heard someone hum the theme back, they could relax, knowing that they were among dancers or people who were friends of dancers.[8]

The company opened a three-week season in Mexico City on 19 May 1947,[9] then returned to the United States for summer performances, including an engagement at the Hollywood Bowl. Following the success of *Madroños,* plans were made for Antonia Cobos to choreograph Stravinsky's *Scènes de Ballet* during the 1947-48 season.[10] The ballet was never staged, however, and later that season the Sadler's Wells Ballet in London premiered Frederick Ashton's *Scènes de Ballet,* which some critics consider the definitive treatment of the score. Searching for new choreographers, Denham allowed two company members to undertake ballets. One dancer's project, which had a peculiar scenario about stealing the crown jewels from the Tower of London, was soon abandoned. The second, Ruthanna Boris's *Cirque de Deux,* went on to become a hit.

Boris had been pestering Denham, asking him to allow her to choreograph. Denham's reply invariably was, "Why should I permit you—an unknown American—to choreograph?" Hearing this, Boris declared that, yes, she was an American, but she was certainly not unknown as a dancer, and even as a choreographer she had a small reputation, since for several years she had staged dances for summer theatre musicals, working with such entertainers as Danny Kaye and Imogene Coca. Her pleading did her no good and when she learned that Denham had permitted another dancer, with absolutely no choreographic experience, to proceed with the Tower of London ballet, she was so aghast that, unable to control herself, she burst into tears one night at a party given by Richard Hammond, of the Hammond Organ firm.

A few days later, Denham relented, telling her that she could produce "a little pas de deux" (but entirely at her own expense) for the company's Hollywood Bowl season. Her dreams of grandiose productions tumbling about her, Boris screamed, "A pas de deux! That's nothing but a circus!" Almost immediately, she had second thoughts: "A circus?" she wondered. "Hmm . . ." *Cirque de Deux* was born.

Set to the Walpurgis Night music from Gounod's *Faust,* the ballet was a showpiece for a ballerina, her cavalier, and two attendants. Commenting upon the circuslike elements present in most virtuoso pas de deux, it treated adagio, variations, and coda as though they were circus acts. After an *entrée,* conceived as a parade with flying capes, came an adagio in which the ballerina sustained poses on a mobile platform which the pages wheeled around, displaying her to the audience at various angles, flattering and otherwise. The male variation, a dance with a jeweled stick, suggested tightrope maneuvers, while the female variation, in which the ballerina carried a whip, was reminiscent of an equestrian act. Not the least of the charms of *Cirque de Deux* was its ability to maintain a balance between affection and parody. Ann Barzel called it "a gentle spoof that neither satirises nor burlesques ballet dancing, but just points to some of its *clichés* with the attitude that even if they are trite, when well done they are mighty pretty, and we believe in them."

When Denham decided that he wished to view the work-in-progress to ascertain whether it was worth producing, Boris arranged a showing to which she invited Walter Terry and John Martin. At the end of the run-through, before anyone else had an opportunity to speak, she turned toward Martin and asked. "Do I have any talent, Mr. Martin?" "And then some, miss," he replied. After the ballet's premiere at Hollywood Bowl, 1 August 1947, Richard Hammond came backstage with Judith Anderson and Ramon Novarro. "Are you happy now?" he asked Boris. Later, she learned that, as one of the directors of the Hollywood Bowl Association, Hammond had insisted upon a new work by her during the 1947 engagement.[11]

Cirque de Deux received its New York premiere 10 September 1947, one of two novelties offered during the Monte Carlo's 7-21 September season at City Center. The other, Edward Caton's *Lola Montez,* though it had Danilova in the title role, was possibly the company's biggest flop since *Saratoga.* Originally choreographed in 1946 for a small company called Ballet for America, the ballet, with a score by Fred Witt, utilized the settings Raoul Pène Du Bois had designed for *Ghost Town* and chronicled the visit of Lola Montez to a California mining community. Early in rehearsals, Caton realized that his ballet was flawed and requested that it be withdrawn, but the management, having promised it, felt it had to be presented and it went on against Caton's wishes. John Martin called it "formless, pointless and a general waste of time. . . ."[12]

That autumn saw the end of an old quarrel when Federal Judge John Bright awarded $52,250, plus costs, to Universal Art in a suit brought against Colonel W. de Basil. At issue was the 1938 contract which had intended to merge the two Ballets Russes and which involved the turning over to Universal Art of the complete legal title to six ballets. Since the merger never occurred and Universal Art never received the ballets, Judge Bright found de Basil guilty of breach of contract.[13]

The company returned to City Center for a four-week

season beginning 15 February 1948. The season's highlights included Alexandra Danilova's first New York performance in the title role of *Giselle* (on 24 February) and a Ruth Page ballet that confirmed her reputation for unconventionality.

Although her Myrtha had been much acclaimed in previous seasons, Danilova, as Giselle, received mixed notices. Her characterization was, as both its defenders and critics acknowledged, "broad and theatrical" (to quote Anatole Chujoy), but whereas for Chujoy this conception, if not yet perfect, was potentially first rate, others found *Giselle* "totally unsuited to her in nearly all respects. Her performance was technically unsteady and psychologically unconvincing" (to quote Robert Sabin).[14]

The Ruth Page ballet was *Billy Sunday,* based upon the life and sermons of an ex-ballplayer turned evangelist who was fond of exhorting the faithful to "hit a home run and knock the devil out of the box." Page's own Chicago company presented the world premiere of *Billy Sunday* in 1946. Originally, Page had hoped that Jerome Moross, composer of *Frankie and Johnny,* would also write the music for *Billy Sunday.* But Moross had other commitments and Page instead commissioned a score from music critic Remi Gassman. It was, she now believes, an unwise commission, for Gassman's music, though workmanlike, was "dry and academic," and not at all suited to the rowdy tone of the ballet. *Billy Sunday* was first produced by the Ballet Russe on 29 January 1948 in York, Pennsylvania. The New York premiere occurred 2 March.

Taking the form of a series of dramatized sermons on temptation, it retold in burlesqued fashion the stories of Joseph, Samson, and David. What made *Billy Sunday* unique was that its dancers were required to speak a text inspired by Sunday's actual sermons. The prospect of hearing such idols as Frederic Franklin (Billy) and Alexandra Danilova (Mrs. Potiphar) speak attracted throngs of curious balletomanes. Ann Barzel considered the situation "analogous to the beginning of sound movies after two decades of the silent art. Audiences could not believe it was British Freddy Franklin who, as Billy Sunday, was declaiming in the broad nasal accents of the American Middle West. They waited breathlessly for Danilova's first words and shrieked with delight at her hilarious lines in Russianized English."

As sometimes happens with ballets by Ruth Page, critics found the conceptions and production ideas superior to the choreography. Thus Reed Severin thought that the ballet's union of speech and dance suggested that Page might be a successful stager of musical comedy, but judging *Billy Sunday* on purely choreographic terms, he pronounced it "empty, rambling, listless and not very important. . . ." That it may have been—but it was also controversial. Billy Sunday's widow wrote an angry letter, accusing Page of mocking her husband. And she refused to be placated when Page pointed out that text and choreography had been based upon Sunday's own pulpit imagery. A group of prominent Protestant churchmen informed City Center that they considered the ballet's tone offensive. Denham invited them to a performance, after which Page discussed the ballet with them. Her reaction to all objections to *Billy Sunday* on moral grounds was "The Bible is filled with sex, especially the Old Testament. And anyway, you can't be very sexy on your toes."[15]

    After the New York engagement, but before the touring season ended, the Ballet Russe offered another Ruth Page ballet, *Love Song,* to an arrangement of Schubert piano pieces. A new version of a work originally choreographed in 1936, it was premiered on 5 April 1948 in Rochester, New York. Usually, when the company premiered a new ballet on the road, the New York premiere followed shortly thereafter. But New Yorkers had to wait until 1 March 1949 to see *Love Song.* Most critics wondered whether it was worth the wait. Somewhat vague in theme, *Love Song,* if it concerned anything, concerned a woman who sinks into melancholy when her lover leaves her for a more frivolous girl. "Its sentimental romantic theme," said Walter Terry, "provided the noted choreographer with little opportunity to display those gifts of wit, ingenuity and adventuresomeness which distinguish many of her compositions." And John Martin said, " 'Love Song' is not bad; it is just not good." Today, Ruth Page recalls *Love Song* with malicious glee. "I was supposed to be a shocking choreographer," she says, "so this time I shocked people by doing a ballet that wasn't shocking at all. I felt like doing a poetic classical ballet. So that's what I did."[16]

    Love Song was Page's last production for the Ballet Russe. She says that she did no further works for the company because "I felt it was starting to decline." That suspicion disturbed other people, including people associated with the company. To insure the maintenance of standards, there began to be talk of a Ballet Russe school. In the summer of 1948 Denham considered the possibility of establishing a company school in Houston, but his proposals were rejected. That same summer, the ballet department of the Jacob's Pillow Dance Festival was supervised by the Ballet Russe, company members teaching classes and appearing in festival performances.[17]

Gloomy intimations of decline were soon banished, however, by what appeared to be an incredible stroke of good luck. The Ballet Russe was to know at least one more triumphant season.

This came about because Sol Hurok announced that he was through with ballet forever. At least, that is what he thought then. He was sufficiently sincere about it, though, to relinquish his rights to the pre- and post-opera weeks at the Metropolitan Opera House, making the Met available to companies not under his auspices.[18] Therefore in 1948 the Ballet Russe de Monte Carlo could celebrate its tenth anniversary in the theatre in which it had made its American debut. Since the spring of 1944, the company had been associated with the City Center. Although it had developed an enthusiastic audience there, the theatre was uncomfortable and had nowhere near the prestige of the Met. Moving to the Met for a gala season, 18 September-10 October 1948, the company acknowledged its City Center devotees by preserving the "popular" City Center ticket price scale of 60¢ to $3.[19]

The decision to leave City Center in 1948 now appears to have been one of the turning points in the history of the Ballet Russe. In 1948 Ballet Society became the New York City Ballet and, although other troupes also appeared there, City Center was regarded as that company's home. Yet for years before Ballet Society came into existence, City Center had served as home for the Ballet Russe. If the Ballet Russe had not left City Center in 1948, it might have been possible to regard City Center as the home of two ballet companies, and how that would have affected the development of American ballet is a matter for speculation.

In 1948, however, the opportunity to dance at the Met seemed too auspicious to refuse. The company asked Massine to restage *Seventh Symphony* and *Rouge et Noir*, augmented its ranks so that it might have a sufficient number of dancers to appear in these vast compositions, and invited Alicia Markova, Mia Slavenska, Anton Dolin, Agnes de Mille, and José Torres as guests. Opening night, one of the most socially glamorous occasions in years, was entirely sold out, and the SRO sign went up for many subsequent performances. Dancers remember that the importance of the anniversary inspired them to give their best, and critics agreed that the dancing attained a distinguished level. "It has been a long time since Ballet Russe de Monte Carlo has had as thrilling and glamorous a season," said Anatole Chujoy.[20]

Balletomanes excitedly compared the Giselles of Markova, Danilova, and Slavenska and the Albrechts of Dolin and Franklin, while Agnes de Mille received a warm welcome as the

Cowgirl in *Rodeo.* Massine's revivals aroused mixed feelings. For some dancers, working with Massine was an inspiring experience. Others regarded him as a relic from the past. For one American dancer, Massine was so much the personification of all that she considered retrogressive in ballet that, when the entire company was asked to assemble on the Met's stage for possible casting in Massine's revivals, she obeyed the letter of the law by arriving as ordered, yet hid behind a curtain in the hopes that Massine would not notice her.

The novelties were slight. Opening night, 18 September, offered the company's first presentation of Anton Dolin's *Pas de Quatre* with Alicia Markova (Taglioni), Mia Slavenska (Grisi), Nathalie Krassovska (Grahn), and Alexandra Danilova (Cerrito)—an all-star cast almost as impressive as the original. Yet some critics considered the performance excessively broad, Ann Barzel deploring the way dancers gave "over-acid interpretations of the gentle anecdote."[21] When plans for the anniversary season were being made, there were reports that Dolin would also stage Ninette de Valois's *Job,*[22] but the production never materialized.

The season's one large-scale new work was a romp—a romp of peculiar origins. After the success of *Cirque de Deux,* Denham suggested that Ruthanna Boris choreograph another comedy: this time, a satire on Martha Graham. Years before, Boris had studied at the Graham school. She admired Graham's choreography enormously and felt that it was still insufficiently appreciated. A satire on Graham struck Boris as being a concession to the Philistines. She offered Denham a proposal of her own: a serious ballet, set in Columbus Circle, concerning the maturation of a group of adolescents. Denham rejected it on the grounds that it would be too costly. In those days, Columbus Circle was dominated by a huge Coca-Cola sign, and friends of Boris used to joke that she ought to ask Coca-Cola to finance her ballet for her. Soon, Boris found herself involved in a ballet financed in just such a fashion.

Planning to reintroduce Quelques Fleurs, a scent unavailable in American during the war, the Houbigant perfume company decided it would sponsor a new ballet as part of its promotional campaign. The work could be on any subject, officials at Houbigant said, the sole stipulation being that its title be *Quelques Fleurs.* When Denham approached Boris about this, she scorned the offer as crass commercialism. Later she discussed the proposal with theatrical writer Leo Lerman. "Would the choreographer really have a free hand?" Boris remembers Lerman asking.

"Apparently," she replied. Then, Lerman said, "You'd be a fool to refuse."

Boris accepted the commission. Although she had been promised total freedom, she was nevertheless cautious enough to utilize a scenario that had at least something to do with perfume. She invented a story about a haughty Contessa who, unsuccessful in her attempts to snare a young man, seeks help from an alchemist who presents her with three wondrous perfumes which cause the young man to swoon at their loveliness. Ultimately, this gift proves to be of no avail, since the youth still rejects the Contessa, preferring the fragrances to the woman. Danced to an Auber potpourri arranged by Harry G. Schumer, *Quelques Fleurs* presumably pleased Houbigant, although someone wishing to take its nonsense seriously could have argued that, because it showed that perfume cannot disguise lack of true beauty, Boris's ballet was essentially anti-cosmetic. Walter Terry called it "not as hilarious as her 'Cirque de Deux,' but it generates constant smiles and frequent chuckles."[23]

Guest artist José Torres (who also appeared in *Madroños*) presented a suite of *Spanish Dances* on 29 September 1948. Hiring a Spanish dancer for a company that performed few works inspired by Spain seemed a mysterious extravagance. Perhaps Denham hoped that the vitality of Spanish dancing would add spice to the season. Unfortunately, Lillian Moore wrote of Torres:

> He is a vivid theatre personality, who knows how to project his ego to the farthest reaches of the balcony, and since he is a well-built, good-looking young man, this alone should ensure him of a certain popularity. His basic technical equipment for the Spanish dance, however, is somewhat less than complete; his castanets are often hesitant, and his taste in dance arrangement borders upon the vaudevillian.

Mincing no words, Walter Terry called *Spanish Dances* "the nadir of the season."[24]

Proud of its fine dancing and bearing enthusiastic reviews, the company embarked upon its autumn tour. The Chicago engagement (15 October-1 November 1948) made news with a bigger advance sale and more sold-out performances than any other ballet company had ever had in that city. Company spirits soared. And there were lavish parties, the most lavish of all being one featuring roast pheasant and vintage wines hosted by the restaurateur—and ballet lover—known as "Ric" Ricardo.

It was during that Chicago engagement that critic Ann Barzel played the title role in a great classical ballet with the Ballet Russe. She appeared as Coppélia in *Coppélia*. Usually, the role of the mechanical doll who sits on a balcony and blows kisses to Frantz was given to a super. One night, the super never arrived. Barzel happened to be backstage photographing dancers when ballet master Frederic Franklin, distraught over the super's absence, looked at Barzel and realized she would fit the *Coppélia* costume. Despite her protests, on she went.[25]

If an extended residency on tour elated dancers, as the Chicago residency did, endless one-night stands could prove exhausting. When the Ballet Russe returned to Manhattan for a 21 February-20 March 1949 season at City Center, the repertoire was virtually the same as it had been for the acclaimed autumn season at the Met. Yet the company had grown so weary that its performances were what Walter Terry termed "subadequate."[26] Markova and Dolin appeared for much of the season, but the company's regular stars were missing, as Danilova and Franklin went to London to dance as guests with the Sadler's Wells Ballet.

The only novelties were Ruth Page's *Love Song* and a revival of Fokine's *Carnaval*, notable for Leon Danielian's performance as Harlequin. "It is impossible to find a flaw in his effortless, brilliant, instinctively right performance of this role," wrote Lillian Moore. "From his perfectly timed pirouettes à la seconde to the witty little gestures of head and hands and the expressive pantomime of the entire body, Danielian's Harlequin is perfect." The editorial staff of *Dance* named Danielian's Harlequin and Maria Tallchief's Eurydice in *Orpheus* the two finest individual performances of the 1948-49 season.[27]

The New York season over, the company continued touring. It was on this tour, on 31 March 1949 in Montreal, that Nathalie Krassovska made her debut in *Giselle* (with Roman Jasinski as Albrecht and Mary Ellen Moylan as Myrtha), giving a performance that S. Morgan-Powell of the *Montreal Daily Star* spoke of as "a brilliant success. . . . Her dancing was characterized by a purity of line not often seen nowadays in ballet. . . ."[28]

One of the dancers who joined the Ballet Russe in 1948 was Polish-born Nina Novak, who had studied at the Warsaw Opera Ballet School and, as a member of the Polish Ballet, had toured in Europe and had appeared at the 1939 New York World's Fair. When she returned to Poland, war broke out and, eventually she and her brother were sent by the Nazis to labor camps. After the war she emigrated to American in 1947 and began studying at Tatiana Chamié's school. Chamié, Denham's trusted friend, acted as an adviser to the company and often brought students to Denham's attention.

There began to be talk about "this new Polish girl," and Denham sent members of the company, including Michel Katcharoff and Roman Jasinski, to look at her. They found, as Chamié had promised, a character dancer of unusual style and flair and recommended that Denham hire her. As a member of the company she began receiving solo parts, but initially no special favoritism was shown toward her. Then, however, Denham began to encourage her, preparing her for leading roles in the entire repertoire— not only the character and demi-caractère roles for which she would be ideally suited, but classical roles as well.[29]

Novak soon became one of the company's most versatile—and controversial—dancers. In her first season, Anatole Chujoy singled her out for special mention as the Can-Can Dancer in *Gaîté Parisienne*. The same virtues and faults that he commented upon in 1948 were to be noticed by critics throughout her career. Novak, said Chujoy, "is very strong technically and she does an excellent manège and fouettés. But she is also very mannered and has a tendency to overact and mug into the audience, dangerous things for a young dancer."[30]

The 1949-50 season was one of many in the company's history that promised a revival of *St. Francis,*[31] reportedly one of Denham's favorite ballets. Yet touring conditions discouraged its revival, since Hindemith's score could not be quickly mastered by musicians on the road. The company did manage to offer several new productions during its 16 September-3 October 1949 engagement at the Metropolitan Opera House, including on opening night the premiere of Antonia Cobos's new version of *The Mute Wife.*

As produced by Ballet International in 1944, *The Mute Wife* had a score by Vittorio Rieti based upon themes of Paganini and was designed by Rico Lebrun. The Ballet Russe staging, re-choreographed from scratch, was set to a Soulima Stravinsky score adapted from Scarlatti and was designed by Castillo. The scenario (borrowed from Anatole France) in both cases concerned a husband seeking a cure for his mute wife; when the cure is found, she becomes such a chatterbox that the husband finds relief only by having his eardrums pierced and becoming deaf. Walter Terry thought the choreographic changes were for the worse: "Originally, if memory serves, 'The Mute Wife' was a charming ballet, light, quick and amusing. The present version is long, slow and not at all amusing until the closing episode is reached."

A conceit of the original version was the use of castanets played by the wife as she danced to indicate her clacking tongue. During the first season that the Ballet Russe presented the new production, Nina Novak still had not mastered the castanets and an offstage musician played them instead. Terry considered this disastrous: "The point, therefore, is pretty nearly lost." By the following spring, however, Novak had learned to play castanets and met with Terry's approval.[32]

The Ballet Russe called itself a guardian of Russian classical tradition. Yet several of its major attempts to produce unfamiliar Russian classics were greeted with bewilderment. Like *The Magic Swan* in 1941 and *Raymonda* in 1946, the divertissements from Petipa's *Paquita* (staged by Alexandra Danilova) received a tepid press when the Ballet Russe presented them on 20 September 1949. The way in which Petipa assembled his ballets, placing variation next to variation like pearls on a string, was considered old-fashioned by audiences of the 1940s. Danilova says that her choreography consisted of the traditional steps as she remembered them from the Maryinsky, filled in at times with choreography of her own. Costumed by Castillo and danced against one of Eugène Berman's settings for *Devil's Holiday*, the divertissements reminded surprisingly many viewers of a Radio City Music Hall routine. Walter Terry looked upon it indulgently as "a show piece . . . unabashedly sentimental, swoopy and bombastic by turns." Doris Hering had no use for it: "The material for the various combinations of dancers is surprisingly unsophisticated. It is done mostly in straight lines and unison and makes the girls resemble a cross between Rockettes and trapeze performers warming up for the clinch. It is at best only a feeble foreshadowing of Balanchine's *Ballet Imperial.*"[33]

The novelty on the next night, 21 September 1949, was warmly greeted, although today it might be considered less sophisticated than Petipa. Sophisticated or not, audiences have always loved David Lichine's *Graduation Ball.* Created for the Original Ballet Russe and later danced by Ballet Theatre, the Monte Carlo's revival was supervised by Vladimir Dokoudovsky and utilized the set by Mstislav Doboujinsky that had been designed for Ballet Theatre but which was owned by Hurok, from whom Denham acquired it. Walter Terry echoed popular sentiment that the ballet had retained "its inherent charm," while John Martin grumbled that "youth is rampant to the point of becoming positively repellent."[34]

Tatiana Chamié made her debut as a choreographer for the company with *Birthday*, to pieces by Rossini arranged by Lucien Cailliet. Intended as a vehicle for Mia Slavenska, *Birthday*'s leading role was danced by guest artist Nana Gollner at the 27 September 1949 premiere, because Slavenska had injured herself. Later performances were headed by Mary Ellen Moylan. *Birthday* was about a woman who, on her fiftieth birthday, remembers a party she had attended on her fifteenth and, particularly, a young man who was one of the guests. By making everything end happily, Chamié managed to avoid dealing with the melancholy that may accompany aging. Instead, according to Doris Hering, she devised "a neat combination of all the elements that have been used since time immemorial to please an audience without causing it to rise above a level of gentle euphoria." Chamié may not have been a profound choreographic thinker, but she was a respected teacher. So it is not surprising that Walter Terry should have found *Birthday* interesting primarily from a technical standpoint. Air turns usually restricted to men were assigned to women, and Terry noted "Other twists to traditional movements . . . the result is dancing which, though basically academic, is buoyant and novel."[35]

Despite the new productions, most critics considered the engagement (in John Martin's words) "a shoddy season." Doris Hering elaborated on the faults: "There was more bounding about than genuine dancing; more gushing than acting; more activity than vitality."[36]

The company returned to the Met in spring. Denham approached Ballet Theatre, which also planned spring performances, to suggest a shared season during which each company would dance two ballets at every performance. Ballet Theatre declined, and the Ballet Russe went into the Met alone 9-30 April 1950. It was to be the company's last New York season for seven years,[37] a season distinguished for its dancing, rather than for new choreography. Walter Terry was happy because "the raggedness, the air of desperate improvisation noticeable last autumn are gone and in their place one now finds unity of action and poise."[38] Particularly remarkable were the guest performances by the French ballerina Yvette Chauviré.

Yet these performances also revealed one of the company's weaknesses: its lack of rehearsal time. Being a touring ensemble, it was forever rushing to or from somewhere, and there was seldom time for the ballet master to take stock and appraise the company. The Ballet Russe had always been known for the individual styles of its principals. When guided by such choreographers as Massine or Balanchine, these personal styles existed harmoniously together. But without strong artistic direction, there were times when a performance could contain several clashing interpretations. Chauviré's first appearances with the Monte Carlo were troublesome in this fashion. Reviewing her in *Giselle,* Lillian Moore praised Chauviré's "exquisite delicacy of phrasing" and "her really lovely arms," yet also was conscious of a "disturbing contrast between her very French style and the broader, bolder, and in many ways simpler manner of the American corps de ballet." John Martin analyzed the stylistic dilemma after Chauviré's *Swan Lake*:

> In the hands of a director of taste and real capacities, what a dancer she would be! She commands an extraordinary technique, with that combination of steel and velvet which is the essence of academic technique. . . .
>
> Her Swan Queen, however, as it now stands, has no continuity; it leaps from virtuosity to virtuosity with blank spots between them. One may perhaps admire, but is never carried along with a sense of formal development or dramatic line to the satisfaction of artistic completeness. This is manifestly the director's lack, rather than the dancer's, for she has the capacity for long phrases and the dynamic range to put them together, if only she were made to realize the value of utilizing them. The very shortcomings of the performance, then, revealed in a paradoxical way the inherent powers of the dancer.[39]

Chauviré brought three productions from France along with her. *Mort du Cygne* (premiered 11 April 1950) was not Fokine's *Dying Swan,* but a little ballet to Chopin choreographed by Serge Lifar for the French film of that name (released in America as *Ballerina*) starring Chauviré, Slavenska, and the young Janine Charrat. Chauviré's Ballet Russe production, restaged by her husband Constantin Nepo (ordinarily a stage designer by profession) showed a hunter pursuing a swan. At last, said Walter Terry, "the swan dies gracefully (after many a summer, one might add). . . ."[40]

Roméo et Juliette, with Franklin and Chauviré in the title roles on 18 April 1950, was a digest version of Shakespeare's tragedy set to Tchaikovsky's tone-poem. Choreographically, said Anatole Chujoy, "it is naively obvious pantomime mounted in a homemade high school dramatic-group fashion with the enchaînements never leaving the limits of an advanced adagio class." Just who choreographed this production is by no means clear. Basically, it was a version of the *Roméo* created in 1942 by Lifar for the debut of Ludmilla Tcherina. The ballet was later danced by Chauviré. But Ballet Russe programs said only that it had been staged by Nepo and some programs on tour attributed the choreography to Chauviré herself. Yvonne Chouteau remembers that Chauviré introduced substantial changes (and, in Chouteau's estimation, improvements) into the ballet. It was the one work imported by Chauviré that remained in the repertoire after her departure, when it was danced by Chouteau and Oleg Tupine.[41] Finally, there was Victor Gsovsky's virtuoso duet, *Grand Pas Classique*, to Auber, which Chauviré and Tupine offered on 25 April 1950. John Martin called it "no great shakes as art, but . . . a first-rate exhibition piece."[42]

On 12 April 1950 occurred what purported to be a revival of Fokine's *Prince Igor*, superintended by Jean Yazvinsky. Although Yurek Lazowski made a guest appearance as the Warrior, the ballet was intended as a showcase for Nina Novak, and the choreography was altered. For Ann Barzel, "the general intentions of the ballet were distorted with the addition of showy tricks. . . ."[43]

Reviewing the season, Doris Hering chided the management for the extravagance of importing Chauviré in flimsy works when the same money could have been spent to commission substantial new ballets.[44] The Ballet Russe very much needed substantial new ballets. The eclecticism in the commissioning of new works that the company had adopted since Balanchine's departure—a policy that had initially seemed admirably experimental to John Martin—had resulted in items of varying merit. Yet it in no way helped the company to formulate a coherent artistic policy. By 1950 it was obvious that, creatively, the Ballet Russe was drifting rather than developing. Company members sensed this and it disturbed them. Ruthanna Boris and Mary Ellen Moylan resigned in 1950. During the 1949-50 tour, Robert Lindgren expressed his doubts in letters home to his mother, one letter saying,

> There are a good many people who are not satisfied with the company, internally, and who may not stay much longer. It is too long a story to write here, but in ballet the most important thing is to be creative, progressive, artistic, and inspired—if one can't work like this, then the small salary, the hard work, the traveling is [sic] for nothing.[45]

In the past, the Ballet Russe had been a stronghold of classic tradition and a champion of innovation. Now it seemed that other companies were surpassing it in both areas. The Ballet Russe could not hope to mount the classics on a lavish scale equal to that of the evening-long productions that the Sadler's Wells Ballet brought to America in 1949; and as for innovation, surely the center for that had become the New York City Ballet. The Ballet Russe was starting to look provincial.

It also started to avoid New York. There was no New York engagement during the 1950-51 season. Nor was there one during 1951-52. After negotiations with AGMA concerning a new contract (which secured unemployment benefits for the dancers for the first time), the company opened the 1950-51 season on tour. The first major stop was Chicago, for a two-week engagement beginning 16 October. Boris and Moylan had departed and, after a few performances, Franklin left on a sabbatical. But, following a year's absence, Krassovska was back, and Chauviré, Nina Stroganova, and Vladimir Dokoudovsky were guests.

Ann Barzel found much to admire in the dancing of two young principals. Gertrude Tyven, said Barzel, "is a perfectionist and there is something extra special about her correctness—the straight back, the quiet unfolding of a high extension, the well placed arms and general ease." When Nina Novak danced Swanilda in *Coppélia* she created, said Barzel, "Something of a sensation . . . . Not only did she have technical mastery of the part, but her roguishness and charm filled in the characterization and her bravura style was very right for the dancing."[46]

There were two premieres. *Prima Ballerina,* Tatiana Chamié's second choreographic effort (to music of Lecoq, orchestrated by Lucien Cailliet) was a comic account of backstage intrigue: when a ballerina walks out on a company after slapping her partner's face, her understudy is given a chance to shine. "An entertaining trifle, but hardly a ballet," said Barzel after seeing its first performance, 25 October 1950.[47] However, balletgoers familiar with the Ballet Russe hierarchy might have thought that Chamié was indulging in some in-jokes by casting Danilova as the departing ballerina and Novak as the ambitious understudy.

Victor Gsovsky's *Nocturne* (premiered 26 October 1950) was simply an excuse for Chauviré to look lovely while portraying a lady gambled for in a card game and fought over in a duel by two ardent admirers. Set to Mozart's "Eine Kleine Nachtmusik," it "breathed the taste and chic we recognize as Parisian, and partook of the emptiness of that style," said Barzel.

Among its attractions were its costumes by Balmain, which in-cluded a genuine diamond necklace for Chauviré. Essentially, *Nocturne* was a triumph of couture over choreography.[48]

After the Chicago engagement, the rest of the season was constant touring.

So was the 1951-52 season—except that it was also more turbulent, being filled with rumors, quarrels, reunions, and farewells. The reunions provided reasons for rejoicing. Chauviré and Slavenska returned for guest appearances, as did Léonide Massine, dancing with the company for the first time since 1942. His performances in *Beau Danube, Capriccio Espagnol,* and *Gaîté Parisienne* during the 15-30 October 1950 engagement in Chicago were his last on the American stage. The departures from the company were crucial enough to suggest that history was passing the Ballet Russe by, leaving it to languish in a balletic twilight. Danielian went off to Les Ballets des Champs-Elysées as a guest artist, and at the end of the season Franklin announced that he and Slavenska were resigning to organize a company of their own. Eternally optimistic, Denham announced ambitious plans: revivals of *Snow Maiden, Chopin Concerto,* and the oft-promised *St. Francis;* a three-act *Swan Lake;* reconstructions of pieces from the Pavlova repertoire; a new ballet by Karel Shook, and a new ballet by Carmelita Maracci adapted from a Hemingway story, with music by George Antheil (this became *Capital of the World,* choreographed by Eugene Loring for Ballet Theatre). Despite these announcements, there were no new productions whatsoever during 1951-52.[49]

The season's most devastating event occurred in Hous-ton on 30 December 1951. Alexandra Danilova gave her last per-formance as a regular member of the Ballet Russe. When the curtain fell upon *Gaîté Parisienne,* many in the filled auditorium were in tears, and when in an on-stage ceremony Denham presented the ballerina with a gold bracelet, the audience rose to its feet in a standing ovation.

Her farewell was surrounded with gossip. There were rumors that Danilova could not agree with the present policies of the company, particularly with Denham's determination to grant ballerina status to one of the young dancers. Music critic Hubert Roussel, long a friend of the Ballet Russe, commented that "Sergei Denham is determined to bring up a ballerina from his own ranks. But the present candidate for this position, who enjoys the status of a protégée extraordinaire, and who does not enjoy the full artistic respect of the rest of the company, is the fundamental cause of the trouble."[50]

Roussel named no names. But for the past two or three seasons other critics had begun to wonder whether Nina Novak, though undeniably gifted, was being pushed too quickly into roles for which she was not ready. Thus Doris Hering spoke of Novak as "an exceptional dancer—with spirit, temperament, versatility, and an incredibly accurate sense of rhythm. Moreover, she looks lovely and projects even when she is not dancing. But she is being thrown helterskelter into all shapes and sizes of roles. She is being allowed to tire herself unmercifully, instead of being carefully nurtured into the mature and richly faceted artist she could someday become."[51] From Danilova's retirement onward, Novak increasingly dominated the company.

The Ballet Russe went to Mexico City in August 1952, then traveled on to Caracas. When the company returned to America, its dancers went on leave. For the next two seasons the company would exist in a very different form. The old Ballet Russe de Monte Carlo had temporarily come to a halt.[52]

NOTES FOR CHAPTER 7

1. *The Bells*—Edwin Denby, *Looking at the Dance*, p. 198; Robert A. Hague, "Bells and Ghouls," *PM*, 11 September 1946; John Martin, *Ruth Page*, p. 116; conversations with Ruthanna Boris and Ruth Page.
2. John Martin, "The Dance: Repertory of the Ballet Russe," *New York Times*, 26 January 1947.
3. *Virginia Sampler*—John Martin, "The Dance: Sampler," *New York Times*, 9 March 1947; Anatole Chujoy, "The Season in Review," *Dance News*, April 1947, p. 5; conversation with Valerie Bettis.
4. "Phyllis Nahl Bride of John de Cuevas," *New York Times*, 4 February 1953.
5. John Martin, "The Dance: Futures," *New York Times*, 24 August 1947.
6. *Madroños*—Versions and premiere: John Martin, "The Dance: Premieres," *New York Times*, 23 March 1947; "Attitudes and Arabesques," *Dance News*, May 1947, p. 4; conversations with Ruthanna Boris, Robert Lindgren, George Verdak. Reviews: Anatole Chujoy, "The Season in Review," *Dance News*, May 1950, p. 7; John Martin, "The Dance: Premieres," *New York Times*, 21 September 1947.
7. John Martin, " 'Bells' Is Offered by Ballet Russe," *New York Times*, 10 March 1947.
8. *Scheherazade*—Paul Hume, "Ballet Russe Brings Best Company Yet," *Washington Post*, 18 February 1951; conversations with Michel Katcharoff, Robert Lindgren, Gilbert Reed.
9. "Mexico Salutes Ballet Russe," *Dance News*, June-August 1947, p. 1.
10. Letter from S.J. Denham to Lauder Greenway, 10 July 1947.

11. *Cirque de Deux* — Robert Lawrence, *The Victor Book of Ballets and Ballet Music,* pp. 112-113; Walter Terry, "The Ballet," *New York Herald-Tribune,* 11 September 1947; Ann Barzel, *Ballet Annual #3,* p. 116; conversation with Ruthanna Boris.

12. *Lola Montez* — Ann Barzel, *Ballet Annual #3,* p. 119; John Martin, "Miss Boris Stars in Caton Ballet," *New York Times,* 13 September 1947.

13. "Head of Ballet Russe Must Pay $52,250 by Court Order for Breaking a Contract," *New York Times,* 18 September 1947.

14. *Giselle* — Anatole Chujoy, "The Season in Review," *Dance News,* April 1948, p. 5; Robert Sabin, "Ballet Talks Again in Ruth Page's 'Billy Sunday,' " *Dance Observer,* April 1948, p. 43.

15. *Billy Sunday* — Walter Terry, *Ballet: A New Guide to the Liveliest Art,* p. 61; A.G., "Enthusiastic Ovation for Ballet Russe 'Billy Sunday': World Premiere, Hailed," *York Gazette and Daily,* 30 January 1948; Ann Barzel, *Ballet Annual #3,* p. 119; Reed Severin, "The Season in Review," *Dance,* April 1948, p. 14; "Three Churchmen Object to 'Billy,' " *PM,* 4 March 1948; "The Devil's Due," *Time,* 15 March 1948; John Martin, *Ruth Page,* pp. 120-123; conversation with Ruth Page.

16. *Love Song* — "Ballet Russe de Monte Carlo Winds Up Season," *Dance News,* May 1948, p. 1; Walter Terry, "The Dance: Ballet Looks Ahead," *New York Herald-Tribune,* 13 March 1949; John Martin, "Ruth Page Ballet Feature at Center," *New York Times,* 2 March 1949; John Martin, *Ruth Page,* p. 89; conversation with Ruth Page.

17. Mrs. Peter Sherwood, "Dixie Rejects Ballet Russe Cultural Offer," *Dance,* August 1948, p. 4; John Martin, "The Dance: Festival," *New York Times,* 28 March 1948.

18. John Martin, "The Dance: Era's End," *New York Times,* 30 November 1947.

19. John Martin, "The Dance: Premiere," *New York Times,* 15 August 1948.

20. Anniversary season — Ann Barzel, *Ballet Annual #4,* pp. 130-131; "Attitudes and Arabesques," *Dance News,* October 1948, p. 4; Anatole Chujoy, "The Season in Review," *Dance News,* November 1948, p. 5.

21. Ann Barzel, *Ballet Annual #4,* p. 130.

22. John Martin, "The Dance: Markova," *New York Times,* 4 July 1948.

23. Walter Terry, "The Dance: A Refreshed Ballet Russe," *New York Herald-Tribune,* 10 October 1948.

24. Lillian Moore, "Reviewer's Stand," *Dance,* November 1948, p. 12; Walter Terry, "The Dance: A Refreshed Ballet Russe," *New York Herald-Tribune,* 10 October 1948.

25. Chicago — "Attitudes and Arabesques," *Dance News,* December 1948, pp. 4-5; "Chicago," *Dance,* December 1948, p. 51; conversation with Ann Barzel.

26. Walter Terry, "Dance: Ballet Looks Ahead," *New York Herald-Tribune,* 13 March 1949.

27. Lillian Moore, "The Dance in Review," p. 27; "Dance Magazine Awards," p. 16, *Dance,* May 1949.

28. S. Morgan-Powell, "A Great Giselle by Krassovska," *Montreal Daily Star,* 1 April 1949.

29. Novak — Saul Goodman, "Nina Novak Revisits Warsaw," *Dance Magazine,* November 1961, p. 21; Harvey Taylor, "From Prisoner to Ballet Star," *Detroit Times,* 21 December 1950; conversations with Michel Katcharoff and Roman Jasinski; letter from Nina Novak to Jack Anderson, 20 December 1977.

30. Anatole Chujoy, "The Season in Review," *Dance News,* October 1945, p. 5.

31. Walter Terry, "Dance: Ballet Looks Ahead," *New York Herald-Tribune*, 13 March 1949.

32. Walter Terry, "The Season Opens," *New York Herald-Tribune*, 17 September 1949; "The Ballet," *New York Herald-Tribune*, 12 April 1950.

33. *Paquita*—Walter Terry, "The Ballet," *New York Herald-Tribune*, 21 September 1949; Doris Hering, "The Season in Review," *Dance*, November 1949, p. 16; conversation with Alexandra Danilova.

34. *Graduation Ball*—Robert Lawrence, *The Victor Book of Ballets and Ballet Music*, p. 224; Walter Terry, "The Ballet," *New York Herald-Tribune*, 22 September 1949; John Martin, " 'Graduation Ball' Revived by Ballet," *New York Times*, 22 September 1949.

35. *Birthday*—Doris Hering, "The Season in Review," *Dance*, November 1949, p. 16. Walter Terry, "Better Late Than. . . ,"*New York Herald-Tribune*, 28 September 1949.

36. John Martin, "The Dance: Victims," *New York Times*, 25 September 1949; Doris Hering, "The Season in Review," *Dance*, November 1949, p. 16.

37. "BT May Also Have Easter Opening," *Dance News*, March 1950, p. 1.

38. Walter Terry, "The Dance World," *New York Herald-Tribune*, 16 April 1950.

39. Lillian Moore, "A New Choreographer," *The Dancing Times*, June 1950, p. 540; John Martin, "Chauviré Dances Swan Queen Role," *New York Times*, 14 April 1950.

40. Walter Terry, "The Ballet," *New York Herald-Tribune*, 12 April 1950.

41. *Roméo et Juliette*—Anatole Chujoy, "The Season in Review," *Dance News*, May 1950, p. 7; Ann Barzel, *Ballet Annual #6*, p. 125; conversation with Yvonne Chouteau.

42. John Martin, "2 Ballet Groups Offer Premieres," *New York Times*, 26 April 1950.

43. Ann Barzel, *Ballet Annual #5*, p. 122.

44. Doris Hering, "The Season in Review," *Dance Magazine*, June 1950, pp. 40-41.

45. Letter from Robert Lindgren, 8 February 1950.

46. Chicago—"Via the Grapevine," *Dance Magazine*, October 1950, p. 6; "Ballet Russe de Monte Carlo Begins Oct. 10," *Dance News*, December 1950, pp. 8-9; Ann Barzel, *Ballet Annual #6*, p. 125.

47. Ann Barzel, *Ballet Annual #6*, p. 125.

48. Ann Barzel, *Ballet Annual #6*, p. 122; "Dance in Review," *Dance News*, December 1950, p. 9.

49. 1951-52 season—"Ballet Russe de Monte Carlo Opens U.S. Season," *Dance News*, October 1951, p. 3; John Martin, "Notes from the Field," *New York Times*, 30 September 1951; "Via the Grapevine," *Dance Magazine*, September 1951, p. 8, and November 1951, p. 1.

50. Houston—"Curtain of Tears for Danilova," *Dance Magazine*, February 1952, p. 3; Hubert Roussel, "In Homage to a Very Grand Theatre Lady and a Sage Audience," *Houston Post*, 1 January 1952.

51. Doris Hering, "The Season in Review," *Dance*, November 1949, p. 40.

52. Latin America—Patricia Fent Ross, "Notes from Mexico," *Dance Magazine*, October 1952, p. 57; advertisements in *La Esfera*, *El National*, and *El Universal*, Caracas, 19-30 September 1952.

8 REORGANIZA- TION (1954-1957)

WITH its intrigues and tearful leave-takings, the Ballet Russe de Monte Carlo was demoralized by the end of the 1951-52 season and much of its old prestige had vanished. Denham sought a total reorganization of the Ballet Russe on a grand scale and called a halt to most company activities. Instead of a Ballet Russe de Monte Carlo with full corps de ballet and orchestra, there was a Ballet Russe de Monte Carlo Concert Company, which toured during the seasons of 1952-53 and 1953-54 under the auspices of Columbia Artists Management. This troupe of fifteen dancers, plus technical staff, did one-night stands by bus and truck with a single program consisting of *Swan Lake, Cirque de Deux, Bluebird,* and *Gaîté Parisienne.* Musical accompaniment was provided by two pianists, one of them the loyal and reliable Rachel Chapman. Sophie Pourmel, another old associate of the Ballet Russe, traveled along to oversee the wardrobe.

During the 1952-53 season the company was headed by Moscelyne Larkin, Anna Istomina, Roman Jasinski (who also served as ballet master), Victor Moreno, and Fernando Schaffenburg. The next season, the announced principals included Nina Novak, Larkin, Moreno, Jasinski, and Schaffenburg, but Larkin took maternity leave during the tour and was replaced by Gertrude Tyven. Ann Barzel saw the Concert Company in Park Ridge, Illinois, on 20 November 1952, and although admitting to a prejudice

153

against "truncated ballet," she was happy to discover that the troupe "managed to make a good impression."[1]

While the Concert Company was on the road, Julius Fleischmann was in Monte Carlo negotiating with local authorities about the possibility of re-establishing the full company in the Principality. He proposed that the Ballet Russe move there with most of its present dancers, give Christmas and Easter seasons in Monte Carlo, and tour for the rest of the year. Tamara Toumanova was mentioned as a possible ballerina. Fleischmann also tried to interest Sol Hurok in managing an American tour for the company in 1954. Although these negotiations were to no avail, they indicate that Denham and Fleischmann were trying to provide stability for the nomadic company, as did the establishment, at long last, of a Ballet Russe School in March 1954. Strictly speaking, the school was not completely new, the Ballet Russe having taken over the respected Swoboda School on West 57th Street. Faculty for the first term of the school under Ballet Russe supervision included Frederic Franklin, Marie Swoboda, Igor Schwezoff, Anatole Vilzak, Valerie Bettis, Leon Danielian, and Duncan Noble.[2]

The full-scale Ballet Russe de Monte Carlo returned to the scene for the 1954-55 season under Columbia Artists Management. Even before it had danced a step, the revived company attracted enormous interest. Of 179 dates that had been booked, 70 were guaranteed for $250,000, while the remaining 109 were expected to bring in something over $300,000. Because of the increasing costs and complications of rail travel, the personnel toured in buses, while scenery and costumes were carried in trucks as they had been for the Concert Company. Ballet Russe dancers say that the 1954-55 tour, which covered 20,127 miles by motorcade, was the first undertaken by a major ballet company in the now common bus-and-truck manner. Despite the extensive itinerary and rigorous touring schedule, the company was put up every night in hotel beds, never sleeping in transit, as sometimes occurred in the era of rail travel.[3]

Frederic Franklin returned as ballet master, and back with the company were several dancers from previous seasons. Yet many other dancers were new, and the company was predominantly young. Some Ballet Russe veterans maintain that the season of reorganization is the demarcation between the old (and for them, the real) Ballet Russe and what was, in effect, an entirely different company. Yet the new dancers were excited to be with the Ballet Russe simply because it was the Ballet Russe. For some, the Ballet Russe was the first company they had ever seen, the company that had inspired them to dance. As students, they had known and loved the repertoire. Now they were being given a chance to dance that repertoire. No wonder that there was a spirit of excitement and adventure about preparatory rehearsals. "We were in the Ballet Russe because we loved it," says Rochelle Zide, who was fifteen at the time.[4] "And we learned the repertoire fast. In one week alone Frederic Franklin taught us *Swan Lake, Sylphides, Gaîté, Nutcracker*, and *Scheherazade*. We had more spirit and energy than finesse, and there were extreme dichotomies in dancing style that season because we all came from different schools. But we were there because we wanted to be there."

Denham invited Salvador Dali to design a general front curtain for the company, but Dali never completed it. However, another of Denham's schemes did come to pass: he secured the National Symphony Orchestra of Washington, D.C., for the company's Washington and Baltimore performances, including opening night 1 October 1954.[5] On that night also occurred the first of the season's two world premieres, a ballet version of *The Mikado*, choreographed by Antonia Cobos to an arrangement of Sir Arthur Sullivan's music by Vittorio Rieti. Baltimore critic Weldon Wallace considered the reorganized company's debut an important occasion, but thought the new ballet made only "a modest entrance into the world of the theater." Audiences, however, seemed to enjoy *The Mikado*. It remained around for several seasons, although critics complained that the story was not well told. P. W. Manchester labeled the ballet "simply a divertissement arranged to some famous music." On the other hand, Harry MacArthur, a Washington critic who liked Cobos's ballet, detected a story of sorts—as much of a story, at any rate, as he thought a ballet needed:

> Even to one unfamiliar with "The Mikado" . . . the general outlines of the action must have been clear. It is obvious in this ballet "Mikado" that a young fellow in a black wig and a girl in another black wig are smitten on sight. It is further obvious that their mutual yen is painful to three sinister parties, one of who [sic] is wearing a bright blue wig instead of the conventional black.
>
> There probably isn't much more you need to know about the plot of a ballet, since this is one corner of the theatrical arts where the playing rather than the play . . . is the thing. The Ballet Russe "Mikado" was executed with both skill and spirit.
> . . .

Ann Barzel defended Cobos's sketchy approach to dramatization: if Cobos "merely hung amusing, stylised dances on to the highly danceable music . . . this may make it a longer lasting ballet, one to see again for the ever-interesting dancing rather than for a borrowed literary content which soon loses point."⁶

The other new ballet of the season brought Léonide Massine back to the Ballet Russe. For one thing, it was legally convenient for him to be in America. A naturalized citizen, he had been residing abroad. Immigration policies, however, required that naturalized citizens return to the United States every five years in order to retain citizenship. Denham had been writing Massine conciliatory letters, assuring him "that our organization is the only one Russian organization that remains today and which is still carrying the flag of good taste and love for the great traditions." At first, Denham and Massine envisioned presenting, with new décor by George Rouault, the American premiere of *Laudes Evangelii,* a dance pageant created in Italy in 1952 that retold the story of the life of Christ from the Annunciation to the Resurrection. But the dimensions of this work, which required thirty dancers, twenty-four supers, and a chorus of ninety, obviously made it impracticable for a touring company.

Massine settled instead upon a symphonic ballet to Berlioz's *Harold in Italy.* Oddly enough, in the last dance column he wrote before induction into the armed forces in World War II, Robert Lawrence hoped that Massine would one day choreograph that score. Now, more than a decade later, his wish was coming true.⁷ Scheduled for a premiere in Washington, D.C., the first performance was canceled because of an injury to Frederic Franklin, who had been cast as Harold. The ballet was delayed until the company reached Boston in the middle of October. There, the date of the first night was again changed, the premiere finally occurring 14 October 1954, with Leon Danielian assuming the title role at two days' notice.

Choreographed in a style strange to younger dance-goers, *Harold in Italy* received mixed notices. Yet Ann Barzel praised it as "a grand-scale conception," and its presence in the repertoire made P.W. Manchester hope that, with the return of Massine's ballets, the company would once again attain distinction. In *Harold in Italy* she saw "the beginnings of a style" which, provided Massine and the dancers had opportunities to work together over a long period of time, might give the company " its own individual character."⁸ There was talk of further association with Massine and of producing his *Usher,* based on Poe and created for the Teatro Colón. But *Harold in Italy* was the final collaboration between Massine and the Ballet Russe.⁹

The new Ballet Russe was not yet a polished ensemble and performances that first season varied considerably. Boston critic Elliot Norton was appalled to behold "disappointing exhibitions by certain soloists and a generally ridiculous performance by a corps de ballet that was poorly trained and downright amateurish." Yet less than two weeks after Norton wrote that notice, an unsigned review in a Hartford paper said the Ballet Russe demonstrated "that if ballet is again to reach the golden pinnacle it attained in this country during the Thirties, this is the company that will lead the way to it" because of its "special attribute of style," as well as "technical skills and poise."[10]

The guest artist for the 1954-55 season was Maria Tallchief, who had been lured away from the New York City Ballet by a salary of $2000 a week, at that time an unheard-of sum.[11] "There I was," Tallchief recalls, "being offered this huge amount—more than I had ever made before. So I went to Balanchine and asked what to do, and he told me, take the money." Yet she found the tour "horrendous" because bus travel proved intolerable to her. She also says that she was annoyed because, on the inevitable triple-bill of *Swan Lake, Nutcracker,* and *Scheherazade,* she—a noted classicist—was often cast in the mimed role of Zobeide, while Nina Novak, a fine character and demi-caractère dancer, appeared as the Swan Queen.

Among the newcomers to the company was Irina Borowska, an Argentine dancer of Polish parentage who had been a member of the ballet at the Teatro Colón in Buenos Aires, where Massine discovered her. At Massine's recommendation, Denham accepted her into the Ballet Russe. "She is markedly different in style from the American dancers," said P.W. Manchester, "with a greater feeling for *épaulement* and the use of the arms, but not so clean and strong in the purely technical aspects. She would remind English audiences of the pre-war Ballet Russe."[12]

There was no New York season, but on 9 July 1955 the company appeared at Lewisohn Stadium, with Mia Slavenska as guest artist, drawing a record audience of 17,000 persons.[13] The company's well-wishers, and there were many, hoped along with Lillian Moore that the Ballet Russe had really undergone "a reformation and regeneration."[14]

Certain aspects of the 1955-56 season led observers to hope that this had indeed come to pass. If the dancing during the first season of reorganization was uneven because the ensemble was new, during this next season critics such as John Voorhees in

Seattle were to note that the "Ballet Russe has definitely acquired more spirit and more feeling of a company than shown in its lackluster appearances last season. There's more dash and excitement in the corps than last year (when it was more 'corpse' than 'corps')."[15]

The biggest excitement of the season was the presence of Alicia Alonso and Igor Youskevitch. The balletgoers who were surprised the previous season when Tallchief left the New York City Ballet to appear with the Monte Carlo were positively flabbergasted to learn that Alonso and Youskevitch had left Ballet Theatre to join the company, Alonso dividing her time between the Ballet Russe and her own company in Cuba, Youskevitch appearing with the Ballet Russe full-time and also bearing the title of artistic adviser. In 1955 Alonso and Youskevitch were probably the most famous couple in American ballet. A decade earlier, that distinction had belonged to Danilova and Franklin—the stars of the Ballet Russe. Now, the most famous couple in American ballet were again the stars of the Ballet Russe.

Youskevitch says he accepted Denham's offer to rejoin the company that had introduced him to America because he was starting to feel restless and thought he was being taken for granted at Ballet Theatre. The post of artistic adviser tempted him, for he was curious to try himself out as a director. Yet, though termed adviser, he was seldom called upon for advice, and he says that most of the advice he tried to give was never taken. "The Ballet Russe desperately needed revitalization in order to keep its standing among American companies," he says, "but whenever I suggested a new work or recommended refurbishing an old, Denham was reluctant to spend a penny. Costs of ballet production were going up and Denham hated to be financially extravagant."

If Youskevitch failed to help the company with direct advice, he and Alonso had an enormous influence upon the dancers through their sheer presence. Uniting imagination and intelligence with physical skill, they awed not only audiences, but their fellow dancers—who, impressed by their artistry, were inspired to dance at their own best level. Perfectionists, Alonso and Youskevitch even rehearsed together after performances were over, and each performance they gave was meticulously detailed and wholeheartedly danced. There was almost something supernatural about their rapport. Alonso, whose sight had long been impaired, was almost blind at the time and members of the corps were required to assist her to ensure that her entrances and exits were made without a hitch. Thus dancers posted offstage would snap fingers to indicate the direction of an exit or hold up will skirts so that she could see a white blur where the exit was. Yet she somehow always seemed to know what every other dancer on stage was doing, right or wrong. Los Angeles critic Patterson Greene summed up the electric quality of the two stars when he said,

> It seems there were two dancers.
> One was named Alicia Alonso. The other was named Igor Youskevitch.
> And whenever or wherever they danced, the world became perfectly wonderful.[16]

The most celebrated of their ballets was *Giselle,* and together they reworked the old Ballet Russe production, trying to strengthen it dramatically and to make motivation and stage business clear. Typical of their approach was their attitude toward Hilarion, who tends to be portrayed either as a scowling villain or as a fine young man of Giselle's own social class. Youskevitch, as producer, had somewhat different ideas about how Hilarion ought to be played. Hilarion, claims Youskevitch, feels superior to Albrecht because he is the head gamekeeper, whereas Albrecht, so far as he can tell, is a mere peasant. Rethinking his own role of Albrecht, Youskevitch invented many details, including a piece of business that has been widely imitated by danseurs ever since: When Hilarion rushes at Albrecht with a knife, Albrecht in a reflex action grabs for where his sword would be if he were wearing one. Hilarion is astonished: peasants don't wear swords, he thinks, so who can this fellow be? This sequence is now so common that it almost seems traditional. But Youskevitch swears that before he got the idea for it, he had never known any other danseur to do that bit of stage business.

The Alonso-Youskevitch *Giselle* was admired by John Martin for its unusual dramatic clarity, when he saw it in 1957. But Martin also added a faint warning about playing too fast and loose with the ballet: "There are . . . numerous accommodations of tempo, which are justifiable on practical rather than artistic grounds, and several choreographic alterations which at least do no harm."[17]

The season's major new production, though not a total success, seemed evidence that the company was again willing to stage serious ballets. In prospect, *La Dame à la Licorne* sounded exciting. Although its choreographer, Heinz Rosen (who had created the ballet in Munich in 1953), was virtually unknown in

America, the scenario and décor were by none other than Jean Cocteau, who adapted his designs from the unicorn tapestries in the Cluny Museum in Paris. Jacques Chailly's score was based upon troubadour songs, and one of Cocteau's conceits was to place a small group of musicians on stage, like a medieval consort. The ballet derived from the legend that unicorns eat only from the hand of a virgin. When a Lady becomes enamored of a Knight, her Unicorn dies. Rueful, the Lady spurns the Knight, and is left alone. A banner is then lowered bearing the enigmatic emblem that appears in the Cluny tapestries. *Mon seul désir.*

Youskevitch was the Knight; Nina Novak, the Unicorn. And Irina Borowska looked ravishing as the Lady (a role she had earlier danced at the Colón). The entire ballet was visually beautiful, and after its premiere (14 October 1955 in Toronto) Fraser Macdonald confidently declared that the "Ballet Russe de Monte Carlo has a masterpiece on its hands." When the company brought Rosen's ballet to Chicago, George Jackson, correspondent for England's *Ballet Today*, called it the "best new ballet seen in Chicago during 1955." Other critics were not so enthusiastic. P.W. Manchester was among the commentators who complained that the action "was strung out interminably so that each situation became boring long before the choreographer had finished with it." For Jackson, however, Rosen's "sparse use of movement" seemed "intentional and purposeful." That the ballet looked weak was because it "was not . . . given an ideal production. . . . The girls of the corps were not up to the split second timing which the choreography for the unicorns demands; Nina Novak's classic proportions were not suited for the role of the white unicorn. . . ."

Rochelle Zide agrees with the critics who called the ballet "absolutely endless." She also says that Rosen was "an odd man—he was a choreographer, yet he seemed to know little about dance. He moved us about as though he were a stage director—I could imagine him directing operas—and when he gave us technical things to do, they were strange: he wanted us to do things on pointe that were impossible. Not things that were difficult or challenging, but things that were literally impossible, things that could ruin your feet."[18]

More gratifying to the dancers was Balanchine's Minkus *Pas de Trois*. It joined *Bluebird*, the *Don Quixote* pas de deux, and *Black Swan* (which the company usually billed as *Pas de Deux Classique*) as one of the virtuoso showpieces that could be added to a mixed bill. Staged for the company by Michel Katcharoff, who had learned it while serving as guest régisseur for the de Cuevas

Ballet, it was usually performed by Gertrude Tyven, Yvonne Chouteau, and the young American danseur, Alan Howard, who, with "exceptional elevation and beats, carried off special honours," according to Ann Barzel. [19]

The 1955-56 tour, which began 9 October in Newark and ended 14 April in Philadelphia, was an unusually long and an unusually successful one, the Ballet Russe doing better at the box office nationally than any other ballet company that season, with the exception of the visiting Sadler's Wells. The Christmas season in Chicago—where the Ballet Russe was always welcome— amassed a whopping $77,021.74 gross. [20] Yet, despite the electrifying presence of Alonso and Youskevitch and an attempt to produce new works, the Ballet Russe still seemed worrisome to critics who saw it on its travels. If John Voorhees detected an improvement in the corps and was forced to acknowledge that the Ballet Russe drew larger audiences in Seattle than the New York City Ballet did, he nevertheless had the impression that the Ballet Russe was living in the past.

Doris Hering was similarly bothered by the company's lack of firm artistic direction: "The element that moulds a group of dancers into a ballet company is a point of view—a consistent esthetic base from which all of the dancers, no matter how individual, are required to work. It is a long time since the Ballet Russe de Monte Carlo has had this base. Instead, it allows its dancers to pursue the path of 'uncontrolled eclecticism.' " Thus, said Hering, at one performance she saw four ballerinas, all talented, but "all looking as though they had descended upon the company from different epochs in the history of dance." There was Gertrude Tyven, with "a fundamentally simple, athletic, contemporary style. But she is still dancing in the shadow of Danilova." Nina Novak, on the other hand, "clings to an approximation of the late Nineteenth Century Russian style, with the bent knee arabesque and a determined brittleness of attack." In such company, Irina Borowska seemed an anachronism because, though young, she had the "slightly exaggerated line of the Ballet Russe style of the Nineteen Thirties." And then there was Alicia Alonso, a "dancing body performing as a glorious and natural extension of the music." [21]

Eyebrows were raised when Nina Novak declared that she was leaving the company at the end of the season because of her "dissatisfaction with the quality and quantity of her roles in the repertoire." But two months after she made her pronouncement, *Dance News* reported that her differences with the management had been amicably resolved. [22]

During the summer of 1956 the company played such outdoor theatres as Lewisohn Stadium, Red Rocks, Ravinia, and the Greek Theatre. It was for one of these, Washington, D.C.'s Carter Barron Amphitheatre, that Leon Danielian choreographed his first ballet, *Sombreros,* which was premiered 18 June 1956. Danielian recalls that Denham decided he would risk a new work in Washington and wondered whether Danielian cared to try his hand at choreography. Later that night, a friend played some Mexican music on the phonograph and Danielian got the idea for a Mexican ballet, a suite that offered romantic and humorous dances in a blending of ballet and Mexican folk styles. *Sombreros*'s music consisted of folk tunes orchestrated by the company's conductor, Ivan Boutnikoff.

As often happened at the Ballet Russe, Danielian was given only a short time in which to get the ballet ready—"twelve minutes and two blinks of an eye," he jokes. But he was pleased with his cast, led by Irina Borowska and Deni Lamont, and critics who saw the ballet during the next few seasons were also pleased. "Altogether a pleasing work," declared Ann Barzel. John Martin found it had "quality and invention and a gentle humor and a manifestly creative attitude to its every detail. If Mr. Danielian can do this the first time, he should be able to do even better the next time. . ."[23]

With the 1956-57 season the Ballet Russe parted company with Columbia Artists and the tour, beginning 21 October 1956, was booked by the company's old friend David Libidins in collaboration with Kenneth Allen Associates. Frederic Franklin was absent from that tour, having left to join his former Ballet Russe colleagues Alexandra Danilova, Sonja (Taanila) Tyven, and Robert Lindgren for a tour of South Africa. The first major stop for the Ballet Russe was a two-week season in Chicago, beginning Christmas night.[24]

En route to Chicago, company member Salvador Juarez made his choreographic debut by premiering a ballet in South Bend, Indiana, 15 December 1956. *Tragedy in Calabria,* set to themes from Leoncavallo's *Pagliacci,* re-enacted the love triangle from that opera, with Juarez, Nina Novak, and Alan Howard as the unhappy commedia dell' arte players. Trying to be fair, a local critic called the ballet "stilted," yet immediately added that he thought it "nicely put together" with "good opportunities for both solo and ensemble work." But when the ballet received its first Chicago performance, Claudia Cassidy let it be known that "I can't think of a better word than ludicrous to describe 'Tragedy in Calabria,' an unbelievably amateurish raid on Leoncavallo's 'Pagliacci' which the Ballet Russe de Monte Carlo charged money for in the Civic Opera House. . . ."[25]

Another ballet, Boris Romanoff's *Harlequinade*, received its premiere in Chicago on 27 December 1956. *Harlequinade* was an adaptation of Drigo's *Les Millions d'Arlequin* which, choreographed by Petipa, was presented at St. Petersburg's Hermitage Theatre in 1900. Romanoff had choreographed an earlier *Harlequinade* for his Théâtre Romantique Russe which toured Europe in the 1920s, and in 1965 George Balanchine did his own *Harlequinade* for the New York City Ballet. All versions tell the same basic story about the attempts of Harlequin, aided by the Good Fairy, to win Columbine from Pantalon. Romanoff, a pupil of Fokine in St. Petersburg, had choreographed *La Tragédie de Salome* for Diaghilev and for many years was ballet master of the Metropolitan Opera. Eugene Slavin remembers him as a nervous, high-strung man who yelled a lot. Meredith Baylis says he used to make dancers giggle irreverently because of his love of using a dime-store toy department frog clicker as a sort of metronome to set rhythms in rehearsal and when he taught classes. A limited amount of time in which to put the ballet together forced him to work under great pressure, and the ballet was still not quite finished at the premiere, the dancers filling in details of characterization and choreography on their own.

Nevertheless, says Rochelle Zide, "he used all the people in the cast very well, he really used them as individuals. Eugene Slavin was a wonderful Pierrot and Romanoff capitalized on all of Youskevitch's charm as Harlequin. And Alonso! Romanoff used her beautifully as Columbine. She was such a fine adagio dancer that I never realized how well she could jump until Romanoff made one of her solos a jump-variation. She had a wonderful jump, very light, she could cover the stage with her elevation." Miguel Terekhov received a good character role as Pantalon, and Rochelle Zide and Dorothy Daniels charmed audiences as two little Blackamoors who sat at the side of the stage, commenting upon the action.

Designed by Rolf Gérard, with some costumes borrowed from Eugène Berman's *Devil's Holiday* and *Bourgeois Gentilhomme, Harlequinade* was greeted with enthusiastic applause. Those who liked it liked it because, as Ann Barzel said, Romanoff "was successful in setting a period style and in providing the dancers with usable dance material." Audiences who found commedia dell' arte revelry too sweet for their taste were less amused.

Claudia Cassidy acknowledged that the ballet was a pastiche, but added that, in her opinion, "Pastiche is a polite word for hodgepodge, or, in the vernacular, 'This is really a mess.' I'm afraid they all apply to 'Harlequinade.' " When P.W. Manchester encountered *Harlequinade* later that season, all she saw in it were "interminable jolly jigglings by an ensemble of merrymakers who do not have anything in particular to be merry about."

When asked to compare Romanoff's *Harlequinade* with Balanchine's, Meredith Baylis used a phrase similar to one employed by Claudia Cassidy. "Romanoff's *Harlequinade* was nothing like Balanchine's, except for the story," she said. "Romanoff's was an archaic hodgepodge, terribly heavy-handed Russianized commedia dell' arte." However, she did add that that was how it looked to her at the time. "Romanoff himself," she said, "seemed terribly ancient to me. Since I was only in my 20s, almost everybody seemed ancient to me, then. Now that I'm older, I'm more tolerant."[26]

By the mid-1950s two prominent Chicago critics, Ann Barzel and Claudia Cassidy, had developed radically different ideas about the state of the Ballet Russe. Sanguine in her attitudes, Barzel observed the Chicago season and concluded that the Ballet Russe was dancing "in a thoroughly professional manner. Giving an honest performance is really the greatest compliment performers can pay their audiences and everyone in Ballet Russe is obviously interested in what he is doing and, moreover, knows what he is doing." In contrast, after observing that same season, Cassidy declared, "We are brazenly told that such goings-on 'keep the great tradition alive.' Well, there always was a fate worse than death."[27] Audiences must have agreed with Barzel. Once again, the Ballet Russe broke box office records at the Civic Opera House (grossing $102,000) and, said Barzel, "the greatest demonstration since Callas sang Lucia was given Alicia Alonso and Igor Youskevitch after a *Giselle* greater than the great ones that have gone before." Growing awareness of, and interest in, Soviet ballet led Alonso to stress the arched back and fluid arms of the Soviets, and she and Youskevitch added high Soviet lifts to their pas de deux.[28]

The company traveled on, reaching Canada in the spring of 1957. On 8 April the bus and truck fleet, delayed on the highway, arrived late in Montreal. Therefore the program that night was late in starting. In a sense, the program was also early in ending, for at 11:30 p.m., halfway through *Le Beau Danube*, the curtain came down. The curtain fell at that precise moment because if it had stayed up one minute longer, the management would have had to grant overtime payment to the dancers, stage-hands, and musicians. Outraged, Igor Youskevitch attracted the attention of Canadian newspapers and American dance pub-lications by threatening to resign from the company and by di-vulging that, far from being an isolated incident, the cutting— indeed, the brutal curtailment—of ballets occurred "at least once a month."[29]

Few practices of the Ballet Russe have received more justifiably adverse criticism than that of abridging ballets or of bringing down a curtain during a ballet simply to avoid overtime payments. It occasionally happened in the earlier days of the com-pany. In the later days, when mounting expenses made penny-pinching necessary, it happened often. "It happened more often than I care to admit," says Rochelle Zide. "Sometimes it happened once a week." There was one program of *Swan Lake, Sombreros,* and *Coppélia* in Mobile, Alabama, when, as Zide records in her diary, "We really ran late, so Nina's 2nd & 3rd Act Variations, Prayer, Dawn, and Alan's variation were cut." On fortunately rare occasions, *Beau Danube* came to an end before the "Blue Danube Waltz." The most frequently cut ballet was *Gaîté Parisienne,* which had three possible early endings: just before the barcarolle, at the splits in the can-can, and, if the program happened to be drasti-cally overlong, at the end of the waltz just before the can-can. At one *Graduation Ball* performance, in order to save time, Denham ordered the pas de deux cut. Yet while he relayed his commands to the dancers, he forgot to tell the musicians, who struck up the pas de deux music at the proper time. Since no one appeared for the pas de deux, the dancers on stage were forced to improvise a scene of their own.

Since Denham in the late years refused to countenance overtime, why, then, did he plan programs that had a chance of going beyond 11:30? Régisseur Michel Katcharoff believes that several factors were involved in this. Although he hated to pay anyone extra, Denham did sincerely want to give his audiences their money's worth. Moreover, local managers in requesting bal-lets had no idea how long certain works were. The Ballet Russe toured at a time when the triple-bill was standard. A program containing less than three works was considered skimpy by some managers. *Coppélia,* in particular, posed difficulties. Managers insisted upon regarding it as a single entity, similar to any ordinary one-act ballet, rather than as a work consisting of three long acts. Eventually, Denham might agree to lengthy programs, but he always demanded that the curtain go up promptly. If ballets were truncated, that was because they occurred on long programs that started late. Sometimes weather or traffic conditions made the company unavoidably late in arriving at a theatre. The most annoying occasions, however, were those in communities where ballet performances were also social events at which the curtain might be held until some prominent citizen had taken his seat. In one city, the curtain was held for more than half an hour until the arrival of the mayor, who, all that time, was fully visible enjoying a leisurely dinner in a restaurant across the street from the theatre. By making headlines, Youskevitch called national attention to a deplorable practice. It was not the only time that season that a curtailed ballet got into the news.[30]

During the spring of 1957, the Ballet Russe returned to New York for its first season at the Metropolitan Opera House since 1950—and what would also be its last season there, ever. In terms of attendance and intake, the 21 April-4 May engagement broke all records for an American ballet company at the Met, gross receipts amounting to $150,445.[31] New Yorkers were introduced to such ballets as *La Dame à la Licorne, Harlequinade, Sombreros,* and *The Mikado.* Alonso and Youskevitch were rapturously received. And critics saw great promise in some of the younger dancers. Of Alan Howard, John Martin wrote that he "has a remarkable technical facility, and can, indeed, do everything in the book. He has some postural problems, however, that need serious attention, and as yet he has not learned the performer's secret of inward quiet and command."[32]

In some ways it was just like old times. Alexandra Danilova, Frederic Franklin, and Leon Danielian returned as guest artists, Danilova's opening-night entrance in *Gaîté Parisienne* stopping the show for several minutes, as it always had. She danced with extraordinary energy in *Gaîté* and *Beau Danube,* and fans fell in love with her all over again.

Yet, for two reasons, that Met engagement was not entirely a happy time for her. Realizing that her dancing career was drawing to a close, she hoped that during the season Denham would grant her a gala New York farewell performance. Denham refused. To this day, she does not know why.

Another Ballet Russe dancer, upon hearing this story, pondered a moment, then speculated, "As long as the Ballet Russe never formally announced a farewell performance by her, Danilova was always, at least potentially, a part of the company. She may not have danced with it for years; she might never dance with it again. Yet the Ballet Russe could still be 'Danilova's company.' Once she officially retired, that tie would be broken forever."

Danilova's second reason for being unhappy was that on 30 April 1957 Denham ordered the curtain down on *Gaîté Parisienne* before the ballet had ended, although the Met was crowded to standing room with an audience that had come to see Danilova as the Glove Seller. As usual, the reason was a reluctance to pay overtime. Danilova called the action "amateurish, unprofessional." Denham tried to convince reporters that he had used an "alternate finale" that was "artistically sound" and that he had even heard some audience members say that the short version constituted a "good ending."[33]

Few balletgoers concurred. It was this sort of thing that made John Martin complain, "At present the company is definitely a road-show company; it has cut everything down to the irreducible minimum. . . . The physical productions with few exceptions are poor and shoddy. The general style of the dancing is coarse-grained and often appears to have been scaled to Yankee Stadium." Yet on the occasions in which such scaling did not occur, Martin was pleased that the company's "unusually good" corps was still able to "take on variations of style."

The company's style was starting to disturb critics. Increasingly, it seemed to be losing stylistic distinctiveness until now, according to Walter Terry, it had "no particular style, nothing which says 'we are the Ballet Russe and this is our special quality.' " Agreeing, Doris Hering thought this was because

> the dancers have been allowed to go their own way. They are neither motivated nor inspired by any discernable artistic direction. They just simply dance.
>
> And they do so with the open heartiness that one associates with that typically American theatre form, the musical comedy. They jump as high as they can. They czardas as hard as they can. They turn as multiply as they can. The result is overly emphatic. But it is curiously heartwarming. For secretly we all like to know that performers are giving their utmost.

"They just simply dance," she said. For five seasons more, the Ballet Russe de Monte Carlo would do just that. It would just simply dance, often with heartwarming results. Yet this very energy could also make the dancers seem pathetic. For (to quote Hering once more) "they are a gallant and often gifted group. They richly deserve a more inspired artistic framework."[34] Unfortunately, during those five last seasons, the Ballet Russe consistently lacked such a framework.

NOTES FOR CHAPTER 8

1. Concert Company—"Footnotes on the Dancing Scene," *Dance Magazine,* November 1952; Ann Barzel, "Ballet Russe de Monte Carlo Concert Company," *Dance News,* January 1953, p. 9; conversations with Moscelyne Larkin and Roman Jasinski.
2. Plans—"Ballet Russe de Monte Carlo May Return to Original Home," *Dance News,* February 1953, p. 1; John Martin, "The Dance: Futures," *New York Times,* 14 March 1954.
3. Tour—"Ballet Russe de Monte Carlo Slated for Strong Comeback," *Dance News,* September 1953, p. 1; "The Sitter Out," *The Dancing Times,* November 1954, p. 76; company brochure 1955-56 season.
4. Conversation with Rochelle Zide. Henceforth all statements for which no printed source is given were made in conversation with the author.
5. "Ballet Russe de Monte Carlo Adds to Cast," *Dance News,* September 1954, p. 1; John Martin, "The Dance: Revival," *New York Times,* 12 September 1954.
6. *The Mikado*—Weldon Wallace, "Balletomanes Out en Masse at Premiere of 'The Mikado,' " *Baltimore Sun,* 2 October 1954; P.W. Manchester, "Ballet Russe de Monte Carlo," *Dance News,* November 1954, p. 7; Harry MacArthur, "Sorry, W.S., Ballet Russe 'Mikado' Is Lively Stuff," *Washington Evening Star,* 5 October 1954; Ann Barzel, *Ballet Annual #10,* p. 118.
7. Massine—Léonide Massine, *My Life in Ballet,* p. 247; Letter from S.J. Denham, to Léonide Massine, 2 July 1953; Letter from Léonide Massine to S.J. Denham, 1 October 1953; Robert Lawrence, "Ballet Farewell," *New York Herald-Tribune,* 20 June 1943.
8. *Harold in Italy*—Ann Barzel, *Ballet Annual #10,* p. 118; P.W. Manchester, "Ballet Russe de Monte Carlo," *Dance News,* November 1954, p. 7.
9. "Rosen to Choreo For Ballet Russe de Monte Carlo," *Dance News,* September 1955, p. 1.
10. Elliot Norton, "Public Badly Treated by Ballet Russe," *Boston Globe,* 17 October 1954; "Ballet Russe Is Splendid at Bushnell," *Hartford Courant,* 30 October 1954.
11. Walter Terry, *Dance: A New Guide to the Liveliest Art,* p. 172.
12. Saul Goodman, "Irina Borowska," *Dance Magazine,* October 1955, p. 35; P.W. Manchester, in A.H. Franks, *Ballet: A Decade of Endeavour,* p. 55.
13. "In the News," *Dance Magazine,* August 1955, p. 4.
14. Lillian Moore, in A.H. Franks, *Ballet: A Decade of Endeavour,* p. 55.
15. John Voorhees, "Thoughts on Ballet Russe," *Seattle Post-Intelligencer,* 24 January 1956.
16. Alonso and Youskevitch—"Alonso, Youskevitch Move to Ballet Russe de Monte Carlo," *Dance News,* June 1955, p. 1; Patterson Greene, "Alicia, Igor Spell Perfection," *Los Angeles Examiner,* 12 February 1959; conversations with Meredith Baylis, Yvonne Chouteau, Eugene Slavin, Igor Youskevitch.
17. *Giselle*—John Martin, "Ballet: Monte Carlo Troupe Back," *New York Times,* 22 April 1957; conversation with Igor Youskevitch.
18. *La Dame à la Licorne*—"Ballet Russe de Monte Carlo Adds to Cast," *Dance*

News, September 1954, p. 1; George Jackson, "Chicago," *Ballet Today,* April 1956, p. 9; Fraser Macdonald, "Toronto Has Two Premieres; New Troupe; New Production," *Dance News,* November 1955, p. 3; P.W. Manchester, "The Season in Review," *Dance News,* June 1957, p. 9; conversation with Rochelle Zide.

19. *Pas de Trois*—Ann Barzel, *Ballet Annual #11,* p. 130; conversation with Michel Katcharoff.

20. Ann Barzel, *Ballet Annual #11,* pp. 129-130; "Chicago-ings On," *Dance News,* March 1956, p. 6.

21. John Voorhees, "Thoughts on Ballet Russe," *Seattle Post-Intelligencer,* 24 January 1956; Doris Hering, "Reviews," *Dance Magazine,* August 1956, p. 3.

22. "Novak to Leave Ballet Russe," *Dance News,* November 1955, p. 3; "Nina Novak Will Not Leave Troupe," *Dance News,* January 1956, p. 4.

23. *Sombreros*—Ann Barzel, *Ballet Annual #12,* p. 133; John Martin, "The Dance: Summing Up," *New York Times,* 5 May 1957; conversation with Leon Danielian.

24. 1956-57—"Libidins, Allen to Book Ballet Russe," *Dance News,* January 1956, p. 1; "Dance Scene USA," *Dance Magazine,* November 1956, p. 6; "Dancers Overseas," *The Dancing Times,* August 1956, p. 631; Irving Sabolosky, "Ballet Russe to Open Yule Night," *Chicago Daily News,* 24 November 1956.

25. *Tragedy in Calabria*—Frank A. Schmidt, " 'Swan Lake' Sparks Ballet Presentation," *South Bend Tribune,* 16 December 1956; Claudia Cassidy, "On the Aisle," *Chicago Tribune,* 3 January 1957.

26. *Harlequinade*—Ann Barzel, " 'Harlequinade' Holds Promise," *Chicago American,* 28 December 1956; Claudia Cassidy, "On the Aisle," *Chicago Tribune,* 28 December 1956; P.W. Manchester, "The Season in Review," *Dance News,* June 1957, p. 9; conversations with Meredith Baylis, Eugene Slavin, Rochelle Zide.

27. Ann Barzel, "Ballet Russe Shows Professional Ease," *Chicago American,* 27 December 1956; Claudia Cassidy, "On the Aisle," *Chicago Tribune,* 31 December 1956.

28. Ann Barzel, "Ballet Russe de Monte Carlo," *Dance News,* February 1957, p. 8; *Ballet Annual #12,* pp. 133-135; "Ballet Russe Met Season," *Dance Magazine,* March 1957, p. 3.

29. "Attitudes and Arabesques," *Dance News,* May 1957, p. 8; "Curtain Is 12 Minutes Early, Ballet Russe Dancer Quits," *Toronto Globe and Mail,* 12 April 1957.

30. Curtains—Rochelle Zide, unpublished diary entry for 8 March 1957; conversations with Michel Katcharoff, Gilbert Reed, Igor Youskevitch, Rochelle Zide.

31. 1957-58 souvenir book; "Ballet Russe Bulletins," *Dance Magazine,* June 1957, p. 3.

32. John Martin, "The Dance: Summing Up," *New York Times,* 5 May 1957.

33. *Gaîté Parisienne*—"Ballet Russe Bulletins," *Dance Magazine,* June 1957, p. 3; Walter Terry, "Met Curtain Rung Down as Ballet Runs Overtime," *New York Herald-Tribune,* 2 May 1957.

34. Reviews—John Martin, "The Dance: Summing Up," *New York Times,* 5 May 1957; Walter Terry, "Ballet Summary; Phoenix Premieres," *New York Herald-Tribune,* 12 May 1957; Doris Hering, "Reviews," *Dance Magazine,* June 1957, pp. 14, 87.

9 THE LAST YEARS (1957-1962)

AFTER 1957 occurs the steady and irreversible decline of the Ballet Russe de Monte Carlo. The artistic direction became increasingly uncertain and the company waned in importance. Yet up to the end there were good performances by gallant and talented dancers. If there were no major additions to the repertoire during the company's final years, there nevertheless were new ballets; and if their quality varied considerably and none proved of lasting value, a few, in their unassuming way, were genuinely pleasant. Two such works were offered at the beginning of the 1957-58 season.

Nina Novak's *Variations Classiques* received its premiere on 6 October 1957 at the University of Puerto Rico. The ballet, Novak's first attempt at choreography, was one of the company's contributions to the Casals Festival, at which it had been invited to perform for a week beginning 3 October. An abstraction to Brahms's "Variations on a Theme of Handel," orchestrated by Ivan Boutnikoff, *Variations Classiques* attracted favorable attention for its taste, simplicity, and lack of bombast. Later that season Doris Hering wrote, "Unlike most neophyte choreographers confronted with Romantic music, Miss Novak keeps her approach essentially modest and brisk. . . . The ballet's twelve variations were clear in dance material and pleasingly symmetrical to the eye. The rhythmic base tended at times to be rigid, and the work lacked a positive climax. But for a first attempt, it was laudable."[1] Although other critics echoed these sentiments and encouraged Novak to continue choreographing, *Variations Classiques* was to be her only ballet for the company, except for a little pas de deux in 1961.

The company's annual American tour got underway 18 October 1957, in Hartford, at which performance Leon Danielian's second ballet, *The Mazurka*, was presented. Set to pieces by Chopin, Tchaikovsky, and Strauss, arranged by Boutnikoff, the ballet was a ballroom suite offering a portrait of the many facets of the mazurka. Originally, Danielian wanted to intensify the illusion of a ballroom by having all the music played on stage by a pianist. But he was advised that audiences would not accept a ballet accompanied only by a piano. Today, Danielian muses, "Who knows? If they had let me have the piano, I might have done an Eliot Feld ballet before there were any Eliot Feld ballets." (Ironically, in 1975 Feld choreographed his own *Mazurka*, set to mazurkas by Chopin for solo piano.) After its premiere, Hartford critic George W. Stowe said he thought Danielian's ballet had "snap and vigor," although he thought the performance "marred by considerable imprecision." By the time the Ballet Russe reached Chicago the following spring, the imprecision apparently had vanished, for Ann Barzel praised Danielian's work because it possessed the "dash and style of his own dancing."[2]

Alonso and Youskevitch appeared for part of the 1957-58 season, as did Yvette Chauviré (who danced the classics and *The Dying Swan*). Two former members of the Ballet Russe, Tatiana Grantzeva and George Zoritch, rejoined the company. Zoritch was to demonstrate over the next few years that he was "the perfect cavalier" (to quote Walter Terry). For Ann Barzel, Zoritch's "great elegance was the backbone of the classics." New to the company in 1957 were two Polish dancers, Edmund Novak (Nina Novak's brother) and his wife, Irina Kovalska. They were both essentially character dancers, and Edmund Novak's roles included Dr. Coppelius. Except for three performances at the Brooklyn Academy of Music in October, there was no New York season. As always, however, there was an extended Chicago engagement (7-13 April 1958), on the basis of which Ann Barzel reluctantly had to admit that the Ballet Russe appeared to be having "the least auspicious season of its career."[3]

It was in Chicago that Nina Novak danced her first *Giselle* (with Alan Howard as Albrecht). Barzel thought it "honest and creditable." Yet it was also, as George Jackson put it, "a novel characterization," for "Nina Novak's Giselle is far from frail and shy;

she is almost bold in her loving and dancing." This strong-mindedness bothered Doris Hering when she saw Novak's Giselle the following season: "Gestures were immediate, rather than evocative. Character development was monochromatic."[4]

Hering made these remarks after watching the company dance 25 October 1958 at the Brooklyn Academy of Music at the start of its 1958-59 tour. On this occasion, Hering called attention to several problems that were plaguing the company, including "Economics and the vicissitudes of touring" which

> have made the Ballet Russe de Monte Carlo lose sight of the fact that ballet is a theatre art. The physical elements of their two New York performances were neglected to the point of drabness.
>
> But dancers have a sweet obliviousness of their own. Most of them—and especially the corps—romped through *Coppélia* and waltzed through *Giselle* as though the sets weren't wrinkled, the lighting wasn't funereal, the props weren't makeshift. In fact, despite a certain beginning-of-the-season raggedness, the corps were often the most heartening part of the performances.

Hering was also disturbed by the company's casting policy: "The major classical roles fall to Nina Novak, despite the fact that she is not a classical dancer."[5]

Alonso and Youskevitch were back with the company, and Tatiana Grantzeva was appointed régisseur, replacing Michel Katcharoff, who had gone to work with Ruth Page's group.[6] Although the souvenir book made much of the fact that 1958 marked the company's twentieth anniversary and dwelt nostalgically upon past productions, the new works scheduled for the anniversary year were modest in proportions.

Two were presented during a 24 December 1958-4 January 1959 Chicago engagement. Once again, Tchaikovsky's *Romeo and Juliet* served as a star vehicle, this time for Alonso and Youskevitch, who appeared in a version by Alberto Alonso that reduced the action of Shakespeare's tragedy to a dramatic pas de deux, first performed 26 December 1958. "The dancing was inspired," Ann Barzel reported, but the choreography received even less praise than Constantin Nepo's staging for Chauviré, Claudia Cassidy scorning it as "a tawdry makeshift."[7]

The other novelty, Edmund Novak's *Springtime* (premiered 29 December 1958), was also a pas de deux—a duet for Nina Novak and Eugene Collins to a score commissioned from

Hazel Archibald Draper, a Boston patron of the Ballet Russe. The music, which Ann Barzel found "not particularly inspiring," was supposedly part of an evening-long ballet that Draper was composing for the company. (As it turned out, nothing more from this projected work was ever staged by the Ballet Russe.) Whatever choreographic interest *Springtime* had was due to its use of the Soviet acrobatic tricks that had started to fascinate Western dancers. But while audiences applauded Novak flinging herself from a great distance at Collins, "the piece was not yet in a condition to be appraised for its choreographic merit" (said Barzel).[8]

Despite the absence of substantial new works, the Ballet Russe again broke records at Chicago's Civic Opera House, drawing $115,767.15, which topped all ballet engagements there except for the Royal Ballet. Barzel detected "a new silky loveliness" in Alonso's dancing, while Nina Novak, "spurred by the presence of great stars, did the best dancing of her career. . . ."[9]

If *Springtime* reflected interest in Soviet virtuosity, the season's third new work, Edmund Novak's *Slavonic Dances* (to a potpourri of Slavic pieces), appears to have been inspired by the success of such folk dance troupes as the Moiseyev and the Beryozhka on their first American tours. Like *Springtime*, the imitation did not have the impact of the real thing. After its premiere 25 January 1959 in Seattle, John Voorhees said, "Though trying to achieve a kind of carefree atmosphere, as opposed to more formal ballet, Novak wound up with formless but frenzied activity that became extremely tiresome to watch. . . . At times it looked like total improvisation."[10]

During the summer of 1959 the Ballet Russe was invited to appear in Central Park at the Wollman Memorial Rink, which had been turned into a theatre-in-the-round. With Alonso, Youskevitch, Nathalie Krassovska, and Leon Danielian as guests, the company offered a repertoire consisting of *Swan Lake, Variations Classiques, Gaîté Parisienne, Les Sylphides, Sombreros, Nutcracker,* and various pas de deux, 10-16 August. Each of these ballets had to be specially adapted for arena staging, the task of arranging them going to Nina Novak, who, in John Martin's opinion, did "A first-rate job."[11]

Successful though that summer engagement was, the attitude of a growing number of critics toward the company was that expressed in a headline that appeared in a Pittsburgh newspaper: "Ballet Russe Pleases But Not Overmuch."[12]

There was only one new work during 1959-60, Jan

Cieplinski's *Ballad,* to a score commissioned from Los Angeles composer and critic Herbert Donaldson. An experienced choreographer and ballet master, Cieplinski had danced with the Pavlova and Diaghilev companies and had choreographed in his native Poland and for such companies throughout the world as the Royal Swedish Ballet, the Budapest State Opera Ballet, and the Ballet of the Teatro Colón in Buenos Aires before opening a New York studio in 1959. Despite his background, his first work for an American company was considered disappointing, although after its premiere in Pittsburgh, 24 October 1959, local critic Donald Steinfirst did say, "Its music is interesting and its choreography is modern in concept, yet with a classical base."

Essentially, *Ballad* was nothing more than an extended pas de trois in which Nina Novak, George Zoritch, and Alan Howard tried to sustain a poetic mood. However, just what specific mood this mood was supposed to be was left annoyingly vague. Claudia Cassidy described the action after seeing *Ballad* in Chicago:

> George Zoritch and Alan Howard hold Nina Novak as high aloft as they can manage, and she has one leg thrust even higher. She is dressed in pink coverall tights hung with scarlet scarves and streamers. . . .
>
> The men leave the stage and Miss Novak scampers around wildly, streamers waving in the breeze. The men return and all engage in emotional calisthenics, with serpentine arms, heaving chests, and gleaming glances. Finally the men heave Miss Novak aloft, and all retire.

Sharing Cassidy's opinion, Ann Barzel also faulted *Ballad* for its lack of clarity and logic and thought that among its silly touches was the way, when one man danced with Novak, the other was required to pose on stage, although it was never clear "whether he was sulking, brooding, or politely waiting his turn."[13]

Nathalie Krassovska returned for the entire season and when she appeared as Giselle in Houston, Herbert Roussel praised her for "an utterly pure and beautiful interpretation. . . . Dancing with a new maturity of concept and plasticity of phrase, Krassovska, with her rare physical beauty and inner grace, was a completely poetic and immaculate performer. . . ."[14]

Another unusual interpretation of a classic occurred during the company's 25 December 1959 - 3 January 1960 season in Chicago. It was on 26 December, in a performance headed by Alonso and Youskevitch, that Ann Barzel said she saw for the first time by an American company a version of *Swan Lake* in which

Odette and Siegfried danced their adagio without the assistance of Benno. The elimination of Benno from Ivanov's adagio is now standard practice, but in the late 1950s only the Soviets dispensed with him. Barzel applauded the change, scorning Benno as a "fifth wheel" and praising Alonso and Youskevitch for having achieved, despite the emendations, a "sensible presentation of the famous dance with little tampering with the basic choreography." Some observers also claim that Benno's appearance in the adagio to assist Siegfried makes Siegfried seem to lack strength of character. However, Benno's defenders argue that, with Benno, the adagio becomes a formal aristocratic courtship, Benno serving as an official emissary between one monarch and another. Moreover, these same balletgoers argue, Benno's absence enables Odette to swoon with romantic ardor far less effectively than in stagings in which there is one man to let her fall and another to catch her again. [15]

During the 1959-60 season Nina Novak, who now exerted great influence upon company policy, was named maîtresse de ballet and her brother Edmund became régisseur, their assistants being Tatiana Grantzeva and Gwenn Barker. Later that same season, the Polish-born teacher and choreographer Vadim Sulima joined the Ballet Russe, receiving the title of régisseur-general. [16]

The 1960-61 tour was supposed to have begun 24 October 1960 in Reading, Pennsylvania, but performances were delayed because the Ballet Russe and the American Guild of Musical Artists failed to agree on terms of a new contract. While neither side was willing to specify publicly the precise points of difference that caused negotiations to be stalled, Denham accused AGMA of "inexcusable delay" and charged the union with making "prohibitive demands." After nine weeks of touring had been canceled, a contract was signed that provided for a minimum wage of $115 on tour and rehearsal pay of $60 a week. [17]

The Ballet Russe opened 27 December 1960 in Los Angeles. Igor Youskevitch again headed the male roster and there were two imported ballerinas from Paris, Hélène Trailine (who returned with her husband Juan Giuliano the following season) and Tania Chevtchenko (who has also danced under the name of Tania Karina). [18] The most important new offering was a three act *Swan Lake* (minus the first act), staged by Nina Novak and Anatole Vilzak and designed by Rolf Gérard.

Theoretically, this production should have been of great

importance, since the third and fourth acts of *Swan Lake* were still relatively unfamiliar to Americans, while visits by the Royal Ballet and the Bolshoi Ballet were steadily developing an interest in multi-act classics. Instead, what could have been a major attempt by an American company to stage one of the great works of the nineteenth century in virtually its entirety seemed, as Ann Barzel puts it, "wasted effort." The Ballet Russe simply did not have the resources to produce *Swan Lake* on the scale that the ballet deserved. Therefore tacking on two "unspectacular acts merely violates the poetic 2nd act, that in the usual version can stand alone quite well," Barzel said. She also thought the happy ending of the fourth act—which occurred after Siegfried tore a wing off von Rothbart, who thereupon fell dead—"quite prosaic."

The casting of Nina Novak as Odette/Odile also displeased some balletgoers—not Los Angeles critic Richard D. Saunders, however, who after *Swan Lake's* premiere, 30 December 1960, wrote that Novak "differentiated the two characters deftly, emphasizing warmth and emotion with Odette and mocking brilliance with Odile." But after a later Chicago performance Claudia Cassidy said, "Nina Novak is a pathetic Odette, without the technique, the line, the style or even the mood to create the illusion."[19]

The season's other new work, Vadim Sulima's *Bach Concerto* (to the F-minor keyboard concerto), was premiered in Los Angeles on 29 December 1960. Reviewing its first performance, Viola Hegyi Swisher observed, "Though it is developed with a persistent emphasis on diagonal patterns and employs a few mild balletic distortions, the Bach Concerto is conformist and conventional rather than baroque in choreographic design." The first performance was headed by Hélène Trailine, although Meredith Baylis replaced her at most later presentations on tour. Claudia Cassidy had no use for it when she encountered it in Chicago:

> As decor three white arches were lined up in front of a dingy green backdrop. Lined up in front of them were four miserably lighted couples plus Meredith Baylis and James Capp. They wore cheap white wigs, apparently plastic, and oddly ugly blue tights, with skimpy, stiff tutus to make the girls even more unsightly. The "choreography" would not be tolerated by a self-respecting ballet school on graduation day.[20]

Balletgoers were losing patience with the Ballet Russe, which seemed to be growing ever more inexplicable in its policies. It had been a long time since a new work had added luster to the repertoire. Sometimes the stodgy repertoire could be overlooked because of the brilliance of star dancers. But Trailine and Chevtchenko, the imported stars of 1960-61, were not only dancers of whom most Americans had never heard, they failed to make any impression, other than that of causing audiences to wonder why they had been imported in the first place. Ann Barzel thought that they were "excelled by most of the ensemble members and their style is wrong."

After the 25 and 26 March 1961 performances at the Brooklyn Academy of Music, Doris Hering analyzed the Monte Carlo's strengths and weaknesses:

> It is unusual to see a company in which the corps outweighs the soloists. Yet that is the current state of the Ballet Russe.
>
> The credit for this reversal of emphasis—some of the blame, too—would seem to lie with Nina Novak. Miss Novak tandems as ballet mistress and prima ballerina.
>
> As ballet mistress, she is most knowledgeable in her drilling of the corps. The *Swan Lake, Act II* was particularly impressive. The corps moved as one, stood still as one. . . .
>
> The distribution and execution of solo roles was another matter. To begin with, Miss Novak persists in casting herself as a classic dancer—a Giselle, to which she is temperamentally unsuited—an "assoluta" in *Ballet Imperial,* to which she is muscularly unsuited. By the same token, the roles which she could have enhanced with her natural gifts as a soubrette—the Glove Seller in *Gaité Parisienne* and the Street Dancer in *Beau Danube*—were turned over to other dancers. As a result, everything seemed just a little out of focus. . . .[21]

In June Nina Novak was invited to Warsaw to appear at the Festival of International Ballet Stars. Returning to Poland for the first time since 1947, she danced *Swan Lake* and *Giselle* with the Warsaw Opera Ballet, partnered by Zbigniew Strzalkowski of the Opera Ballet company, and she also danced *Swan Lake* in Poznan. It was a homecoming of happy tears. She met once again several dancers she had known when she was a student, and "We had such a wonderful time when we first met that we cried and cried." Novak also visited with her mother, two sisters, a brother, and several nephews and nieces, and this "was a most exciting family reunion . . . and we all cried and cried. . . . We had such a good time!"[22]

If the April 1938 performances of the company in Monte Carlo can be said to be the beginning of the Ballet Russe de Monte

Carlo as an independent entity, then the 1961-62 season would constitute the company's twenty-fifth anniversary, since those April 1938 performances would officially count as part of the 1937-38 theatrical season. To celebrate this silver anniversary, Denham decided to commission three new works from three former company members—Frederic Franklin, Leon Danielian, and James Starbuck. The first of them, Franklin's *Tribute* (to César Franck's "Symphonic Variations") was premiered at the Boston Arts Center, 20 July 1961. A plotless work, it employed the same score and the same division of cast (three couples) as Frederick Ashton's *Symphonic Variations,* one of that English choreographer's most acclaimed ballets for Sadler's Wells. Yet it was altogether different in mood, and while in no way equal to the Ashton, balletgoers (including Walter Terry) found it "pretty, peppy and pleasant to watch."[23] It has also proven to be a durable ballet, for it was later produced by both the National Ballet of Washington and by the Pittsburgh Ballet Theatre.

With Nina Vyroubova as guest star, the 1961-62 tour began unusually late, on 24 December, in Chicago, where Denham's other two anniversary commissions were premiered.[24] Leon Danielian's *España,* which received its first performance on the company's opening night, contained atmospheric Spanish dances (to pieces by Breton, Chapi, and Granados) that hinted at some sort of emotional relationship between a Lady with a Black Mantilla (Andrea Vodehnal) and a Man with a Black Cape (Mario Ignisci). Seeing the ballet in New York, Walter Terry confessed that he could not fathom its dramatic complications, but thought the dances attractive "and the steps and formations for the corps were bouncy and vital and touched with a chuckle or two."[25]

The new ballet most in demand by local managers that season was James Starbuck's *The Comedians* (premiered 30 December 1961). Starbuck was well known at the time as a choreographer for television, and audiences were eager to see his frolicsome romp to Kabalevsky's familiar suite. Starbuck says that, although Denham insisted that he very much wanted him to choreograph for the Ballet Russe, the terms of the contract he was offered were not generous. He ended up putting the ballet on at his own expense, Denham later paying him $1000 for it. Jan Scott's décor made use of eight scrim panels before and behind which the dancers cavorted, but the economies of touring reduced the number of scrims to three—thereby also, thinks Starbuck, reducing the ballet's visual effectiveness.

Seeing it the following spring, Walter Terry conceded

that *The Comedians* did "make a stab at liveliness," but he never-theless thought it wound up as "rather routine stuff." The Chicago premiere, however, was for Ann Barzel, "a resounding success. . . . The clever choreography uses a ballet vocabulary that is not entirely easy, yet not demanding. It is used meaningfully and the pace is fast. There are five couples in a series of zany situations."[26]

One further premiere took place in Chicago on 27 December 1961. Using some of the Drigo music from *Harlequinade,* Nina Novak choreographed a *Harlequinade Pas de Deux* for herself and Juan Giuliano. "The style is the coyness of Harlequin and Columbine," said Ann Barzel, "but there are some showy technical pas, such as a circle of fouetté turns that Novak executed with brio."[27]

The company's guest star policy sometimes led to stylistic problems in the 1950s and '60s. Alonso, who because of worsening political relations between the United States and Cuba could no longer dance here, had no trouble adapting her own style to that of the Ballet Russe. Having danced for most of her career in America, she knew the Ballet Russe and had been trained by teach-ers familiar with the Ballet Russe style. But even so great an artist as Chauviré was, at the outset, not seen at her best with the company because her way of dancing did not always harmonize with that of the ensemble. In 1960-61 Trailine and Chevtchenko had failed to make any impression. Now, in 1961-62, Vyroubova was to en-counter difficulties. While recognized as a great dancer, she never-theless bewildered audiences. Walter Terry describes what she was like:

> You have to see her to believe her. Oh, yes, she is an excellent technician, definitely a ballerina but I haven't witnessed such hamming since Tamara Toumanova last chewed up the scen-ery here. Vyroubova who, in profile, looks surprisingly like a Mayan glyph, flirts with her partner and her public, indulges in all manner of mannerisms, from rhapsodic flourishes to minx-ish coquetries. She's outrageous . . . but her dancing powers are considerable. She knows the stage and the ham she prof-fers is delectable and of the highest grade.[28]

The tour ended with performances at the Brooklyn Academy of Music, 13-14 April 1962, which, because the company was celebrating its silver anniversary, were analyzed at some length by many of New York's dance critics. Doris Hering tried to compare the company of 1938 with that of 1962. In terms of stars, she thought the 1962 roster weak, yet suspected that the technical level of the company as a whole was "probably as strong, if not stronger." "As for the repertoire," she speculated, "the present one is not appreciably inferior or superior to a quarter century ago"— surely an overstatement, since the 1938 repertoire had contained such works as *St. Francis, Seventh Symphony, Don Juan,* and *L'Épreuve d'Amour.* The performances also put Anatole Chujoy into good spirits. He maintained, "It has been quite a while since Ballet Russe de Monte Carlo has had as technically strong and stylistically proper a troupe as this." Yet he did chide Nina Novak for choreographic changes which she introduced into the second act of *Swan Lake:* apparently, said Chujoy, "what the charming ballerina must have thought was that the 67-year-old ballet could stand rejuvenation. The truth is that it cannot."

A more cautious appraisal came from Walter Terry. Although he, too, praised the precision of the ensemble, he found the dancers indifferent in terms of style and characterization, and in *Gaîté Parisienne* only George Zoritch (the one dancer from 1938 still with the company) "really knew what this lively, elegant ballet was all about." In sum, this was "Bargain basement ballet: some excellent buys along with materials destined for the rummage sale."

Nobody knew it then, but those performances in Brooklyn were to be the last ever given by the Ballet Russe de Monte Carlo. Ironically, Nina Novak, who had become the company's indisputable prima ballerina, was unable to appear in any of them since she had twisted her arm a week before while dancing *Swan Lake* in Wilmington.[29]

Of all the things said about the Ballet Russe during 1961-62, one of the most significant, in terms of its implications, was the seemingly casual remark by *Dance Magazine's* San Francisco correspondent Clifford Gessler that this season the company had failed to fill the San Francisco War Memorial Opera House and the Oakland Auditorium, its two traditional big stops in the Bay Area.[30] The Ballet Russe was not doing as well on tour as it once had and production costs were rising.

Meredith Baylis, who worked for Denham as an assistant régisseur during the company's final seasons, says that in the Ballet Russe offices she caught glimpses of the financial records for the 1961-62 tour. They were not encouraging. Although rumors drifted through the company that the Ballet Russe was in a bad state, no one was unduly alarmed when Denham did not discuss contracts for the next season: Denham loved to procrastinate and would often delay such discussions until the last minute.

However, Sophie Pourmel, the wardrobe director, began to be seriously worried. It had always been her custom to spend the summer before an autumn tour refreshing the costumes in preparation for the new season. Yet whenever she approached Denham about this matter in the summer of 1962, Denham would say, "Wait, wait. Not yet, not yet." Finally, Denham was forced to admit to her that the Ballet Russe was no more.

The September 1962 issue of *Dance Magazine* contained the following statement: "Because of a substantial loss last season, Ballet Russe de Monte Carlo has decided not to tour in the season 1962-63. Instead, it plans to make a thorough study of the touring potential in the United States from a general business aspect. It also wants to re-appraise its own standing with regard to repertoire, personnel and tour management."[31]

The dancers dispersed. The Ballet Russe de Monte Carlo had, very quietly, come to an end.

Not quite. Sergei Denham never really gave up. Nor did the company's faithful supporter, Julius Fleischmann. Hoping to avoid the expenses of American touring, they dreamed of founding a new ballet company on a grand scale abroad. In 1963 Fleischmann thought it might be possible to establish a company in Tunis with the support of the Tunisian government. But funds proved insufficient. The next year, Fleischmann proposed starting a ballet company in Greece. But political instability made this impossible.[32] Early in 1966 Denham paid two visits to Monte Carlo to discuss reestablishing a Ballet Russe there. This time he was in luck, and Denham's new Ballets de Monte Carlo gave its first performance 19 November 1966, before an invited audience at the Fête du Prince, honoring Prince Rainier III of Monaco.

Denham envisioned that the company would dance in Monte Carlo during high season and tour for the rest of the year, but not in America because of what he termed the "impossible demands" made by American trade unions. But many of the dancers were Americans, having been chosen at auditions in New York conducted by Léonide Massine. Several associates of the Ballet Russe in the past returned to work with the new troupe. Rachel Chapman was, as always, staff pianist, and Paul Strauss, a Ballet Russe conductor in the late 1940s and early '50s, served as conductor. Michel Katcharoff was régisseur, and Michael Subotin, who for years had assisted Denham in one way or another, was company manager. Lorca Massine, the choreographer's son, was among the male dancers, and Nina Novak, though not a member of the company at the outset, arrived mid-season to star in *Ballet Imperial*.

The opening night program included *Les Sylphides* (staged by Serge Lifar), the *Flower Festival at Genzano* pas de deux (with guest stars Josette Amiel and Flemming Flindt), a revival of *Bacchanale*, and *Gaîté Parisienne*. Guest stars were featured throughout the course of what proved to be the company's only season: among the dancers who appeared on one occasion or another were Magdalena Popa, Amatto Checiulesco, Michel Bruel, Marilyn Burr, Nina Stucky, Olga de Haas, and André Simon. In addition to *Ballet Imperial* and the ballets offered on opening night, the repertoire included *Swan Lake* (Act II), Pavel Smok's *Fresques* (Martinu), Lorca Massine's *Andante* (Prokofiev), and *Raymonda* (Act III), plus virtuoso pas de deux and divertissements performed by the guests.[33]

The company was not a good one. Nor was it well organized. So, at least, say two of its members, Alexandra Nadal and Eugene Slavin, who had previously danced with the Ballet Russe. There was much turnover in personnel and the dancers represented what Nadal calls "a mishmash of styles," there being a great disparity between the Europeans and the Americans in the troupe. Some of the Europeans, says Nadal, were surprisingly—even shockingly—lazy. Classes were infrequent at best and were taught by several teachers, none of whom stayed long enough to make much impression upon the company, although many of the dancers particularly enjoyed the classes taught by Alexandre Kalioujny. Morale was seriously undermined at the very outset during rehearsals for the revival of *Bacchanale*. Massine's ballet so bewildered the younger dancers that they could never decide whether it was a horror or an idiosyncratic masterpiece. Then, for reasons that are still obscure, some unknown person mailed to the company copies of all the most unfavorable reviews *Bacchanale* had received at its premiere in 1939, thereby precipitating a loss of ensemble self-confidence.

After Monte Carlo performances in the spring of 1967, impresario Boris Trailine took the company on a tour of Spain. Then the organization disbanded.[34]

The old days were over. First the Ballet Russe, then the new Monte Carlo company collapsed. Having lost its lease, the Ballet Russe School closed its doors 30 June 1967.[35] On 22 October 1968 Julius Fleischmann died at the age of sixty-eight. Although respected as a director of the Metropolitan Opera, a member of the advisory committee of the Yale School of Drama, and a member of the executive committee of the United States National Commission for UNESCO, Fleischmann had also moved in circles which, in those days of outrage against the Vietnam War, were being called questionable by some social commentators. For he had been president of the arts and music committee of the Congress for Cultural Freedom, an organization allegedly infiltrated and partially supported by the CIA.[36]

And Denham? Denham never stopped dreaming about a new ballet company. He mulled over several schemes, then thought he had what might be a workable one. Chicago. Chicago had always loved the Ballet Russe. Why not a new Ballet Russe in Chicago? On 30 January 1970 he telephoned Ruth Page in Chicago to consult with her about the proposal and to ask if she cared to become involved with it. Why not a Chicago Ballet Russe?

Within an hour after he made that telephone call from his New York office, Denham stepped off a curb at Madison Avenue and East 57th Street and was struck by a bus. He died shortly thereafter. His sudden death came as a blow to his family and to the dance world. Yet, in retrospect, his daughter Irina Pabst thinks it may have been a kind of blessing. Denham, an active man, had always dreaded wasting away in old age, crippled or bedridden. He died as he had lived much of his life—making plans for a ballet company.[37]

NOTES FOR CHAPTER 9

1. Doris Hering, "Ballet Russe de Monte Carlo," *Dance Magazine*, December 1957, p. 84.
2. *The Mazurka*—George W. Stowe, "Ballet Full of Kinks in Familiar Dances, Few Artists Shine," *Hartford Times*, 19 October 1957; Ann Barzel, "Ballet Russe de Monte Carlo," *Dance News*, May 1958, p. 9; conversation with Leon Danielian.
3. 1957-58 season—"Ballet Russe Season," *Dance Magazine*, October 1957, p. 3; "Chauviré Joins Ballet Russe," *Dance Magazine*, February 1958, p. 3; "Ballet Russe de Monte Carlo Begins Coast-to-Coast Tour," *Dance News*, November 1957, p. 4; "Ballet Russe de Monte Carlo in B'lyn Academy," *Dance News*, October 1957, p. 1; Ann Barzel, *Ballet Annual #13*, pp. 130-131. George Zoritch—Walter Terry, "Ballet Russe de Monte Carlo," *New York Herald-Tribune*, 11 August 1959; Ann Barzel, "Ballet Russe de Monte Carlo," *Dance News*, February 1962, p. 9.
4. Novak—Ann Barzel, "Chicago News," *Dance Magazine*, May 1958, p. 6; George Jackson, "Chicago," *Ballet Today*, April 1959, p. 21; Doris Hering, "Ballet Russe de Monte Carlo," *Dance Magazine*, December 1958, p. 25.
5. Doris Hering, "Ballet Russe de Monte Carlo," *Dance Magazine*, December 1958, p. 25.

6. John Percival, in *Ballet Annual #14*, p. 156; "Ballet Russe Begins Tour," *Dance Magazine*, October 1958, p. 3.
7. *Romeo and Juliet*—Ann Barzel, "Ballet Russe de Monte Carlo," *Dance News*, February 1959, p. 7; Claudia Cassidy, "On the Aisle," *Chicago Tribune*, 29 December 1958.
8. *Springtime*—Louis R. Guzzo, "Ex-Seattleite's Ballet to Be Introduced Here," *Seattle Times*, 21 January 1959; Ann Barzel, "Ballet Russe de Monte Carlo," *Dance News*, February 1959, p. 8.
9. Ann Barzel, "Chicago News," *Dance Magazine*, February 1959, p. 96.
10. John Voorhees, "Ballet Russe Performances Show New Vitality," *Seattle Post-Intelligencer*, 26 January 1959.
11. "Summer Dance Attractions Keep New York Lively," *Dance News*, September 1959, pp. 4, 13; John Martin, "The Dance: Schedule," *New York Times*, 16 August 1959.
12. *Pittsburgh Post-Gazette*, 28 November 1958.
13. *Ballad*—Donald Steinfirst, "Large Audience Enjoys Ballet Russe Premiere," *Pittsburgh Post-Gazette*, 26 October 1959; Claudia Cassidy, "On the Aisle," *Chicago Tribune*, 30 December 1959; Ann Barzel, "Ballet Russe de Monte Carlo," *Dance News*, February 1960, p. 10.
14. Herbert Roussel, "Ballet Russe Brilliant in Two Opening Shows," *Houston Post*, 13 March 1960.
15. Ann Barzel, "Ballet Russe de Monte Carlo," *Dance News*, February 1960, p. 10; "Tradition Out in 'Swan Lake,'" *Chicago's American*, 28 December 1959.
16. Souvenir programs 1959-60, 1960-61.
17. *Dance Magazine:* "Ballet Russe Cancels 9 Tour Weeks," October 1960, p. 3; "Ballet Russe—AGMA Pact," November 1960, p. 3.
18. "French Dancers Join U.S. Troupe," *Dance News*, January 1961, p. 1.
19. *Swan Lake*—Ann Barzel, "Chicago News," *Dance Magazine*, April 1961, p. 6; Richard D. Saunders, "Ballet Russe Gives Fine Performance," *Hollywood Citizen-News*, 31 December 1960; Claudia Cassidy, "On the Aisle," *Chicago Tribune*, 8 March 1961.
20. *Bach Concerto*—Viola Hegyi Swisher, "Ballet Premiere of Concerto Presented," *Los Angeles Mirror*, 30 December 1960; Claudia Cassidy, "Shameless Makeshift Masquerades as Denham's 'New' Ballet," *Chicago Tribune*, 9 March 1961; conversation with Meredith Baylis.
21. Ann Barzel, "Ballet Russe Needs Overhaul," *Chicago's American*, 11 March 1961; Doris Hering, "Ballet Russe de Monte Carlo," *Dance Magazine*, May 1961, pp. 20, 65.
22. "Novak Dances in Native Poland," *Dance News*, September 1961, p. 6.
23. Walter Terry, "25 Years of Ballet Company," *New York Herald-Tribune*, 29 April 1962.
24. "Notes from the Field," *New York Times*, 17 December 1961.
25. Walter Terry, "25 Years of Ballet Company," *New York Herald-Tribune*, 29 April 1962.
26. *The Comedians*—Walter Terry, "25 Years of Ballet Company," *New York Herald-Tribune*, 29 April 1962; Ann Barzel, "Ballet Russe de Monte Carlo," *Dance News*, February 1962, p. 9; conversation with James Starbuck.
27. Ann Barzel, "Ballet Russe de Monte Carlo," *Dance News*, February 1962, p. 9.
28. Walter Terry, "25 Years of Ballet Company," *New York Herald-Tribune*, 29 April 1962.
29. Brooklyn engagement—Doris Hering, "Spring Surge," *Dance Magazine*, June

1962, p. 31; Anatole Chujoy, "Ballet Russe Ends Season," *Dance News,* May 1962, p. 3; Walter Terry, "25 Years of Ballet Company," *New York Herald-Tribune,* 29 April 1962; "Nina Novak, Ballerina, Injured," *New York Times,* 9 April 1962.

30. Clifford Gessler, "San Francisco Bay Area News," *Dance Magazine,* March 1962, p. 75.
31. Disbanding—"Ballet Russe to Sit Out Season," *Dance Magazine,* September 1962, p. 4; conversations with Meredith Baylis and Sophie Pourmel.
32. Michael Subotin, unpublished biography of Sergei Denham.
33. Monte Carlo company—"Will Monte Carlo Have Company?" *Dance News,* April 1966, p. 6; "Americans Make Up Nucleus of Monte Carlo Company," *Dance News,* October 1966, p. 7; "Correction on Monte Carlo," *Dance News,* December 1966, p. 7; "Monte Carlo Had Easter Season," *Dance News,* May 1967, p. 19; Irène Lidova, "Petits Tours de Paris," *Dance News,* September 1967, p. 8; posters and programs in collection of Alexandra Nadal and Eugene Slavin; conversations with Michel Katcharoff, Alexandra Nadal, Eugene Slavin.
34. Michael Subotin, unpublished biography of Sergei Denham.
35. "Ballet Russe School Closes," *Dance Magazine,* July 1967, p. 3.
36. "Julius Fleischmann Dies at 68, Stage Producer and Art Patron," *New York Times,* 24 October 1968; Christopher Lasch, *The Agony of the American Left,* pp. 100-110.
37. John Martin, *Ruth Page,* p. 135; conversation with Irina Pabst.

PART TWO

Life in the Company

10 SERGEI J. DENHAM: COMPANY DIRECTOR

SERGEI J. DENHAM was born Sergei Ivanovich Dokouchaiev (a surname also transliterated as Dokootshieff) on 22 October 1896 in Samara, a Russian city on the Volga today known as Kuibyshev.[1] His father, a member of the gentry, died when he was young, and Denham was raised by two remarkable women: his cultivated mother, whom he adored, and a French governness known as Madame Marie, who taught him to make cutout dolls and scenery for toy theatres, thereby helping to instill in him a love for the theatre. The Dokouchaiev family included, in addition to young Sergei, three daughters and four sons. There had also been an older son named Sergei who died before Denham was born and after whom he was named.

Denham's childhood friend, Michael Subotin, characterizes him[2] as a lively boy fond of theatregoing and music, and his daughter, Irina Pabst, suspects that, when young, her father's ambition was to become a pianist. Subotin recalls that whenever Denham, as a youngster, went to silent films that had live musical accompaniment, he would wave his arms about, pretending to be an orchestra conductor.

When Denham had reached the Russian equivalent of the American fourth grade, the family moved to Moscow, where his mother mingled with the intelligentsia and invited scholars, scientists, and musicians to her home. Among her acquaintances was

189

the composer Scriabin, who gave Denham a few piano lessons and whose music Denham admired ever afterward.

Denham was sent to a boarding school at Tsarskoye Selo (a town now called Pushkin), near St. Petersburg. The school was presided over by a Madame Levitsky, who possessed what Denham once described as a "stern, icon-like face." She ran her establishment according to strict principles. Rooms were unheated, meat was forbidden, and Madame Levitsky tried to make her pupils aware of the importance of patriotic ideals, a sense of duty, and fidelity to the teachings of the Orthodox Church.[3]

Despite his love of music, it was not at a conservatory but at the Moscow Commercial Institute that Denham received his college education. Art and business were to make demands upon him for the rest of his life. At the Commercial Institute Denham met once again his old friend Michael Subotin from Samara, and except when the Revolution separated them for several years, he was to remain in close contact with Subotin for the rest of his life. In 1915 Denham married Valentina Nikolaevna Yershova (whose Christian name was usually transliterated as Valentine), a member of a wealthy merchant family whose home had once belonged to Pushkin. They became the parents of two daughters, Irina and Valentine.

When World War I broke out Denham worked for the Red Cross. But after the Revolution of 1917 he and his family left for Uralsk, where they had relatives. As the Bolsheviks approached they moved further eastward, eventually arriving in Vladivostok, where Denham became director of the dormitories at the University of Vladivostok. Then Admiral A.V. Kolchak appointed him a representative of his anti-Bolshevik Siberian government, in charge of procuring funds to support his troops. Denham was in Shanghai on a financial mission when the Kolchak regime fell. This led Denham to decide to emigrate to the United States with his wife and children.

The family left by ship for San Francisco in 1921. On board, the charming young Russian met an American lawyer, Watson Washburn, and they became lifelong friends, Washburn serving as attorney for the Ballet Russe throughout the company's existence. Arriving at San Francisco without any prospect of employment, Denham left his family there while he went job hunting in Chicago and New York. He finally found a job in a New York antique store on West 59th Street. Cultivated, suave, and persuasive, Denham had a knack for striking up acquaintanceships with the socially prominent people who visited the shop. About that time, a friend and a fellow émigré named I.I. Milberg was employed by Gaston and Company, a private banking firm. One night he came to Denham for help. Milberg had been asked to translate documents from Russian into English, and knowing that Denham had a flair for languages, he wanted to ask him some questions about idiom. The translations pleased Milberg's employers, and when they heard of the assistance that Denham had provided, they sent similar assignments his way. Soon he was traveling about on business for the firm. A career in banking had opened for Denham.

He then went to work for Bankers Trust, eventually becoming a vice-president. His position involved visiting European cities and overseeing the establishment of branch offices. Significantly, it was the prospect of traveling to the great cities of the world that made this post so attractive to Denham. It was not until he had become a successful banker, however, that he thought of changing his name to some form that would be less difficult for Americans to pronounce. His daughter Irina remembers that, as a child, she had to endure the taunts of her schoolmates who liked to mock her for possessing what was to them an outlandish name. Sergei Ivanovich Dokouchaiev pored over lists of English names and finally decided upon Denham, his choice being in part a tribute to a friend, Charles Denby (father of dance critic Edwin Denby), who worked for the State Department and who had helped sponsor Dokouchaiev as an immigrant to the United States. Late in his life, Denham included Charles Denby's name on a list of "friends whose memory I will always bless, who in one way or the other helped me to start a new life, to understand the new world. . . ." Denham kept his Russian first name and adopted the middle initial of J (for John, the English equivalent of his patronymic).[4]

Because of the economic and political problems of the 1930s, Bankers Trust opened fewer branches abroad and Denham was confined more and more to a desk in a New York office. The routine of office work bored him and he felt trapped. He was rescued from drudgery by ballet. Denham had met Colonel de Basil's dancers on an ocean voyage, and when de Basil and Massine began to quarrel he became involved with ballet politics. Years later, Denham told reporters that as a young banker in Paris he had encountered Serge Diaghilev in a bookshop and, after a conversation had started up between them, Diaghilev predicted that the time was coming for America to be a supporter of ballet.[5] As director of the Ballet Russe de Monte Carlo, Denham would play a major role in helping to bring about an American ballet.

Virtually all of Denham's associates—those who liked him as well as those who were forever annoyed by him—are agreed upon one thing: as Michel Katcharoff put it in conversation, "Denham had class!"[6] Tall, dignified, and somewhat portly, Denham could charm anyone he talked to with what Americans would recognize as an old-world Continental manner. Fluent in several languages, he could discourse upon music, literature, and painting. Always in control of a situation, always assured, he could flatter and cajole prospective backers and soothe the tempers of volatile dancers. During that brief period in the mid-1940s when he cast an inquiring eye upon modern dance, Denham not only investigated Valerie Bettis's choreography, but attended several of Pauline Koner's rehearsals. Koner says she found him "very sweet and dear—and terribly, terribly Russian."

The suavity was the external manifestation of an underlying sense of order and efficiency. His years in banking stood him in good stead when he became a ballet director. At all times the Ballet Russe de Monte Carlo was run with admirable business acumen. Dancers who were members of both the de Basil and the Denham companies say that whereas one could not always be sure that payday would be a day in de Basil's calendar week, Denham's dancers never failed to receive their salary payments at the appointed time. Some of these same dancers also add, however, that while paychecks always arrived when they were supposed to, Denham never paid anyone a penny more than he had to.

That Denham was so obviously a combination of the cultivated gentleman and the shrewd businessman has made the estimations of some people who knew him curiously ambivalent in tone. Agnes de Mille has described him in her memoirs as looking "like an old world diplomat. . . . He tiptoed through large circumventions and maneuverings with pussy-cat elegance. . . ." In conversation, she has been more outspoken, calling him "a smooth operator who talked a great blather." Says de Mille, "He always tried to get away with murder—and very often he managed to."[7] Similarly, Ruth Page characterizes him as "a charming scoundrel," yet adds that he invariably gave her whatever she requested in terms of rehearsal time and personnel when she was staging a ballet.

Denham was a man of contradictions. Blessed with a full measure of joie de vivre, he loved the good things in life. He adored fine music and wine and was fond of hosting elaborate parties conspicuous for their shish kebabs and flaming desserts. If such gestures satisfied his artistic as well as his culinary appetites—and he most definitely rated the fine art of cooking very highly—the businessman in him occasionally made him cut corners. At some parties for company members he served cheap wine, with the result that the next morning he might have a very queasy corps de ballet. And while a champagne party on the last night of a season was a Ballet Russe tradition, behind his back dancers sang an equally traditional Ballet Russe song about "Mr. Denham and his cheap champagne!"

Denham carefully separated his family life from his life as a ballet director. His granddaughter Stephanie Fenwick says—and her mother, Irina Pabst, concurs—that "ballet was not part of our daily life. It was always something distant, apart from us. In some families where the father is involved with theatre or dance, all the kids turn into little 'theatre rats.' That was not true of us." More accurately, Denham could be said to have had two families. One was the family of wife and daughters who lived at 1200 Fifth Avenue, totally removed from the world of ballet. This home was Denham's castle, and to insure privacy he had an unlisted telephone number long before unlisted numbers became fashionable.

Denham's other world was the Ballet Russe de Monte Carlo, which he ruled like a patriarch. The lord and master of the Ballet Russe, he (like a Hollywood film director) had his own special chair, with his name painted on it, on which he sat to watch the company rehearse. When he was out front watching a performance, Denham deliberately coughed a lot with a special recognizable cough to make sure that company members knew he was present. He gave advice to his dancers as though these boys and girls were his own sons and daughters, and, like an old-fashioned father, he fussed over matters of dress and grooming. He was concerned with the length of the boys' hair and was distressed whenever any boy tried to wear jeans on a tour. He was even more concerned with the appearance of his girls. The Ballet Russe girls were never at any time permitted to wear slacks, not even while relaxing during an arduous tour. He considered gum chewing a barbarism and had his own favorite theories of hair styling and fashion design.

Today, members of a ballet company might—and with some justification—consider this to be excessive interference into areas of private life that had no connection with rehearsal or performance. But, as Denham himself liked to say, the Ballet Russe was one big family—his family. Moreover, as several dancers have admitted, Denham's suggestions on clothing were often sound ones. Denham could teach girls to be simply but fashionably dressed: "He could teach you to look like a princess," says Moscelyne Larkin.

Unlike the directors of some companies who mingle

casually with their dancers and are ready at any time to discuss company affairs informally, Denham kept his distance. Seldom did he call dancers by their first names. One was almost always referred to as "Mr." or "Miss." Yet formality did not make the Ballet Russe stuffy in atmosphere. Rather, some dancers have said, it could at times help intensify self-respect. Touring may have made dancers tired and bedraggled, but to be called "Mr." or "Miss" suggested that they were considered important.

There are two charges that are frequently brought against Denham as a director: first of all, that he was an intolerable snob; second, that, despite his pretensions, his artistic taste was unreliable. Agnes de Mille bluntly refers to him as "the greatest snob I have ever met." And several dancers have told stories that are variants upon this one:

Traveling with the Ballet Russe on a tour of one-night stands, Denham went out to eat with the company after a performance in a small Midwestern town. The restaurant into which they piled was scarcely more than a diner, yet it was the only place in the community that stayed open late. Seemingly oblivious to the nature of the cafe, Denham ordered a fine French wine. After the waiter recovered from his surprise, he rummaged frantically about the premises and from somewhere managed to unearth a bottle of cheap sweet wine which he brought to Denham's table, proud to have been able to do at least something to fill this elegant gentleman's order. Denham took one glance at the bottle and contemptuously sent it back.

While rehearsing *Rodeo*, de Mille found one of the Russian male dancers habitually surly, lazy, and hung over. She complained of this to Denham and Denham recommended, "Agnes, appeal to his class; remember, he's a count." At that, de Mille threw back her head and howled, then primly told Denham that such aristocratic considerations were out of place in democratic America and that she refused to countenance snobbery of any kind. Today, she admits, "Of course, everyone is snobbish in some way about *something* or other. But I certainly wasn't going to concede *that* to a man like Denham!"[8]

Denham knew well that his courtliness made him attractive to socially important people, and his banker's eye instantly told him just how financially important each new person he met was. Seeking out benefactors for the Ballet Russe, he flattered heiresses and talked business with industrialists. He was apparently irresistible, and his letters to prospective donors remain models of persuasiveness. A favorite practice was to take socialites backstage to watch a company class. Even though the visitors would have a view of little more than sweaty bodies in leg warmers, Denham's silken tones would convince them that they had just glimpsed all the magic of the theatre. And, believing Denham, the socialites would walk away, dazzled, straight to their checkbooks.

The ways in which Denham sought out the rich and famous have struck some observers as distasteful. Yet all this may have been necessary. The Ballet Russe existed at a time before there were state arts councils or national arts trusts and before philanthropic foundations became regular supporters of dance. For the Ballet Russe to survive, it had to depend upon the contributions of private donors. If being able to mingle with high society somehow appealed to Denham's personal vanity, it also kept the Ballet Russe alive.

Often, Denham had to use every bit of ingenuity he possessed and all his wiles as a diplomat to keep his socialites, and potential donors, happy. A notebook entry contains this description of an evening when *Billy Sunday* was on the bill:

> *Society!* A very known Lady (with capital L) asked me to reserve six tickets. I did, On the same evening we went to a very elegant dinner . . . with two butlers, silver plates, etc. As usually, —we never got to the theatre until well after 9. . . . I went through the stage door & the ladies with their escorts went through "the entrance of the nobles." Ten minutes later an attendant rushes to me and says that there are no tickets for my ladies in the box office!! Error & horror . . . What to do?? Thank God for the solution: we were giving at that memorable night the "Billy Sunday" and the scene called for supers—women and men—(part of Sunday's audiences)—neurotics and drunks. . .
>
> My suggestion to the elegant ladies to *perform on* the stage, instead of looking on it, was cheerfully received & we garbed them all in the garbs of the neurotics. Hiding the beautiful dresses, jewels & putting on dishevelled wigs!! But . . I was saved.[9]

Clearly, the rich ladies must have adored the opportunity to appear as supers with the Ballet Russe. A potentially embarrassing situation had been turned into a lark that might well have predisposed these high society folk to increase their contributions to the ballet.

Alexandra Danilova has stated, "Mr. Denham had a marvelous capacity for getting wealthy people involved with ballet." But she has added, "Little by little, though, he lost almost everyone."

The gloomy coda to Danilova's remarks about Denham's fund-raising capabilities refers to his vagaries of taste as a director. On a season-by-season basis, Denham's record as an artistic director is often laudable, particularly during the years before the company's temporary cessation in 1952. Following the departure of Massine as choreographer, Denham commissioned new ballets from Nijinska, appointed Balanchine as resident choreographer, made a tentative (but historically important) foray into modern dance, offered experimental pieces by Ruth Page, sanctioned the production of *Rodeo,* and allowed Todd Bolender and Ruthanna Boris to stage their first works for a major company. On the basis of these accomplishments alone, Denham must rank as one of the important directors of American ballet.

Unfortunately, when Denham's directorial record is assessed in terms of long-range goals and well-defined policies, the results are not so impressive. Essentially, Denham had no clearly articulated goals. What he did have was a passion for ballet. Denham was a cultivated fan and he ran his company with a fan's enthusiasm. Ballet permitted Denham the banker to live in a world of glamour and creativity he had always known existed, but which he might not have been able to be a part of if it had not been for the Ballet Russe. Without a Ballet Russe, the young Russian-born banker who considered traveling to European cities to be the most pleasant part of his job might have matured into yet another businessman in a gray flannel suit, seemingly successful, yet inwardly gnawed by a sense of emptiness.

Denham appears to have possessed a genuine creative impulse. However, creative impulses sometimes manifest themselves in maddening forms and Denham's took one of the most maddening forms of all: Denham's was the miscellaneous creative impulse directed toward no single art but toward the arts in general. Denham dabbled in various arts, crafts, hobbies, and avocations. He played the piano (and, by reports, played it well), he had an attractive tenor voice and liked to sing, he took up sculpture under the influence of Malvina Hoffman, he collected old glass and invented crossword puzzles. Fond of carpentry, he built castles for his grandchildren and cabinets for his own home. He treated the farm property that he acquired in Connecticut as his personal toy, attaching stereo loudspeakers to the trees so that he could listen to music outdoors and tying special bells around the necks of the sheep he raised there.[10]

If the sheer variety of these pursuits indicates that Denham was always active, always inquisitive, it also suggests that his creative urges remained, in some fundamental way, unchanneled. If as director of a ballet company he had the thorough professionalism of a born manager, he also had the aesthetics of a dilettante. He respected the Russian ballet tradition and wished to bring ballets, old and new, to the American public. Yet the answers Denham gave to the questions of how tradition ought to be preserved and what sort of new works should enter the repertoire tended to be vague. In the late years of the company, the answers were also often dictated by economic considerations.

That the Ballet Russe survived as long as it did is a tribute to Denham's business sense. During its best years, Denham the businessman and Denham the artistic director ruled in harmony together. But when mounting expenses caused Denham to count his pennies even more carefully than usual, business practicality often triumphed over artistic vision. Out of a desire to economize, Denham sometimes reduced the décor of a ballet to its barest essentials and he seldom had more than forty dancers in his company. While this may have been good business, it made critics complain that productions were unattractively Spartan and that the dancers looked obviously overworked.

Increasingly, Denham the businessman hesitated to take the risk of commissioning new productions. Igor Youskevitch says that when he was artistic adviser to the Ballet Russe, he was able to persuade his friend José Limón to make *The Moor's Pavane* available to the company. Denham refused it, not because he disliked the work, but because he was loath to spend the money necessary to produce it. The Ballet Russe thereby lost the opportunity to be the first classical ballet company to take an acknowledged modern dance masterpiece into its repertoire. At about the same time Yvonne Chouteau, after having studied with Antony Tudor, urged Denham to hire Tudor as a guest choreographer. Again Denham refused. Such refusals may have been made for good business reasons, but they did nothing to increase the artistic stature of the Ballet Russe. No wonder, then, that many critics began to regard the Ballet Russe as an organization of waning creative importance.

Artistic matters were not helped by one aspect of Denham's casting policy: his determination to make Nina Novak the company's prima ballerina. No one, not even those who criticize Denham most bitterly on this issue, will deny that Novak was a gifted dancer. What is open to question is whether she was quite as versatile as Denham thought she was. To attempt to develop a ballerina from the ranks of his own company was surely laudable. But Denham's infatuation with Novak led to the mistaken belief that one single ballerina could suffice for all genres of ballet. By emphasizing Novak so much, Denham, instead of strengthening her position with the company, made her more vulnerable to critical attack.

Nevertheless, despite his lack of a coherent artistic policy, Denham possessed to an extraordinary degree one cardinal virtue that any ballet director ought to possess: tenacity. Denham refused to be daunted. He kept the Ballet Russe going under difficult conditions that might have caused less hardy directors to disband the company. His commitment may explain why he once told his granddaughter Stephanie that "You must have something in life that is absolutely yours. No matter what may befall you, that certain something always remains yours." The force that guided Denham for much of his adult life was his devotion to the Ballet Russe. This is why some Ballet Russe dancers, after reciting a catalogue of complaints against him, may then—rather grudgingly, perhaps—agree with Nathalie Krassovska's summation that "Mr. Denham could be a terribly difficult man. And yet I think he tried his best."

However gratifying it may have been, it was not easy to be director of the Ballet Russe. So it is not totally surprising that, although surrounded by dancers, musicians, designers, socialites, and philanthropists, Denham in his journals should nevertheless refer to his position as one in which he at times felt great "Loneliness. Because, at the command of everybody & everything, I was solely responsible for discipline. Thus I had to remain rather aloof from everybody (our big family). I began to understand the loneliness of the 'old man' commanding a Navy ship at sea."[11]

NOTES FOR CHAPTER 10

1. Although the unpublished biography of Denham by his friend Michael Subotin gives 1895 as his date of birth, many reference works say 1897. The date of 1896 is supported by a passport dated 5 May 1937.
2. Michael Subotin, unpublished biography of Sergei Denham. Except as noted, all basic biographical information is taken from this account.
3. S.J. Denham, notebook entry dated 20 January 1968.
4. S.J. Denham, notebook entry dated 17 March 1963. Also conversations with Edwin Denby and Irina Pabst.

5. Philip Kappel, "Denham to Address Art Assn. on Ballet," *The Washington New Preston (Conn.) News,* 29 September 1960.
6. Conversation with Michel Katcharoff. Henceforth, all statements for which no printed source is given were made in conversation with the author. Particularly helpful have been conversations with Yvonne Chouteau, Laura Clandon, Leon Danielian, Alexandra Danilova, Agnes de Mille, Stephanie Fenwick, M. Hornyak, Roman Jasinski, Pauline Koner, Nathalie Krassovska, Moscelyne Larkin, Robert Lindgren, Irina Pabst, Ruth Page, Michael Subotin, Sonja Taanila, Miguel Terekhov, George Verdak, Igor Youskevitch, Rochelle Zide.
7. Agnes de Mille, *Dance to the Piper,* p. 271, and conversation.
8. Agnes de Mille, *Dance to the Piper,* pp. 287-88, and conversation.
9. S.J. Denham, notebook entry dated March 1948.
10. Avocations—Margy Braggiotti, "His Ballet Dream Come True," *New York Post,* 6 September 1945; S.J. Denham, notebook entry dated 17 June 1960; conversations with Stephanie Fenwick, Irina Pabst, Michael Subotin.
11. S.J. Denham, undated notebook entry.

Alexandra Danilova in *Song of Norway* surrounded by (from left) Alfredo Corvino, Alexander Goudovitch, Alan Banks, Serge Ismailoff, and Michel Katcharoff. Photo: The Photo-Colotype Co.

Maria Tallchief, Nicholas Magallanes, and Mary Ellen Moylan in
Balanchine's *Danses Concertantes.*

Above: Merriam Lanova, Bernice Rehner, Myrna Galle, Sonja Taanila, Patricia Wilde, Constance Garfield, Joy Williams, and Pauline Goddard in Balanchine's *Serenade*. Photo: Fred Fehl.

Below: The Pas de Sept from Balanchine's *Le Bourgeois Gentilhomme*. Photo: Fred Fehl.

Above: The funeral scene from Page and Stone's *Frankie and Johnny* with Frederic Franklin (as Johnny) in coffin mourned by Ruthanna Boris, at left as Frankie, and Pauline Goddard (at right).

Below: Alexandra Danilova, in *Mozartiana* costume, with George Balanchine and Frederic Franklin.

Right: The masquerade costumes from Balanchine's *Night Shadow*, 1946, designed by Surrealist painter Dorothea Tanning.

Below: Alexandra Danilova and Nicholas Magallanes as Sleepwalker and Poet in Balanchine's *Night Shadow*. Photo: Maurice Seymour.

Above: Rachel Chapman and George Balanchine play the score for
Raymonda while Barth Cummins, Peter Deign, Harding Dorn, and Claire
Pasch listen. Photo: Frank Hobi.

Below: Alexandra Danilova in Balanchine's *Raymonda*.

Alexandra Danilova, Frederic Franklin, and Nikita Talin in Ruth Page's *The Bells.*

Leon Danielian and Ruthanna Boris in Boris's *Cirque de Deux,* 1947.

Above: Mary Ellen Moylan.

Below: Yvonne Chouteau and Vida Brown in Bettis's *Virginia Sampler*.

Alexandra Danilova and Oleg Tupine in *Paquita*. Photo: Maurice Seymour.

Right: Oleg Tupine and Yvette Chauviré in Lifar's *Roméo et Juliette,* 1950. Photo: Maurice Seymour.

Below: Yvonne Chouteau as Juliet. Photo: Easton's Studio.

Alan Howard and Nina Novak. Photo: Maurice Seymour.

Right: Gertrude Tyven. Photo: Constantine.

Below: Group from Massine's *Harold in Italy* with Teri de Mari (on floor) as the Simpleton and Leon Danielian as Harold.

Three moments from a famous triple bill.

Left: Alexandra Danilova as the Sugar Plum Fairy in *Nutcracker.* Photo: Fred Fehl.

Below: Nathalie Krassovska and Jean Yazvinsky in *Scheherazade.* Photo: Fred Fehl.

Right: Moscelyne Larkin as Odette in *Swan Lake.* Photo: Maurice Seymour.

Left: Rachel Chapman, staff pianist.

Below: Sophie Pourmei, wardrobe director. Photo: Maurice Seymour.

11 DANILOVA AND FRANKLIN: COMPANY STARS

THERE was a ballet performance in Columbus, Ohio, in 1944 by an organization which, although it featured a large ensemble in *Swan Lake, Red Poppy,* and *Prince Igor,* was listed on the first page of the program as "Mlle Danilova, Frederic Franklin and Company." It was only by reading the small print on page three that a member of the audience would have learned that the real name of this group was Ballet Russe de Monte Carlo.[1]

That first-page listing was of course a printer's error. Yet it told a truth about the Ballet Russe. For thousands of dancegoers from 1938 until the 1950s did indeed regard the Ballet Russe as "Mlle Danilova, Frederic Franklin and Company." Although the Ballet Russe always had other stars—stars such as Alicia Markova, Nathalie Krassovska, Mia Slavenska, Igor Youskevitch, and André Eglevsky, for example, or such young Americans as Ruthanna Boris, Mary Ellen Moylan, Maria Tallchief, and Leon Danielian—Danilova and Franklin were the stars who shone brightest for American audiences. Not only were they brilliant individually; together they formed one of the great partnerships of twentieth-century ballet. Both were, as George Amberg once said of Danilova, "adored by the public and respected by . . . colleagues."[2]

At their best, there was a champagne-like sparkle about Ballet Russe performances, and it is no accident that Léonide Massine once compared Danilova with champagne, saying that he

201

particularly valued her as an interpreter of demi-caractère roles because "It is easier to be tragic on the stage than to be champagne."[3] Yet Danilova, although she excelled in light comedy, could be wistful or tragic, as well as gay. With her heart-shaped face, heavily-lidded hazel eyes, Grecian nose, and dark brown hair, her very appearance on stage was striking. She also possessed what were, in her day, the most celebrated and photogenic legs in all ballet—"legs like luminous wax," Lincoln Kirstein called them. Even as a young dancer at the Maryinsky Theatre in Petrograd, Danilova's legs were famous, in part possibly because she made sure that audiences noticed them. Thus as the Diamond Fairy in *The Sleeping Beauty* she would always stand in a position that would display her legs to best advantage during the variations of the other soloists.[4]

Danilova's stage presence was remarkable. She was, above all, a dancer who realized that a ballet was not simply a succession of steps, but an opportunity for a performance. Frederic Franklin has said, "Danilova was, essentially, a theatre person. The moment she came on stage you knew that *there* was a great personality."[5] Yet never did critics chide her for being cheap or brassy. Rather, they tended to agree with Anatole Chujoy that her virtues included "elegance, simplicity, dignity, correctness of style . . . an unsurpassed taste, a feeling for the right thing in the right place, an absence of mannerisms and ostentation . . . a magnificent personality, a radiant projection . . . ."[6]

On several occasions another admirer, Edwin Denby, tried to isolate the qualities that made her performances memorable. One was the "special gift" of joyousness: "At the height of a classical variation, while she is observing all the restrictions of the grand style, she seems suddenly to be happy to be dancing, with a pleasure like a little girl's. It gives her a sort of natural grace that is unique." But joyousness is a theatrical illusion. What, specifically, helped create that illusion? At least in part, thought Denby, it was a mastery of rhythm: "In all the severity of exact classicism Danilova's dancing rhythm fills the time quantities of the music to the full; it does not, like the rhythm of lesser dancers, jab at a stress and then drag for a moment till the music catches up. Stress and release in all their variety are equally vivid, equally expressive to watch." After a performance of *Le Beau Danube* Denby observed,

> She has by nature and by artistry a wonderful legato that gives to all the sharp accents and spurts of cancan steps that the part calls for a musical grace none of the younger dancers have

learned. In comparison to her they seem to trust to luck for their balance, and so their dancing loses flow and sweetness. Danilova makes her temperamental vivacity count because the movements are so well placed. Where others look happy she scintillates. But it is her feminine presence, her air of dancing for the delight of it, that captures the audience's heart.[7]

Maryinsky-trained, Danilova grew up knowing the Petipa repertoire and some of the early ballets of the young Fokine (and at various times she has helped stage, in whole or in part, such works as *Raymonda, Paquita, Les Sylphides,* and *Le Pavillon d'Armide*). She also participated in some of the daring experimental productions of Soviet ballet in the 1920s, and, along with George Balanchine, was a member of the cast of *Dance Symphony,* Fyodor Lopukhov's pioneering abstract symphonic ballet of 1923. As a member of the Diaghilev Ballet, Danilova encountered the works of Massine, Nijinska, and Balanchine, many of them collaborations with the most advanced composers and artists of the time. With Colonel de Basil's Ballets Russes she appeared in the controversial symphonic ballets of Massine, and one of the reasons why she left de Basil to join the Ballet Russe de Monte Carlo was to continue working with Massine. With the Monte Carlo she also danced works by Nijinska and Balanchine and spoke dialogue in Ruth's Page's unconventional *Billy Sunday.* To this day she retains an artistically inquisitive mind and, very significantly, has said, "I have been so lucky: all my life I have worked with the avant-garde. That developed me enormously as an artist, much more than if I had done just *Swan Lake* and *Giselle.*" Danilova's passion for dancing strikes close associates as being virtually an instinctive need, and Danilova herself, after first admitting to be puzzled by the remark, finally agreed when Walter Terry told her that, if she had been denied ballet training, she might still have become a dancer—a sort of Russian Isadora Duncan, perhaps.

Versatile though she was, Danilova did possess limitations. Although admired as a classical stylist, such passages as the thirty-two fouettés in the Black Swan pas de deux did not come easily to her. And although her range as a dance-actress was wide, some dancegoers thought that she lacked sweet naive simplicity when she portrayed Giselle. She is probably best remembered for her performances in ballets of plot and character, although *Danses Concertantes* was created for her and she has danced such abstractions as *Serenade* and *Chopin Concerto.* She has said, "I like best . . . the ballets where the role, she have a character of her own."[8]

That character—Giselle notwithstanding—could be convincingly tragic. There was an ineffable sadness about Danilova's Odette because in her view of the Swan Queen, "You see, no one have ever loved her enough, and so they cannot save her . . . ."[9] As the betrothed girl in *Le Baiser de la Fée* she had a curious elusiveness, and when someone remarked that she looked more unearthly than the Ice Fairy herself, she remarked, "That is as it should be. I am what he want and can never get!"[10] Balanchine again made use of that same elusiveness when he cast her as the Sleepwalker in *Night Shadow*.

But it was the roles demanding gaiety and *joie de vivre*—the champagne roles—for which Danilova was most beloved. Her Swanilda, said Grace Robert, was notable for "authoritative style, exquisite sparkle, and inimitable pantomime." And Robert is only one of countless balletgoers for whom Danilova's performances in Massine's *Gaîté Parisienne, Beau Danube,* and *Boutique Fantasque* formed "a triptych of that gaiety of which she alone possesses the secret." In such ballets, Danilova set "a standard of balletic elegance."[11]

The only partner capable of equaling the irrepressible high spirits of Danilova was Frederic Franklin. "There is no stage grin in the world to match that of Frederic Franklin," Walter Terry has written.[12] According to Agnes de Mille, who cast him in *Rodeo,* "With the exception of Massine, he has the most exact sense of timing of any man in the dance world."[13]

When Danilova stepped onto the stage during a performance by the Ballet Russe de Monte Carlo, she brought to her intepretation of a role a wealth of experience gained in dancing at the Maryinsky and for Diaghilev. Franklin, too, could draw upon a wealth of performing experience—but that experience was of a very different order. During an interview, Franklin kept insisting, "I'm not a hothouse product. I grew up in the vaudeville theatre and in musical comedy," and he kept returning to that point: "I'm not a hothouse product."

And he is right. He is not. Born in Liverpool, he began his studies locally with Mrs. E.M. Kelly, Marjorie Kelly, and Shelagh Elliott-Clarke. Although he wanted most of all to become a ballet dancer, there were few opportunities for British ballet dancers at the time. So Franklin worked in Paris at the Casino de Paris, where he sang, played the piano, tap-danced, and once did a number with

Mistinguette. In London he appeared in musical comedy and vaudeville (where he was a tap dancer in an act called the Lancashire Lads) and formed a supper-club dance team with Wendy Toye, who went on to become a successful musical comedy choreographer and director. All the while, he continued ballet studies with Nicolas Legat, Lydia Kyasht, Lydia Sokolova, and Anton Dolin. He became a member of the Markova-Dolin Ballet in 1935, and one of his important roles was the Bluebird, opposite Alicia Markova's Enchanted Princess. He so impressed Bronislava Nijinska that she created a buffoon's dance for him in the *Nutcracker* divertissements. [14]

He remembers that at one London performance in 1937 almost the entire de Basil company was in the audience. During an intermission George Zoritch came backstage with a note informing him that Massine wished to see him. Massine had liked his dancing, Franklin learned, and wanted him to sign a four-year contract with the new Ballet Russe de Monte Carlo that he was forming. Said Franklin, "I just looked into Massine's eyes—they were deep pools of brown—and he could have made me sign anything." Once the spell wore off, however, he realized that he should not have signed any such document, since he was still under contract to the Markova-Dolin Ballet. He explained the situation to Massine, who told him, "Come when you're ready." That time came sooner than he expected, for Massine had also signed Markova for his company. With the dissolution of the Markova-Dolin Ballet, Franklin joined the Ballet Russe de Monte Carlo. Shortly thereafter, he met David Lichine on the street. Lichine urged him, "Don't go with Massine. De Basil and I want you in our company. I'm even planning a new ballet with a wonderful part in it for you." On the basis of Lichine's description, Franklin now thinks that this role must have been that of the Drummer in *Graduation Ball* (although *Graduation Ball* was not premiered until 1940).

Franklin's motley career in show business, plus his classical ballet training, made him an unusually versatile performer adept at many styles of dancing. His roles extended from Albrecht in *Giselle* to the Champion Roper in *Rodeo*. His rough-and-tumble vaudeville background may also explain why Franklin was a fast learner, a tireless worker, and a fervent believer that, come what may, the show must go on. Agnes de Mille marveled at this and, during the creation of *Rodeo*, drew strength from Franklin's energy:

He was as strong as a mustang, as sudden, as direct, and as

inexhaustible. There was no slacking off at the end of a long effort, no marking. He came into the room briskly, dressed and ready at the first minute of the rehearsal, and he worked full out without a second's deviation of attention until the rehearsal finished, and the last lift was as precise and as vigorous as the first.[15]

Like Danilova, Franklin was a striking stage personality; and, just as Edwin Denby attempted to explain the reasons for Danilova's appeal, so he tried to explain that of Franklin:

> His line is large and open, his deportment is convincing, his extension is clean, his support is sure and easy. He has variety of attack and he ends with assurance. Though he has no startling brilliance or Slavic subtlety, he dances with a continuity of rhythm and a clarity of phrasing that are rare indeed. Franklin's dancing always makes perfect sense; like a true artist, he is completely at the service of the role he takes, and his straight delight in dancing, his forthright presence and openhearted nature give his version of the great classic roles a lyric grace that is fresh and sweet.[16]

Franklin says that it was Massine who first suspected that he had directorial abilities. Even when Franklin was still a comparative newcomer to the tightly enclosed world of Russian ballet, Massine would ask him to conduct rehearsals. Balanchine recognized similar talents in Franklin, and it was at Balanchine's recommendation that he became maître de ballet in 1944. Franklin proved to be sensible, efficient, and organized. Until his appointment, solo roles did not invariably have understudies. If a dancer happened to be indisposed, someone would be almost literally thrown on as a replacement. While such incidents did occur throughout the entire history of the company, Franklin tried to insure that they would happen as seldom as possible by establishing a roster of understudies for every solo part. He also became famous for his speed in setting a ballet. "He taught quickly and always very clearly," Rochelle Zide remembers, and Franklin to this day has not lost his ability to mount big productions in a short time. When André Eglevsky died unexpectedly in 1977, Franklin was called in to stage the production of *Giselle* that the Eglevsky Ballet had announced as its next attraction. He managed to do it in five rehearsals. And when, at one rehearsal, he discovered that the wrong tape had been brought to the studio, he simply went ahead, humming the music as he worked.

Speaking of Franklin in rehearsal, Rochelle Zide says, "He was absolutely marvelous. I adored him, we all adored him, we'd have done anything for him." But she also adds this about Franklin (and her comments are seconded by other dancers): "Freddie gave few individual corrections. He never really coached. For one thing, there usually wasn't much time for that." Yet Franklin was always thorough and his energy was boundless. No wonder, then, that Agnes de Mille called him "the inner motor of the Ballet Russe, the reason why they get through the sheer amount of labor involved in each tour."[17]

Danilova and Franklin were first paired together as Glove Seller and Baron in *Gâité Parisienne.* As Franklin puts it, "The chemistry worked." Offstage, however, relations between them remained stiffly formal for a long time. As a struggling English dancer almost nobody had ever heard of, Franklin had adored Danilova, the great ballerina of de Basil's Ballets Russes. He never dreamed that he would ever have a chance to dance with her. And now that he found himself her partner, he was still in awe of her. "I called her Madame Danilova for the longest time," he says.

At one performance of *Saratoga,* however, Danilova suffered a memory lapse and Franklin prompted her by naming the steps as they danced together. When they reached the wings, Danilova was furious: "How dare you do that! You know you must never speak to me on stage!" A few moments later, she apologized, and then told Franklin, "You may call me Shoura," the nickname which only her closest friends are permitted to use when they address her.

Danilova and Franklin were indefatigable. They danced everywhere, night after night, often several times a night. Not only did they star in many of the ballets, but Franklin as maître de ballet rehearsed the repertoire and Danilova, by her example, set the style for every girl in the company, on stage and off. Danilova always looked the image of a glamorous ballerina and insisted that every other girl do so too. When Sonja Taanila joined the Ballet Russe she wore saddle shoes on tour until Danilova lectured her that, since she was now a member of one of the world's great companies, she should wear high heels: ballerinas always wore high heels, Danilova said.

Danilova could at times be remarkably generous to younger dancers, giving them technical pointers in class. According to Moscelyne Larkin, "If she really liked you, she would even fix your hair or wash your tights if she thought you looked tired." Yet James Starbuck also notes, "Danilova could tear you to shreds." He adds, however, "If you managed to get beyond your anger and listened carefully to what she had to say, her goading could help you develop as an artist."

Danilova and Franklin ruled the company, and their reign was one of the glories of the Ballet Russe. But their reign also, inadvertently, contributed to the company's problems. On the road, local managers insisted upon them. Therefore, they always danced. But because Danilova and Franklin were always there to dance, some observers believe that the Ballet Russe made no systematic attempt to develop its younger ballerinas and danseurs and that this neglect ultimately hurt the company. Thus during the 1946-47 season both Grace Robert and Walter Terry made similar comments. Grace Robert complained, "Unfortunately, the management of the Monte Carlo company has not seen fit to develop the potentialities of the talents that might be found among its own lesser members." Consequently, the company was always at a disadvantage when neither Danilova nor Franklin could appear. Robert also speculated, "No doubt it is difficult to express much individuality in the shadow of such an overpowering personality as Danilova." Noting slight but curious weaknesses in the Monte Carlo's performances, Walter Terry declared, "This hint of weakness is due, I think, to the failure of the management to groom certain of the company's most advanced members to the point where they could share stellar burdens with Danilova and Franklin and to the failure of many of the dancers to rectify those flaws which hold them in the classification known as 'promise.' "[18]

There are some former members of the Ballet Russe who will agree with Grace Robert about the power of Danilova's personality. At times, Danilova was a second mother to the young women in the company. But, like many mothers, she was not certain how to react when daughters started growing up. She could be the very incarnation of devotion and helpfulness when she coached a girl in a small solo. But should a girl start receiving more important parts, then—perhaps understandably—her attitude toward that girl became more ambiguous. A dancer who had graduated into leading roles recalls that one day Danilova came up to her and frankly told her, "Outside the theatre, I'm your friend. Inside the theatre, I have no friends." And that young dancer was not merely astonished by the remark, she was oddly touched by its candor.

Another dancer—a dancer who successfully performed

some very important roles—says this: "To survive in the presence of Danilova and Franklin—and to be noticed—you had to develop your own style as a performer. That style had to be totally unlike theirs. But it also had to be just as valid." For what no one can deny is that Danilova and Franklin were great artists. Moreover, it was their devotion to ballet that gave artistic focus to the Ballet Russe, particularly in seasons when the artistic direction was shaky. It was their sheer nerve as performers that could make lackluster ballets seem little choreographic jewels and masterpieces seem the great treasures they were.

Whatever Danilova and Franklin did, they did with zest and enthusiasm. No matter how small a small town was on tour, no matter how small the audiences were in the theatre in that small town, Danilova and Franklin never refused to dance. They danced everywhere the Ballet Russe danced, before intellectuals and farmers, before big city industrialists and small town merchants. With amazing unanimity, their colleagues insist that Danilova and Franklin never cut corners. They never simplified their makeup, not even in the tiniest of one-night-stand tank towns, and they never altered or simplified the choreography because they were tired. Somehow, they never seemed to be tired. They loved ballet above all other arts and the Ballet Russe de Monte Carlo above all other companies. No wonder, then, that audiences in return loved them.

NOTES FOR CHAPTER 11

1. Program for Memorial Hall, Columbus, O., 4 January 1944.
2. George Amberg, *Ballet,* p. 68.
3. A.E. Twysden, *Alexandra Danilova,* p. 134.
4. Legs—Lincoln Kirstein, "Let's Go Native," *Town and Country,* January 1939, p. 50; A.E. Twysden, *Alexandra Danilova,* p. 50.
5. Conversation with Frederic Franklin. Henceforth all statements for which no printed source is given were made in conversation with the author. Invaluable help has come from Danilova and Franklin themselves. Also helpful have been conversations with Meredith Baylis, Ruthanna Boris, Yvonne Chouteau, Leon Daniellan, Roman Jasinski, Moscelyne Larkin, Robert Lindgren, James Starbuck, Sonja Taanila, and Rochelle Zide.
6. Anatole Chujoy, "Dance in Review," *Dance News,* June 1943, p. 4.
7. Denby on Danilova—*Looking at the Dance,* pp. 143, 164-165; "Monte Carlo Minus Franklin," *New York Herald-Tribune,* 13 September 1944.
8. A.E. Twysden, *Alexandra Danilova,* p. 133.
9. A.E. Twysden, *Alexandra Danilova,* p. 141.
10. A.E. Twysden, *Alexandra Danilova,* p. 145.

11. Grace Robert on Danilova—*The Borzoi Book of Ballets:* on *Coppélia,* p. 91; on Massine, p. 70.
12. Walter Terry, "Dancing Gentlemen," *New York Herald-Tribune,* 2 November 1941.
13. Agnes de Mille, *Dance to the Piper,* p. 286.
14. Franklin biography—Lillian Moore, "Frederic Franklin," *The Dancing Times,* February 1939, pp. 609-610; "The Sitter Out," *The Dancing Times,* April 1939, p. 5; Ann Barzel, "Lancashire Lad to Ballet Master—Frederic Franklin," *Dance,* February 1946, p. 12.
15. Agnes de Mille, *Dance to the Piper,* p. 286.
16. Edwin Denby, *Looking at the Dance,* pp. 165-166.
17. Agnes de Mille, *Dance to the Piper,* p. 287.
18. Grace Robert, in *Ballet Annual #2,* pp. 102-105; Walter Terry, "Ballet Russe de Monte Carlo: A Survey of Dancers' Talents," *New York Herald-Tribune,* 16 March 1947.

12 AMERICANS IN THE BALLET RUSSE

THE Ballet Russe de Monte Carlo was never totally "Russe." Its ranks included dancers from Great Britain and several Western European nations, and from the Western Hemisphere as well. Among the Canadians in the company were Anna Istomina, Nora White, Patricia Wilde, Robert Lindgren, Ian Gibson, and Duncan Noble. Ramon Segarra came from Puerto Rico; Luis Trapaga, from Cuba. During the final years of the Ballet Russe there were many dancers from Latin American nations in the company—such dancers as Yelle Bettencourt, Irina Borowska, Giaconda Filippini, Fernando Schaffenburg, Lupe Serrano, Eugene Slavin, Miguel Terekhov.

And always, of course, there were dancers from the United States. There were Americans in the Ballet Russe from its inception. By the time it disbanded, most of its dancers were Americans. In 1940 *Dance* could note with alarm, "The Russian-born members of the Ballet Russe de Monte Carlo refer to the Americans in the company as 'foreigners.' " Less than a decade later, in 1949, the Boston critic Elinor Hughes could state that "the term, 'Ballet Russe,' is actually without meaning," because the company had become thoroughly Americanized.[1]

World War II helped speed the process of Americanization. Yet even if the Ballet Russe had not spent the war years here, it would have had to become at some time something other than

211

predominantly "Russe," since it did not have access to dancers from the Soviet Union and one could not expect that there would be an unlimited supply of dancing children of Russian émigré parents. The word "Russe" in the name remained significant, however, for it was emblematic of a great tradition. To American dancers of the 1930s and 1940s, the Ballet Russe was a company one longed to join, since acceptance meant that one was deemed worthy of being part of the great tradition, or it was a company one scorned to join because one believed that the tradition it represented was by no means the only valid tradition.

Dancers of the early years of the Ballet Russe have different, and often contradictory, memories about how Americans were treated. Nathalie Krassovska, a Russian-Scottish ballerina noted for her sanguine disposition, is convinced that there was very little prejudice against Americans. "We were all one big family," she says. "The Americans and the Russians got along very well. No one cared what nationality anyone was. What was important was how well you danced. Oh, sometimes we'd quarrel, but then we'd always make up."[2] Maria Tallchief hotly disagrees about the early 1940s. "Back then, the Russians treated Americans miserably," she remembers. "We were scorned and derided." Ruthanna Boris concurs, saying she sensed a "subtle prejudice" against Americans when she joined the company. She recalls that in Bronislava Nijinska's *Ancient Russia* she and Dorothy Etheridge were the American members of a group of captive princesses, the others in the group being Russians. During rehearsals, if anyone made a mistake, Nijinska would automatically growl, "Dumb Americans!" even when the offender was one of the Russians. Yet Nijinska could also battle ferociously to insure that her own American protégées—among them, Tallchief—received the roles she thought they deserved.

On the other hand, Milada Mladova, an American dancer with the company from the beginning, says that she was never aware of any particular prejudice against her. She speculates that this may have been because the dancers knew she came from a Czech family background, which meant that she was, if not Russian, at least Slavic. Born in Oklahoma City, Mladova grew up in a cultivated family, both of her parents being violin teachers. She studied dance in Oklahoma and showed such promise that her mother, anxious to have an expert appraisal of her daughter's abilities, arranged for an audition with Massine. Massine declared that he liked Mladova's Spanish dancing, but thought her ballet uneven. He recommended study in Paris with Olga Preobrajenska.

Mladova's parents took her to Europe, and soon afterward Massine invited her to join his new company in Monte Carlo. It was the management of the Ballet Russe that gave Mladova her alliterative name. The Milada was real, her Christian names being Annabel Milada. But it was thought that her surname, Mraz, was unsuitable as a stage name. So Milada Mladova she became—although she herself confesses that she always found the alliteration bothersome.

Like Mladova, Charles Dickson, another American with the Ballet Russe during its first season, recalls no great prejudice against Americans. But he wonders whether men escaped prejudice simply because male dancers were always scarce and therefore there did not exist as many people—Russian or non-Russian—to quarrel over who should dance male roles as there were to quarrel over the female roles. Dickson also thinks that the fact that the company's backing was predominantly American helped influence the way in which Americans were treated. Thus, although Americans were occasionally encouraged to adopt Russian names, no concerted efforts were made to force them to do so, whereas in Colonel de Basil's Ballets Russes, American names were changed as a matter of course.

Dickson grew up in Altoona, Pennsylvania, and as a small child loved to watch dancing in movies. Fred Astaire became his idol and he started taking tap lessons from a local teacher, who also recommended ballet. Dickson auditioned for the de Basil Ballets Russes in Pittsburgh and was accepted. Yet he never actually appeared with the company, for Massine asked him to join the new Ballet Russe that he was forming. Dickson decided that, as a youngster, it might be better to start off with a totally new organization than to be in competition with experienced dancers in an already famous troupe. He sailed for Europe—third class—on the same ship on which Massine and Delarova were traveling first class. Also in third class on that ship were two other young Americans joining the Ballet Russe, Rosella Hightower and Dorothy Etheridge. Although he declares that he never felt prejudice against him in the Ballet Russe, Dickson also admits that one reason why he left to join Ballet Theatre for its debut season in 1940 was that Ballet Theatre proudly proclaimed itself an American company.

James Starbuck, who joined the Monte Carlo in its second year, says that the Russians were initially suspicious of Americans. When Massine asked Starbuck to understudy a role in *Gaîté Parisienne*, a Russian dancer informed him, "You'll do that role over my dead body." Gradually, however, Americans became accepted by the Russians, as was perhaps inevitable, considering the fact that the same group of people had to travel together for months on end. The Americans started teaching English to the Russians and, in turn, the Americans mastered the peculiar blending of French and Russian that was the company language at rehearsals. Americans also soon learned Russian words of praise and blame and an assortment of Russian curses. An American could feel he had arrived as a dancer when someone said of him, "He's really Russian at heart." Yet one could also discover that to be metaphorically Russian was not the same as being Russian by birth. Starbuck remembers being denied admission to a party given by some of the Russians in the company, angry guests turning to him and saying, "What are you doing here? You don't belong here. This party is for Russian dancers. Get out."

An orphan, Starbuck was raised by foster-parents in Oakland, California, where he acted with local drama groups until Oakland teacher Raoul Pausé recommended that he also study dance. After studies with Pausé, he joined the San Francisco Ballet. When the de Basil Ballets Russes came to town he auditioned for Lichine, who said he would be hired if he was able to pay his own travel expenses to Europe. But Starbuck at that time had only $9 to his name. Nor was he much richer the next year, when he auditioned for Massine and received a similar offer. But his foster-mother, who worked in a department store, realized that he wanted more than anything to dance and managed to save enough money to pay for a Greyhound bus ticket to New York, where the Ballet Russe de Monte Carlo was playing. He attracted attention for his performances in the Massine repertoire, and in 1943 he was singled out for praise by John Martin for his interpretation of Massine's own role of the Peruvian in *Gaîté Parisienne:* "Mr. Starbuck had the excellent sense to realize that he could not possibly play it in the way Massine had played it, and managed accordingly to give it his own colors and to come through with them flying."[3]

Mladova, Dickson, and Starbuck concur that Massine liked American dancers. Apparently he admired their combination of exuberance and discipline. Also, unlike some of the Russians, the Americans were starry-eyed and rather overawed at finding themselves members of a fabled ballet company. Consequently, they were tractable and seldom indulged in outbursts of temperament. Massine seemed particularly fond of four young Americans who came to Monte Carlo in the spring of 1938—Dickson, Dorothy Etheridge, Rosella Hightower, and Robert Irwin—and served as a sort of cultural mentor to them. Even when the other members of the corps de ballet were dismissed for the day, Massine would ask the Americans to remain and watch rehearsals. Then he would examine them: "Which couple did you like best in *Swan Lake*? Which in *Les Sylphides*? Why do you think that? Why was so-and-so good in *Lac* and not so good in *Sylphides*? Tell me why, please." Even though it was now 10 or 11 at night and the young Americans were exhausted, Massine's questioning continued. "It was his way of educating us," says Dickson.

Americans may have been the workhorses of the company, but they were poorly paid. Yet no one, except for some of the top stars, was ever paid very much in the early days of the Ballet Russe. That is why, says Agnes de Mille, Ballet Russe dancers were notorious for the way they wolfed caviar and champagne at parties given by socialites in the cities they visited on tour. The dancers were always ravenous and they never had enough money. In summer, when the ballet company closed down and dancing jobs were scarce, some dancers literally went broke and, to survive, often borrowed on their salaries for the coming season. "They lived like indentured servants," says de Mille.

It is persistently rumored that in the de Basil Ballets Russes and in the early days of the Ballet Russe de Monte Carlo there were dancers, particularly American and English dancers, who were paying for the privilege of appearing with the company. These dancers were regarded as "apprentices" and the money they paid the management was considered the equivalent of the fee that might be charged for lessons at a ballet school. Today, dancers seem loath to talk about this questionable practice. Most of them admit that they had indeed heard of it, yet add that, to their knowledge, none of their acquaintances had paid to dance with the Ballet Russe. Charles Dickson says, "All of us had to pay our own boat fare to get to Europe. But that was standard practice at the time. Once we reached Monte Carlo, however, we received a salary—a pitifully small one, yet a salary."

Nevertheless, there does exist a document, signed by a British Army officer and dated 8 March 1939, suggesting that a form of apprenticeship existed at least once in the history of the Ballet Russe de Monte Carlo. The officer states,

> I hereby agree that my daughter . . . shall be taken as a student in the Ballet Company of which Leonide Massine is artistic director for a period of one year, beginning about 10

April 1939, with the understanding she will provide her living expenses during the one year of her studentship. . . .

My daughter is to have free tuition and will be given the opportunity to take part in the Ballet Repertoire. . . .

At the termination of [her] studentship, Mr. Massine shall do his best to recommend her for engagement in the company as a regular artist with remuneration, provided, she will prove satisfactory to him in his work.

I . . . hereby agree to contribute . . . the sum of One Thousand Pounds for the production of ballets with Mr. Massine's choreography.[4]

Among the American women who appeared with the Ballet Russe were Ruthanna Boris, Eleanor D'Antuono, Rosella Hightower, Marie-Jeanne, Mary Ellen Moylan, and Maria Tallchief. Some of these dancers (among them D'Antuono, Hightower, and Tallchief) essentially began their careers with the Ballet Russe, but achieved their greatest fame after they had left the company. Marie-Jeanne, on the other hand, was already known—to ballet devotees, if not to the general public—as a ballerina of Balanchine's American Ballet and the Ballet Caravan before she joined the Monte Carlo. Mary Ellen Moylan was also known to ardent ballet fans before her arrival at the Ballet Russe because in 1942 she had danced *Ballet Imperial* with the ballet ensemble of the New Opera Company. During her seasons with the Monte Carlo, Moylan was much admired for her classical perfection; according to Ann Barzel, "Together with Nana Gollner, Mary Ellen Moylan is the nearest thing to a classical ballerina America has developed. . . . She is beautiful, musical and is growing more lyric."[5]

However, the first American ballerina to become a star of the Ballet Russe de Monte Carlo was Ruthanna Boris, and she remains best known today because of her association with the company. Boris was the first American in the Ballet Russe to dance the full range of classical ballerina roles, including Odette, Swanilda, the Sugar Plum Fairy, the Bluebird and Black Swan pas de deux, and Giselle (although she never was seen as Giselle in New York).

Boris is, as her fellow dancer Yvonne Chouteau admiringly calls her, "a fighter." A native New Yorker, Boris was trained at the Metropolitan Opera Ballet School, where she became a special favorite of her teacher, Rosina Galli. When the de Basil company arrived on its first American tour, Galli and the Met's other specialists in the Italian style forbade their students to see the Russians because, says Boris, "They told us that the Russian style would corrupt us. But trying to forbid me to see dancing was like waving a red flag at a bull. I went anyway, and was overwhelmed. I vowed then that someday I would dance with the Ballet Russe." Before that time came, Boris appeared with the American Ballet, where she came under the influence of Balanchine, who profoundly affected her artistic development, and after that company disbanded she served as prima ballerina of the Metropolitan Opera Ballet.

When Mia Slavenska left the Monte Carlo during the 1942-43 season, Boris reasoned, "The company needs another ballerina. Now is my chance." But Sergei Denham appeared unimpressed by her credentials, telling her, "No American comes into this company as a principal dancer. They must all start in the corps, so they can learn our style." Boris was distressed to hear this, but she now realizes that Denham's comment was not merely anti-Americanism, but a tactic used by directors the world over who want to try out possibly valuable dancers without having to pay them top salaries. Nevertheless, Denham did permit her to audition for the company. Present at that audition was Leon Danielian, who advised her to do all that she could to get into the Ballet Russe because he was looking for a regular partner to dance with and thought that the combination of Boris and Danielian would prove a good one. Then he added, "We Americans have got to show those Russians that we can dance as well as they can."

And they did, the partnership of Boris and Danielian achieving a fame surpassed only by that of Danilova and Franklin. Championing the cause of American ballet, they would whoop with joy whenever one of their pas de deux or variations got more applause than an equivalent item by a Russian dancer. "People even nicknamed us 'Mr. and Mrs. Borden,' " says Boris, "because of our ability to milk our curtain calls." Partners on stage, they were also personal friends. "When, for one reason or another, things started going bad for us, we'd arrange to meet at a delicatessen," Boris says, "and then Leon would say, 'Okay, let's talk dirty,' and we'd let our hair down and cry over all our problems."

Boris's gifts extended beyond an ability to milk curtain calls. Ann Barzel termed her "a technical perfectionist and performer of great intelligence." Other critics were astonished at her range. Not only did she dance the classics, she was praised for her interpretations of ballets by such disparate twentieth-century choreographers as Fokine, Balanchine, and Ruth Page. John Martin said of her, "No role to her is merely a vehicle for the display of her talents; her talents rather become the vehicles for publishing the role's intent. . . . It would be difficult to name another dancer who has so clear a sense of these stylistic differences as Miss Boris has or who so unfailingly makes them clear to the spectator."[6]

As for Leon Danielian, "Mr. Borden" of the "Mr. and Mrs. Borden" team, "The boy can dance like a house afire," said John Martin.[7] The son of Armenian immigrant parents, Danielian was taught folk dancing by his mother when he was scarcely more than a baby. "I've never not danced," he says. "I honestly can't remember when I first learned about the five positions. They were always there, something I always knew." After study with various teachers, Danielian joined the Mordkin Ballet and in 1940 became a charter member of Ballet Theatre. But when Ballet Theatre increasingly emphasized Russian ballet, Danielian, like other young Americans in that company, felt slighted. "Finally," he says, "I decided that if Ballet Theatre was going to be a Russian ballet, I would join a *real* Russian ballet." He joined Colonel de Basil's Original Ballets Russes, but when that company left for South America he chose to remain in New York. After a stint of nightclub work, he was accepted by the Ballet Russe de Monte Carlo. Although he made guest appearances with other companies (including Les Ballets des Champs-Elysées), Danielian was primarily associated with the Ballet Russe, and it was as a principal dancer of the Ballet Russe that he became popular with audiences from coast to coast.

Ann Barzel analyzed the qualities that made him such a favorite: "Leon Danielian is one of the best classical dancers, with a *batterie* unequaled for brilliance and a technical neatness few male dancers can match. With them he has an engaging personality and is a natural comedian, not a slapstick one, but the suave witty kind."[8]

One American dancer who is remembered with admiration by many connoisseurs of classical technique is Gertrude Tyven. Tyven (who died in 1966) devoted her entire dancing career to the Ballet Russe. Her Finnish immigrant parents became friends of the ballet teachers Vecheslav and Maria Swoboda, and when the Swobodas caught a glimpse of little Gertrude they called her "a beautiful sparrow of a child" and exclaimed, "She must study!" Therefore Gertrude and, later, her sister Sonja received dancing lessons and both eventually became members of the Ballet Russe, Gertrude joining the company in 1942 and remaining with it until 1959. Until the 1945-46 season she danced under the stage name of Svobodina, as a tribute to her teachers.

The year she reverted to her real name was the year

that her sister joined the company. Now there were two Tyvens in the Ballet Russe. That would not do, George Balanchine told them. Therefore Sonja, being the younger, would have to find herself a new name. What should it be? Balanchine suggested that she adopt a Finnish name. And what was a Finnish name? "Something with double vowels," said Balanchine. So Sonja Tyven became Sonja Taanila, although later she danced with other companies under the name of Sonja Tyven and under her married name of Sonja Lindgren.

"Gertrude was a totally natural dancer," her sister remembers. "To this day, Mme Swoboda still claims that she never encountered a young body that was such perfect material for classical ballet. Other dancers may have had more flash. But Gertrude was always an honest, true dancer." But her very modesty as a performer disturbed some critics. P.W. Manchester observed, "Gertrude Tyven has a superbly complete classic technique and a marvellous line. Yet her work is strangely pallid. The spectator would sometimes gladly sacrifice so much correctness for a little fire."

"Gertrude needed artistic direction," her sister concedes. "I sometimes think she stayed too long with the Ballet Russe, for the years when she was coming into her full powers as a dancer were also the years when the Ballet Russe started to decline artistically." Yet if her dancing never blazed, one could say along with Olga Maynard that "she burned like a wax candle with a steady, mellow gleam."[9]

Four ballerinas of American Indian descent were at one time or another members of the Ballet Russe. The first of them, Rosella Hightower, was a member of the corps during the company's opening season. But it was only after she left the Monte Carlo in 1941 to join, first, Ballet Theatre and then, much later, the de Cuevas Ballet that she became widely known. The other American Indian ballerinas, however, are closely associated with the Ballet Russe.

Denham invited Maria Tallchief to join the company the first time he saw her working in a Los Angeles studio. But her mother considered her still too young to tour the country with a ballet troupe. Later, the ballerina Tatiana Riabouchinska set out by train from Los Angeles to make a visit to New York, and because Tallchief's mother considered Riabouchinska a suitable chaperone, Tallchief was permitted to travel with her to see what her current prospects of joining the Ballet Russe were. Once in New

York, Tallchief made an appointment to see Denham. Unfortunately, Denham had now forgotten both her and his invitation to her. Yet he took her on a Canadian tour as a replacement for one of the dancers who, because of passport difficulties, was not permitted to cross the border during wartime. Shortly thereafter, she became a regular member of the company.

Like Boris, Tallchief was proud to be an American dancer. She was willing to adopt a variant of her middle name, Marie, for the stage (her real first name was Elizabeth and she had danced as Betty Tallchief in California), but she adamantly refused to listen to those who tried to persuade her that it would be so easy to Russianize her name by changing it to Tallchieva. She firmly believes that some of the Russian dancers disliked her intensely. But she had a strong ally. For she enjoyed the protection of Bronislava Nijinska, who had been one of her teachers in California.

By 1945 Edwin Denby was writing that "Tallchief has a thrilling power of momentum that one misses in most of our young dancers, men as well as girls. Her style would gain in warmth if her arms could curve and yield and float more easily, but her honesty in all she does is completely winning and everybody loves her."[10] Eventually, Tallchief became an internationally celebrated ballerina of the New York City Ballet.

Yvonne Chouteau, another of the Indian ballerinas, devoted most of her career to the Ballet Russe, just as Gertrude Tyven did. As long as she has been a dancer, wags have joked that if the syllables of her last name are reversed, Chouteau becomes "Toeshoe"; pronounce her name without reversing the syllables, but with a Southwestern accent, and one has "Show toe." Her first name has also caused some trouble. Thus a *New York Herald-Tribune* reporter, perhaps taking down his information by telephone, announced in 1944 that two members of the Ballet Russe were Indians, Maria Tallchief and a boy, "Ivan Chouteau."

The Oklahoma-born dancer is part Indian, part French, and bears one of the most distinguished surnames in the Midwest and Southwest. She is the great-great-great-granddaughter of Jean-Pierre Chouteau, who in 1796 established the first white settlement in what is now Oklahoma. His brother, Auguste, founded the city of St. Louis.

Yvonne Chouteau's father was determined that his only daughter be either a ballerina or an opera singer, and at the age of two she received her first dancing lesson. In 1941, accompanied by her mother and a beloved spitz dog, she came to New York to study at the Vilzak-Shollar School. Soon afterward she was awarded a scholarship to the School of American Ballet. Danilova saw her in class and recommended to Denham that she be hired for the Ballet Russe, despite Balanchine's objection that she was still too young. But Danilova countered by saying that this would be the opportunity of a lifetime for her. She joined the company in 1943. She was 14, the company's baby.

She became a very special sort of dancer. P. W. Manchester called her "A dancer who does not fit into any exact classification. . . . Like the prewar Tatiana Riabouchinska, she can give performances in certain parts that no one else can touch. Although tall and strongly built, she is very light and at times brings an ecstatic quality to her dancing. She has the technique for the classic roles, but in temperament is more suited to *demi-caractère*. . . ." Describing a performance of *Coppélia* in 1945, Edwin Denby noted, "On this occasion Miss Chouteau celebrated her sixteenth birthday by dancing alone a 'Prayer' that was lovely in every way." In 1957—her last year with the company—Chouteau, then expecting her first child, was still dancing "Prayer" in *Coppélia*.

That fact suggests both some of her artistic virtues and some of the limited ways in which she was regarded by the company. Chouteau's dancing was blessed with an enormously appealing sweetness and clarity. But she entered the company as the baby, and she herself concedes, "For some people at the Ballet Russe, I was always the baby, no matter how old I was." Her great protector was Danilova, who watched over her like a second mother. It was Danilova who had recommended that Chouteau dance "Prayer" in *Coppélia* because that had been Danilova's own first solo role. In 1956 when Chouteau wished to marry dancer Miguel Terekhov, the prospective bridegroom had to consult Danilova as though she were a surrogate parent. If Danilova always tried to make sure that Chouteau was safe and comfortable, she also tried to impart a bit of worldly wisdom to the shy and deeply religious girl. Chouteau recalls how annoyed Danilova sometimes used to be "when she saw me studying my missal. She kept saying that I ought to be reading something like *Madame Bovary*, instead."

Taking maternity leave in 1957, Chouteau fully expected to return to the Ballet Russe, but then decided "that a life of constant touring would not be fair to the baby. Besides, it was now clear to me that the company had gone into a decline. It was just not an inspiring company to go back to." She remained in Oklahoma, teaching in Oklahoma City and, with her husband, at the University of Oklahoma in Norman. She has also danced in ballet productions at the university. Her native state has honored her as both dancer and teacher. In 1957 the State Senate proclaimed her "Miss Oklahoma Semi-Centennial," and a year later a portrait of Yvonne Chouteau was installed in the Oklahoma Hall of Fame.[11]

P.W. Manchester said of Moscelyne Larkin, "She is tiny and sparkling, with a magnificent jump and a spectacular way with turns."[12] Larkin is the daughter of a Russian mother and an Indian father. Her mother, Eva Matlagova, toured America in musical comedy until she married, settled down in Oklahoma, and later opened a dancing school in Tulsa. Larkin was studying with Vilzak in New York when, at the age of fifteen, she was hired by the de Basil company. The Russians promptly changed her last name to Larkina. Because they considered her curious first name unpronounceable (named after a friend of the family, Larkin suspects that Moscelyne is a corruption of Marceline), they substituted the Russian name, Moussia, which today is her nickname. Later, Anatole Chujoy encouraged her to revert to her own name. She spent the war years with the Original Ballet Russe in South America, marrying Roman Jasinski in Buenos Aires on Christmas Eve 1943.

The Jasinskis returned to the United States with the de Basil company in 1946 and then accompanied it on the European tour that followed. But Jasinski, who was traveling on a Polish passport, was advised that it would be politically wise for him to settle in America and become a citizen. Back to the United States he and Larkin came, and they joined the Ballet Russe de Monte Carlo, a move that also helped put them on their financial feet. "With de Basil," says Larkin, "you never knew whether there'd be a payday. But Denham's company, by the late 1940s, was paying pretty good salaries." When it became evident that the Monte Carlo had started to decline, the Jasinskis left the company, toured in a concert group with Danilova, then went to Tulsa, where they currently direct the Tulsa Ballet Theatre.

In 1956, by hiring Raven Wilkinson, the Ballet Russe de Monte Carlo became the first American touring ballet company to hire a black dancer. For Wilkinson, the next five years were to be tumultuous, inspiring, dismaying, and exhausting. Like most little girls, Wilkinson danced about the house to music on the phonograph or radio. Her parents, seeking to develop her artistic abilities, gave her lessons in Dalcroze eurythmics and, as a special treat on her ninth birthday, took her to her first ballet class. Wilkinson's mother had investigated several New York studios and had decided that the best one for her daughter was the Swoboda School, from which came many Ballet Russe dancers.

When she became old enough to think of dancing as a career, Wilkinson attended Ballet Russe auditions. Invariably, she was rejected—always, she thought, because she was not good enough. But shortly before one audition, someone told her that it was futile to try to get into the Ballet Russe: the Ballet Russe—indeed, ballet itself—would remain forever closed to her because of her race. That remark enraged her, just as, years later when she was contending with prejudice while on tour with the Ballet Russe, she was enraged when a supposedly well-meaning person suggested, "Why don't you get a company of your own together and do African dances?" Wilkinson specifically wished to be a classical dancer and, never having studied jazz or modern dance, was exclusively classically trained. To her surprise, she was finally accepted by the Ballet Russe at the next audition she attended. She is not sure why: possibly she really had improved as a dancer; she also suspects that she was supported by Danilova, Franklin, and Danielian, who had seen and liked her dancing.

To this day, no one quite knows what made Denham, ordinarily a cautious man, decide to risk having a black dancer in a company that annually toured the segregated South. Perhaps, thinks Igor Youskevitch, who was with the company at the time, Denham, for all his years of residence in the United States, was not fully aware of how great a risk he was taking. Says Youskevitch, "Denham, so far as I could tell, never seemed to have any particular racial prejudice. Many Russians of his social class don't. In the social circles in which he was raised, race was simply never an issue. So he may not have realized how violent an issue it could be for some Americans."

At first, Wilkinson's presence with the company, on and off stage, aroused no criticism and she progressed from the corps into such solo roles as the Waltz in *Les Sylphides.* If audiences in segregated cities suspected that she was black, they declined, possibly out of sheer politeness, to raise objections. But as the civil rights struggles of the 1950s became increasingly intense, the forces of reaction also intensified. Local managers started to complain. In some cities she was forbidden to perform on the same stage with white dancers or to stay at white hotels. Once when she was evicted from a hotel in a city and forced to move to a black hotel, her roommate, Eleanor D'Antuono, staunchly declared, "This is terrible! I'm going with you, Raven." Then Wilkinson had to explain, "Ellie, you can't. They won't let you. It's just as much against the law here for you to be in my hotel as it is for me to be in yours." In another city it was considered wisest for her never even to attempt to dance, for that city was playing host to a Ku Klux Klan rally that weekend. With grim amusement, Wilkinson recalls eating alone in the whites-only dining room of her hotel while all around her sat Ku Klux Klan members (their sheets and hoods piled on vacant chairs), who apparently never suspected that she was black. Occasionally, protests against her were so strong that she had to leave the tour, fly back to New York, and remain there until the company's itinerary took it north again.

During all these difficulties, her colleagues were totally supportive. "The other dancers were just wonderful," she says. "They did all sorts of things to help me. If they thought anyone in a town was suspicious of me, they'd start talking to me in French, as though trying to convince people that I was some sort of exotic— but white—dancer from overseas. And there were occasions when, after a performance, four strong boys would suddenly appear at my dressing room and say, 'We're walking you home, Raven.' That's all they needed to say. It was enough to let me know that they thought trouble might be brewing and they wanted to protect me. Then there was the horrible afternoon when we were rehearsing on stage in one Southern theatre and the manager—a real redneck— burst in shouting, 'Okay, where's the nigra?' Nobody said a word, not a word. So he went up to each of us in turn and asked, 'Where's the nigra?' Still, nobody said a word. He came up to me, too, looked at me and said, 'Where's the nigra?' And when I didn't say anything, he went on to the next person. He never did find his nigra."

But, she notes, "I didn't dance that night. It was thought safest for me not to." When it was thought "safest" for her not to dance in a growing number of cities—"I felt like a freak some- times"—she decided to leave the company. But that, she soon discovered, led to a whole new set of problems: "I'm surprised now at how naive I was then. I simply thought that because I already had been a soloist with one major ballet company, I'd have no problem getting into another ballet company." Yet although she has danced in opera-ballet and with the National Ballet of Holland, she points out, "I was never accepted by another ballet company in America."

Raven Wilkinson's tours with the Ballet Russe left her shattered, and, crushed by her inability to find work with other companies, for a time she retired to a convent and contemplated taking religious orders. But today she thinks she may have "made a point" by being with the Ballet Russe and hopes that her precedent might, in some way, encourage other black ballet dancers to take heart.

 Few other American dancers with the Ballet Russe had to undergo such grueling experiences. Yet many of the American dancers with the company do talk of something akin to making a point when they discuss their years with the Ballet Russe. Their presence with the Ballet Russe demonstrated the ability of American dancers and the validity of American ballet training. "Despite the troubles I had at the Ballet Russe," says Ruthanna Boris, "I'd still do it all over again. I think I helped the cause of American dancers—and in so doing I had the opportunity to dance a repertoire I loved. My years with the Ballet Russe were some of the most tempestuous and exciting years of my life—and some of the funniest, too."

NOTES FOR CHAPTER 12

1. "Entr'acte," *Dance,* November 1940, p. 6; Elinor Hughes, "Ballet in America Worthy More Study and Appreciation," *Boston Sunday Herald,* 15 May 1949.
2. Conversation with Nathalie Krassovska. Henceforth, all statements for which no printed source is given were made in conversation with the author.
3. John Martin, "The Dance: Honor Roll," *New York Times,* 29 August 1943.
4. Contract signed 8 March 1939.
5. Ann Barzel, in *Ballet Annual #5,* p. 122.
6. Ann Barzel, in *Ballet Annual #5,* p. 122; John Martin, "The Dance: An Artist," *New York Times,* 2 March 1947.
7. John Martin, "The Dance: Honor Roll," *New York Times,* 29 August 1943.
8. Ann Barzel, in *Ballet Annual #4,* p. 131.
9. Gertrude Tyven—"Gertrude Tyven Dies in New York," *Dance News,* March 1966; p. 7; P.W. Manchester, in A.H. Franks, *Ballet: A Decade of Endeavour,* p. 114; Olga Maynard, *Bird of Fire: The Story of Maria Tallchief,* p. 109; conversation with Sonja Taanila.
10. Edwin Denby, "The Ballet: Some Reflections on Monte Carlo's Fall Season," *New York Herald-Tribune,* 23 September 1945.
11. Yvonne Chouteau—"Ballet Theatre and Ballet Russe Both Will Open Here on April 9," *New York Herald-Tribune,* 5 March 1944; P.W. Manchester, in A.H. Franks, *Ballet: A Decade of Endeavour,* p. 114; Edwin Denby, *Looking at the Dance,* p. 118; Eugene Palatsky, "Yvonne Chouteau Gets Settled in Oklahoma's Hall of Fame," *Dance Magazine,* January 1959, pp. 12-13; conversation with Yvonne Chouteau.
12. P.W. Manchester, in A.H. Franks, *Ballet: A Decade of Endeavour,* p. 115.

13 PEOPLE BEHIND THE SCENES

"THE Ballet Russe isn't a company of employees, but a family," Sergei Denham liked to tell reporters.[1] Many of his dancers also insisted that the Ballet Russe de Monte Carlo was indeed one big family. The company inspired loyalty, and people remained with it for years, sometimes cursing it, sometimes crying over it, yet sticking with it. Not only the dancers were loyal: the technical assistants and the office staff could be just as devoted. In 1949 the Boston critic Elinor Hughes wrote that eighty per cent of the personnel of the Ballet Russe, including the stage crew, had been together for eight or nine years.[2]

Many people worked behind the scenes at the Ballet Russe, people dancers remember fondly and speak of with affection. There was, for instance, George Ford, who in 1961 had served as company manager for eighteen years. His father, Henry Clay Ford, had been in Ford's Theatre on the night of Lincoln's assassination, and Ford's uncle, John T. Ford, was that theatre's proprietor. From these relatives George Ford acquired a love of theatrical history and a fascination with the life of Lincoln. He became an expert on both subjects and could talk about them endlessly—and persuasively, too. For it was Ford, with his love of theatrical history, who prompted George Verdak, as a young dancer with the Ballet Russe, to develop an interest in dance history. Today Verdak, director of Indianapolis Ballet Theatre, possesses one of the outstanding private dance collections in America.[3]

An important man backstage was Lewis L. Smith (nick-named Cat), who joined the company as an electrician in 1943. When he retired in 1956 he bore the title of "assistant to the director on stage," and was in charge of all properties, scenery and lighting. Interviewed in 1958, he told a reporter, "I still get calls from the ballet asking me where something is stored in its store-house in Hackensack." Smith fascinated impecunious dancers be-cause he always seemed to have huge sums of money about him in ready cash, and stories began to circulate about mysterious sources of income upon which he could draw. George Verdak, who became a friend of Smith, dismisses most of these stories as mere fantasies. "Lew was invaluable," Verdak says, "and Denham knew it. So he was probably the best paid member of the Ballet Russe. Lew made lots of money and liked to keep cash on hand." Verdak also says—and his colleagues concur—that Smith was always willing to use some of that cash to help a dancer in need.[4]

Other dancers talk of Jean Cerrone, who served as "ex-ecutive assistant and assistant director" for the company from its inception to its temporary dissolution in 1952. Before that, he had worked for René Blum's company in his native Monte Carlo. In more recent years he has been on the staff of such organizations as the Harkness Ballet, Maryland Ballet, and American Ballet Theatre. Also devoted to the Ballet Russe were such figures as Julius Fleischmann, the company's most important patron, and Watson Washburn, the company's lawyer from its birth to its demise. Dur-ing all that time, Washburn worked for the company without any payment, says Denham's daughter, Irina Pabst.[5]

When Denham was faced with important decisions, yet was unsure of what course of action he would follow, he might postpone affairs by saying, "Before I act on this, I want to consult my board of directors." Sometimes he would then confer with Fleischmann or Washburn. But he was more likely to sit down and have a talk with Michael Subotin, who was listed in programs as the director's "special assistant" or "special representative." In reality, Subotin was "Mr. Denham's one-man board of directors," as Ruth-anna Boris puts it. He was more than that. He was probably Den-ham's oldest and best friend.

Subotin and Denham grew up together in Samara, and both attended the Moscow Commercial Institute until the Revolu-tion separated them. Not wishing to fight fellow Russians in what he interpreted as a kind of civil war, Subotin fled to Kiev, then went on to various other towns that kept being claimed first by the White Russians, then by the Bolshevik forces. Eventually, he was able to reach Paris, where he found work driving a taxi.

Denham learned of Subotin's whereabouts and, on one of his banking trips to Paris, looked him up. In those days, Denham used to stay at the exclusive Chambord Hotel on the Champs-Elysées, and the hotel's concierge was perpetually mystified that Denham not only had a friend who was a mere chauffeur, but also was willing to lower himself in social dignity by sitting in the front seat when they went out for a drive. Denham kept urging Subotin to emigrate to the United States and in 1928 was able to secure him a visa. In New York, Subotin again drove a taxi and for some years worked for a match company.

When Denham became associated with the Ballet Russe, he recommended that Subotin work there, too. But Subotin, knowing little about ballet companies, wondered how he could possibly be of use. "You could sell the souvenir programs," Denham suggested. And that is what Subotin did. He was the rosy-cheeked man who stood in the lobby of every theatre on tour calling out, "Ballet book! Get your ballet book!" He also assisted George Ford, eventually becoming company manager for the Ballet Russe's final season.

To this day Subotin still, in a sense, works for the Ballet Russe, for the Ballet Foundation retains a small office in New York City's Steinway Hall. There, every morning, the octogenarian Subotin goes to guard the Ballet Foundation's collection of documents and scores and to transact any business with which the foundation may be involved.

Not the least of the remarkable people associated with the Ballet Russe were the women who worked in the Ballet Russe offices. In the later years of the company, Doris Luhrs served as staff assistant, while Natalie Riley was executive secretary. But, before that, there was an assistant to the director who signed herself simply M. Hornyak.

The "M." stands for Margaret, but friends call her Peggy. She is a vivacious blonde who seems not in the least the dour sort of person who might want to be known as M. Hornyak. But there was a reason for that austere signature. Born in New York and raised in Connecticut, Hornyak longed to be a dancer, but her parents did not consider dancing a proper profession for a respectable girl. To keep her from dancing, they gave her trips to Europe and sent her through college. By the time she had graduated, she knew that it was probably too late for her to start dancing. But, as it turned out, it was not too late for her to become involved with dance. When she was looking for work, an employment agency told her that the Ballet Russe needed someone to help in the office. "That did it!" she says. "I ran straight to the Ballet Russe and signed the contract. It didn't matter to me what the wages and hours were. All that mattered was that I was going to work for the Ballet Russe." She recalls this as being "about 1940." She remained with the Ballet Russe until 1948.[6]

It was her first job. And now that she was actually with the Ballet Russe, she suddenly felt scared and vulnerable. To hide her youthful inexperience, she tried to appear coolly authoritative. One way that she did so was to adopt the professional name of M. Hornyak—a name, she thought, that would make her sound neither youthful nor inexperienced. Nor would that name necessarily indicate that the person behind the signature was a woman. Asked whether the adoption of such a name might, in today's terminology, be considered something of a feminist gesture, Hornyak replied, "Yes, I suppose you could say that."

Inexperienced she may have been, but she was also reliable and intelligent. Eventually, as assistant to the director, her duties included supplying printers with program information, supervising the preparation of the souvenir books, seeing to it that contracts were signed and in order, and making sure that publicity materials were sent out to local sponsors on the road. During the run of *Song of Norway* she had to attend one performance of the musical each week in order to ascertain whether the dance sequences were being kept in good shape. She was even permitted to make suggestions about program building. In programming she stressed variety, both in the tone of the ballets and in the kinds of physical demands they made upon the cast. Thus she tried to follow a strenuous pointe ballet with one performed in soft slippers or one that emphasized character dancing. Because Denham's private office was a sanctum to which few were admitted, Hornyak found that dancers started taking some of their troubles to her and she would have to calm tempers, soothe wounded feelings, dole out sympathy and encouragement, and diplomatically handle troublesome cases—for instance, that of the company member who never wanted to go to Canada because the age listed on her passport revealed that she was two years older than she cared to admit.

Hornyak also takes credit for two bright ideas. She believes it was she who first got the idea of photographing nothing of Danilova but her fabled legs and of using that photograph as company publicity. Another bright idea affected programming for years to come. One of her tasks was to tabulate receipts as they came in from the road. Occasionally, she would note the strange phenomenon that the Ballet Russe would do well in a city one year and very poorly in that same city the next year. She began to wonder why and decided that choice of repertoire might have something to do with it. After devising elaborate charts showing which ballets had been presented in which cities in which years, she concluded that business was always good when *Swan Lake* and *Scheherazade* were billed together on the same program. It did not really matter what else was on that program: business would still probably be good. But her tabulations inclined her to believe that business would be especially good if the third ballet happened to be *Nutcracker.* She says, "I think I invented the triple-bill of *Swan Lake, Nutcracker,* and *Scheherazade"* — the triple-bill that became the Ballet Russe trademark.

At the time that Frederic Franklin became maître de ballet in 1944, Jean Yazvinsky resigned as régisseur and was replaced by Michel Katcharoff. Except for a season or two during which he worked with other companies, he remained régisseur until 1959. It was a job that, without his knowing it, Katcharoff had been preparing for all his dancing days. Born in Iran of Armenian parents, he was raised in Baku and had his first dance training at the Baku Opera School. After moving to Paris, he danced briefly with companies headed by Bronislava Nijinska and Ida Rubinstein and in 1932 joined the new Ballets Russes of Colonel de Basil. It was Serge Grigoriev, de Basil's régisseur, who first noticed that Katcharoff had a good eye and a good memory. He urged Katcharoff to watch the rehearsals of all the ballets in the repertoire and to study their steps. Gradually, if replacements were needed in certain works, Grigoriev started asking Katcharoff to teach the new dancers their roles. "I now realize," Katcharoff says, "that Grigoriev by doing this was teaching me how to become a régisseur."

When the split came between de Basil and Massine, Katcharoff sided with Massine, in part because he knew the Massine company was planning to visit America and he wished to stay in America and take out citizenship papers. Like Grigoriev, Massine admired Katcharoff's ability to remember details and occasionally called upon him to assist at rehearsals.

Katcharoff found that as régisseur he had to take on more duties and responsibilities than a régisseur would probably have to assume in a company today. As a régisseur does today, he was required to conduct repertoire and replacement rehearsals and to oversee the performance at night. But he not only had to watch over performances generally, he also had to serve as a supervisory stage manager. Since there was never enough money in the Ballet Russe budget for assistants, the régisseur had to see that the scenery was hung, he gave lighting cues to the electricians and masterminded the curtain calls, and even had to go to the dancers' dressing rooms and call "Places"—tasks now usually performed by the stage manager or his assistants. "But back then," says Katcharoff, "the régisseur had to be everywhere and get there in a hurry."[7]

During the 1960-61 season Vadim Sulima became régisseur. But because Sulima spoke almost no English, it proved necessary to give him an assistant. Named to the post was a California-born dancer, Meredith Baylis. Of Scottish-Irish descent, Baylis came from a theatrical family. On her mother's side were several Highland dancing masters, while her great-aunt was Lilian Baylis, director of London's Old Vic Theatre. Baylis had joined the Ballet Russe in 1951-52, the season before the company temporarily disbanded. Like many young American dancers of her day, she specifically wanted to be with the Ballet Russe because she knew and loved the repertoire. Therefore she returned to the Ballet Russe when it was reorganized in 1954 and remained with it until its demise in 1962.

As assistant régisseur, she rehearsed ballets and made suggestions as to casting, subject to the approval of Denham and Sulima—and also to the approval of Nina Novak, who now had influence over almost every aspect of company activities. Another of Baylis's jobs was that of keeping the official company diary, a document that recorded every move the Ballet Russe made (and at what time of day that move was made), the casting of each ballet at every performance, and the exact times that performances began and ended.

Of all the Ballet Russe staff members, none are spoken of more often by dancers—and with more respect and affection—than Rachel Chapman, the company pianist, and Sophie Pourmel, the wardrobe director. Both were associated with the Ballet Russe de Monte Carlo from its first day to its last, and both were totally dedicated to it.

No one ever called Rachel Chapman anything other than Rachel. And Rachel was always pronounced "Rah-SHEL"— "Just like the French actress," she used to advise strangers uncertain about her name. But although one could call her by her first name, one never treated her lightly. Rachel Chapman was the company's irreplaceable musical authority. Conductors came and went. Dancers and choreographers came and went. But always there was Rachel. She played for all rehearsals and in the evening she played with the orchestra in the pit. If a ballet was set to a piano concerto, it was usually Rachel Chapman who played the solo part. Because *Ballet Imperial* figured for so many seasons in the repertoire, she believes she may have played Tchaikovsky's second piano concerto more often than any other pianist in history. She played on grand pianos in the opera houses of large cities and on rickety uprights with stuck keys in the gymnasiums of small town high schools. "I'm the queen of the uprights," she said of herself.

In some ways more important than any conductor, Chapman was responsible for the tempos and musical style of each work in the repertoire. One never quarreled with her, for her memory and her taste were impeccable. She could even coach dancers in choreographic details. Meredith Baylis says it was Chapman who taught her both the Black Swan pas de deux and Myrtha in *Giselle*. Afraid of no one, Chapman had no hesitations about reprimanding famous ballerinas over errors in musicality and phrasing and she was known to snort contemptuously at choreographers for their musical gaffes. Yet neither was Chapman a pedant, for she always sought to keep a balance between musical strictness and a comfortable dancing tempo. Dancers therefore trusted her.

Chapman was born Rachel Bodenstein in Warsaw. A member of a musical family, she studied to be a concert pianist and her brother became one of the founding members of the Palestine Orchestra, today the Israel Philharmonic. In 1933 she came to the United States, where she married Philip Chapman, who was killed while serving with the army in the Pacific during World War II. Because the blonde Chapman is such a flamboyant woman—"She looked and acted like a Polish lioness," is how Agnes de Mille describes her—many stories grew up about her, not all of them necessarily true. Perhaps the most puzzling is the story that, when she was very young, she was a pianist for Diaghilev. Ann Barzel remembers hearing this, and, during the heyday of the Ballet Russe, newspaper articles would occasionally link Chapman to the Diaghilev Ballet. Was this only a publicist's extravagance? Perhaps—for Chapman, in an interview with Israeli critic Giora Manor, has denied ever having any connection with Diaghilev.

Instead, Chapman insists that her "first encounter with ballet" came when she arrived one day at a de Basil Ballet rehearsal as a stand-in for one of the company's indisposed accompanists. Her playing attracted such favorable attention that only a few days later she received a telegram inviting her to become a regular pianist for the company. She was to devote the rest of her professional life to ballet, most of it to the Ballet Russe de Monte Carlo. When Denham attempted to organize a new company in Monte Carlo in 1966, Chapman was again the staff pianist. When that company folded, she worked for Hurok, playing for the various visiting foreign companies that the impresario imported. In 1974 she retired to Tel Aviv.[8]

Chapman was noted for emotional fireworks. Although blessed with remarkable stamina—she could play for hours on end—she had no patience with choreographers or dancers who appeared to be merely dithering in rehearsals. She particularly loathed the sort of choreographer who could never make up his mind about what he wanted for a certain passage in a ballet. She would scare the wits out of such a choreographer by announcing, after he had been fussing repeatedly and to no avail over a phrase, "I've played this passage quite enough. I'll only play it twice more. So you'd better get it right, because I won't play it again." That ultimatum had a magical effect, for choreographers always somehow managed to complete the bothersome passages.

A *New York Times* reporter, sent to do a backstage story on the Ballet Russe in 1948, was nonplussed to find Chapman angrily slamming down the piano lid during rehearsals, berating the dancers, and telling conductor Paul Strauss that he knew almost nothing about conducting ballet music. When a dancer left some personal belongings on the top of the piano, she shouted, "This is my territory. Nobody puts anything here but me. This is not a garbage dump and it is not a clothes closet and it is not a bookcase. This is my piano. This is my territory."

Because Chapman could rule so well over her "territory," on a number of occasions she saved the company's musical life. One such occasion was an Ottawa appearance in 1942, when wartime passport regulations made crossing the border into Canada a tortuous matter. An Ottawa newspaper reported that passport control was so strict and inspections were so thorough that, although the dancers and staff members managed to reach Ottawa in time for the performance, most of the musicians who toured with the company were still back at the border when the curtain went up. John Martin tells the same story, but adds something the Ottawa paper did not mention, perhaps for reasons of local pride: lacking experienced first-chair players to guide them, the local pickup musicians in Ottawa complained that the scores were too difficult. Therefore Denham dispensed with an orchestra altogether and had Chapman play solo for a triple-bill consisting of *Magic Swan, Scheherazade,* and *Gaîté Parisienne.*

Igor Youskevitch and Eugene Slavin both speak of an occasion, some time in the mid-1950s, when the conductor did not arrive for a performance in a town in upstate New York. He had been traveling in a private car, rather than on the company bus, and that evening was delayed for some reason that neither dancer can now recall—weather conditions, perhaps, or mechanical breakdown. Denham told the manager of the local theatre not to worry: Rachel Chapman would cue the orchestra from the piano. Yet that failed to please the manager. He pointed out that the contract stated that the Ballet Russe would appear with orchestra *and* conductor. Since that was what the contract promised, that was what he demanded, and neither blizzards nor flat tires would make him alter his demands. Denham was dismayed: there simply was no conductor to be had.

Then he thought of a plan. It was risky, yet it might just work. Denham marched up to the theatre manager and announced, "Tonight I shall bestow a great favor upon your community. Tonight I, Sergei J. Denham, director of the Ballet Russe de Monte Carlo, will personally conduct the orchestra." The manager was overjoyed, for the publicity value of such an event was enormous. So that night, Denham (who, after all, had had early musical training) stepped before the orchestra and magisterially waved his arms about. But he knew and the players knew (even if the manager did not) that the real musical force behind that performance was Rachel Chapman, who was cueing the orchestra from the piano, just as she had said she would.

No wonder people forgave her tantrums. She was always dependable. Sometimes, after a particularly stormy outburst, she might suddenly smile, turn sweet, and ask anyone around her, "Am I not the most beautiful blonde pianist you ever saw?" And everyone was happy to say yes, of course she was.[9]

If Rachel Chapman was always referred to by her first name, nobody ever called Sophie Pourmel anything other than Madame Pourmel. It was Madame Pourmel's task to keep the wardrobe in good condition, and she managed to do this so well that Ballet Russe dancers are eternally grateful to her. Eugene Slavin calls her "the best wardrobe lady in the whole world," while Meredith Baylis says, "Madame Pourmel made wardrobe a fine art."

Born in St. Petersburg, Sophie Pourmel received an

academic education at the Alexanderskaya Gymnasia, and was a member of the last class to graduate before the Revolution. She was regularly taken to ballet performances with her classmates and she became particularly fond of the dancing of Lubov Egorova. In 1920 she and her husband, George Jacobson, decided to leave Russia and settle elsewhere. Her husband was Latvian and when Latvia gained its independence after World War I he became involved with a scheme whereby Latvians residing in Russia were exchanged with Russians who were then living in the Baltic nation. Pourmel and her husband were able to make their way to Riga. But after investigating several cities as possible places of residence, they moved to Paris. In Paris, their daughter Adda showed talent as a dancer and was taken to study with Olga Preobrajenska.

Fokine and René Blum wanted Adda to join their Ballets de Monte Carlo, and permission was granted when her mother was told that she would be allowed to accompany her daughter on tour. It was while she was traveling with the Blum company that Sophie Pourmel became involved with stage costumes. En route to South Africa, shipboard mice destroyed the dragon's costume in *L'Épreuve d'Amour,* a vast papier-mâché construction with a tail that could cover a large part of the stage. Amidst the consternation, Pourmel suggested that she might be able to sew pieces of material together and devise a new costume. She did such a good job that when the post of wardrobe mistress fell vacant, she was urged to take it. Because it was a salaried position that would bring money to the family, she accepted. She has been involved with wardrobe ever since: first, with Blum's company, then for the entire history of the Ballet Russe de Monte Carlo. When the Ballet Russe disbanded, she joined the staff of the New York City Ballet.

As wardrobe director, Pourmel had to look after all the costumes, see that they were clean and in the right place at the right time at each performance, and cope with emergencies. She did such a good job that, despite the wear and tear of constant touring that caused scenery to become soiled and wrinkled, Ballet Russe costumes managed to look remarkably attractive.

Pourmel could not have accomplished this without establishing a formidable set of regulations that had to be followed at all times by everyone. Thus she and Cornelie ("Corrie") de Brauw, the former vaudeville dancer who served as her assistant, often seemed to be stern figures to new dancers in the company. But dancers soon realized that this sternness was only a sign of Pourmel's extraordinary single-mindedness. Because she believed that good costumes make the stage look special when the curtain goes up, the list of rules that had to be followed was extensive: no dancer could eat, drink, or smoke while wearing a costume; sitting down in a costume was forbidden; so was leaning against anything while wearing a costume; to put one's hands on one's hips while wearing a costume was a major crime (if Pourmel saw anyone doing that, she would run up and swat the offender's hands away); personal clothes and stage costumes could not be hung together on the same rack; and when a ballet was over, costumes had to be removed immediately, lest perspiration ruin them. Demanding of dancers, Pourmel was equally demanding of herself. One of her rules required her to inspect every costume each time it was worn because, if small rips in the material were not corrected immediately, they could easily develop into catastrophic rents and tears.

Pourmel's resourcefulness knew no bounds. She had a solution for every problem. So a costume did not fit properly? "Then we'll make it fit!" she would say, getting to work. So one's character shoes were too big and there were no substitutes available? "Then wear two pairs of socks," she would recommend. She knew what cleaning facilities were available in each town on tour. Once in Phoenix, Arizona, she commandeered an entire laundromat to get the full set of *Les Sylphides* and *Swan Lake* costumes clean. The invention of nylon, Pourmel thinks, was a godsend for touring companies, for nylon was easy to care for and, unlike some materials that could shrink unpredictably after washing or cleaning, nylon was seldom responsible for nasty surprises.

Each ballet had its own special problems. However, the costumes that were subject to the most strain were those of *Gaîté Parisienne*. Because it was invariably the last ballet on a program, the costumes usually had to be packed away while they were still damp. Thus they decayed easily, a set of *Gaîté* costumes barely lasting out a tour. "Costumes need air," Pourmel explains. "They ought to be able to hang properly before they're packed away. Otherwise, they'll lose their shape and get twisted."

Ruthanna Boris once said of Sophie Pourmel, "She could have been the director of the Ballet Russe. If she wanted to, she could be President of the United States." Pourmel has entertained no such grandiose ambitions. She is one of the former staff members of the Ballet Russe who chose to devote herself to one activity—in her case, to caring for wardrobe. But her devotion was total and selfless. "How strange," she muses today. "At first, working on costumes was just a way to make extra money. But here

I still am, still busy, still working on costumes. I do not regret it. I've never been a dancer. But I adore ballet. And I dance each ballet along with the dancers. Ballet has become my fate."[10]

NOTES FOR CHAPTER 13

1. Eileen Summers, "Ballet Reflects 'Family' Format," *Washington Post, Times and Herald,* 5 August 1959.
2. Elinor Hughes, "Ballet in America Worthy More Study and Appreciation," *Boston Sunday Herald,* 15 May 1949.
3. Kathryn Boardman, "Ballet Manager Authority on Lincoln Assassination," *St. Paul Dispatch,* 1 December 1959; conversation with George Verdak.
4. Clyde Bolton, "It Was 'Old Home Week' for 'Cat' Smith and Many Other Former Ballet Troupers," *Gadsden (Ala.) Times,* 23 November 1958; conversation with George Verdak.
5. Conversation with Irina Pabst. Henceforth all statements for which no printed source is given were made in conversation with the author.
6. Letter from M. Hornyak to S.J. Denham, 27 February 1948.
7. Michel Katcharoff, unpublished autobiography, pp. 55-56; and conversation.
8. Rachel Chapman—Agnes de Mille, *Dance to the Piper,* p. 289; correspondence with Giora Manor, who interviewed Chapman at the author's request; conversations with Ann Barzel, Meredith Baylis, Robert Lindgren, Alexandra Nadal, Eugene Slavin, Sonja Taanila, Rochelle Zide.
9. Chapman anecdotes—"Temperamental Blonde Bombshell Smites the Keys for Ballet Troupe," *New York Times,* 18 October 1948; Isabel C. Armstrong, "Artistic Season Opens with Gaiety and Color," *Ottawa Evening Citizen,* 6 October 1942; John Martin, "Monte Carlo Troupe at the Metropolitan," *New York Times,* 11 October 1942; conversations with Ruth Page, Eugene Slavin, Igor Youskevitch.
10. Sophie Pourmel—Saul Goodman, "Meet Sophie Pourmel," *Dance Magazine,* January 1961, pp. 18-21; conversations with Meredith Baylis, Ruthanna Boris, Moscelyne Larkin, Alexandra Nadal, Sophie Pourmel, Eugene Slavin, Rochelle Zide.

14 THE COMPANY ON TOUR

THE Ballet Russe de Monte Carlo spent most of its time on the road. It was a touring company, and it toured on a scale that most ballet companies today would not attempt to equal. During the 1949-50 season, for instance, there were 191 performances in 86 cities. When the company was reorganized in 1954-55, there were 188 performances in 104 cities. The next season saw 161 performances in 95 cities.[1] A career with any ballet company during the 1940s and '50s inevitably involved much touring. But the Ballet Russe toured more than most.

A typical day on tour, particularly during a series of one-night stands, often involved rising as early as 6 a.m. in order to be ready to catch a train (or bus) some time between 7 and 8:30. The company would usually reach the next city by early afternoon. The dancers would then dash to their hotel and assemble at the theatre in the early evening for warmup, makeup, and performance. After the performance, dinner would have to be found somewhere (which was often no easy task), and after dinner one might fall exhausted into bed.

"I couldn't do all that now," says Leon Danielian. "I don't even know how I was able to do it back then. I certainly wouldn't approve of any of my students living that kind of life. It was grueling and it destroyed you."[2]

Other dancers disagree. "We looked forward to going

239

on tour," Sonja Taanila says. And while Meredith Baylis, like Danielian, says that she could not survive today on the sort of touring schedule she knew as a young dancer, she adds, "We had rather a good time on tour." Régisseur Michel Katcharoff has no regrets at all: "Touring? It was a wonderful life!"

The company's manner of touring changed significantly several times over the years. Until the middle of the 1950s the Ballet Russe almost always traveled by train. The era of rail transportation, however, can be divided into two distinct periods. At the beginning of the company's life, during the late 1930s, the Ballet Russe had its own special train. Those were the posh days of train travel for the company, and James Starbuck believes that the private train encouraged the preservation of a hierarchical structure within the company: "Each car on the train held a different group. There was a car for the stars, a car for the corps, a car for the orchestra, and so on. Barriers were set up at the end of each car, and no fraternizing between cars was permitted."

Often, during those days, artistic director Léonide Massine traveled totally apart from his company. He bought a trailer and had it fitted out with a kitchen and a bed-sitting room. Georgi Labourinsky, who came from an old Cossack family, served as chauffeur. Also part of the entourage was an Italian cook, who was brought along because Massine and his wife, Tatiana Orlova, disliked most hotel food. Sometimes, Massine dispensed with hotels entirely. When the Ballet Russe played San Francisco in 1941, he parked his trailer downtown on Market Street and lived in it for the company's engagement, entertaining visitors and even hosting champagne parties there.[3]

World War II changed that sort of life. Gasoline rationing made keeping a trailer impractical. The necessity of transporting military personnel by rail made private trains unavailable. From World War II onward, the Ballet Russe would usually travel in special cars attached to regularly scheduled trains. Sometimes, during the war, there were no special cars to be had or the cars would be claimed by weary servicemen. Dancers stood in the aisles for long journeys, and some of the women of the company stuffed shoes or practice clothes under their dresses, trying to look pregnant in the hope that polite gentlemen might rise and give them seats. Looking pregnant also protected them from the advances of amorous soldiers and traveling salesmen.

Despite the hardships, the World War II years were important because they helped democratize the Ballet Russe. War broke down the old class distinctions in the company and brought everybody together. Principals mingled with corps members, and all the dancers mingled with the servicemen and civilians who shared the train with them. The wartime hotel shortage also hastened this process of democratization. People bunked together, when there were rooms to be had, and made do as best they could when there were no rooms. Once in San Francisco there were no rooms available for any of the dancers. So the company bedded down in a hotel ballroom, Agnes de Mille (who was rehearsing *Rodeo* at the time) spending her nights sprawled across a table.

Only a minority of the servicemen encountered on the wartime train rides were rowdy or lecherous. Most were simply young men far from home and, beneath their show of bravado, lonely and scared. Many, looking for companionship and intrigued by the dancers, would wander into the Ballet Russe coaches to strike up a conversation or a card game. They found the Ballet Russe dancers sympathetic listeners, voluble talkers, and mean poker players.

After the war, the company continued to travel in private coaches until the decline of rail service made touring by train all but impossible. When the Ballet Russe was reorganized in 1954 it started touring in special buses, and bus remained the mode of transportation until the company disbanded. Many dancers who lived through the eras of both train and bus travel now state that they preferred traveling by train, principally because train seats seemed less cramped than bus seats and one could always stretch one's legs by walking up and down the corridor. "Buses!" exclaims Nathalie Krassovska. "They were awful! There was no room. And the bus was so jiggly and bumpy you couldn't even darn toe shoes." Rochelle Zide recalls that dancers in 1954 were frightened to hear Frederic Franklin glumly speculate that every year spent on a bus would take two years off one's performing career.

But bus travel has its defenders. Among them is Meredith Baylis, who also knew the days of train travel. She says, "People simply have forgotten how terrible some of those old trains were. They were dirty and uncomfortable—far more uncomfortable than any bus. Yes, the bus was cramped. But there were meal stops and frequent rest stops. The best thing about bus travel was its convenience. The bus was entirely your own. It took you to the door of your hotel and from your hotel to the theatre. It left in the morning at whatever time was necessary to get you to the next town, and if the next town was nearby, then it left late and you got extra sleep. With trains, you were always at the mercy of the railroad line. The next town may have been a mere twenty miles away.

But if the only passenger train of the day to that town left at seven in the morning, then that's the time you had to be at the station. As for getting from the hotel to the station or from the station to the hotel—those could be major problems in themselves. Remember, you'd always be weighted down by luggage. When you were playing some remote community, the train might let you off in the yards or on a siding and you'd have to walk for what seemed like miles through gravel or over rail ties before you got anywhere where there might conceivably be a taxi. Don't romanticize the trains. The trains were terrible."

Whether the dancers liked the bus or not, the bus was home. For one dancer the bus was literally home. Because he had a wife and children to support, he never stayed in hotels but spent every night on the luggage rack of the bus, a practice that enabled him to send home the money he would otherwise spend on hotel rooms. Seats on the bus were assigned according to a rigid system. The first seat of the bus—the seat with the best view—was shared by Sophie Pourmel and Rachel Chapman. Maria Tallchief, when she was ballerina with the company in 1954, claimed the entirety of the back seat so that she could stretch out full-length and nap. New members of the corps de ballet received the least desirable seats, the seats directly on top of the wheels. The longer one stayed with the company, the better the seat one got. Desirable or undesirable, one's place was one's place for the duration of the tour. Seats were regarded almost as though they were rooms in a house, and at Christmas dancers would vie with one another in decorating their seats and windows.

Staff members, including the musicians, toured along with the dancers. The Ballet Russe usually traveled with an orchestra of twenty players. In large cities, this number was considerably augmented and the company occasionally appeared with some of America's greatest symphony orchestras in the pit. These could be musically glorious performances. Other performances were not so glorious. Often, in small towns, only the touring orchestra of twenty played, because no other musicians could be found. In other cities, union contracts required hiring extra musicians, but some of these local musicians were never actually used because they were either totally unfamiliar with the ballet repertoire or downright incompetent.

No wonder, then, that the company's musical standards varied so much. One could never predict what the pickup musicians would be like. During the same tour, orchestral playing could range from the admirable to the execrable. Moreover, the size of a city was no guarantee of expert musicianship. Thus in 1956 Los Angeles music critic Albert Goldberg complained that during the company's local engagement audiences paid "top prices to hear ballet music slaughtered by an orchestra that most of the time played as if it belonged in a Main Street burleycue house." Yet only a few days before, Fresno critic Eldred J. Renk had praised the orchestra because it "made up in quality what it may have been lacking because of its rather modest proportions . . . it showed much precision in attack and release, and the strings displayed uniform, silky tones in true intonation."[4]

Many of the musicians who toured with the Ballet Russe, particularly those who toured during the 1940s, were émigré Russians, some of whom had played in the orchestras of St. Petersburg theatres. These musicians were almost as colorful as the dancers. They were certainly distinctive looking, for in an effort to lighten the weight of their luggage they tended to make their tuxedos their regular daily apparel outside the theatre as well as inside it. Luggage, always a problem for dancers on tour, was an especially complicated one for the musicians since, in addition to clothes and personal effects, they also had to tote their instruments. Robert Lindgren says that the musicians of the Ballet Russe were the first people he ever encountered to have hit upon the idea of attaching casters to their suitcases.

Traveling with the Ballet Russe during its early years were several people who were not officially part of the company's staff, yet who were, in their own way, very much a part of the Ballet Russe. Among them were Janet Roughton, who served as secretary to Frederic Franklin, and A.E. Twysden, the Englishwoman who was Danilova's secretary, companion, and biographer. People never referred to Twysden informally. She was always "Miss Twysden." A "very, very British lady whose solution for everything was smelling salts" (as one dancer described her), Twysden tended to be snobbish in attitudes and schoolteacherish in manner. In addition to assisting Danilova, she kept a governess's eye upon the very young girls who were members of the company, and in large cities she would book them into YWCAs instead of into hotels. In proper British fashion, she made sure that her girls kept their windows open, even in midwinter; and, a pious Roman Catholic, she encouraged young dancers to attend church on Sundays.

During the early years, several "ballet mothers" went on tour—not as many as used to travel with de Basil's company, dancers hasten to add: de Basil's company sometimes seemed to be "all mothers." Yet the Monte Carlo had its share. Usually they were parents of young women in the company, yet at least one of the men—Marcel Fenchel—traveled regularly with his mother. Most of the ballet mothers were Russian émigrés, and since many no longer had any place they could call home, home might just as well be the Ballet Russe for them. What did the mothers do? They fussed over their children, they applauded their children's performances, and they cursed the critics who wrote unflattering notices and the company management that denied their children the roles they knew the children deserved. They also cooked. The mothers were forever miraculously whipping up meals on hotplates. They cooked in theatres and in their hotel rooms. The former was dangerous; the latter, both dangerous and illegal. Sometimes there were so many hotplates going simultaneously backstage in a theatre that the mothers would overload the electrical system and cause a power failure. And on more than one occasion mothers accidentally set hotel carpets afire.

Then there were the pets. Dogs and cats, mostly, but other animals as well. Nathalie Krassovska, herself an animal lover, remembers that one time there were, in addition to the dogs and cats, several pet birds, a monkey, and a mouse aboard the Ballet Russe train. ("I never much cared for the mouse," she adds.) Mia Slavenska traveled with a cat, as did Tamara Toumanova. Slavenska's cat, Mickey, was plump and tiger-striped, and Slavenska was devoted to it. Toumanova was equally devoted to Moura, a white Persian cat that had finicky eating habits. It hated milk and drank water only from a glass. But among its loves were chicken, ice cream, honeydew melon, oranges, and American cheese. Moura even had a part in one of the ballets, for in *The New Yorker* she portrayed the pet of a society lady.[5]

Léonide Massine and conductor Efrem Kurtz both traveled with dogs. But the company's most ardent dog fancier was Nathalie Krassovska. Krassovska always seemed to have a dog with her, and she tried to take her dogs everywhere. Once when a headwaiter refused to let her bring her dog into a hotel restaurant, she pointed toward one of the diners and declared, "My dog is just as clean as that man over there!" Some of her dogs were adored by the entire company, but a few were dogs that only Krassovska loved.

One dog precipitated a company scandal and was indirectly responsible for a serious illness. This was a puppy that Krassovska had been given by an elderly couple in the Midwest. It was a cute puppy. But it was also incontinent. One afternoon, as the company was traveling by train toward Chicago, it urinated on the shoe of régisseur Jean Yazvinsky. Even though Yazvinsky and his wife traveled with a dog of their own that they treated like a baby, he declared that he was no longer willing to put up with the misbehavior of Krassovska's puppy. "That puppy must go!" he ordered. Krassovska turned equally indignant. "If my puppy goes," she said, "I go with it." "Then both of you go," Yazvinsky shouted.

They did. At the next station Krassovska and her puppy got off the train. She found herself in a howling blizzard. Nevertheless, there she stood in the snow, glaring at the train, her dog in her arms. The train departed. And there Krassovska remained, still standing in the snow. Now, however, she knew she would have to do something. For one thing, she had no idea where she was. All she knew was that she was in a small town somewhere in the Midwest. She trudged through the snow until she came to a hotel where she booked herself a room.

Once she got herself settled, she realized that she was not feeling very well. She was coughing and sneezing and possibly running a fever. She was also suffering an attack of remorse. She thought to herself, "Chicago is coming up and I am supposed to dance in Chicago. But how can I dance in Chicago when I am here in this hotel room? Yet everyone has always said that Krassovska is a professional who never misses a performance. So I must go back to the company. I must not miss a performance." Back to the railroad station she went, back through the blizzard, still clutching her dog and now running a high temperature. She waited in the drafty depot until the next train for Chicago came along. A true professional, she danced her scheduled performance, after which she was rushed to a hospital where her condition was diagnosed as pneumonia.

Never staying long in any single place on tour posed special problems of dress and grooming. One could not travel with an extensive wardrobe. Yet one still had to look neat. Dancers rejoiced when they found all-night laundromats. But, because of the time it took, dry cleaning was seldom possible. Dancers therefore had to do the best they could. They gave each other haircuts, and clothes were worn until they almost fell apart. The men favored dark blue shirts, even though such shirts made them look like Chicago gangsters. These shirts were nicknamed "5000-mile shirts," because a dancer supposedly could tour the whole country in one without having to have it laundered.

The women had their own problems of dress, especially

since Sergei Denham decreed that no women in the company were permitted to wear slacks, not even on the train or the bus. He was adamant on this matter. So at all times of the day the Ballet Russe women wore dresses. During the days of bus travel, they often wore girdles as well, since the belief was then prevalent that girdles would keep a dancer's flesh from spreading after sitting all day long. The Ballet Russe women also used to complain that they got less sleep than the men, because they always had to wash and dry their hair before going to bed.

One year the lot of the Ballet Russe woman was improved because in the company that season was a dancer with a rich boy friend who kept sending her expensive dresses, more dresses than she could hope to carry around on tour. She would therefore hold periodic "bargain sales" in her dressing room at which she sold off her clothes at greatly reduced prices. "That was the season," says Frederic Franklin, "when we probably had the most chic corps de ballet in the world."

Just as dancers seldom had enough time, so they seldom had enough money. Dancers, particularly corps de ballet dancers, were often underpaid. In the earliest days of the company the salaries of corps members were so low that James Starbuck remembers having to stay on occasion in real flophouses consisting of dormitories partitioned off by chicken wire into tiny cubicles.

The need to economize led to the practice known as ghosting, whereby one dancer would legally register for a hotel room and then share it with as many as six other dancers (the "ghosts"). The cost of the room would be paid collectively, each dancer thereby spending less for a night's accommodation than he would if he had stayed in a room of his own. Once the legal occupant of the room had registered, the ghosts would sneak up to it as best they could without attracting the suspicion of desk clerks or bellboys. They would then pull the bed apart, some sleeping on the springs, some on the mattress, some even rolling themselves up in the extra blankets and sleeping on the floor.

Because they were better paid, principal dancers usually did not have to ghost. But they sometimes did so during the war when hotel accommodations were scarce. Once, passing through a hotel lobby, Frederic Franklin was startled to find Alexandra Danilova lurking mysteriously behind a potted palm. "Whatever are you doing, Shoura?" he inquired. "Ssh," she whispered conspiratorially. "Tonight I am the spook!"

The ghosts were seldom caught, and some managers,

guessing what was going on, seemed willing to overlook the practice of ghosting. But a few were sticklers. One, who was clearly aware that dancers were occupying rooms illegally, kept all the keys himself and then personally escorted each dancer upstairs. After unlocking the door, he would search the room to see whether anyone was hiding in it. When that manager told James Starbuck that he wished to inspect his room, Starbuck feigned a violent temper tantrum. While the manager stood with his mouth agape, Starbuck rushed to the elevator and went to his room where he told the four ghosts who were staying there that the manager was on his way and they had better hide quickly. They ran down the hall and piled into a broom closet just as the manager, in pursuit of Starbuck, stepped from the elevator. The manager poked his head into every nook and cranny of Starbuck's room. Much to his disappointment, he found no illegal occupants. The only things he did find that aroused his suspicion were two suitcases—*two* suitcases. What did this mean? Starbuck simply looked haughtily at the manager and said, "Can't a gentleman travel with more than one suitcase?"

Not all ghosts were so lucky. Some were caught. One night, as a ghost was showering, getting ready for bed, there was a knock at the door. It was the house detective. He asked the room's legal occupant when his "guest" was going to leave, adding that, of course, any "guests" were welcome to stay the night. But if they wished to do that, they must first go down to the lobby and register. The room's legal occupant stoutly declared that he had no guests. Unwilling to take his word for it, the detective demanded to enter the room. He peeked into the closet. There was nobody there. He stormed into the bathroom, then peered under the bed. Again he found no one. The room did indeed seem empty. The detective was about to leave when he noticed a pair of bare feet sticking out from beneath the window drapes. The drapes were pulled aside and there stood the ghost, totally naked and dripping from the shower. Detective and ghost stared at each other for one surprised second, then the ghost, still naked, marched jauntily toward the hall, saying, "Well, I guess I'd better go downstairs and register."

Sometimes touring seemed to be one misadventure after another. The scenery, costumes, and orchestral parts for certain ballets were occasionally sent off by mistake to the wrong city. Once in Dayton the Ballet Russe danced a whole program, including *Rodeo* and *Scheherazade,* in bits of street clothes and practice dress, with the musicians clustered about the piano, trying to deduce their parts from the piano score. Slippery floors were hazards everywhere and the company used to curse those misguided janitors who subscribed to the notion that one way to make a theatre pleasant for dancers was to wax the stage. After a Detroit performance that was all slipping and sliding, Danilova announced to the house manager, "If you want a smooth performance, give us a rough floor."[6]

Some ballets required supers, who had to be recruited locally in each city on tour. Often, the supers were students at the town's leading ballet school. But there were places in which dance students were unavailable and supers had to be taken from colleges or even military bases. Since these supers usually knew little about ballet and were given instructions by people who babbled at them with a foreign accent, it is not surprising that they sometimes made mistakes. At one performance, the supers portraying the Shah's warriors in *Scheherazade* were told, "When there is great excitement on stage, you rush in and stab everyone." Curious to see what ballet was like, the boys stood backstage in their exotic costumes, watching the performance. They noticed that things on stage were getting quite lively and started to wonder whether they had missed their cue. Now convinced that they had indeed missed their entrance, they dashed out, daggers drawn, and proceeded to stab all the cowboys in the square dance scene of *Rodeo*.

Because of constant touring, some sets became very disheveled. Robert Sabin in 1944 complained that the scenery for *Les Sylphides* looked "as if it had been through the Johnstown flood."[7] Similar complaints were made about other productions, and Denham was often blamed for their shabbiness. Although Denham dearly loved to economize, Leon Danielian thinks that Denham was just as unhappy about the shabby productions as his critics were. "You may not have always liked Mr. Denham's artistic taste," Danielian says, "but he tried to put on a good-looking show. He did sincerely try."

Touring wore out the dancers as well as the scenery. Danielian believes that the strain of touring made dancers unusually accident-prone. Because the company was so small that one could not always be easily replaced if one missed a performance, one tended to keep dancing in a show-must-go-on spirit, even after one had sustained an injury. This, in turn, made injuries slow to heal.

The Ballet Russe almost never canceled performances, even though weather and travel conditions made some performances difficult to get to. Bound for a performance in upstate New

York one winter, the Ballet Russe train was so cold that the dancers wrapped newspapers around their legs to keep warm. On another tour, the train froze on the tracks near Boise, leaving the dancers snowbound for two days. The wartime trains were the worst. Waiting for one train that would supposedly take them to a town in Texas, the dancers learned that their train had been delayed. They waited through the night in a dingy station. Because there was no food to be had anywhere nearby, a few of the dancers managed to steal some fruit by breaking into a shipment in a boxcar that was off on a siding. When the train did pull in, it was jammed. It was also very late. And it kept getting later. To make sure that the dancers would arrive for their next scheduled performance, they were transferred to a bus at the next stop. The bus had a blowout. When the dancers finally reached the town in which they were supposed to appear, no hotel rooms were available and they had to wait for several hours in a bowling alley.

Unrelenting dreariness made that Texas trip unforgettable. Even more unforgettable for all who were on board the train was 7 October 1947. The Ballet Russe dancers were speeding along across Indiana. A few were reading. A few more were napping. Others, including Ruthanna Boris, were discussing Tennyson with Miss Twysden. When the conversation turned from Tennyson's poetry to his title, Miss Twysden clucked, "Oh, you Americans! You say you're democratic, yet you're obsessed with titles." Then there was a horrendous crash and, as Boris puts it, "The world came to an end." The train had hit a construction machine and had jumped the tracks. Three train crew members were killed, but of the dancers only Yvonne Chouteau and Harding Dorn were injured, and they only slightly. The Ballet Russe's next performance—in Dayton, the following night—took place as scheduled.

Fortunately, accidents on tour were rare. Far more common were boredom and fatigue. When South American dancer Eugene Slavin joined the company, he thought he would have an exciting time seeing the United States. For two weeks he stared out the window of the bus all day long. "But then," he says, "I got tired of seeing the countryside and I did what everyone else did: I slept." Sometimes there was not even much to see. "A not-too-long trip with a lunch stop at Howard Johnson's and a view of the State Cancer Hospital brought us today to Kansas City," Rochelle Zide noted in her diary for 9 January 1958. Zide kept a diary throughout her years with the Ballet Russe in which she commented upon the hotels, restaurants, and theatres she encountered. All too often, she entered comments such as this one for 13 January 1958: "Stage was tiny and filthy; dressing rooms were unbearably hot with *no* water (Corrie [de Brauw] got us a pitcher of the precious liquid) and no place to hang clothes."

Nevertheless, travel did broaden people, sometimes in unexpected ways, as it did in the case of one dancer. While touring with the Ballet Russe he first learned (and nearly choked to death on the discovery) that fish had bones, something he had not known before because his mother had always served fish fillets at home. On tour, the dancers read: they read everything from classics to detective stories. They talked lots—sometimes far into the night. And they observed. They may have complained that all they ever saw of the places they visited were stages and dressing rooms, yet they managed to get a better sense of what life in America was like than many of their stay-at-home contemporaries did.

Several dancers managed to pursue hobbies on the road. George Verdak and William Glenn took four-hand piano music on tour and played through scores in orchestra pits before the musicians arrived for the evening's performance. Verdak was also a book collector and seemed to be acquainted with every antiquarian bookshop in America. A few dancers might be called pilferers. These were the dancers who liked to steal towels from hotels or silverware from restaurants. There is a possibly apocryphal story that, during a long engagement in one city, a dancer managed to steal a chandelier from a hotel ballroom without anyone on the hotel staff being aware of it, simply by dismantling it one or two pendants at a time.

Touring acquainted one with many life-styles. During the war years, when people felt that they had to live each minute as intensely as possible, and in the peacetime euphoria that followed immediately after the war, there was a mania for parties. An extraordinary camaraderie prevailed. Total strangers would come up to the dancers after a performance and invite them en masse to a party. And off to the party the dancers would troop. "We sometimes never knew what sort of a party it would be," Robert Lindgren says, "whether it would be a high society party with champagne or a drag party with gay servicemen. But we'd all go, anyway—and if it was possible to have a good time, we'd have one."

The Ballet Russe brought ballet to many places where there had never been dance before. Because they knew they were pioneers, the Ballet Russe dancers soon grew used to strange audience reactions. But even the company's hardiest veterans were disconcerted by a performance in one town at which there was no applause whatsoever. Three ballets were danced and the curtain rose and fell in total silence upon each. When the manager of the theatre came backstage after the performance, the dancers, quaking with trepidation, asked what had gone wrong. Nothing had gone wrong, the manager replied. The audience had liked the performance very much and had responded to it as they would have done to a movie, the only form of entertainment most of those people knew. As it would have meant at a movie, their silence indicated their absorption in what they were watching.

At a San Diego performance of *Swan Lake* starring Ruthanna Boris, a woman in the first row of the audience tapped conductor Lucien Cailliet on the shoulder and said with great indignation, "Will you *please* be good enough to *sit down?*" The theatre manager in another city once got a call from someone who asked, "Would you tell me, please, in what language does the company perform?"[8]

As late as 1950, ballet was still considered risqué in certain communities. Commenting upon a performance of *Les Sylphides,* that most chaste of ballets, a Portland, Maine, critic said that because of her "startlingly brief costume," Ruthanna Boris "was initially responsible for thoughts of Minsky's." That same critic, commenting upon a Bluebird pas de deux with Gertrude Tyven and Robert Lindgren, said, "When the curtain parted . . . the close-fitting costumes of the dancers drew gasps from spectators."[9]

Scheherazade had a reputation for being "naughty," and there were dancegoers who found it so. During a long engagement in one large city, members of a religious group were offended by a performance of *Scheherazade.* Calling the ballet immoral and Mary Ellen Moylan and Robert Lindgren as Zobeide and the Favorite Slave "downright lascivious," they campaigned to have future performances of the work canceled in their town. Denham told them that *Scheherazade* was not immoral in the least, and to prove it he was willing to arrange a special run-through of the ballet for members of the religious group. If there were any immoral moments, he would like to be told which they were. Shrewdly, Denham had the run-through occur in practice clothes and without Bakst's opulent setting. When the performance was over, the would-be censors had to concede that Denham was right, their leader scratching his head and remarking, "It really wasn't so bad, after all. Somehow, it just seemed worse on stage."

Each dancer had his own personal list of cities he liked best and least on tour. Chicago was an almost universal favorite. Chicago audiences loved the Ballet Russe, and there were many parties. Since the Chicago season was always a long one, dancers could unpack their suitcases and do their laundry. Charm and sophistication made San Francisco popular. As the Ballet Russe train neared Los Angeles, many of the women would take special care to pretty themselves up in the hope that someone might discover them and offer them a movie contract. When the company reached Dallas, some dancers would drop their bags at the hotel and run immediately to the stylish Neiman-Marcus department store. Dancers liked Milwaukee for its first-rate German cooking. And because Denham's daughter, Irina, had married Robert E. Pabst, a member of one of the Beer City's brewing families, there were always special brewery tours for the dancers. Houston and New Orleans also had their champions. Usually, a dancer's choice of favorite cities was totally idiosyncratic. As Leon Danielian puts it, "You tended to like the places where the critics liked you or where you had an affair."

Most seasons, the company traveled westward from New York to California across the northern half of the United States and returned eastward through the South. Although some dancers liked the Southern leg of the tour because they could send their winter clothes back home, others dreaded it. For one thing, it consisted of almost nothing but one-night stands—sometimes for as long as six weeks. In addition, many parts of the South in the 1940s and '50s were not very pleasant places. Whereas the cooking in private homes in the South was often of the highest quality, restaurant food in Southern small towns tended to be horrendous. And everywhere there was evidence of segregation.

Sometimes cities seemed to go by in a kind of blur. "All those cities in Ohio," Rochelle Zide replied when she was asked which cities she liked least. "Akron, Dayton, Columbus . . . I couldn't tell them apart. They all looked alike to me. I never could remember where I was." This inability to remember sometimes got her into trouble. These were the times when she would forget the number of her hotel room and go to the number of the room she had had in the hotel at which she had stayed the previous night. Since hotel keys often fit, or with a bit of jiggling can be made to fit, several locks, she occasionally found herself walking in upon total strangers.

Touring taught dancers a lot about life. And yet, as Sonja Taanila says, "In some ways it was all rather innocent. For instance, we never had any acquaintance with the drug scene and almost nobody drank to excess. Oh, there were a few legendary drinkers, but it was their very rarity that helped make them legends. We all liked to have fun. But few of us did anything scandalous. We liked to go to parties or to a nightclub after a performance. And if we wanted what we thought was a really risqué time, we'd go to a burlesque show or to a drag club."

Touring was tough. It could be unnerving and exhausting. Yet the dancers seemed proud of their life—"unnaturally proud," as Agnes de Mille has observed. Why? Because "They think they are doing the most difficult and interesting work in the theater."[10] Looking back upon the changes that have occurred in American ballet, Frederic Franklin observes, "Dancers today *do* have it easier. They ought to. They have it easier because of what we had to go through. Ballet itself was an unknown quantity in America when we toured. Today, in many ways thanks to us of the Ballet Russe, ballet is known."

Most of the members of the Ballet Russe, however, never paused to meditate upon the arduousness of their life on tour. They simply accepted it. Was touring tough? Nathalie Krassovska was asked. She replied, "I really don't know. I never stopped to think about it. Touring was just something I did, something I've always done all my life."

NOTES FOR CHAPTER 14

1. Touring figures—1949-50: Ann Barzel, in *Ballet Annual #5*, p. 121; 1954-55: company brochure advertising 1955-56 season; 1955-56: advertisement, *Dance News*, October 1955, p. 2.
2. Conversation with Leon Danielian. Henceforth all statements for which no printed source is given were made in conversation with the author. Particularly valuable have been conversations with Meredith Baylis, Ruthanna Boris, Yvonne Chouteau, Frederic Franklin, Michel Katcharoff, Nathalie Krassovska, Robert Lindgren, Alexandra Nadal, Gilbert Reed, Mia Slavenska, Eugene Slavin, James Starbuck, Sonja Taanila, Maria Tallchief, George Verdak, Raven Wilkinson, Igor Youskevitch, Rochelle Zide.
3. Léonide Massine, *My Life in Ballet*, p. 215; "Entr'acte," *Dance*, March 1941, p. 8.
4. Albert Goldberg, "Monte Carlo Ballet Russe Closes Season," *Los Angeles Times*, 20 February 1956; Eldred J. Renk, "Ballet Russe Gives Sprightly Show for Huge Audience," *Fresno Bee*, 10 February 1956.
5. Cats—Slavenska's: "Ballet Dancer Here Stands by Her Cat," *San Antonio Light*, 12 January 1943; Toumanova's: David B. Eisendrath Jr., "Dancer's Music-Loving Cat Hates Milk, Likes Ice Cream," *PM's Weekly*, 26 October 1941.
6. "Smooth Floor—Rough Show," *Dance News*, November 1951, p. 3.

7. Robert Sabin, "Ballet Russe de Monte Carlo," *Dance Observer,* October 1944, p. 101.

8. "Attitudes and Arabesques," *Dance News,* February 1950, p. 4; "Lightly Tripping," *Dance Magazine,* August 1952, p. 1.

9. Roger V. Snow Jr., "Ballet Combines Classical Music, Minsky's Curves to Portlanders," *Portland (Maine) Press Herald,* 9 May 1950.

10. Agnes de Mille, *Dance to the Piper,* p. 296.

15 COMPANY STYLE: ON STAGE AND OFF

ASKED to comment upon the difference between dancers today and the dancers he knew as a member of the Ballet Russe, Leon Danielian quipped, "Dancers today have more money, but less personal style than we did."[1]

The remark is not totally facetious. Even toward the end of its days, the Ballet Russe de Monte Carlo still retained traces of a recognizable style, a style that was unabashedly presentationalistic. Ballet Russe dancers—the members of both the de Basil and the Monte Carlo companies—knew how to present themselves on stage. All could project and each had a distinctive stage presence. P.W. Manchester recalls that as a young balletgoer in London during the 1930s she

> almost never saw a ballet anywhere except up in the gallery of Covent Garden and yet I knew a dancer when she came in. I'd recognize her by an elbow. I didn't need to see the face. It must have been a larger scale than dancers work on today in that particular kind of thing. The movement wasn't nearly so large, of course, in their actual dancing. You didn't get those great expansive leaps that we all take for granted today, but the projection of the dancer as a person and as a character, I think, was much more in a way robust than it is today.[2]

Today's dancers, régisseur Michel Katcharoff concedes, "are much better technicians than most of us ever were. But, artistically, we

255

may have been better in some ways. We were concerned with characterization, period, style—and we always danced full-out. When I was with Colonel de Basil's company, Serge Grigoriev told me that technique is only fifty per cent of dance: the rest is acting, projection, personality. I never forgot that remark. I think all of us at the Ballet Russe recognized the truth of it."

In contrast, Katcharoff now finds that many young American dancers are unable to do pantomime or even to act clearly and naturally. However, Katcharoff believes that their inability to do so has nothing to do with not being Russian. "It makes no difference whether you were born in Russia or America," he insists. "Projection is no special Russian gift. All sorts of people can acquire it. But before you can acquire it, you have to be shown what it is. The young dancers of the Ballet Russe—the Americans as well as the Russians—could study the performances of some of the greatest personalities in ballet. We realized that ballet was an art of the stage and we got lots of stage experience early."

Eugene Slavin says, "At the Ballet Russe you could come out on stage and with your dancing declare, 'I am I and here I am.' " Some of those declarations were powerful indeed. "Massine, Danilova, Franklin," says Meredith Baylis, "when any of them stepped on stage, you knew there was *somebody!* Danilova could simply sit still and audiences would be watching her while all the people around her were dancing their heads off."

Even the members of the corps de ballet managed to give an impression of diversity within an ensemble unity. Harvey Southgate, a reviewer in Rochester, New York, once said this about the Ballet Russe corps: "Here were accurate timing of bodily rhythm and posture, yet without the machine-like quality that one often sees in group dancing. Each dancer preserves his or her individuality to an extraordinary degree. . . ."[3] In some ways, however, the corps de ballet members could not help but seem individualistic. Unlike certain companies today, in which every dancer in the ensemble is chosen because he or she conforms as closely as possible to some ideal body type, the corps members of the Ballet Russe were not necessarily chosen so that they would look alike on stage.

Rochelle Zide believes that this was not simply because the Ballet Russe needed any talented dancers it could get and could not afford to be fussy. Rather, she thinks that it reflected the taste of Denham and his associates. Denham, she says, "didn't seem to care whether all his dancers were from the same school or were the same size and shape. He didn't seem to care what their hair color was or whether they all had the same little turned-up noses and long legs. If he thought you were a good dancer, fine: you were in the company. That meant, though, that a very short girl might be standing next to a very tall girl in the corps, and they sometimes would not appear to be dancing together even when they were in perfect unison."

Although individuality was prized, Igor Youskevitch carefully points out that no dancer was given the license to distort the basic style of a ballet. And many former members of the company insist that—certainly until the late 1950s—one was not allowed to change choreography to suit one's own personal taste. It was the Ballet Russe's tradition of being faithful to a choreographer's intentions that made such an event as Jean Yazvinsky's reworking of *Prince Igor* so bothersome. Today, dancers point out, some companies have what seem to be substantially different versions of standard works for each ballerina or danseur who performs the principal roles in them. Such wholesale changes would not have been tolerated at the Ballet Russe. "We danced what we were supposed to dance," Robert Lindgren says. "The one ballerina who occasionally added embellishments to steps was Slavenska, who, being a virtuoso, liked to make steps harder. But while we admired what she could do, such changes never seemed 'proper' to us."

Ballet Russe dancers also maintain that the company tried to achieve the special style required by each separate work in the repertoire. *Swan Lake* and *Les Sylphides* were not danced alike, even though both were "white" ballets. *Beau Danube* and *Gaîté Parisienne* were not danced alike, even though both were comedies by Massine. This attention to stylistic nuances explains why Michel Katcharoff is able to say, "Young dancers today dance all ballets the same way."

The immediate source of the Ballet Russe style was the Diaghilev Ballet, with which some of the dancers in the Monte Carlo had appeared in their youth. Most of Diaghilev's dancers, in turn, had been trained at the Imperial Ballet Schools of St. Petersburg, Moscow, and Warsaw. The Ballet Russe, then, possessed a link back to Russian classicism. But despite its fine classicists, the Ballet Russe tended to emphasize what in academic terminology would be labeled demi-caractère and character dancing. Many of the works in the Diaghilev repertoire, particularly those of Fokine and Massine, came out of the demi-caractère and character tradition and the enormous influence wielded by Massine made this tradition predominant.

Balanchine's tenure with the Ballet Russe refined the

company's style by introducing a concern for classical elegance. Dancers were not permitted to disguise technical sloppiness with vivacity of stage presence. Yet Balanchine did not totally alter the company's style. He was with the Ballet Russe for too short a period to effect a wholesale transformation, and throughout that period works by Fokine and Massine remained in the repertoire. The repertoire also contained the Americana ballets of de Mille and Ruth Page, which might be called our own native contributions to the character tradition. These ballets, Balanchine's dislike of mannerisms, and American audiences' preference for robust hearty movement made the Ballet Russe style direct and forceful. Thus when Yvette Chauviré first appeared with the company as guest artist in 1950, some observers believed that her dancing, although admirable in itself, seemed to have a "hothouse" quality when seen in comparison with the dancing of the young Americans or of the older Russians who had been performing here for many seasons.

From the mid-'50s onward, stylistic changes occurred. For one thing, the Ballet Russe lacked a distinguished resident choreographer who could develop the company's basic style in valid new ways. As the company became artistically insecure, so it also became stylistically insecure. Some balletgoers thought that the Monte Carlo's heartiness now seemed forced, that it had turned into a mere caricature of its old genial self. Yet even that old heartiness might not have pleased certain dancegoers, for the Ballet Russe was no longer fashionable among the balletic intelligentsia in New York, although the company was still adored on the road. Olga Maynard pointed out in 1959 that, for sophisticates,

> the dancing is altogether too emphatic and the dancers are reproved in New York for being too showy, in the manner of "musical" stars. To the audience outside New York, especially to the cities whose annual visits from the Ballet Russe are the sole link with "live ballet" the requirement and demand is for exhilaration and energy . . .[4]

The ensemble dancing of the Royal Ballet and the New York City Ballet (and, later, of the Bolshoi Ballet on its first American visit in 1959) exerted a profound effect upon audiences. Here were ensembles that truly seemed cohesive entities. In comparison, the Ballet Russe ensemble, that aggregation of disparate individuals, began to seem inadequate, even though its members may have been good dancers. In 1956 San Francisco Bay Area critic Clifford Gessler thought that "The company, in general, now has a gentle, softly rounded style, reminiscent of that of the English companies. Yet each of the ballerinas has her individual accent within that style, or in some cases differing from it."[5]

More often, however, critics at that time complained that increasing accuracy of ensemble dancing was accompanied by energy without subtlety. Doris Hering, in 1957, observed, "This approach . . . makes all ballets—romantic, late Nineteenth Century, and contemporary—similar in intensity. . . ."[6] By 1961, according to Hering, "The corps moved as one; stood still as one . . . ."[7] But unanimity had been achieved at the expense of stylistic differentiation. Whereas previously the Ballet Russe had sometimes looked ragged, yet usually tried to dance each ballet in that ballet's own special style, now it was well drilled, yet danced all ballets alike.

The wonder of the Ballet Russe is that it had ever achieved stylistic distinction at all. Rehearsals on tour were often rough-and-ready brushups, and there was little individual coaching. Rather, young dancers learned by example. They stood in the wings watching their elders dance roles, and when the roles were given to members of the younger generation, the newcomers tried to preserve the style as well as the steps of their predecessors. In such a way were tradition and repertoire passed on.

It was a precarious way to preserve tradition, and eventually tradition was endangered. Robert Lindgren is among the dancers who think that one of the crucial events in the company's history was its temporary cessation in 1952. Even though a Ballet Russe Concert Company did continue to tour, the Ballet Russe itself was no more; and, when it was revived, it was never quite the same. The reorganized Ballet Russe of 1954 did include dancers who had been with the company before 1952. Nevertheless, a gap had occurred in company development. The handing down of a style from one generation of dancers to another had been interrupted.

Lindgren believes that lack of direct contact with the tradition is one reason why younger dancers find Massine's ballets so puzzling today. "They've had no opportunities to see them and absorb them," he says. "They have no models to follow. With us, that style was all around us. No one gave us special lessons in it; it was simply there, and eventually it became second nature to us. And it was a style that we loved."

Ballet Russe dancers who chose to remain with the company for several seasons at any period in the organization's history almost unanimously agree that they were there because, whatever complaints they may have had about company policies, they basically loved the Ballet Russe. Lindgren expresses the attitude of many dancers of the 1940s: "The company was very special. When you were part of the Ballet Russe you felt you were dancing as part of a great tradition. Yet you also felt that you might be dancing perilously for the moment. After all, ballet was still new to America. You could never be sure how strong the ballet craze really was or when a ballet company would fail. Already, by the 1940s, Ballet Caravan had failed, the Littlefield Ballet had failed, the Chicago Opera Ballet had failed—and during the '40s even Ballet Theatre went out of business temporarily. We had no idea how long anything would last, and the notion that a company might survive for ten years was considered wildly optimistic. So we danced for the moment and we danced our hearts out."

Cherishing tradition yet dancing for the moment, the Ballet Russe defied adversity, financial insecurity, and the aches and pains of touring. And it did so gallantly. Flair was encouraged off-stage as well as on. In its early years, the company deliberately cultivated an exotic image. Those were the days when Walter Terry could say that the Ballet Russe dancers were "like freaks, not disfigured in form, but beings from a fictional world whose romantic private lives add glamour to their stage personalities. . . . The unpredictable lives of the Russian ballet's stars will keep us all eager to see more of these exotic beings whose world of make-believe and temperamental dynamite is such a far cry from our own commonplace existence."[8]

A few dancers delighted in inventing eccentric offstage personae for themselves. Most of his former colleagues agree that the master of such impersonation was Nikita Talin, a dancer who, despite his name, hailed from East Cicero, Illinois. Talin liked to dress in a manner related in some way to each city in which the company appeared. No one knows to this day how Talin was able to find and transport all his clothes, yet in San Francisco he turned himself into a Chinatown mandarin in flowing robes, while in Canada he was a prim Englishman. In the Southwest he was a cowboy; in Chicago, a gangster. And when the company toured the South, he became Rhett Butler. George Verdak remembers that once, having been influenced by the pedagogical theories of Enrico Cecchetti, Talin, in homage to the Italian ballet master, decided to look Italian. However, when Talin made himself Italian, he turned out to bear an uncanny resemblance to Benito Mussolini. Since this impersonation occurred during World War II, Talin started to attract attention and in one small town his appearance so disquieted the local citizenry that he was questioned by the police.

Another example of Ballet Russe prankishness was what might be termed the company's booby prize, the Alan Banks Award. Named after an enthusiastic but technically limited dancer who had briefly appeared with the Ballet Russe during the war when there was a shortage of male dancers, this award was a title bestowed upon the dancer who, according to his colleagues, had given the most maladroit performance of the season. Company members often whiled away their hours on tour nominating candidates for the award.

Some dancers were superstitious, believing in all the age-old theatrical charms to ward off bad luck. Others, who may not have been so credulous, nevertheless also paid attention to these superstitions: after all, there was no sense in courting danger. It was considered bad luck to return to the dressing room once one had started toward the stage. It was believed that good luck would occur if one put one's left stocking on first. Stepping out of the dressing room on the right foot and stepping on stage on the right foot also brought good luck. It was bad luck to say a kind word to a dancer about to make a debut in a new role, whereas good luck would follow if a friend gave that dancer a kick and a curse. A dancer singled out by a critic in an unfavorable review would magically try to prevent further criticism by wadding that review inside a slipper at the next rehearsal.

Alexandra Danilova told a reporter for the *Brooklyn Eagle* that she considered black cats bad luck and purple an unlucky color. Nina Novak preserved a silver dollar that she received after her first Metropolitan Opera House performance as a good luck charm. Novak, Eugene Slavin, and Miguel Terekhov kept little brown bear dolls on their dressing room tables. Terekhov also made a habit of picking up a nail from the stage and keeping it on his dressing room table, for good luck, until the performance was over. Alicia Alonso was another hunter of talismanic nails. Gertrude Tyven's good luck charm was a *Swan Lake* headpiece given to her by Danilova, while Deni Lamont always kept an unopened jar of Russian caviar on his dressing table. Kenneth Gillespie carried about two stones from his native Tasmania and two pieces of Egyptian amber that had originally belonged to Pavlova and had been given to him by a ballet teacher in Australia. Irina Borowska trusted in the magic of a toy elephant; however, wherever it was put, its back had to be to a door and it could never face a window.

And so, given all these charms, the Ballet Russe was

always lucky—or so, at least, the dancers told reporters who asked them about superstitions.[9]

The Ballet Russe sometimes needed luck when it brought dance to towns in which ballet had never been seen before. Even in big cities, brash journalists often wrote as though they thought ballet a laughing matter. The company made efforts of several kinds to attract audiences. During its first tour in 1938 it almost brazenly billed itself as though it were an assemblage of Hollywood stars. Thus an advertisement in a Richmond paper informed Virginians that they were about to see the "SEVEN MOST BEAUTIFUL BALLERINAS IN THE WORLD," the beauties being Alexandra Danilova, Alicia Markova, Marina Franca, Nathalie Krassovska, Mia Slavenska, Milada Mladova, and Nini Theilade. Each was described with a few provocative phrases. Krassovska, readers learned, "won a beauty contest in Paris," and when Danilova "stepped on the toe of the former Prince of Wales while waltzing . . . [he] deemed it an honor." Lest ballet still seem something remote, the advertisement told prospective ticket buyers not to be afraid of fancy names: "The ballet called *Gaîté Parisienne* [is] Gay Paree to you."[10]

During extended seasons in New York and other large cities the company arranged to have window displays in stores that would relate the ballets in the repertoire to appropriate merchandise. In 1938, for example, each window of Bonwit Teller contained a placard asking such questions as these: "Did 'Ikare' [sic] make you want a sublime white gown? . . . Did 'Spectre de la Rose' make you want something in Victorian pink?" Accompanying the placards were gowns supposedly inspired by the ballets.[11]

To make sure that ballet would seem respectable and to encourage the wealthy to contribute to the Ballet Russe, Sergei Denham courted high society and tried to make ballet performances social events in the same sense that opera performances were. Before World War II, newspapers regularly sent society writers, as well as music or dance critics, to ballet openings, and syndicated columnists told readers from coast to coast what the rich and famous had worn to the Ballet Russe.

The prewar society audience could often be extravagant in both appearance and behavior. "The audience is the show," wrote James Whittaker in 1939. Robert Sabin provided this analysis of the audience in 1940:

> There is a large sprinkling of tired business men, who regard the ballet as an amusing and fashionable opportunity to look at women's legs. There is a large collection of women gotten

up in costumes which only the ballet season seems to evoke. There is a small group of bilious-looking first-nighters and balletomanes. There are the stenographers and office clerks, who discuss the works eagerly and loudly at intermissions. And, lastly, there is a minority of people who really know and love dancing, a minority which is apt to get lost in the melée.

Despite its social pretensions, the audience could be rude and vulgar. At the opening of the company's autumn season at the Metropolitan Opera House in 1941, Russell Rhodes noted in *The Dancing Times* how

> the incredible first night audience which greets the Russian ballet in New York—an audience in large part totally uninterested and completely lacking in discrimination—roamed through the stately corridors and the classic lobby of the Metropolitan, and stormed the Sherry Bar on the mezzanine between the numbers, wearing the remarkable coiffeurs, exaggerated headgear, fabulous jewels and fantastic costumes that are typical of this occasion. . . .[12]

Denham indulged the whims of New York socialites. They were sources of funds and they inspired social leaders from coast to coast to come to the Ballet Russe. Everywhere the Ballet Russe appeared, there were people eager to make the occasion rival in glamour the New York season at the Met. "New York may have its Metropolitan Opera, its brilliant Diamond Horseshoe," claimed an Atlanta newspaper in 1938, "but Atlanta had the Ballet Russe last night which provided as brilliant a preview of evening fashions as has been seen in many years." Society people across the country could behave as extravagantly as anyone in New York. The most commonly voiced complaint against them was that they considered it fashionable to be late. A Boston society reporter wrote that the "fashionable audience, a little breathless, stole the first half of the opening ballet's show as it sauntered down after the lights were out in its new ermine, sable and silver fox jackets and wraps." Unfortunately, the opening ballet that evening was *L'Épreuve d'Amour*, a work considered unusually delicate in its choreographic texture. Perhaps the antics of too many well-heeled, well-dressed, but ill-mannered balletgoers may explain why it never achieved popularity in America. Its subtleties may have gone unnoticed in the din.[13]

The fashionable audience was also capricious, easily capable of transferring its allegiance from the ballet company it championed one season to another company the following year, or abandoning support of ballet altogether. From the first, the most loyal supporters of the Ballet Russe were what Igor Youskevitch calls "ordinary Americans." For them, the Ballet Russe was always in fashion.

The coming of the war sobered people and made social extravagance seem out of place. During the 1940s the ballet audience became calmer and somewhat less colorful, although there were still firstnighters who longed for what Edwin Denby calls "the pre-war fashion, its odd elegance and its nervous glamour."[14] When the Ballet Russe moved to City Center, its audience became essentially middle class.

The Ballet Russe always had a strong roster of male dancers. Not even the combination of the wartime draft and Balanchine's glorification of the ballerina made the company's male dancing totally negligible. In its early seasons the Ballet Russe could boast of such male dancers as Léonide Massine, Igor Youskevitch, Frederic Franklin, Roland Guerard, George Zoritch, and André Eglevsky. Later, there were Leon Danielian, Nicholas Magallanes, Roman Jasinski, Oleg Tupine, Robert Lindgren, and Alan Howard. And among the men in the company during the last seasons were Eugene Slavin, Deni Lamont, Lawrence Rhodes, Ramon Segarra, and Juan Giuliano. One of the accomplishments of the Ballet Russe was that of demonstrating the validity of male dancing to skeptics around the country.

It was no easy task. Male ballet dancing was constantly being accused, even by people who ought to have known better, of being soft, affected, and effete. Walter Terry in 1940 complained about "the male dancers' tendency toward the limp wrist school of movement." Other critics looked askance upon any choreography that made men seem delicate, tender, or vulnerable. Cleveland critic William N. Gates pronounced Albrecht in *Giselle* unmanly because "the pas allotted to Albrecht . . . left this character in the twilight zone between sexes." Similarly, San Francisco critic Alexander Fried found *Swan Lake* offensive because of "its effeminate conception of male romantic behavior."[15]

Like many other defenders of male dancing in the 1930s and '40s, apologists for the Ballet Russe often called attention to similarities between classical ballet and sports or work activities. Writing about Igor Youskevitch, Walter Terry carefully pointed out that this superb Romantic stylist was also a genuine he-man:

> . . . in his earlier days he laid railway ties, spent months wielding a scythe, walked the tightrope and swung acrobat-

ically from trapezes in a circus. Evidently it takes a he-man to be a classic dancer of the first order and Youskevitch believes that this youthful training in the use of muscles has been of inestimable value to his dancing.[16]

Given the concept of virility and virile dancing implicit in these remarks, it is not surprising that one ballet that proved troublesome to dancegoers and critics was *Spectre de la Rose*. Fokine's curving choreography and Bakst's remarkable petaled costume perfectly exemplify certain aspects of Art Nouveau. And simply because they are such perfect exemplars, they may seem totally grotesque to anyone unsympathetic to that style of design.

The inclusion of *Spectre de la Rose* in the repertoire of the Monte Carlo's fall season in 1939 made Walter Terry declare that "as a male I resent seeing a man impersonate a rose—or even the spirit of one, for that matter." Moreover, he thought that such a ballet would have a terrible effect upon unsophisticated audiences; and, as a believer in the cause of male dancing, he was alarmed both at the decision of companies to include such ballets in their repertoires and at the willingness of men to dance in them. Male dancers, he asserted,

> are strong and muscular, and they probably work harder than a ditch digger. I wish they'd show it. Those of us who want to see the dance a recognized and honored activity for every man and boy would be most grateful for the co-operation of the ballet men. The ballet is a great power in the dance, and let us hope that it raises its standards of masculinity to match its high standards in technique. . . .

When Terry again complained about *Spectre* the following year, he received a long letter from none other than Fokine himself. After pointing out that the Spectre is neither masculine nor feminine but "totally sexless," Fokine challenged what he considered to be Terry's false artistic premises:

> It is regrettable that there is a prevailing opinion that ballet is an exhibition of feminine and masculine charms. Against this very thing I have always fought. I always held that the problem of ballet is not to show the woman or the man, but the human being. People interested only in the demonstration of power and masculinity, those who like athletic physiques and muscular development, should not go to the theater but to sporting events. . . .
>
> Why should a wide range of characters be substituted by one demand, masculinity? Why not approach the ballet with the same demands as when approaching the opera or drama? No

one demands masculinity from all opera singers irrespective of the character of their roles. No one is searching for athletes and sportsmen in the plays of Tolstoy, Chekov, Ibsen, Maeterlinck! Isn't it time to admit that ballet is also an art, that it is a departure from oneself, a departure into a world of creative fantasies?[17]

Hidden behind the fuss about what style of male dancing could properly be termed masculine was the whole matter of whether ballet could be considered a haven for people whose ways of life—including their sexual preferences—differed from socially accepted norms. To the uninitiated, the conventions of ballet must seem strange indeed, and brash newspapermen found that ballet provided good material for wisecracks. Some were harmless enough, as when a *Daily News* reporter facetiously retold the plots of famous ballets, calling *Snow Maiden* a ballet about "a guy who falls in love with a snow flake, only she melts" and *Coppélia* a ballet "about two lovers who spat, spurn and finally spoon."[18]

But some newspaper commentaries were vicious. Journalistic conventions of the day probably forbade printing the outright charge that ballet was an art with wide appeal for homosexuals, yet reviews and features were filled with innuendos concerning ballet companies and the ballet public. Such articles appeared on both sides of the Atlantic. Thus in 1938 London journalist Stephen Williams declared, "I should enjoy ballet very much if the intervals were not marred (for me) by willowy young men who call each other 'darling,' and lissome young women who lean against each other in rapture before futuristic paintings in the foyer and declare that they are just too utterly utter."

An American writer who repeatedly linked ballet with sexual nonconformity was drama critic John Chapman. In 1946 he said, "I'm not sure what it is about ballet that attracts so many sexually abnormal people and inspires them to heights of offensiveness." Two years later, he was charging that "abnormal people" were actually spoiling ballet for normal folk:

> Queer people . . . began taking up the ballet, until frog-voiced, flatfooted women and men with spangles in their hair drove some of the more ordinary audiences out of the theatres with their vocal and sartorial ecstasies.
>
> Today, anybody who goes to the ballet too much is suspect, and a normal and beautiful form of entertainment suffers at the box office. There aren't enough queer people in the country yet to pay for ballet all by themselves, and many of us have quit going because we can't stand the audiences.[19]

Dancers (both gay and straight) grow indignant to this day when such remarks are quoted back at them. Ballet companies of the 1940s, these dancers declare, did contain homosexual dancers (just as ballet companies do today); but there were also many heterosexual dancers. Similarly, among the segments of the audience that constituted the ballet public (segments that also included socialites, the middle class, family groups, and professional people), there was a homosexual contingent. Chapman is at least right about one thing: for whatever reasons, many homosexuals find ballet appealing (as do many heterosexuals). Since, virtually by theatrical tradition, dancers often accept personal foibles without casting moral judgments upon them, homosexuals might have found in the ballet a milieu in which they could escape censure.

Yet, dancers say, despite the journalists, the gay audience was far less noticeable in the 1940s than it is today in large cities where gay liberation movements have encouraged homosexuals to "come out." Indeed, the few spangle-haired youths that were on view back then could even be considered courageous in a way for daring to express themselves so openly. Homosexuality, Ballet Russe dancers insist, was seldom a problem in itself; it was simply an issue that was seized upon by sensationalistic journalists willing to pander to the prejudices of their readers.

That dancers can still be incensed over issues almost two decades after their company ceased operations suggests the remarkable esprit de corps that existed in the Ballet Russe. The Ballet Russe inspired loyalty. "We are all one big family" was more than a favorite catchphrase of Sergei Denham. Like the members of many families, the dancers of the Ballet Russe quarreled, sometimes violently. Yet if they felt that the company was being attacked or if problems had to be surmounted, they became united in their determination.

Several dancers say that there was always someone to go to if one had a problem. On the company's final tour, each new member of the corps was assigned to an older dancer of the company who served as an adviser and confidante in a manner akin to the "big sister-little sister" arrangement prevalent in some college sororities. Usually, however, such formalities were unnecessary. Help was simply there when one needed it.

"The truly astonishing thing about the Ballet Russe was its spirit," Raven Wilkinson says. "It must have been about the last of the real old-fashioned show-must-go-on companies. No matter what problem came up, everyone was always willing to pitch in." Ruthanna Boris concurs. She says that at one time admirers of Ballet Theatre, the Monte Carlo's chief rival, had nicknamed that company, "The Cadillac of ballet companies." That phrase, says Boris, "made us at the Ballet Russe joke that if Ballet Theatre was the Cadillac, then we were the jeep of ballet companies. A jeep may not be fancy, but it always gets where it's supposed to go. And we did, too."

Audiences sensed the spirit of the Ballet Russe. That is one reason why they came back season after season. Frederic Franklin sums up his years with the company very simply: "We were good. And people liked us."

NOTES FOR CHAPTER 15

1. Conversation with Leon Danielian. Henceforth all statements for which no printed source is given were made in conversation with the author. Particularly helpful have been conversations with Meredith Baylis, Ruthanna Boris, Alexandra Danilova, Michel Katcharoff, Nathalie Krassovska, Robert Lindgren, Alexandra Nadal, Duncan Noble, Eugene Slavin, James Starbuck, Sonja Taanila, George Verdak, Raven Wilkinson, Igor Youskevitch, and Rochelle Zide.
2. "A Conversation with P.W. Manchester," *Ballet Review,* v. VI no. 3, p. 84.
3. Harvey Southgate, "Ballet Russe Acclaimed for Color, Dance Skill," *Rochester Democrat and Chronicle,* 1 November 1956.
4. Olga Maynard, *The American Ballet,* p. 85.
5. Clifford Gessler, "Ballet 'Giselle' Gets Warm Reception from Audience," *Oakland Tribune,* 7 February 1956.
6. Doris Hering, "Reviews," *Dance Magazine,* June 1957, p. 14.
7. Doris Hering, "Ballet Russe de Monte Carlo," *Dance Magazine,* May 1961, p. 20.
8. Walter Terry, "The Lure of Ballet," *New York Herald-Tribune,* 31 March 1940.
9. Superstitions—"Left Leg for Luck," *PM,* 22 February 1948; Al Delancey, "Massage Greatest Luxury," *Brooklyn Eagle,* 13 October 1941; "Good Seats Still Available for Ballet Performances," *Thomasville (Georgia) Times-Enterprise,* 6 December 1957; conversation with Alexandra Nadal and Eugene Slavin.
10. Advertisement, *Richmond Leader,* 23 November 1938.
11. "Ballet Russe 'Puts Ideas' into Windows at Bonwit Teller," *Women's Wear,* 25 October 1938.
12. New York audience—James Whittaker, "Gala Ballet Gives Eyeful at the Met," *New York Mirror,* 27 October 1939; Robert Sabin, "When Will the Ballet Grow Up," *Dance Observer,* December 1940, p. 150; Russell Rhodes, "Notes from America," *The Dancing Times,* December 1941, p. 145.
13. Society—"Ballet Russe's Atlanta Appearance Rivals N.Y. Metropolitan's 'Glitter,' " *Atlanta American,* 27 November 1938; Grace Davidson, "Society Greets Ballet Opening," *Boston Post,* 8 November 1938.
14. Edwin Denby, *Looking at the Dance,* p. 397.

15. Men—Walter Terry, "Ballet Russe de Monte Carlo," *Boston Herald,* 17 April 1940; William N. Gates, "Massine Brings New Deal in Ballet to City," *Cleveland News,* 4 December 1938; Alexander Fried, "Twice-Tried Program Launches Season of Ballet Russe Here," *San Francisco Examiner,* 31 January 1940.
16. Walter Terry, "Men in the Ballet," *New York Herald-Tribune,* 24 March 1940.
17. Walter Terry, "Ballet Traditions," *New York Herald-Tribune,* 5 November 1939; Walter Terry, "Dance Argument," *New York Herald-Tribune,* 29 December 1940 (contains Fokine's letter).
18. Robert Wahls, "The City Center's Ballet Is as Pure as Its 'Snow Maiden,' " *New York Daily News,* 9 March 1945.
19. Journalistic attacks—Stephen Williams, "Ballet Would Be Better If . . .," *London Evening Standard,* 27 July 1938; John Chapman, "Those Ballet Audiences!" *Dance,* September 1946, p. 9; John Chapman, "Whoops! Ballets Coming," *New York Sunday News,* 5 September 1948.

16 THE BALLET RUSSE: A SUMMING UP

To speak as harshly as possible, it could be said that the Ballet Russe de Monte Carlo was a company of brilliant beginnings that never attained real fulfillment. It was established in 1938, largely to suit the wishes of Léonide Massine. Yet within two years Massine found his prestige and authority waning, and four years after the birth of the company created especially for him, he departed from it to choreograph for other organizations.

There was another brave beginning in 1944 when George Balanchine came to the Ballet Russe. But that association proved brief, and in 1946 Balanchine left the company to work elsewhere. In 1954 the company attempted a massive reorganization. All that came of it were a few hopeful seasons followed by a slow decline. George Amberg has pointed out that "no choreographer of stature stayed long enough with any of the Ballet Russe-style companies to identify his creative endeavor with the growth of the ensemble."[1]

All this is true. And if this were the only thing that could be said, then it would be simple enough to relegate the Ballet Russe to no more than a paragraph or two in the dance history books. Yet the Ballet Russe was a complex organization that exerted a profound influence.

A theory of company direction advanced by the British critic Fernau Hall[2] may help explain what sort of company the Ballet

271

Russe was, particularly during its early years. Hall calls both the Ballet Russe de Monte Carlo and Colonel de Basil's Ballets Russes "hybrid companies"; that is, they were companies led not by a single charismatic force, as the Diaghilev Ballet had been, but by a group of often quite disparate people. Among the people who at one time or another helped guide the destinies of the Ballet Russe companies from the 1930s on were Massine, Balanchine, Sergei J. Denham, René Blum, Sol Hurok, and, of course, Colonel de Basil himself.

Hybrid companies can do valuable creative work, provided that the personalities and tastes of their various directors are kept in a state of constant tension that assures a kind of equilibrium in the struggle for power. However, it frequently happens that one of the directors may squeeze out the others to gain absolute power, or the other directors may simply resign because they think that more promising opportunities exist for them elsewhere. In either case, the director who remains after these changes in personnel now usually has total control over the company. Hence there may no longer be any behind-the-scenes bickering. But that also means that the company will now reflect a single director's artistic taste and managerial skill. Unfortunately, the director who survives the split often proves deficient in either taste or management. A valuable man to have as a member of a board of directors, he proves inadequate as a company's sole director.

Of the men involved in the hybrid directorate of the Ballet Russe de Monte Carlo in 1938, it was probably inevitable that Denham should have survived as sole director. Blum was somewhat reticent. Massine struck people as aloof and arrogant, and his choreography was going out of fashion. Sol Hurok, of course, was one of the best theatrical businessmen who ever lived. To Hurok must go much of the credit for popularizing ballet in America. Yet if Hurok can be praised for much, he can also be blamed for much. Hurok seems to have been at least partly responsible for some of the difficulties in which the Ballet Russe found itself. During the 1930s and '40s Hurok actively tried to shape and control the policies of the companies he managed. This might have been only annoying at worst—and it could even have been beneficial, for Hurok knew how to turn his attractions into successes—if this tendency to meddle had not also been accompanied by a kind of fickleness. Hurok was constantly switching balletic allegiances, adopting each new company that seemed promising, while at the same time ignoring or even dropping the company that had seemed promising the year before.

Moreover, Hurok appeared to want to control all American ballet. Thus he not only managed supposedly rival companies simultaneously, he even had separate companies share single seasons, as the Ballet Russe de Monte Carlo and Ballet Theatre did at the Metropolitan Opera House. If the general public could not remember which company was which, no matter: Hurok made sure the public knew that both companies were Hurok Attractions. Ultimately, Hurok decided that it would be wise of him to abandon the Ballet Russe, and so he left the Ballet Russe behind.

It was Denham who remained to guide it, and he did so with gallantry and devotion. But Denham was unable to formulate a coherent artistic policy. At first, all went well. There were well-known choreographers upon whom he could call: Nijinska, Balanchine. There were newer or less-known choreographers to be encouraged: de Mille, Page, Boris, Cobos, Bolender, Bettis. Eventually, however, each of those choreographers, for various reasons, moved on from the Ballet Russe. And when all were gone, Denham had no one to whom he could turn. Although Massine did return to stage *Harold in Italy,* Denham, for the most part, seemed unable to win back the choreographers he had lost and he did not possess Marie Rambert's knack for discovering choreographic talent in each new generation.

Gradually, the company boxed itself in artistically. It emphasized what has been nicknamed a ham-and-eggs repertoire. This was partly out of choice, and the choice is defensible: after all, *Swan Lake* and *Les Sylphides* are acknowledged classics, *Ballet Imperial* and *Le Beau Danube* would certainly be considered works of stature by most critics, and *Cirque de Deux* and *Madroños,* if slight, were far from negligible. But the limited repertoire was also a matter of necessity. Local managers on the road kept insisting upon old favorites, and Denham apparently lacked the flair for programming that might have enabled him to widen an audience's horizons by placing an unfamiliar work on a bill along with two already popular works in the hopes that acquaintance with the new work might in time turn it, too, into an old favorite.

The Ballet Russe became fossilized. The company's very conception of tradition and classicism gradually narrowed in the later years. In a letter Nina Novak declares that, for her, the artistic policy of the Ballet Russe de Monte Carlo was "always to keep the classical tradition." Yet because of "the wave of modern dancing . . . the opinions were *contra* the classical tradition, the company was very strongly criticized."[3] Although Novak oversimplifies the rise and influence of American modern dance, few dance lovers would disagree with her about the importance of the classical tradition. However, she speaks of classicism only as something that must be kept, rather than as something capable of development. In contrast, George Amberg says that Balanchine's classicism involves "the perpetual rediscovery and reapplication of . . . basic laws."[4] Classicism, so conceived, is dynamic. At the Ballet Russe in its late years, classicism had become static.

When asked whether she thought the Ballet Russe could have survived—and whether there would have been any point in letting it survive—beyond 1962, Meredith Baylis replied, "Its time for change had already passed by 1962. For the company to have had any real point after that, it would have had to change substantially at least five years earlier, or even ten. Yet if it had managed to change, if it had both preserved the best of its repertoire and traditions and produced important new works, it could have gone on. There would have been a place for the Ballet Russe in America even today."[5]

In its best years the Ballet Russe de Monte Carlo did exemplify Amberg's notion of classicism, the works in its repertoire serving as illustrations of ballet's ongoing evolution. From the nineteenth century came *Giselle, Coppélia,* and the second act of *Swan Lake;* and it was the Ballet Russe that introduced American audiences to *Nutcracker, Raymonda, Paquita,* and the traditional third act of *Swan Lake.* The Diaghilev era was represented by such ballets as *Les Sylphides, Petrouchka, Spectre de la Rose, Prince Igor, L'Après-midi d'un Faune, Scheherazade, Three-Cornered Hat,* and *La Boutique Fantasque.* The continuation of the cosmopolitan tradition was reflected in *Don Juan, L'Épreuve d'Amour, St. Francis, Rouge et Noir, Seventh Symphony, Bacchanale, Gaîté Parisienne, Baiser de la Fée,* and *Chopin Concerto,* while the coming of classical ballet to America was evident both in the specifically Americana pieces by Page and de Mille and in the vigorous abstractions of Balanchine.

"The Ballet Russe," says Meredith Baylis, "was the first blending of the Old World and the New World in ballet. It linked St. Petersburg with America and Canada." Preserving a tradition and letting that tradition grow in new ways in a new land, the Ballet Russe was simultaneously exotic and as American as apple pie.

Through its tours, the Ballet Russe not only introduced thousands of people to ballet, it also served as an inspiration to young dancers. The Ballet Russe was a goal to which one could aspire. The Ballet Russe changed lives. Many dancers tell stories about the profound ways in which they were affected by the Ballet Russe. Years ago, for instance, a performance of *Bourgeois Gentilhomme, Snow Maiden,* and *Rodeo* inspired a little girl in Fort Worth, Texas, to be a dancer. The Ballet Russe gave one performance annually in Fort Worth and that girl was always in the audience. One year, she and a friend were so excited by what they saw that they tried to sneak backstage to get a peep at the dancers. The company manager kept discovering them and evicting them from the theatre. Eventually, the girl's friend gave up and went home. But the little girl decided to make one last try. She slipped through the stage door and hid behind some costume trunks. There she was spotted by Alexandra Danilova, who whispered, "Come quickly," and whisked the girl off to her dressing room. While she packed her things away, Danilova regaled her young admirer with stories of the Imperial Russian Ballet. That little girl left the dressing room starry-eyed.

She grew up to be a dancer whose own performances may have left other little girls similarly in awe. For that little girl was Sallie Wilson, who became the great dramatic ballerina of American Ballet Theatre in the 1960s and '70s.

Many other prominent figures in the dance world have similar stories to tell. Arnold Spohr, director of the Royal Winnipeg Ballet, was reluctantly dragged off to a performance of the Ballet Russe by his sister. That performance transformed him completely, for it made him want to be a dancer. The Ballet Russe also helped change the life of Paul Taylor. A Ballet Russe performance he attended when he was a student at the University of Syracuse made him aware that there was another kind of dancing—a kind more serious than the dancing he had known from movies and musical comedies. Similarly, it was a Ballet Russe performance that inspired the avant-garde choreographer James Waring to study dance. And the Ballet Russe was the first dance company that Alvin Ailey ever saw. The list of dancers whose lives were touched by the Ballet Russe is almost endless.

But perhaps even more important than the Ballet Russe's effect upon dancers was its effect upon dancegoers. As Igor Youskevitch says, "The Ballet Russe tours helped thousands of people to develop a habit of art, that habit which is essential to the growth of any art form." The pioneering of the Ballet Russe helped make America's dance boom.

The Ballet Russe tradition lives on. An extraordinary number of former members of the Ballet Russe de Monte Carlo are still active, particularly as teachers and company directors. Alexandra Danilova teaches at the School of American Ballet and stages revivals for many companies. Frederic Franklin founded the National Ballet of Washington and in recent years has been teacher, coach, choreographer, and stager of works for various organizations. Alicia Markova headed the Metropolitan Opera Ballet for several seasons and has taught at the University of Cincinnati. Anton Dolin has staged ballets around the world. Mia Slavenska has taught for several institutions in Southern California, including the University of California at Los Angeles. Igor Youskevitch teaches at the University of Texas; Ruthanna Boris, at the University of Washington in Seattle. Robert Lindgren and Sonja Taanila direct the North Carolina Dance Theatre and Lindgren is also dean of dance at the North Carolina School of the Arts, where one of his faculty members is Duncan Noble. Maria Tallchief has directed the ballet of Chicago's Lyric Opera. Nicholas Beriozoff has been ballet master for many European companies (including those of Stuttgart and Zurich) and has also taught at Indiana University. Karel Shook is co-director of the Dance Theatre of Harlem. Leon Danielian headed the Ballet Theatre School for many years and Patricia Wilde was a member of his faculty. Nina Novak teaches at her own school in Caracas, Venezuela. Vida Brown has served as ballet mistress for the New York City Ballet. Rosella Hightower was appointed director of the Paris Opéra Ballet in 1980.

Many Ballet Russe dancers are involved in some way—as directors, régisseurs, or members of the managerial staff—with dance companies in communities throughout the United States and Canada. Such companies have become increasingly important now that most large New York and foreign ballet companies have reduced their touring itineraries to performances in only a few big cities. Among the Ballet Russe alumni who have been involved with local professional, semi-professional, or non-professional companies are George Skibine, André Eglevsky, Moscelyne Larkin, Roman Jasinski, Nathalie Krassovska, George Verdak, Natalia Clare, Charles Dickson, Nesta Williams, Sviatoslav Toumine, Thomas Armour, Gilbert Reed, Alan Howard, Eugene Slavin, Joseph Savino, Mary Ellen Moylan, and Gene Marinaccio.

Ballet Russe members who have gone into teaching include George Zoritch, Tatiana Grantzeva, Yvonne Chouteau, Miguel Terekhov, Ana Roje, Dorothy Etheridge, Katia Geleznova, Jeannette Lauret, Eleonora Marra, Milada Mladova, Michel Panaieff, Adda Pourmel, Nina Stroganova, Vladimir Dokoudovsky, Nikita Talin, Anna Istomina, Serge Ismailoff,

Merriam Lanova, William Glenn, Alfredo Corvino, Richard Thomas, Oleg Tupine, Fernando Schaffenburg, Meredith Baylis, Rochelle Zide, Dorothy Daniels, and Gwenn Barker. James Starbuck became a successful television choreographer, while Marc Platt (Platoff) choreographed for the Radio City Music Hall. Other former company members have aided dance in other ways. Thus Herbert Kummel was for several years director of the Dance Notation Bureau and James Brusock was a makeup artist and hair stylist for the New York City Ballet.

Moscelyne Larkin sums up the feelings of many former company members when she says, "For us, Ballet Russe is not a dirty word. For us, Ballet Russe represents a great tradition, a tradition we are passing down to our own students."

The Ballet Russe de Monte Carlo may have been the company with the fancy foreign name. But if there had been no Ballet Russe, ballet in North America would be very different today. During all its years of touring, the Ballet Russe liked to bill itself as "The One and Only."

And that it was. The One and Only.

NOTES FOR CHAPTER 16

1. George Amberg, *Ballet*, p. 40.
2. Fernau Hall, *An Anatomy of Ballet*, p. 402.
3. Letter from Nina Novak to Jack Anderson, 20 December 1977.
4. George Amberg, *Ballet*, p. 63.
5. Conversation with Meredith Baylis. Also valuable have been conversations with Yvonne Chouteau, Roman Jasinski, Moscelyne Larkin, Robert Lindgren, Arnold Spohr, Paul Taylor, Miguel Terekhov, Sallie Wilson, Igor Youskevitch, and Rochelle Zide.

APPENDIX: ROSTER AND REPERTOIRE

WHAT follows is an attempt to provide a season-by-season listing of the dancers and the repertoire of the Ballet Russe de Monte Carlo. However, since the Ballet Russe was primarily a touring company, one cannot always be certain who was who in it and what it was dancing at every moment in its peregrinations.

Of inestimable aid are the company's own souvenir programs. Yet they cannot be absolutely trusted. For one thing, they do not invariably list all the dancers with the company. The earliest programs listed only the principals and soloists. Later programs were comprehensive, but even they were not always able to include new dancers with the company. And, of course, they could not list anyone who joined the company during the middle of a season. Moreover, the souvenir books' repertoire listings are sometimes wildly optimistic, for they may include ballets that the company had not performed for several years. Because of this, I have also consulted other sources: advertisements and announcements of dance attractions in New York newspapers and the nightly programs for performances across the country housed in the Dance Collection of the New York Public Library.

Following theatrical convention, each new season is assumed to start in September and to run through the following summer. However, one exception has been made. Because Ruth Page's *The Bells* entered the repertoire at the very end of August, it is treated here, as it probably was by the company at the time, as the first production of the new season, rather than as the last production of the old.

The preparation of company rosters brings with it a special set of problems. Programs often referred to members of the corps de ballet simply as "M." or "Mlle," and in several instances I have been unable to ascertain the first names of dancers. Other dancers—particularly some of the Russians whose names were difficult to transliterate, but also some of the Americans who were first tempted to adopt, and then later to drop, exotic surnames—changed their names several times. I have usually included dancers under the spellings of their names for which they are best known (thus "Beriozoff" rather than "Beresoff") or which they themselves prefer (thus "Jasinski" rather than "Jasinsky"). But important variants are noted in parentheses.

Michel Katcharoff, the company's former régisseur, has reminded me that some names on a program may be pseudonyms for supers. Occasionally, to create the illusion that the Ballet Russe was an enormous company, if the same super danced in several ballets, he might be listed under a different name for each ballet. A few of these names (particularly the ubiquitous "Ivan Ivanoff") immediately arouse suspicion, but other names invented for supers could be very convincing. Therefore I hope that the members of the Ballet Russe will smile indulgently at me if I have placed the names of totally fictitious people on the roster—and that they will forgive me if I have inadvertently omitted the names of people who did in fact exist. For purposes of convenience, all names are listed alphabetically.

In addition to the ballets included here, the company's principals and guest stars often appeared in such divertissements as the Bluebird, *Don Quixote,* and Black Swan pas de deux (the last-named billed as Pas de Deux Classique) and in *The Dying Swan.*

Spring-Summer 1938

DANCERS:

Barbara Barrie, Nicholas Beriozoff (also known as Beresoff), Tatiana Chamié, Leila Crabtree (also known as Leilanova and Crabovska), Alexandra Danilova, Eugénie Delarova, Charles Dickson, Tatiana Dokoudovska, Vladimir Dokoudovsky, Irene Drosdova, Dorothy Etheridge, Irène Fabergé, Marcel Fenchel (later known as Luipart), Rosalind Firminova, Tatiana Flotat, Marina

Franca, Frederic Franklin, Eugène Gabay, Katia Geleznova, Unity Grantham, Tatiana Grantzeva, Simone Grossman, Roland Guerard, Rosella Hightower, Nicholas Ivangin, Robert T. Irwin, Kari Karnakovsky, Michel Katcharoff, Nathalie Kelepovska, Diana King, Max Kirbos, Pierre Klimoff, Casimir Kokitch, Marina (also Moussia) Korjinska, Waldemar (later Vladimir) Kostenko, Nathalie Krassovska, Yolanda Lacca, Paula Lamonte, Jeannette Lauret, Louis Lebercher, Serge Lifar, Irène Litvinova, Alicia Markova, Eleanora Marra, Arvo Martikainen, Léonide Massine, Eugénie Melnitchenko, Anna Michailova, Milada Mladova, Arved Ozoline, Michel Panaieff, Felix Piotrovsky, Marc Platoff, Adda Pourmel, Ludmilla Rklitzka, Ana Roje, Virginia Rosson, Lubov Rostova, Lubov Roudenko, Anna (also Tina) Scarpova, Simon Semenoff, Youra (later George) Skibine, Mia Slavenska, Nina Stroganova, Nina Tarakanova, Nini Theilade, Nina Tikonova, Sviatoslav Toumine, Tamara Toumanova, Betty Vallentin, M. Voujanitch, Nesta Williams, Jean Yazvinsky, Igor Youskevitch, Maria Zarina

PRODUCTIONS INHERITED FROM BLUM'S BALLETS DE MONTE CARLO:

Don Juan (Fokine/Gluck), Les Éléments (Fokine/Bach), Les Elfes (Fokine/Mendelssohn), L'Épreuve d'Amour (Fokine/Mozart attrib.), Igrouchki (Fokine/Rimsky-Korsakov)

PRODUCTIONS INHERITED FROM OTHER SOURCES:

Le Beau Danube (Massine/Strauss), Carnaval (Fokine/Schumann), Giselle, two acts (Coralli, Perrot/Adam), Petrouchka (Fokine/ Stravinsky), Prince Igor (Fokine/Borodin), Scheherazade (Fokine/Rimsky-Korsakov), Spectre de la Rose (Fokine/Weber), Swan Lake Act II (Ivanov, Petipa/Tchaikovsky), Les Sylphides (Fokine/Chopin), Three-Cornered Hat (Massine/Falla)

NEW PRODUCTIONS:

Gaîté Parisienne (Monte Carlo, 5 April 1938). Choreography: Léonide Massine; Book: Comte Etienne de Beaumont; Music: Offenbach, arr. Manuel Rosenthal; Designs: Comte Etienne de Beaumont. / Glove Seller: Nina Tarakanova; Flower-Girl: Eugénie Delarova; Peruvian: Léonide Massine; Baron: Frederic Franklin; Officer: Igor Youskevitch; ensemble.

Seventh Symphony (Monte Carlo, 5 May 1938). Choreography: Léonide Massine; Music: Beethoven; Designs: Christian Bérard. / Spirit of Creation: Frederic Franklin; Sky: Alicia Markova; Stream:

Nini Theilade; Woman: Jeannette Lauret; Man: Eugène Gabay; Youth: Charles Dickson; Innocent: Max Kirbos; Gods: Alicia Markova and Igor Youskevitch; ensemble.

Nobilissima Visione (St. Francis) (London, 21 July 1938). Choreography: Léonide Massine; Book: Massine and Paul Hindemith; Music: Paul Hindemith; Designs: Pavel Tchelitchev. / St. Francis: Léonide Massine; Knight: Frederic Franklin; Poverty: Nini Theilade; Obedience: Jeannette Lauret; Chastity: Lubov Rostova; Wolf: Frederic Franklin; ensemble.

Icare (London, 28 July 1938). Choreography: Serge Lifar; Music: J.E. Szyfer; Designs: Eugène Berman. / Icarus: Serge Lifar; Daedalus: Louis Lebercher; ensemble.

Coppélia, three acts (London, 20 September 1938). Choreography staged by Nicholas Sergeyev, automatons' dance and betrothal dance by Léonide Massine; Music: Léo Delibes; Designs: Pierre Roy. / Swanilda: Alexandra Danilova; Frantz: Michel Panaieff; Coppelius: Simon Semenoff; ensemble.

1938-39

DANCERS:

Argentinita (guest), Nicholas Beriozoff, Tatiana Chamié, Leila Crabtree, Alexandra Danilova, Eugénie Delarova, Charles Dickson, Dorothy Etheridge, Marcel Fenchel, Tatiana Flotat, Marina Franca, Frederic Franklin, Eugène Gabay, Katia Geleznova, Tatiana Grantzeva, Roland Guerard, Rosella Hightower, Nicholas Ivangin, Robert T. Irwin, Kari Karnakovsky, Michel Katcharoff, Nathalie Kelepovska, Max Kirbos, Pierre Klimoff, Casimir Kokitch, Marina Korjinska, Vladimir (formerly Waldemar) Kostenko, Nathalie Krassovska, Yolanda Lacca, Jeannette Lauret, Serge Lifar, Mlle Likely, Irène Litvinova, Alicia Markova, Léonide Massine, Eugénie Melnitchenko, Anna Michailova, Milada Mladova, Nicolas Orloff, Tatiana Orlova, Arved Ozoline, Michel Panaieff, Felix Piotrovsky, Marc Platoff, Adda Pourmel, Nina Radova, Ludmilla Rklitzka, Virginia Rosson, Lubov Rostova, Lubov Roudenko, Anna Scarpova, Simon Semenoff, George Skibine, Mia Slavenska, Nini Theilade, Tamara Toumanova, Sviatoslav Toumine, Felicity Watt, Jean Yazvinsky, Igor Youskevitch, George (also Youra) Zoritch

REPERTOIRE:

L'Après-midi d'un Faune, Beau Danube, Carnaval, Cimarosiana,

Coppélia, Don Juan, Les Elfes, L'Épreuve d'Amour, Gaîté Parisienne, Giselle, Icare, Petrouchka, Prince Igor, St. Francis (American title for "Nobilissima Visione"), Seventh Symphony, Spectre de la Rose, Swan Lake, Les Sylphides, Three-Cornered Hat

NEW PRODUCTIONS:

Bogatyri (New York, 20 October 1938). Choreography: Léonide Massine; Music: Borodin, B-minor Symphony, A-minor Symphony, Nocturne from Second String Quartet); Designs: Nathalie Gontcharova. / Anastachiuska: Mia Slavenska; Alyosha: Igor Youskevitch; Dobryna: Frederic Franklin; Khanja: Nathalie Krassovska; The Mouromitz: Marc Platoff; Khan: George Zoritch; ensemble.

Capriccio Espagnol (Monte Carlo, 4 May 1939). Choreography: Léonide Massine and Argentinita; Music: Rimsky-Korsakov; Designs: Mariano Andreu. / Gypsy couple: Argentinita, Léonide Massine; Peasant couple: Alexandra Danilova, Michel Panaieff; ensemble.

Rouge et Noir (Monte Carlo, 11 May 1939). Choreography: Léonide Massine; Music: Shostakovitch, First Symphony; Designs: Henri Matisse. / Woman: Alicia Markova; Man: Igor Youskevitch; Black leader: Marc Platoff; Red leader: Frederic Franklin; Yellow leader: Nathalie Krassovska; Blue leader: Michel Panaieff; ensemble.

1939-40

DANCERS:

Argentinita (guest), Thomas Armour, Irina Baronova (guest), Nicholas Beriozoff, M. Bocchino, Vida Brown, Tatiana Chamié, Leila Crabtree, Alexandra Danilova, Eugénie Delarova, Charles Dickson, Anton Dolin (guest), André Eglevsky, Stanislav Egoroff, Dorothy Etheridge, Tatiana Flotat, Marina Franca, Frederic Franklin, Ian Gibson, Katia Geleznova, Paul Godkin, Alexander Goudovitch, Tatiana Grantzeva, Roland Guerard, Rosella Hightower, Yvonne Hill, Robert T. Irwin, Michel Katcharoff, Nathalie Kelepovska, Casimir Kokitch, Moussia Korjinska, Nathalie Krassovska, Yolanda Lacca, Jeannette Lauret, Betty Low (also known as Ludmilla Lvova), Fedja Markoff, Alicia Markova, Eleanora Marra, Léonide Massine, Roy Milton, Milada Mladova, Marina Novikova, Tatiana Orlova, Jan Orwiroff, Marcel Perensky, Marc Platoff, Adda Pourmel, Ludmilla Rklitzka, Sascha Rolanoff, Virginia

Rosson, Lubov Rostova, Lubov Roudenko, Anna Scarpova, Simon Semenoff, Mia Slavenska, Howard Spurling (later Nikita Talin), James Starbuck, Robert Steele, Nini Theilade, Audrée Thomas (later known as Anna Istomina), Jean Vallon, Chris Vokoff, Mlle Wilcox, Nesta Williams, Jean Yazvinsky, Ivan Youroff, Igor Youskevitch, George Zoritch

REPERTOIRE:

L'Après-midi d'un Faune, Beau Danube, Bogatyri, Boutique Fantasque, Capriccio Espagnol, Carnaval, Coppélia, Gaîté Parisienne, Giselle, Igrouchki, Petrouchka, Prince Igor, Rouge et Noir, St. Francis, Scheherazade, Seventh Symphony, Spectre de la Rose, Swan Lake, Les Sylphides, Three-Cornered Hat

NEW PRODUCTIONS

Devil's Holiday (New York, 26 October 1939). Choreography: Frederick Ashton; Book: Vincenzo Tommasini; Music: Tommasini on themes of Paganini; Designs: Eugène Berman./Old Lord: Simon Semenoff; His Daughter: Alexandra Danilova; Young Lover: Frederic Franklin; Fiancé: George Zoritch; Devil: Marc Platoff; Gypsy Girl: Nathalie Krassovska; Old Woman: Tatiana Chamié; Beggar: Robert Irwin; Hat-Seller: Alexander Goudovitch; ensemble.

Bacchanale (New York, 9 November 1939). Choreography: Léonide Massine; Book: Salvador Dali; Music: Wagner, from *Tannhäuser;* Designs: Salvador Dali. / Ludwig II: Casimir Kokitch; Venus: Nini Theilade; Lola Montez: Milada Mladova; Knight of Death: Chris Volkoff; Nymph: Nathalie Krassovska; Faun: André Eglevsky; Sacher Masoch: Marc Platoff; His Wife: Jeannette Lauret; ensemble.

Ghost Town (New York, 12 November 1939). Choreography: Marc Platoff; Book: Richard Rodgers; Historical research: Gerald Murphy; Music: Richard Rodgers; orchestrated by Hans Spialek; Designs: Raoul Pène du Bois. / Eilley Orum: Mia Slavenska; Orson Hyde: Roland Guerard; Ralston: Frederic Franklin; Jenny Lind: Nini Theilade; Bonanza King Comstock: Casimir Kokitch; Hikers: Charles Dickson, Milada Mladova; Old Prospector: Simon Semenoff; Assay Officer: Paul Godkin; Benicia Boy Heenan: Robert Steele; Algernon C. Swinburn: James Starbuck; The Menken: Marina Franca; ensemble.

Nuages (Clouds) (New York, 9 April 1940). Choreography: Nini Theilade; Music: Debussy; Designs: Willam de Kooning. / Night: Lubov Rostova; Day: Frederic Franklin; Twilight: Nini Theilade, George Zoritch; ensemble.

Le Baiser de la Fée (New York, 10 April 1940). Choreography: George Balanchine; Music: Stravinsky; Designs: Alice Halicka. / Bride: Alexandra Danilova; Friend: Nathalie Krassovska; Bridegroom: André Eglevsky; Mother: Nini Theilade; Fairy: Mia Slavenska; ensemble.

1940-41

DANCERS:

Thomas Armour, Nicholas Beriozoff, Vida Brown, Tatiana Chamié, Leila Crabtree, Alexandra Danilova, André Eglevsky, Igor Egoroff, Dorothy Etheridge, Tatiana Flotat, Frederic Franklin, Katia Geleznova, Ian Gibson, Alexander Goudovitch, Tatiana Grantzeva, Roland Guerard, Rosella Hightower, Yvonne Hill, Robert Irwin, Michel Katcharoff, Nathalie Kelepovska, Casimir Kokitch, Moussia Korjinska, Alexis Kosloff, Vladimir Kostenko, Nathalie Krassovska, Yolanda Lacca, Jeannette Lauret, Marie-Jeanne (guest), Alicia Markova, Eleanora Marra, Léonide Massine, Roy Milton, Milada Mladova, Tatiana Orlova, Marc Platoff, Adda Pourmel, Lubov Rostova, Lubov Roudenko, Anna Scarpova, Simon Semenoff, Tatiana Semenova, Mia Slavenska, James Starbuck, Robert Steele, Audrée Thomas, Georges Tomin, Tamara Toumanova, Chris Volkoff, Nesta Williams, Sonia Woicikowska, Jean Yazvinsky, Igor Youskevitch, George Zoritch.

REPERTOIRE:

L'Après-midi d'un Faune, Bacchanale, Baiser de la Fée, Beau Danube, Boutique Fantasque, Capriccio Espagnol, Coppélia, Gaîté Parisienne, Giselle, Petrouchka, Prince Igor, Rouge et Noir, Scheherazade, Seventh Symphony, Spectre de la Rose, Swan Lake, Les Sylphides

NEW PRODUCTIONS:

Poker Game (Jeu de Cartes) (New York, 14 October 1940). Choreography: George Balanchine; Book: Igor Stravinsky; Associate on the book: M. Malaieff; Music: Stravinsky; Designs: Irene Sharaff. / Joker: Frederic Franklin; Queen of Spades: Alexandra Danilova; Queen of Clubs: Nathalie Krassovska; Queen of Hearts: Alicia Markova; Queen of Diamonds: Milada Mladova; Jack of Clubs: André Eglevsky; Jack of Hearts: Igor Youskevitch; Jack of Spades: Ian Gibson; Jack of Diamonds: Thomas Armour; ensemble.

Vienna—1814 (New York, 14 October 1940). Choreography: Léonide Massine; Music: Weber, *Turandot* overture and four-hand piano pieces arranged and orchestrated by Robert Russell Bennett; Designs: Stewart Chaney. / Prince Metternich: Marc Platoff; Princess Lieven: Mia Slavenska; Princess Melanie: Tatiana Orlova; Prince de Ligne: Simon Semenoff; Frederich von Gentz: Casimir Kokitch; Baron Haager: Robert Steele; Baroness Haager: Nesta Williams; Secretaries: Igor Youskevitch, Roland Guerard, Frederic Franklin, Ian Gibson; Debutantes: Alexandra Danilova, Rosella Hightower, Tatiana Grantzeva, Milada Mladova, Audrée Thomas; Lord Castlereagh: James Starbuck; Lady Castlereagh: Katia Geleznova; Talleyrand: Nicholas Beriozoff; Madame de Perigord: Jeannette Lauret; Madame de Sagan: Tatiana Semenova; Saxon Dance: Nathalie Krassovska; Sicilienne: Chris Volkoff; Thème Russe: Mia Slavenska, Marc Platoff; Entrée Chinoise: Alicia Markova, Léonide Massine, Ian Gibson; Pas de Deux: Alexandra Danilova, Igor Youskevitch; Mazurka: Katia Geleznova, Frederic Franklin; ensemble.

Serenade (New York, 17 October 1940). Choreography: George Balanchine; Music: Tchaikovsky; Setting: Gaston Longchamp; Costumes: Jean Lurcat. / Marie-Jeanne, Igor Youskevitch, Frederic Franklin, ensemble.

Nutcracker, one act, three scenes (New York, 17 October 1940). Choreography: Alexandra Fedorova, after Ivanov; Music: Tchaikovsky; Designs: Alexandre Benois. / Sugar Plum Fairy: Alicia Markova; Prince: André Eglevsky; Waltz of the Flowers soloists: Lubov Rostova, Milada Mladova, Tatiana Grantzeva, Chris Volkoff, James Starbuck, Ian Gibson; Spanish dance: Nathalie Krassovska, Casimir Kokitch; Trepak soloist: Frederic Franklin; ensemble.

The New Yorker (New York, 18 October 1940). Choreography: Léonide Massine; Book: Rea Irvin and Massine; Music: Gershwin, songs and excerpts from Concerto in F, Second Rhapsody, *Cuban Overture, Variations on "I Got Rhythm," An American in Paris,* piano preludes, arranged and orchestrated by David Raksin; Designs: Carl Kent, after Rea Irvin and Nathalie Crothers. / Hokinson Lady: Tatiana Chamlé; Timid Man: Léonide Massine; Dowager: Jean Yazvinsky; Eustace Tilley: George Zoritch; Debutante: Nathalie Krassovska; Boy Friends: Igor Youskevitch, André Eglevsky, Roland Guerard; Small Fry: Lubov Roudenko, Ian Gibson; Girl: Alexandra Danilova; Little King: Michel Katcharoff; Gossip Columnist: Frederic Franklin; ensemble.

1941-42

DANCERS:

Leda Anchutina, Nicholas Beriozoff, Vida Brown, Tatiana Chamié, Leila Crabtree, Alexandra Danilova, André Eglevsky, Dorothy Etheridge, Tatiana Flotat, Frederic Franklin, Katia Geleznova, Alexander Goudovitch, Tatiana Grantzeva, Roland Guerard, Yvonne Hill, Anna Istomina (formerly Thomas), Kari Karnakoski, Arthur Karol, Michel Katcharoff, Nathalie Kelepovska, Casimir Kokitch, Maria Korjinska, Alexis Kosloff, Vladimir Kostenko, Nathalie Krassovska, Yolanda Lacca, Harold Lang, Mlle Lidova, Ludmilla Lvova (formerly Low), Eleonora Marra, Léonide Massine, Milada Mladova, Tatiana Orlova, Betty Orth, Michel Panaieff, Armand Picon, Marc Platoff, Lubov Rostova, Lubov Roudenko, Walter Sampson, Anna Scarpova, John Schendy, Tatiana Semenova, Irina Semochenko, James Starbuck, David Tihmar, Tamara Toumanova, Sviatoslav Toumine, Anton Vlassoff (later Robert Pagent), Chris Volkoff, Nesta Williams, Sonia Woicikowska, Jean Yazvinsky, Igor Youskevitch, George Zoritch

REPERTOIRE:

L'Après-midi d'un Faune, Bacchanale, Baiser de la Fée, Bogatyri, Boutique Fantasque, Capriccio Espagnol, Coppélia, Devil's Holiday, Gaîté Parisienne, The New Yorker, Nutcracker, Petrouchka, Poker Game, Prince Igor, Rouge et Noir, St. Francis, Scheherazade, Serenade, Seventh Symphony, Spectre de la Rose, Swan Lake, Les Sylphides, Three Cornered Hat, Vienna—1814

NEW PRODUCTIONS:

Labyrinth (New York, 8 October 1941). Choreography: Léonide Massine; Book: Salvador Dali; Music: Schubert, Ninth Symphony; Designs: Salvador Dali. / Theseus: André Eglevsky; Castor: George Zoritch; Pollux: Chris Volkoff; Ariadne: Tamara Toumanova; Minotaur: Frederic Franklin; ensemble.

The Magic Swan (Swan Lake, Act III) (New York, 13 October 1941). Choreography: Alexandra Fedorova, after Petipa; Music: Tchaikovsky; Designs: Eugene Dunkel. / Odile: Tamara Toumanova; Siegfried: Igor Youskevitch; Mazurka soloists: Eleonora Marra, Marc Platoff; Czardas soloists: Lubov Roudenko, Frederic Franklin; Pas de trois: Leila Crabtree, Dorothy Etheridge, Roland Guerard; Spanish dance: Milada Mladova, Casimir Kokitch;

Tarantelle: Sonia Woicikowska, Harold Lang; Waltz soloists: Lubov Rostova, George Zoritch; ensemble.

Saratoga (New York, 19 October 1941). Choreography: Léonide Massine; Book: Jaromir Weinberger; Music: Weinberger; Settings: Oliver Smith; Costumes: Alvin Colt. / Young Girl: Alexandra Danilova; Jockey: Frederic Franklin; Mother: Tatiana Chamié; Rich Man: Nicholas Beriozoff; ensemble. (A cakewalk was later added for Tamara Toumanova and Massine).

1942-43

DANCERS:

Nicholas Beriozoff, Vida Brown, Tatiana Chamié, Alfredo Corvino, Leila Crabtree, Alexandra Danilova, Agnes de Mille (guest), André Eglevsky, Dorothy Etheridge, Tatiana Flotat, Frederic Franklin, Katia Geleznova, Alexander Goudovitch, Tatiana Grantzeva, Roland Guerard, Yvonne Hill, Serge Ismailoff, Anna Istomina, Kari Karnakoski, Michel Katcharoff, Nathalie Kelepovska, Casimir Kokitch, Maria Korjinska, Vladimir Kostenko, Elena (also Helen) Kramarr, Nathalie Krassovska, Yolanda Lacca, Harold Lang, Ludmilla Lvova, Eleonora Marra, Léonide Massine, Milada Mladova, Betty Orth, Armand Picon, Nina Popova, Ruth Riekman, Lubov Rostova, Lubov Roudenko, Walter Sampson, Anna Scarpova, Tatiana Semenova, Mia Slavenska, James Starbuck, Gertrude Svobodina (later Tyven), Betty (later Maria) Tallchief, David Tihmar, Sviatoslav Toumine, Anton Vlassoff, Nesta Williams, Sonia Woicikowska, Jean Yazvinsky, Igor Youskevitch, George Zoritch

REPERTOIRE:

L'Après-midi d'un Faune, Beau Danube, Capriccio Espagnol, Carnaval, Coppélia, Les Elfes, Gaîté Parisienne, Giselle, Igrouchki, Magic Swan, Nutcracker, Prince Igor, Rouge et Noir, Scheherazade, Les Sylphides, Three-Cornered Hat

NEW PRODUCTIONS:

Chopin Concerto (New York, 12 October 1942). Choreography: Bronislava Nijinska; Music: Chopin, E-minor Concerto; Costumes: Alexander Ignatieff. / Alexandra Danilova, Igor Youskevitch, Nathalie Krassovska, ensemble.

The Snow Maiden (New York, 12 October 1942). Choreography: Bronislava Nijinska; Book: Sergei J. Denham; Music: Glazounov,

The Seasons; Designs: Boris Aronson. / Crow: Tatiana Semenova; Snow Maiden: Nathalie Krassovska; Spring: Alexandra Danilova; Lell: Igor Youskevitch; ensemble.

Rodeo (New York, 16 October 1942). Choreography: Agnes de Mille; Music: Copland; Settings: Oliver Smith; Costumes: Kermit Love. / Cowgirl: Agnes de Mille; Head Wrangler: Casimir Kokitch; Champion Roper: Frederic Franklin; Rancher's Daughter: Milada Mladova; Caller: Anton Vlassoff; ensemble.

1943-44

DANCERS:

Alan Banks, Herbert Bliss, Ruthanna Boris, Vida Brown, Olivia Cardone, Tatiana Chamié, Yvonne Chouteau, Alfredo Corvino, Alexandra Danilova, Leon Danielian, Peter Deign, Dorothy Etheridge, Milton Feher, Frederic Franklin, Pauline Goddard, Alexander Goudovitch, M. Granteff, Tatiana Grantzeva, Yvonne Hill, Julia Horvath, Serge Ismailoff, Anna Istomina, Kari Karnakoski, Michel Katcharoff, Casimir Kokitch, Elena Kramarr, Nathalie Krassovska, Nicholas Magallanes, M. Michailoff, Grant Mouradoff, Mary Ellen Moylan, Mlle Oleova, Armand Picon, Nina Popova, Ruth Riekman, Anna Scarpova, Tatiana Semenova, Karel Shook, James Starbuck, Nat Stoudenmire (later Michael Lland), Gertrude Svobodina, Nikita Talin, Maria Tallchief, Nora White, Jean Yazvinsky, Igor Youskevitch

REPERTOIRE:

Beau Danube, Carnaval, Chopin Concerto, Gaîté Parisienne, Igrouchki, Nutcracker, Prince Igor, Rodeo, Scheherazade, Serenade, Snow Maiden, Swan Lake, Les Sylphides

NEW PRODUCTIONS:

Etude (Cleveland, 9 October 1943). Choreography: Bronislava Nijinska; Music: Bach, from the Brandenburg concertos and orchestral suites; Costumes: Boris Belinsky. / Nathalie Krassovska, Maria Tallchief, Frederic Franklin, ensemble.

The Cuckold's Fair (Cleveland, 9 October 1943). Choreography: Pilar Lopez; Book: after Garcia Lorca and Rivas-Cherif; Music: Gustavo Pittaluga; Designs: Joan Junyer. / Sierra: Alexandra Danilova; Chivato: Frederic Franklin; ensemble.

The Red Poppy (Cleveland, 9 October 1943). Choreography: Igor

Schwezoff; Music: Glière; Designs: Boris Aronson. / Tai-Hoa: Alexandra Danilova; Owner of the Bar: Grant Mouradoff; Russian Sailor: Frederic Franklin; Dancer on the Golden Platter: Ruthanna Boris; Ribbon Dancer: Igor Youskevitch; ensemble.

Ancient Russia (Cleveland, 11 October 1943). Choreography: Bronislava Nijinska; Music: Tchaikovsky, First Piano Concerto; Designs: Nathalie Gontcharova. / Russian Princess: Alexandra Danilova; Russian Prince: Igor Youskevitch; Tartar Chief: James Starbuck; ensemble.

1944-45

DANCERS:

Alan Banks, Herbert Bliss, Ruthanna Boris, Vida Brown, Olivia Cardone, Yvonne Chouteau, Katherine Clark, Alfredo Corvino, Leon Danielian, Alexandra Danilova, Peter Deign, Harding Dorn, Dorothy Etheridge, Frederic Franklin, Pauline Goddard, Alexander Goudovitch, Julia Horvath, Dick Johnson, Michel Katcharoff, Elena Kramarr, Nathalie Krassovska, Lillian Lanese, Yurek Lazowski, Robert Lindgren, Nicholas Magallanes, Mary Ellen Moylan, Ruth Page (guest), Claire Pasch, Galina Razoumova, Ruth Riekman, Edwina Seaver (later Fontaine), Olga Serova, Karel Shook, Bentley Stone (guest), Gertrude Svobodina, Nikita Talin, Maria Tallchief, George Verdak, Jane Wallis, Shirley Weaver, Nora White, Jean Yazvinsky

REPERTOIRE:

Beau Danube, Chopin Concerto, Coppélia, Cuckold's Fair, Gaîté Parisienne, Igrouchki, Nutcracker, Prince Igor, Red Poppy, Rodeo, Scheherazade, Serenade, Snow Maiden, Swan Lake, Les Sylphides

NEW PRODUCTIONS:

Danses Concertantes (New York, 10 September 1944). Choreography: George Balanchine; Music: Stravinsky; Designs: Eugène Berman. / Alexandra Danilova, Leon Danielian, Gertrude Svobodina, Nikita Talin, Nora White, Ruthanna Boris, Alexander Goudovitch, Dorothy Etheridge, Elena Kramarr, Herbert Bliss, Pauline Goddard, Maria Tallchief, Nicholas Magallanes, Mary Ellen Moylan.

Le Bourgeois Gentilhomme (New York, 23 September 1944). Choreography: George Balanchine; Music: Richard Strauss;

Designs: Eugène Berman. / Cleonte: Frederic Franklin; Coviel: Peter Deign; Jourdain: Michel Katcharoff; Lucile: Nathalie Krassovska; Nicola: Vida Brown; Fencers: Nicholas Magallanes, Alexander Goudovitch; Pas de sept: Mary Ellen Moylan, Ruth Riekman, Yvonne Chouteau, Pauline Goddard, Gertrude Svobodina, Galina Razoumova, Lillian Lanese; Harlequinade: Ruthanna Boris, Leon Danielian, Nikita Talin; Danse Indienne: Maria Tallchief, Yurek Lazowski; ensemble.

Ballet Imperial (Chicago, 4 October 1944). Choreography: George Balanchine; Music: Tchaikovsky, Second Piano Concerto; Designs: Mstislav Doboujinsky. / Mary Ellen Moylan, Nicholas Magallanes, Maria Tallchief, Herbert Bliss, Nikita Talin, ensemble.

Frankie and Johnny (Kansas City, 7 January 1945). Choreography: Ruth Page and Bentley Stone; Book: Michael Blandford and Jerome Moross; Music: Moross; Settings: Clive Rickabaugh; Costumes: Paul Dupont. / Frankie: Ruth Page; Johnny: Bentley Stone; Nelly: Vida Brown; Bartender: Nikita Talin; ensemble.

Mozartiana (New York, 7 March 1945). Choreography: George Balanchine; Music: Tchaikovsky; Designs: Christian Bérard. / Gigue: Yurek Lazowski; Prighiera: Dorothy Etheridge; Adagio and variations: Alexandra Danilova, Frederic Franklin; ensemble.

Pas de Deux (Grand Adagio) (New York, 14 March 1945). Choreography: George Balanchine; Music: Tchaikovsky, from *Sleeping Beauty;* Costumes: Eugène Berman. / Alexandra Danilova, Frederic Franklin

---

1945-46

DANCERS:

Gregory Alexandroff, Herbert Bliss, Todd Bolender, Ruthanna Boris, Yvonne Chouteau, Barth Cummins, Leon Danielian, Alexandra Danilova, Peter Deign, Harding Dorn, Frederic Franklin, Constance Garfield, Aaron Girard, Pauline Goddard, Frank Hobi, Julia Horvath, Michel Katcharoff, Nathalie Krassovska, Merriam Lanova, Robert Lindgren, Nicholas Magallanes, Marie-Jeanne, Claire Pasch, Diane Rhodes, Lubov Roudenko (guest), Edwina Seaver, Karel Shook, Nikita Talin, Maria Tallchief, Harriet Toby, Beatrice Tompkins, Gertrude Tyven (formerly Svobodina), Sonja Tyven (later Taanila), George Verdak, Shirley Weaver, Nora White, Patricia Wilde, Joy Williams, Stanley Zompakos

REPERTOIRE:

L'Après-midi d'un Faune, Baiser de la Fée, Ballet Imperial, Beau Danube, Bourgeois Gentilhomme, Chopin Concerto, Coppélia, Danses Concertantes, Frankie and Johnny, Gaîté Parisienne, Mozartiana, Nutcracker, Pas de Deux (Grand Adagio), Red Poppy, Rodeo, Scheherazade, Snow Maiden, Swan Lake, Les Sylphides

NEW PRODUCTIONS:

Concerto Barocco (New York, 9 September 1945). Choreography: George Balanchine; Music: Bach, Concerto for Two Violins. / Marie-Jeanne, Patricia Wilde, Nicholas Magallanes, ensemble.

Comedia Balletica (New York, 17 September 1945). Choreography: Todd Bolender; Music: Stravinsky, *Pulcinella* suite; Designs: Robert Davison. / Ruthanna Boris, Marie-Jeanne, Leon Danielian, Todd Bolender, Beatrice Tompkins.

Night Shadow (New York, 27 February 1946). Choreography: George Balanchine; Music: Vittorio Rieti, on themes of Bellini; Designs: Dorothea Tanning. / Sleepwalker: Alexandra Danilova; Poet: Nicholas Magallanes; Coquette: Maria Tallchief; Host: Michel Katcharoff; Blackamoors: Ruthanna Boris, Leon Danielian; Harlequin: Marie-Jeanne; ensemble.

Raymonda, three acts (New York, 12 March 1946). Choreography: George Balanchine and Alexandra Danilova; Music: Glazounov; Designs: Alexandre Benois. / Raymonda: Alexandra Danilova; Jean de Brienne: Nicholas Magallanes; Emir Abd-er-Raham: Nikita Talin; Pas de trois: Gertrude Tyven, Patricia Wilde, Leon Danielian; Pas Classique Hongrois: Danilova, Magallanes, Marie-Jeanne, Ruthanna Boris, Maria Tallchief, Yvonne Chouteau, Frank Hobi, Nikita Talin, Robert Lindgren, Todd Bolender; ensemble.

1946-47

DANCERS:

Gregory Alexandroff, Valerie Bettis (guest), Herbert Bliss, Ruthanna Boris, Vida Brown, Yvonne Chouteau, Antonia Cobos (guest), Barth Cummins, Leon Danielian, Alexandra Danilova, Peter Deign, Harding Dorn, Frederic Franklin, Myrna Galle, Constance Garfield, Aaron Girard, Pauline Goddard, Tatiana Grantzeva, Shirley Haynes, Frank Hobi, Michel Katcharoff, Casimir Kokitch, Nathalie Krassovska, Merriam Lanova, Robert Lindgren,

Nicholas Magallanes, Marie-Jeanne, Ruth Page (guest), Claire Pasch, Armand Picon, Bernice Rehner, Diane Rhodes, Edwina Seaver, Karel Shook, Sonja Taanila, Nikita Talin, Maria Tallchief, Harriet Toby, Luis Trapaga, Valrene Tweedie, Gertrude Tyven, George Verdak, Shirley Weaver, Nora White, Patricia Wilde, Joy Williams, Stanley Zompakos

REPERTOIRE:

Baiser de la Fée, Ballet Imperial, Beau Danube, Bourgeois Gentilhomme, Comedia Balletica, Concerto Barocco, Coppélia, Danses Concertantes, Frankie and Johnny, Gâité Parisienne, Mozartiana, Night Shadow, Nutcracker, Raymonda, Rodeo, Scheherazade, Serenade, Snow Maiden, Spectre de la Rose, Swan Lake, Les Sylphides

NEW PRODUCTIONS:

The Bells (Jacob's Pillow, 30 August 1946). Choreography: Ruth Page; Music: Milhaud; Designs: Isamu Noguchi. / Bride: Alexandra Danilova; Bridegroom: Frederic Franklin; King of Ghouls: Nikita Talin; ensemble.

Virginia Sampler (New York, 4 March 1947). Choreography: Valerie Bettis; Music: Leo Smit; Designs: Charles Elson. / Mother: Patricia Wilde; Young Girl: Marie-Jeanne; Eligible Young Bachelor: Frederic Franklin; Child: Harriet Toby; Frontiersman: Leon Danielian; General: Casimir Kokitch; Unidentified Lady: Valerie Bettis; Pristine Lovers: Pauline Goddard, Armand Picon.

Madroños (New York, 22 March 1947). Choreography: Antonia Cobos; Music: Moszkowski, Yradier, and others, arranged and orchestrated by Ivan Boutnikoff. / La Niña del Oro: Antonia Cobos; El Menesteroso: Frederic Franklin; El Bonito: Leon Danielian; ensemble. (A Moorish dance was soon added for Ruthanna Boris.)

Cirque de Deux (Hollywood, 1 August 1947). Choreography: Ruthanna Boris; Music: Gounod, Walpurgis Night from *Faust;* Designs: Robert Davison. / Ruthanna Boris, Leon Danielian, Patricia Wilde, Frank Hobi.

1947-48

DANCERS:

Gregory Alexandroff, Ruthanna Boris, Vida Brown, Yvonne Chouteau, Leon Danielian, Alexandra Danilova, Peter Deign,

Harding Dorn, Frederic Franklin, Myrna Galle, Constance Garfield, Evelyn Giles, William Glenn, Pauline Goddard, Tatiana Grantzeva, Shirley Haynes, Reynaldo Herrera, Frank Hobi, Roman Jasinski, Michel Katcharoff, John Kelly, Nathalie Krassovska, Merriam Lanova, Robert Lindgren, Mary Ellen Moylan, Armand Picon, Nina Popova, Bernice Rehner, Edwina Seaver, Sonja Taanila, Nikita Talin, Jeanette Tannan, Richard Thomas, Harriet Toby, Luis Trapaga, Valrene Tweedie, Gertrude Tyven, George Verdak, Shirley Weaver, Nora White, Patricia Wilde, Joy Williams, Stanley Zompakos

REPERTOIRE:

Baiser de la Fée, Ballet Imperial, Beau Danube, Cirque de Deux, Concerto Barocco, Coppélia, Danses Concertantes, Gaîté Parisienne, Giselle, Madroños, Night Shadow, Nutcracker, Raymonda, Rodeo, Scheherazade, Serenade, Swan Lake, Les Sylphides

NEW PRODUCTIONS:

Lola Montez (New York, 12 September 1947). Choreography: Edward Caton; Book: Dr. N. Wolf; Music: Fred Witt, orchestrated by Ivan Boutnikoff; Settings: Raoul Pène du Bois; Costumes: Raoul Pène du Bois and Paolo d'Anna. / Lola Montez: Alexandra Danilova; Hero: Frederic Franklin; ensemble.

Billy Sunday (York, Pennsylvania, 29 January 1948). Choreography: Ruth Page; Book: Page, Remi Gassmann, J. Ray Hunt; Words: Hunt; Music: Gassmann; Settings: Herbert Andrews; Costumes: Paul Dupont. / Billy Sunday: Frederic Franklin; Mrs. Potiphar: Alexandra Danilova; ensemble.

Love Song (Rochester, New York, 5 April 1948). Choreography: Ruth Page; Music: Schubert, orchestrated by Lucien Cailliet; Designs: Nicolas Remisoff. / Sad One: Ruthanna Boris; Romantic One: Leon Danielian; Flirtatious One: Yvonne Chouteau; ensemble.

1948-49

DANCERS:

Gregory Alexandroff, Ann Barlow, Nina Boneck, Ruthanna Boris, Val Buttignol, Patricia Casey, Yvonne Chouteau, Natalia Clare, Leon Danielian, Alexandra Danilova, Agnes de Mille (guest), Anton Dolin (guest), Harding Dorn, Barbara Ferguson, Royes Fernandez, Edwina Fontaine (formerly Seaver), Frederic Franklin, William

Glenn, Shirley Haynes, Mary Haywood, Frank Hobi, Roman Jasinski, Rita Karlin, Michel Katcharoff, John Kelly, Nathalie Krassovska, Erik Kristen, Marian Ladre (guest), Elena Lane, Moscelyne Larkin, Yurek Lazowski (guest), Gerard Leavitt, Robert Lindgren, Alicia Markova (guest), Dorothy Matsie, Mary Ellen Moylan, Nina Novak, Edward Pfeiffer, Liane Plane, Adda Pourmel, Gilbert Reed, Bernice Rehner, Janice Roman, Job Sanders, Irma Sandre, Helena Seroy, Mia Slavenska (guest), Sonja Taanila, Jeanette Tannan, Richard Thomas, José Torres (guest), Sviatoslav Toumine (guest), Luis Trapaga, Eleonore Treiber, Oleg Tupine, Valrene Tweedie, Gertrude Tyven, Alexandra Uzzell, George Verdak, Patricia Wilde, Jean Yazvinsky (guest)

REPERTOIRE:

Ballet Imperial, Beau Danube, Carnaval, Cirque de Deux, Concerto Barocco, Coppélia, Frankie and Johnny, Gaîté Parisienne, Giselle, Love Song, Madroños, Mozartiana, Night Shadow, Nutcracker, Raymonda, Rodeo, Rouge et Noir, Scheherazade, Seventh Symphony, Swan Lake, Les Sylphides

NEW PRODUCTIONS:

Pas de Quatre (New York, 18 September 1948). Choreography: Anton Dolin; Music: Pugni. / Taglioni: Alicia Markova; Grisi: Mia Slavenska; Grahn: Nathalie Krassovska; Cerrito: Alexandra Danilova.

Spanish Dances (New York, 29 September 1948). Choreography: José Torres; Music: Granados, Albeniz, folk tunes; Costumes: Marcel Rigaud. / José Torres.

Quelques Fleurs (New York, 30 September 1948). Choreography: Ruthanna Boris; Music: Auber, arranged by Harry G. Schumer; Designs: Robert Davison. / Contessa Ilaria: Mary Ellen Moylan; Zenobio Bonaventuri: Leon Danielian; Alchemist: Frank Hobi; Fragrant Ladies: Yvonne Chouteau, Gertrude Tyven, Patricia Wilde; ensemble.

1949-50

DANCERS:

Ruthanna Boris, Tamara Chapman, Yvette Chauviré (guest), Yvonne Chouteau, Natalia Clare, Leon Danielian, Alexandra Danilova, Harding Dorn, Donn Driver, Frederic Franklin, William Glenn, Nana Gollner (guest), Shirley Haynes, Mary Haywood, Alan

Howard, Roman Jasinski, Rita Karlin, Michel Katcharoff, Elena Lane, Moscelyne Larkin, Roberta Laune, Yurek Lazowski (guest), Gerard Leavitt, Robert Lindgren, Dorothie (also Dorothy) Matsie, Mary Ellen Moylan, Helen Murielle, Duncan Noble, Nina Novak, Edward Pfeiffer, Gilbert Reed, Bernice Rehner, Janice Roman, Job Sanders, Irma Sandre, Igor Schwezoff (guest), Helena Seroy, Mia Slavenska (guest), Sonja Taanila, Jeanette Tannan, Richard Thomas, Eleonore Treiber, Oleg Tupine, Valrene Tweedie, Gertrude Tyven, George Verdak, Jean Yazvinsky (guest)

REPERTOIRE:

Ballet Imperial, Beau Danube, Cirque de Deux, Concerto Barocco, Coppélia, Les Elfes, Frankie and Johnny, Gaîté Parisienne, Giselle, Igrouchki, Madroños, Nutcracker, Pas de Quatre, Prince Igor, Quelques Fleurs, Raymonda, Rodeo, Scheherazade, Swan Lake, Les Sylphides

NEW PRODUCTIONS:

The Mute Wife (New York, 16 September 1949). Choreography: Antonia Cobos; Music: Domenico Scarlatti, arranged by Soulima Stravinsky; Designs: Castillo. / Wife: Nina Novak; Husband: Leon Danielian; Doctor: Robert Lindgren; ensemble.

Paquita (New York, 20 September 1949). Choreography: Alexandra Danilova, after Petipa; Music: Deldevez and Minkus; Settings: Eugène Berman; Costumes: Castillo. / Alexandra Danilova, Oleg Tupine, Jeanette Tannan, Moscelyne Larkin, Yvonne Chouteau, Gertrude Tyven, ensemble.

Graduation Ball (New York, 21 September 1949). Choreography: David Lichine; Music: Strauss, arranged by Antal Dorati; Designs: Mstislav Doboujinsky. / Cadet: Leon Danielian; Junior Girls: Yvonne Chouteau, Nina Novak; Head Mistress: Jean Yazvinsky; General: Igor Schwezoff; Dancing competition: Moscelyne Larkin, Natalia Clare; Pas de deux: Gertrude Tyven, Oleg Tupine; Drummer: Roman Jasinski; ensemble.

Birthday (New York, 27 September 1949). Choreography: Tatiana Chamié; Music: Rossini, arranged by Lucien Cailliet; Settings: Mstislav Doboujinsky; Costumes: Karinska. / The Lady: Nana Gollner; The Beloved: Oleg Tupine; Leaders of the Ball: Nina Novak, Leon Danielian; ensemble.

Mort du Cygne (New York, 11 April 1950). Choreography: Staged by Constantin Nepo, after Serge Lifar; Music: Chopin. / Swan: Yvette Chauviré; Hunter: Frederic Franklin.

Roméo et Juliette (New York, 18 April 1950). Choreography: Staged by Constantin Nepo, after Serge Lifar; Music: Tchaikovsky. / Romeo: Frederic Franklin; Juliet: Yvette Chauviré; ensemble.

Grand Pas Classique (New York, 25 April 1950). Choreography: Victor Gsovsky; Music: Auber. / Yvette Chauviré, Oleg Tupine.

1950-51

DANCERS:

Franca Baldwin, Peter Bonura, Tamara Chapman, Yvette Chauviré (guest), Yvonne Chouteau, Natalia Clare, Leon Danielian, Alexandra Danilova, Vladimir Dokoudovsky (guest), Frederic Franklin, William Glenn, Shirley Haynes, Mary Haywood, Alan Howard, Roman Jasinski, Rita Karlin, Jack Kauflin, Nathalie Krassovska, Moscelyne Larkin, Roberta Laune, Gerard Leavitt, Robert Lindgren, Dorothy Matsie, Alice Murer, Duncan Noble, Nina Novak, Patricia Peters, Gilbert Reed, Janice Roman, Job Sanders, Irma Sandre, Helena Seroy, Karel Shook, Mia Slavenska (guest), Nina Stroganova (guest), Sonja Taanila, Jeanette Tannan, Eleonore Treiber, Bill Tremaine, Oleg Tupine, Gertrude Tyven, George Verdak, Nancy Warrek, Carolyn Wells

REPERTOIRE:

Birthday, Concerto Barocco, Coppélia, Les Elfes, Gaîté Parisienne, Giselle, Graduation Ball, Madroños, Mute Wife, Nutcracker, Paquita, Prince Igor, Raymonda, Scheherazade, Swan Lake, Les Sylphides

NEW PRODUCTIONS:

Prima Ballerina (Chicago, 25 October 1950). Choreography: Tatiana Chamié; Music: Lecocq, arranged by Lucien Cailliet; Settings: Mstislav Doboujinsky; Costumes: Karinska. / Guest Ballerina: Alexandra Danilova; Understudy: Nina Novak; Premier Danseur: Frederic Franklin; Dancer Who Comes Late: Vladimir Dokoudovsky; Ballet Master: Duncan Noble; ensemble.

Nocturne (Chicago, 26 October 1950). Choreography: Victor Gsovsky; Music: Mozart, *Eine Kleine Nachtmusik;* Costumes: Balmain. / She: Yvette Chauviré; He: Gerard Leavitt; The Other Man: Oleg Tupine; Soubrette: Yvonne Chouteau; ensemble.

1951-52

DANCERS:

Alice Aycock, Meredith Baylis, Peter Bonura, Yvette Chauviré (guest), Yvonne Chouteau, Natalia Clare, Leon Danielian, Alexandra Danilova, Frederic Franklin, William Glenn, Leon Guerard, Shirley Haynes, Alan Howard, Patricia Jennings, Salvador Juarez, Jack Kauflin, Deni Lamont, Roberta Laune, Gerard Leavitt, Nata Lee, Robert Lindgren, Léonide Massine (guest), Dorothie Matsie, Victor Moreno, Alice Murer, Nina Novak, Janice Roman, Job Sanders, Lupe Serrano, Sally Seven, Karel Shook, Mia Slavenska (guest), Barbara Steele, Sonja Taanila, Jeanette Tannan, Eleonore Treiber, Bill Tremaine, Oleg Tupine, Gertrude Tyven, Marianne Vickers, Nancy Warrek

REPERTOIRE:

Ballet Imperial, Beau Danube, Birthday, Capriccio Espagnol, Cirque de Deux, Coppélia, Les Elfes, Gaîté Parisienne, Giselle, Graduation Ball, Grand Pas Classique, Madroños, Mute Wife, Nutcracker, Paquita, Pas de Quatre, Raymonda, Roméo et Juliette, Scheherazade, Swan Lake, Les Sylphides

NEW PRODUCTIONS: none

1952-53

During the 1952-53 and 1953-54 seasons the Ballet Russe existed only as a touring Concert Company presenting a single bill of *Swan Lake,* the Bluebird pas de deux, *Cirque de Deux,* and *Gaîté Parisienne.*

DANCERS:

Keith Allison, Alice Aycock, Joseph Busheme, Diana Coon, Joanna Crist, Christine Hennessy, Robert Hirst, Anna Istomina, Roman Jasinski, Moscelyne Larkin, Nancie Leonie, Barbara McGinnis, Victor Moreno, Glenn Olson, Fernando Schaffenburg

1953-54

Repertoire and personnel were the same as for 1952-53, except that Nina Novak replaced Istomina and, during the middle of the season, Larkin took maternity leave and was replaced by Gertrude Tyven.

1954-55

· DANCERS:

Meredith Baylis, Margery Beddow, Nancy Benson, Irina Borowska, James Brusock, Joseph Busheme, Yvonne Chouteau, Yvonne Craig, Leon Danielian, Dorothy Daniels, Eleanor D'Antuono, Grant De Laney, Teri De Mari, Harding Dorn, Jeanne Elyse, Giaconda Filippini, Frederic Franklin, Christine Hennessy, Jenifer Heyward, Alan Howard, Salvador Juarez, Deni Lamont, Leonore Lovering, Barbara McGinnis, Irene Minor, Victor Moreno, Nina Novak, Glenn Olson, Paul Roget, Joseph Savino, Fernando Schaffenburg, Sally Seven, Mia Slavenska (guest), Eugene Slavin, Valerie Smith, Maria Tallchief, Miguel Terekhov, Gertrude Tyven, Walda Welch, Rochelle Zide

REPERTOIRE:

L'Après-midi d'un Faune, Ballet Imperial, Beau Danube, Capriccio Espagnol, Cirque de Deux, Coppélia, Gaîté Parisienne, Madroños, Mute Wife, Nutcracker, Prince Igor, Raymonda, Scheherazade, Swan Lake, Les Sylphides

NEW PRODUCTIONS:

The Mikado (Baltimore, 1 October 1954). Choreography: Antonia Cobos; Music: Sullivan, arranged by Vittorio Rieti; Designs: Bernard Lamotte. / Ko-Ko: Leon Danielian; Nanki-Poo: Joseph Savino; Yum-Yum: Irina Borowska; Pitti-Sing: Gertrude Tyven; Peep-Bo: Yvonne Chouteau; Katisha: Frederic Franklin; Mikado: Victor Moreno; ensemble.

Harold In Italy (Boston, 14 October 1954). Choreography: Léonide Massine; Music: Berlioz; Designs: Bernard Lamotte. / Poet: Leon Danielian; Happy Couple: Irina Borowska, Alan Howard; Pilgrim: Yvonne Chouteau; Simpleton: Teri de Mari; Shepherds: Nina Novak, Deni Lamont; Brigand: Victor Moreno; Captive: Gertrude Tyven; ensemble.

1955-56

DANCERS:

Alicia Alonso (guest), Gwenn Barker, Meredith Baylis, Margery Beddow, Lois Bewley, Irina Borowska, James Brusock, Joseph Busheme, Yvonne Chouteau, Yvonne Craig, Leon Danielian,

Dorothy Daniels, Eleanor D'Antuono, Teri de Mari, Giaconda Filippini, Frederic Franklin, Christine Hennessy, Alan Howard, Salvador Juarez, Louis Kosman, Deni Lamont, Leonore Lovering, Gene Marinaccio, Barbara McGinnis, Irene Minor, Victor Moreno, Nina Novak, Glenn Olson, Joseph Savino, Sally Seven, Mia Slavenska (guest), Eugene Slavin, Valerie Smith, Miguel Terekhov, Gertrude Tyven, Dzinta Vanags, Raven Wilkinson, Igor Youskevitch, Rochelle Zide

REPERTOIRE:

Beau Danube, Capriccio Espagnol, Cirque de Deux, Coppélia, Gaîté Parisienne, Giselle, Harold in Italy, Mikado, Mute Wife, Nutcracker, Pas de Quatre, Raymonda, Scheherazade, Swan Lake, Les Sylphides

NEW PRODUCTIONS:

Pas de Trois (Toronto, 12 October 1955). Choreography: George Balanchine; Music: Minkus; Costumes: Castillo. / Gertrude Tyven, Yvonne Chouteau, Alan Howard.

La Dame à la Licorne (Toronto, 14 October 1955). Choreography: Heinz Rosen; Music: Jacques Chailly; Book: Jean Cocteau; Designs: Cocteau. / Lady: Irina Borowska; Knight: Igor Youskevitch; Unicorn: Nina Novak; ensemble.

Sombreros (Washington, D.C., 18 June 1956). Choreography: Leon Danielian; Music: Mexican folk tunes, orchestrated by Ivan Boutnikoff; Costumes: William Cecil. / Irina Borowska, Deni Lamont, ensemble.

1956-57

DANCERS:

Alicia Alonso (guest), Gwenn Barker, Meredith Baylis, Margery Beddow, Vada Belshaw, Lois Bewley, Irina Borowska, Perry Brunson, James Capp, Yvonne Chouteau, Thatcher Clarke, Yvonne Craig, Viola Crucil, Leon Danielian, Dorothy Daniels, Alexandra Danilova (guest), Eleanor D'Antuono, Hester FitzGerald, Frederic Franklin (guest), Kenneth Gillesple, Roy Harsh, Alan Howard, Josephine Jeffers, Salvador Juarez, Louis Kosman, Deni Lamont, Gene Marinaccio, Nina Novak, Libby Salerno, Howard Sayette, Sally Seven, Eugene Slavin, Paula Tennyson, Miguel Terekhov, Gertrude Tyven, Dzinta Vanags, Raven Wilkinson, June Wilson, Igor Youskevitch, Rochelle Zide, Aleck Zybine

REPERTOIRE:

Beau Danube, Cirque de Deux, Coppélia, Dame à la Licorne, Gaîté Parisienne, Giselle, Mikado, Mute Wife, Nutcracker, Pas de Trois, Raymonda, Scheherazade, Sombreros, Swan Lake, Les Sylphides

NEW PRODUCTIONS:

Tragedy in Calabria (South Bend, Indiana, 15 December 1956). Choreography: Salvador Juarez; Music: Leoncavallo. / Pagliacci: Salvador Juarez; Columbine: Nina Novak; Harlequin: Alan Howard.

Harlequinade (Chicago, 27 December 1956). Choreography: Boris Romanoff; Music: Drigo; Settings: Rolf Gerard; Costumes: Gerard, and Eugène Berman (costumes from *Devil's Holiday* and *Bourgeois Gentilhomme*). / Harlequin: Igor Youskevitch; Columbine: Alicia Alonso; Pierrot: Eugene Slavin; Pantalon: Miguel Terekhov; Fairy of Goodness: Irina Borowska; Harlequin's Friends: Deni Lamont, Kenneth Gillespie; Blackamoors: Rochelle Zide, Dorothy Daniels; ensemble.

1957-58

DANCERS:

Alicia Alonso (guest), Gwenn Barker, Meredith Baylis, Margery Beddow, Irina Borowska, Perry Brunson, James Brusock, James Capp, Patricia Carleton, Yvette Chauviré (guest), Viola Crucil, Dorothy Daniels, Eleanor D'Antuono, Hester FitzGerald, Kenneth Gillespie, Tatiana Grantzeva, Roy Harsh, Betsy Herskind, Alan Howard, Josephine Jeffers, Irina Kovalska, Deni Lamont, Susan May, Edmund Novak, Nina Novak, Wakefield Poole, Libby Salerno, Howard Sayette, Sally Seven, Eugene Slavin, Paula Tennyson, Miguel Terekhov, Gertrude Tyven, Andrea Vodehnal, Richard Wagner, Howard White, Raven Wilkinson, June Wilson, Igor Youskevitch (guest), Rochelle Zide, George Zoritch, Aleck Zybine

REPERTOIRE:

Beau Danube, Cirque de Deux, Coppélia, Dame à la Licorne, Gaîté Parisienne, Giselle, Harlequinade, Mikado, Mute Wife, Nutcracker, Pas de Trois, Raymonda, Scheherazade, Sombreros, Swan Lake, Les Sylphides

NEW PRODUCTIONS:

Variations Classiques (San Juan, Puerto Rico, 6 October 1957). Choreography: Nina Novak; Music: Brahms, *Variations on a Theme*

by Handel, orchestrated by Ivan Boutnikoff; Costumes: Karinska. / Nina Novak, Gertrude Tyven, Alan Howard, Kenneth Gillespie, ensemble.

The Mazurka (Hartford, 18 October 1957). Choreography: Leon Danielian; Music: Chopin, Tchaikovsky, Strauss, arranged by Ivan Boutnikoff; Designs: Rouben Ter-Arutunian. / Nina Novak, Eugene Slavin, ensemble.

1958-59

DANCERS:

Wally Adams, Alicia Alonso (guest), Jeanne Armin, Gwenn Barker, Meredith Baylis, Roberta Berson, Irina Borowska, Perry Brunson, James Capp, Eugene Collins, Leon Danielian (guest), Eleanor D'Antuono, Hester FitzGerald, Olivia Fiumara, Michele Franchi, Kenneth Gillespie, Tatiana Grantzeva, Roy Harsh, Betsy Herskind, Carol Hines, Alan Howard, Gail Israel, Josephine Jeffers, Irina Kovalska, Nathalie Krassovska (guest), Carole Kroon, Herb Kummel, Beatrice Lismore, Susan May, Edmund Novak, Nina Novak, Lawrence Rhodes, Audrey Ross, Howard Sayette, Ramon (also Raymond) Segarra, Nancy Sklenar, Eugene Slavin, Richard Tarczynski, Paula Tennyson, Gertrude Tyven, Andrea Vodehnal, Richard Wagner, Raven Wilkinson, June Wilson, Franklin (also Frank) Yezer, Igor Youskevitch (guest), George Zoritch

REPERTOIRE:

Ballet Imperial, Beau Danube, Coppélia, Gaîté Parisienne, Giselle, Harlequinade, Mikado, Nutcracker, Pas de Trois, Raymonda, Scheherazade, Sombreros, Swan Lake, Les Sylphides, Variations Classiques

NEW PRODUCTIONS:

Romeo and Juliet (Chicago, 26 December 1958). Choreography: Alberto Alonso; Music: Tchaikovsky; Designs: Leo Vigildo. / Alicia Alonso, Igor Youskevitch.

Springtime (Chicago, 29 December 1958). Choreography: Edmund Novak; Music: Hazel Archibald Draper; Costumes: Karinska. / Nina Novak, Eugene Collins.

Slavonic Dances (Seattle, 25 January 1959). Choreography: Edmund Novak; Music: Milutin, Khachaturian, Wieniawski, Polish and Russian folk tunes; Costumes: Karinska. / Eleanor D'Antuono,

Eugene Slavin, Irina Kovalska, Edmund Novak, James Capp, ensemble.

1959-60

DANCERS:

Wally Adams, Alicia Alonso (guest), Jeanne Armin, Gwenn Barker, Meredith Baylis, Roberta Berson, Irina Borowska, Perry Brunson, James Capp, Marina Chapman, Eugene Collins, Leon Danielian (guest), Eleanor D'Antuono, Olivia Fiumara, Michele Franchi, Kenneth Gillespie, Tatiana Grantzeva, Alan Howard, Mario Ignisci, Gail Israel, June Kantor, Michael Kelder, Irina Kovalska, Nathalie Krassovska, Carole Kroon, Herb Kummel, Beatrice Lismore, Susan May, Edmund Novak, Nina Novak, Lawrence Rhodes, Audrey Ross, Howard Sayette, Ramon Segarra, Nancy Sklenar, Paula Tennyson, Andrea Vodehnal, Richard Wagner, Raven Wilkinson, June Wilson, Franklin Yezer, Igor Youskevitch (guest), George Zoritch

REPERTOIRE:

Ballet Imperial, Coppélia, Gaîté Parisienne, Giselle, Graduation Ball, Harlequinade, Mute Wife, Nutcracker, Raymonda, Slavonic Dances, Sombreros, Swan Lake, Les Sylphides, Variations Classiques

NEW PRODUCTION:

Ballad (Pittsburgh, 24 October 1959). Choreography: Jan Cieplinski; Music: Herbert Donaldson; Costumes: Karinska. / Nina Novak, George Zoritch, Alan Howard.

1960-61

DANCERS:

Tom Adair, Meredith Baylis, Roberta Berson, Yelle Bettencourt, Perry Brunson, James Capp, Marina Chapman, Tania Chevtchenko (also known as Tania Karina), Eugene Collins, Myron Curtis, Olivia Fiumara, Michele Franchi, Jose Gutierrez, Mario Ignisci, Gail Israel, June Kantor, Michael Kelder, Joe King, Alexis Kotynski, Margery Lambert, Beatrice Lismore, Roni Mahler, Carolyn Martin, Nina Novak, Marlene Rizzo, Ramon Segarra, Nancy Sklenar, Richard Tarczynski, Paula Tennyson, Hélène Trailine, Andrea Vodehnal, Shirley Weishaar, June Wilson, Franklin Yezer, Igor Youskevitch, George Zoritch

REPERTOIRE:

Ballet Imperial, Beau Danube, Coppélia, Gaîté Parisienne, Giselle, Nutcracker, Pas de Trois, Scheherazade, Sombreros, Les Sylphides

NEW PRODUCTIONS:

Bach Concerto (Los Angeles, 29 December 1960). Choreography: Vadim Sulima; Music: Bach, Keyboard Concerto in F-minor. / Hélène Trailine, George Zoritch, ensemble.

Swan Lake (Acts II, III, IV) (Los Angeles, 30 December 1960). Choreography: Nina Novak and Anatole Vilzak, after Petipa-Ivanov; Music: Tchaikovsky; Designs: Rolf Gerard. / Odette/Odile: Nina Novak; Siegfried: Igor Youskevitch; ensemble.

Tribute (Boston, 20 July 1961). Choreography: Frederic Franklin; Music: Franck, *Symphonic Variations*. / Andrea Vodehnal, Eugene Collins, Meredith Baylis, Perry Brunson, Roni Mahler, James Capp.

1961-62

DANCERS:

Robin Adair, Tom Adair, Meredith Baylis, Roberta Berson, Yelle Bettencourt, Emily Byrne, James Capp, Marina Chapman, Eugene Collins, Kenneth Creel, Myron Curtis, Anita Dyche, Juan Giuliano, Christine Hennessy, Harald Horn, Mario Ignisci, Gail Israel, Michael Kelder, Margery Lambert, Delfino Larrosa, Beatrice Lismore, Roni Mahler, Hillel Markman, Carolyn Martin, Rudi Menchaka, Alexandra Nadal, Nina Novak, Vadim Repeskov, Naomi Richardson, Marlene Rizzo, Nancy Sklenar, Paula Tennyson, Hélène Trailine, Andrea Vodehnal, Nina Vyroubova (guest), June Wilson, Franklin Yezer, George Zoritch

REPERTOIRE:

Bach Concerto, Ballet Imperial, Les Elfes, Gaîté Parisienne, Giselle, Grand Pas Classique, Nutcracker, Pas de Trois, Raymonda, Scheherazade, Sombreros, Swan Lake, Les Sylphides, Tribute

NEW PRODUCTIONS

España (Chicago, 24 December 1961). Choreography: Leon Danielian; Music: Breton, Chapi, Granados. / Lady with the Black Mantilla: Andrea Vodehnal; Man with the Black Cape: Mario Ignisci; ensemble.

Harlequinade Pas de Deux (Chicago, 27 December 1961). Choreography: Nina Novak; Music: Drigo. / Nina Novak, Juan Giuliano.

The Comedians (Chicago, 27 December 1961). Choreography: James Starbuck; Music: Kabalevsky; Designs: Jan Scott. / Meredith Baylis, Christine Hennessy, Carolyn Martin, Marlene Rizzo, June Wilson, Tom Adair, James Capp, Harald Horn, Vadim Repeskov, Franklin Yezer.

SELECTED
BIBLIOGRAPHY

THIS bibliography is restricted to books and lengthy magazine articles. Newspaper and magazine reviews, news items, and short features are cited in the notes to each chapter.

"AGMAzine Visits Sergei Denham." *AGMAzine,* December 1958, pp. 1 ff.

Amberg, George. *Ballet: The Emergence of an American Art.* New York: Mentor Books, 1949.

Balanchine, George. *Balanchine's Complete Stories of the Great Ballets,* ed. Francis Mason. Garden City: Doubleday and Company, Inc., 1954.

Balanchine, George. "Notes on Choreography." *Dance Index,* 2, Nos. 2-3 (February-March 1945), pp. 20-31.

"Ballet Girls on Tour." *Life,* 3 December 1945, pp. 129-135.

"Ballet Russe de Gotham," *Newsweek,* 24 September 1945, pp. 110-111.

Barzel, Ann. "Lancashire Lad to Ballet Master—Frederic Franklin." *Dance,* February 1946, pp. 12-13.

Beaumont, Cyril W. *Ballets Past and Present.* London: Putnam, 1955.

Beaumont, Cyril W. *Complete Book of Ballets.* New York: Grosset and Dunlap, 1938.

Beaumont, Cyril W. *Supplement to Complete Book of Ballets.* London: Putnam, 1952.

"A Conversation with Alexandra Danilova." *Ballet Review*, 4, No. 4 (1973), pp. 32-51; 4, No. 5 (1973), pp. 50-60.

"A Conversation with P.W. Manchester." *Ballet Review*, 6, No. 3 (1977-78), pp. 57-89.

de Mille, Agnes. *Dance to the Piper.* Boston: Little, Brown and Company, 1952.

Denby, Edwin. *Looking at the Dance.* New York: Pellegrini and Cudahy, 1949.

Fay, Anthony. "Ballet Russe Retrospective." *Ballet Review*, 4, No. 6 (1974), pp. 91-97.

Fokine, Michel. *Memoirs of a Ballet Master,* trans. Vitale Fokine, ed. Anatole Chujoy. Boston: Little, Brown and Company, 1961.

Franks, A.H., ed. *Ballet: A Decade of Endeavour.* London: Burke Publishing Co. Ltd., 1955.

Franks, A.H. *Twentieth Century Ballet.* London: Burke Publishing Co. Ltd., 1954.

Goodman, Saul. "Meet Sophie Pourmel." *Dance Magazine,* January 1961, pp. 18-21.

Haggin, B.H. *Ballet Chronicle.* New York: Horizon Press, 1970.

Hall, Fernau. *An Anatomy of Ballet.* London: Andrew Melrose, 1953.

Haskell, Arnold, ed. (vols. 1-14) with Mary Clarke (vols. 15-18). *The Ballet Annual.* 18 vols. London: Adam and Charles Black, 1947-1959.

Haskell, Arnold L. *Dancing Round the World.* London: Victor Gollancz Ltd., 1937.

Hurok, S., in collaboration with Ruth Goode. *Impresario.* New York: Random House, 1946.

Hurok, S. *S. Hurok Presents: A Memoir of the Dance World.* New York: Hermitage House, 1953.

Katcharoff, Michel, with Jenny Schulman. Unpublished autobiography.

Kirstein, Lincoln. *Three Pamphlets Collected.* Brooklyn: Dance Horizons, Inc., 1967.

Krokover, Rosalyn. *The New Borzoi Book of Ballets.* New York: Alfred A. Knopf, 1956.

Lasch, Christopher. *The Agony of the American Left.* New York: Vintage Books, 1969.

Lawrence, Robert. *The Victor Book of Ballets and Ballet Music.* New York: Simon and Schuster, 1950.

Manor, Giora. "Lioness in the Orchestra Pit." English version prepared for Jack Anderson of an article written for *Israel Dance '77.*

Markova, Alicia. *Giselle and I.* London: Barrie and Rockliff, 1960.

Martin, John. *Ruth Page: An Intimate Biography.* New York: Marcel Dekker, Inc., 1977.

Martin, John. *World Book of Modern Ballet.* Cleveland: World Publishing Company, 1952.

Massine, Léonide. *My Life in Ballet,* ed. Phyllis Hartnoll and Robert Rubens. New York: St. Martin's Press, 1968.

Maynard, Olga. *The American Ballet.* Philadelphia: Macrae Smith Company, 1959.

Maynard, Olga. *Bird of Fire: The Story of Maria Tallchief.* New York: Dodd, Mead and Company, 1961.

Moore, Lillian. "Frederic Franklin." *The Dancing Times,* February 1939, pp. 609-610.

Palmer, Winthrop, and Anatole Chujoy, eds. *Dance News Annual 1953.* New York: Alfred A. Knopf, 1953.

Pischl, A.J. "A Catalogue of Souvenir Dance Programs." *Dance Index,* 7, Nos. 4-5 (April-May 1948), pp. 76-127.

Quiros, Rod. *Igor Youskevitch.* Chicago: Dance Press, 1956.

Reynolds, Nancy. *Repertory in Review: 40 Years of the New York City Ballet.* New York: The Dial Press, 1977.

Robert, Grace. *The Borzoi Book of Ballets.* New York: Alfred A. Knopf, 1946.

Subotin, Michael. *Sergei Denham,* trans. Anna Kisselgoff, unpublished.

Taper, Bernard. *Balanchine.* New York: Harper & Row, 1963.

Terry, Walter. *Ballet: A New Guide to the Liveliest Art.* New York: Dell Publishing Co., 1959.

Terry, Walter. *The Dance in America.* Revised ed. New York: Harper & Row, 1971.

Twysden, A.E. *Alexandra Danilova.* New York: Kamin Dance Publishers, 1947.

Vaughan, David. *Frederick Ashton and His Ballets.* New York: Alfred A. Knopf, 1977.

Youskevitch, Igor. "Ballet Is a Theatre Art." *Dance News,* June-August 1945, p. 4.

Youskevitch, Igor. "Russian Ballet in America." unpublished essay.

The following works have been consulted as general reference sources:

Chujoy, Anatole, and P.W. Manchester, eds. *The Dance Encyclopedia.* Revised and enlarged ed. New York: Simon and Schuster: 1967.

Koegler, Horst. *The Concise Oxford History of Ballet.* London: Oxford University Press, 1977.

LIST OF DANCERS

This listing indicates the seasons in which these dancers were members of the company.

Adair, Robin, 1961-62
Adair, Tom, 1960-1962
Adams, Wally, 1958-1960
Alexandroff, Gregory, 1945-1949
Allison, Keith, 1952-1954
Alonso, Alicia, 1955-1960 (guest)
Anchutina, Leda, 1941-42
Argentinita, 1938-1940 (guest)
Armin, Jeanne, 1958-1960
Aycock, Alice, 1951-1954

Baldwin, Franca, 1950-51
Banks, Alan, 1943-1945
Barker, Gwenn, 1955-1960
Barlow, Ann, 1948-49
Baronova, Irina, 1940 (guest)
Barrie, Barbara, 1938-39
Baylis, Meredith, 1951-52, 1954-1962
Beddow, Margery, 1954-1958
Benson, Nancy, 1954-55
Beriozoff, Nicholas, 1938-1943

Berson, Roberta, 1958-1962
Bettencourt, Yelle, 1960-1962
Bettis, Valerie, 1947 (guest)
Bewley, Lois, 1955-1957
Bliss, Herbert, 1943-1947
Bocchino, M., 1939-40
Bolender, Todd, 1945-46
Boneck, Nina, 1948-49
Bonura, Peter, 1950-52
Boris, Ruthanna, 1943-50
Borowska, Irina, 1954-60
Brown, Vida, 1939-45, 1946-48
Brunson, Perry, 1956-61
Brusock, James, 1954-56, 1957-58
Busheme, Joseph, 1952-56
Buttignol, Val, 1948-49
Byrne, Emily, 1961-62

Capp, James, 1956-62
Cardone, Olivia, 1943-45
Carleton, Patricia, 1957-58
Casey, Patricia, 1948-49
Chamié, Tatiana, 1938-44
Chapman, Marina, 1959-62
Chapman, Tamara, 1949-51

311

Chauviré, Yvette, 1950-52
(guest), 1957-58 (guest)
Chevtchenko, Tania, 1960-61
Chouteau, Yvonne, 1943-52,
1954-57
Clare, Natalia, 1948-52
Clark, Katherine, 1944-45
Clarke, Thatcher, 1956-57
Cobos, Antonia, 1947 (guest)
Collins, Eugene, 1958-62
Coon, Diana, 1952-54
Corvino, Alfredo, 1942-45
Crabtree, Leila, 1938-43
Craig, Yvonne, 1954-57
Creel, Kenneth, 1961-62
Crist, Joanna, 1952-54
Crucil, Viola, 1956-58
Cummins, Barth, 1945-47
Curtis, Myron, 1960-62

Danielian, Leon, 1943-52,
1954-57, 1958-60
(guest)
Daniels, Dorothy, 1954-58
Danilova, Alexandra, 1938-52,
1956-57 (guest)
D'Antuono, Eleanor, 1954-60
Deign, Peter, 1943-48
DeLaney, Grant, 1954-55
Delarova, Eugénie, 1938-40
DeMari, Teri, 1954-56
DeMille, Agnes, 1942 (guest),
1948 (guest)
Dickson, Charles, 1938-40
Dokoudovska, Tatiana, 1938-39
Dokoudovsky, Vladimir, 1938-39,
1950-51 (guest)
Dolin, Anton, 1939-40 (guest),
1948-49 (guest)
Dorn, Harding, 1944-50,
1954-55
Driver, Donn, 1949-50
Drosdova, Irene, 1938-39
Dyche, Anita, 1961-62

Eglevsky, André, 1939-43

Egoroff, Stanislav, 1939-41
Elyse, Jeanne, 1954-55
Etheridge, Dorothy, 1938-45

Fabergé, Irène, 1938-39
Feher, Milton, 1943-44
Fenchel, Marcel, 1938-39
Ferguson, Barbara, 1948-49
Fernandez, Royes, 1948-49
Filippini, Giaconda, 1954-56
Firminova, Rosalind, 1938-39
FitzGerald, Hester, 1956-59
Fiumara, Olivia, 1958-61
Flotat, Tatiana, 1938-43
Fontaine, Edwina, 1944-49
Franca, Marina, 1938-40
Franchi, Michele, 1958-61
Franklin, Frederic, 1938-52,
1954-56, 1956-57
(guest)

Gabay, Eugène, 1938-39
Galle, Myrna, 1946-48
Garfield, Constance, 1945-48
Geleznova, Katia, 1938-43
Gibson, Ian, 1939-41
Giles, Evelyn, 1947-48
Gillespie, Kenneth, 1956-60
Girard, Aaron, 1945-47
Giuliano, Juan, 1961-62
Glenn, William, 1947-52
Godkin, Paul, 1939-40
Gollner, Nana, 1949 (guest)
Goudovitch, Alexander, 1939-45
Granteff, M., 1943-44
Grantham, Unity, 1938-39
Grantzeva, Tatiana, 1938-44,
1946-48, 1957-60
Grossman, Simone, 1938-39
Guerard, Leon, 1951-52
Guerard, Roland, 1938-43
Gutierrez, Jose, 1960-61

Harsh, Roy, 1956-59
Haynes, Shirley, 1946-52
Haywood, Mary, 1948-51

Hennessy, Christine, 1952-56,
    1961-62
Herrera, Reynaldo, 1947-48
Herskind, Betsy, 1957-59
Heyward, Jennifer, 1954-55
Hightower, Rosella, 1938-41
Hill, Yvonne, 1939-44
Hines, Carol, 1958-59
Hirst, Robert, 1952-54
Hobi, Frank, 1945-49
Horn, Harald, 1961-62
Horvath, Julia, 1943-46
Howard, Alan, 1949-52, 1954-60

Ignisci, Mario, 1959-62
Irwin, Robert T., 1938-41
Ismailoff, Serge, 1942-44
Israel, Gail, 1958-62
Istomina, Anna, 1939-44,
    1952-53
Ivangin, Nicholas, 1938-39

Jasinski, Roman, 1947-51,
    1952-54
Jeffers, Josephine, 1956-59
Jennings, Patricia, 1951-52
Johnson, Dick, 1944-45
Juarez, Salvador, 1951-52,
    1954-57

Kantor, June, 1959-61
Karlin, Rita, 1948-51
Karnakovsky, Kari, 1938-39,
    1941-44
Karol, Arthur, 1941-42
Katcharoff, Michel, 1938-50
Kauflin, Jack, 1950-52
Kelder, Michael, 1959-62
Kelepovska, Nathalie, 1938-43
Kelly, John, 1947-49
King, Diana, 1938-39
King, Joe, 1960-61
Kirbos, Max, 1938-39
Klimoff, Pierre, 1938-39
Kokitch, Casimir, 1938-44,
    1946-47

Korjinska, Marina, 1938-43
Kosloff, Alexis, 1940-42
Kosman, Louis, 1955-57
Kostensko, Vladimir, 1938-43
Kotynski, Alexis, 1960-61
Kovalska, Irina, 1957-60
Kramarr, Elena, 1942-45
Krassovska, Nathalie, 1938-49,
    1950-51, 1958-59
    (guest), 1959-60
Kristen, Eric, 1948-49
Kroon, Carole, 1958-60
Kummel, Herb, 1958-60

Lacca, Yolanda, 1938-43
Ladre, Marian, 1948-49 (guest)
Lambert, Margery, 1960-62
Lamont, Deni, 1951-52, 1954-58
Lamonte, Paula, 1938-39
Lane, Elena, 1948-50
Lanese, Lillian, 1944-45
Lang, Harold, 1941-43
Lanova, Merriam, 1945-48
Larkin, Moscelyne, 1948-51,
    1952-54
Larrosa, Delfino, 1961-62
Laune, Roberta, 1949-52
Lauret, Jeannette, 1938-41
Lazowski, Yurek, 1944-45,
    1948-50 (guest)
Leavitt, Gerard, 1948-52
Lebercher, Louis, 1938-39
Lee, Nata, 1951-52
Leonie, Nancy, 1952-54
Lidova, Mlle, 1941-42
Lifar, Serge, 1938
Likely, Mlle, 1938-39
Lindgren, Robert, 1944-52
Lismore, Beatrice, 1958-62
Litvinova, Irene, 1938-39
Lovering, Leonore, 1954-56
Low, Betty, 1939-40, 1941-43

Magallanes, Nicholas, 1943-47

Mahler, Roni, 1960-62
Marie-Jeanne, 1940-41 (guest),
    1945-47
Marinaccio, Gene, 1955-57
Markman, Hillel, 1961-62
Markoff, Fedja, 1939-40
Markova, Alicia, 1938-41,
    1948-49 (guest)
Marra, Eleanora, 1938-43
Martikainen, Arvo, 1938-39
Martin, Carolyn, 1960-62
Massine, Léonide, 1938-43,
    1951-52 (guest)
Matsie, Dorothy, 1948-52
May, Susan, 1957-60
McGinnis, Barbara, 1952-56
Melnitchenko, Eugénie, 1938-39
Menchaka, Rudi, 1961-62
Michailoff, M., 1943-44
Michailova, Anna, 1938-39
Milton, Roy, 1939-41
Minor, Irene, 1954-56
Mladova, Milada, 1938-43
Moreno, Victor, 1951-56
Mouradoff, Grant, 1943-44
Moylan, Mary Ellen, 1943-45,
    1947-50
Murer, Alice, 1950-52
Murielle, Helen, 1949-50

Nadal, Alexandra, 1961-62
Noble, Duncan, 1949-51
Novak, Edmund, 1957-60
Novak, Nina, 1948-52, 1953-62
Novikova, Marina, 1939-40

Oleova, Mlle, 1943-44
Olson, Glenn, 1942-56
Orloff, Nicolas, 1938-39
Orlova, Tatiana, 1938-42
Orth, Betty, 1941-43
Orwiroff, Jan, 1939-40
Ozoline, Arved, 1938-39

Page, Ruth, 1944-45 (guest),
    1946-47 (guest)

Pagent, Robert, 1941-43
Panaieff, Michel, 1938-39,
    1942-43
Pasch, Claire, 1944-47
Perensky, Marcel, 1939-40
Peters, Patricia, 1950-51
Pfeiffer, Edward, 1948-50
Picon, Armand, 1941-44,
    1946-48
Piotrovsky, Felix, 1938-39
Plane, Liane, 1948-49
Platoff, Marc, 1938-42
Poole, Wakefield, 1957-58
Popova, Nina, 1942-44, 1947-48
Pourmel, Adda, 1939-41,
    1948-49

Radova, Nina, 1938-39
Razoumova, Galina, 1944-45
Reed, Gilbert, 1948-51
Rehman, Bernice, 1946-50
Repeskov, Vadim, 1961-62
Rhodes, Diane, 1945-47
Rhodes, Lawrence, 1958-60
Richardson, Naomi, 1961-62
Riekman, Ruth, 1942-45
Rizzo, Marlene, 1960-62
Rklitzka, Ludmilla, 1938-40
Roget, Paul, 1954-55
Roje, Ana, 1938-39
Rolanoff, Sascha, 1939-40
Roman, Janice, 1948-52
Ross, Audrey, 1958-60
Rosson, Virginia, 1938-40
Rostova, Lubov, 1938-43
Roudenko, Lubov, 1938-43,
    1945-46 (guest)

Salerno, Libby, 1956-58
Sampson, Walter, 1941-43
Sanders, Job, 1948-52
Sandre, Irma, 1948-51
Savino, Joseph, 1954-56
Sayette, Howard, 1956-60
Scarpova, Anna, 1938-44

LIST OF REPERTOIRE

This listing indicates the seasons in which these ballets were in the repertoire.

Ancient Russia, 1943-44
Après-midi d'un Faune, L',
    1938-43, 1945-46,
    1954-55

Bacchanale, 1939-42
Bach Concerto, 1960-62
Baiser de la Fée, Le, 1940-42,
    1945-48
Ballad, 1959-60
Ballet Imperial, 1944-50,
    1954-55, 1958-62
Beau Danube, Le, 1938-41,
    1942-52, 1954-59,
    1960-61
Bells, The, 1946-47
Billy Sunday, 1948-49
Birthday, 1949-52
Bogatyri, 1938-40, 1941-42
Bourgeois Gentilhomme, Le,
    1944-46
Boutique Fantasque, La, 1939-42

Capriccio Espagnol, 1939-43,
    1951-52, 1954-56
Carnaval, 1938-40, 1942-44,
    1948-49
Chopin Concerto, 1942-46
Cimarosiana, 1938-39
Cirque de Deux, 1947-50,
    1951-58
Comedia Balletica, 1945-47
Comedians, The, 1961-62
Concerto Barocco, 1945-51
Coppélia, 1938-43, 1944-52,
    1954-61
Cuckold's Fair, The, 1943-45

Dame à Licorne, La, 1955-58
Danses Concertantes, 1944-48
Devil's Holiday, 1939-40,
    1941-42
Don Juan, 1938-39

Élèments, Les, 1938-39
Elfes, Les, 1938-39, 1942-43,
    1949-52, 1961-62
Épreuve d'Amour, L', 1938-39
España, 1961-62
Etude, 1943-44

317

INDEX

DUE